W. E. Gladstone

Studies subsidiary to the works of bishop Butler

W. E. Gladstone

Studies subsidiary to the works of bishop Butler

ISBN/EAN: 9783743336681

Manufactured in Europe, USA, Canada, Australia, Japa

Cover: Foto ©Thomas Meinert / pixelio.de

Manufactured and distributed by brebook publishing software
(www.brebook.com)

W. E. Gladstone

Studies subsidiary to the works of bishop Butler

STUDIES

SUBSIDIARY TO THE WORKS
OF BISHOP BUTLER

London

HENRY FROWDE

Oxford University Press Warehouse
Amen Corner, E.C.

STUDIES

SUBSIDIARY TO THE WORKS

OF BISHOP BUTLER

BY

THE RIGHT HON. W. E. GLADSTONE

Oxford

AT THE CLARENDON PRESS

1896

OXFORD : PRINTED AT THE CLARENDON PRESS
BY HORACE HART, PRINTER TO THE UNIVERSITY

CONTENTS

PART I: BUTLER

CHAPTER I

PART II: SUBSIDIARY

SUBSIDIARY STUDIES

PART I

CHAPTER I

THE METHOD OF BUTLER [1]

Iт is important, in any attempt at a thorough examination of Butler, to dwell upon the *method* of the author, as well as upon the arguments of his principal works : upon those characteristics of his work and working, which lie outside the express indications of the text. I have here particularly in view the relation of his form of argument to subjects lying beyond his declared, perhaps even his conscious, purpose.

In offering to the world essays which are meant to be supplementary to the works of Butler, I assign the foremost place to the consideration of his method, for the following reason. While maintaining the direct value of the argument of his largest work, the *Analogy,* to be unabated, I hold that the value of his method is greater still. If so, it constitutes the weightiest among the reasons which may be adduced to show that this is no obsolete or antiquated treatise ; and it therefore provides a principal part of the warrant for endeavouring, in a new edition of his works, to supply an increase of facilities for their study.

The first feature of Butler's method which we have to note is, that it was an inductive method. Butler was a collector of facts, and a reasoner upon them. Herein he departed from the more common practice of his age, which had been given to argumentation in the abstract, and to

---

[1] Some chapters of Part I, and principal parts of others, have already been printed in *Good Words,* and are now reprinted, with corrections.

speculative castle-building. He notices, in the *Analogy*, his having forgone the advantages which he might have drawn from a procedure resembling that of Clarke in his *Demonstration of the Being and Attributes of God.*

The main thing, however, to be here considered, is not the mere question between induction and deduction, but that Butler chose for his whole argument the sure and immovable basis of human experience, from his earliest tracings of natural government, up to his final development of the scheme of revealed religion. It is probable that this great feature of Butler's method supplies the explanation of the singular fact that a work, rarely presenting to us the graces of style, not produced in connexion with any academic institution or learned class, singularly difficult to master from the nature of the subject, and running directly counter to the fashionable currents of opinion, should at once have taken hold upon the educated mind of the country, and should, as will appear from the language of Hume, very rapidly have acquired for its author a high position in the literary and philosophic world.

I shall submit, in the most succinct manner, a variety of features which appear to me to characterize the method of Butler, and to recommend his works, in conjunction with what has been already stated, for permanent and classical study by the more thoughtful minds.

It would be difficult to name a writer who in the prosecution of his work has aimed at, and effected, a more absolute self-suppression. His use of the first person singular is rare, and whenever it occurs, we at once perceive that it is a grammatical vehicle, and not the entrance of a caparisoned figure on the stage for presentation to an audience. We attain indeed a solid and rather comprehensive knowledge of the man through his works; but this is owing, if I may so speak, to their moral transparency, which is conspicuous amidst all the difficulties of gaining and keeping a continuous grasp of his meaning.

From beginning to end the *Analogy*, and the *Sermons* to some extent, are avowedly controversial: and the prosecution of such work powerfully tends to cast the mind into a controversial mould. But in Butler this tendency is effectually neutralized by his native ingenuousness, by the sense that his pen moves under the very eye of God, and by the knowledge that the sacred interests of truth must be eventually compromised by over-statement. In any case the result is that his concessions to the presumed opponent are not niggardly, but such as may sometimes excite the surprise of the friendly reader; the discounts from the full breadth of his propositions are so large, that it seems as if they were always tendered in ready and cheerful deference to the supreme calls of justice and of candour. This brave adherence to the principles, which can alone establish mental honesty in its highest sense, has exhibited itself in the fearlessness which has led this habitually circumspect writer into collateral observations of a boldness such as is shown in his strong statements of the ruin of the world through sin, of the rarity of real care for the public interest, of the wide range of waste in creation at large, and of the capacities of progress which may possibly be latent in the animals inferior to man.

But there is one broader and deeper result of the method of Butler, which must be stated at somewhat greater length. He exhibits in himself, and he powerfully tends to create in his reader, a certain habit of mind which is usually far from common, and which at the present day, and amidst the present tendencies, both of the average and even of the more active mind, may justly be termed rare. The politician, the lawyer, the scientist, the theologian, are all of them, apart from any strong controlling action, due to individual character, marked by a certain habit of mind incidental to the profession or pursuit. Butler's pursuit, and the labours of those who study him, are incessantly conversant with the relation between the lower and the higher world, between all the shapes of human character and experience on the one side, and a great governing agency on the other. Such a pursuit will not fail to build up its own habit of mind; and it does not coincide with the habit of mind belonging to any of the professions, as such, that have been mentioned. He does not write like a person addicted to any profession or pursuit; his mind is essentially free. He is the votary of truth, and is bound to no other allegiance.

In these matters we see through a glass darkly; and the propositions appropriate to them will rarely take a sharp edge. To pass from the work of the mathematician to the proper work of those who graze in Butler's pastures, has some resemblance to the transition from the primitive forms of painting without atmosphere or perspective, to the modern chiaroscuro, the subtle art of light and shade. Butler himself supplies us with some guidance on this subject. When he speaks of 'morals, considered as a science, concerning which speculative difficulties are daily raised,' he comes strictly upon his own ground, that aspect, namely, of morals which they present to us in their relations with the unseen world. And he proceeds, 'For here ideas never are in themselves determinate, but become so by the train of reasoning and the place they stand in [1].' His readers know that these ideas, after they have been thus handled and their relative positions ascertained, become determinate only in a qualified sense, and that at every step we feel how truly he has told us both that probable evidence is the guide of life [2], and that probability has this for its essential note, that it is matter of degree [3]. In truth, the general rule for inquiry in this department cannot be better put than as it has been stated by Aristotle, who takes it for the distinctive note of a cultivated mind to estimate with accuracy, in each kind of mental exercise, the degree in which its propositions can be made determinate.

Πεπαιδευμένου γάρ ἐστιν ἐπὶ τοσοῦτον τἀκριβὲς ἐπιζητεῖν καθ' ἕκαστον γένος, ἐφ' ὅσον ἡ τοῦ πράγματος φύσις ἐπιδέχεται [4]. The philosopher takes for his example of determinate science that of mathematics; for the indeterminate, the business of the rhetorician. The vast extension of the sphere of politics since his time has greatly enhanced its aptitude to be treated as an example in this region. But Aristotle's view of morals was barred, so to speak, on the spiritual and immaterial side. His powerful insight enabled him to connect them with the constitution of our natures [5]; but the light in the beginning, and now again

---

[1] Preface to the Sermons, § 3.
[2] Analogy, Introd. § 4.
[3] Ibid. § 1.
[4] Eth. Nic. I. iii. 3.
[5] Eth. I. ii. 4, where Πολιτική is said to be κυριωτάτη καὶ μάλιστα ἀρχιτεκτονική.

adequately thrown on the dependence of both upon the Creator and Moral Governor of the world had become darkness for him, as it had also become darkness for the otherwise marvellously illuminated intellect of Greece in general. We visit actions with praise and blame, but we ought to do it under the conviction that such a judgement is only partial, superficial, and provisional. Greece did not know of the sovereign rule by which every action must principally be judged; and we, who do know and can in a measure apply it, yet ought to be aware that the roots of action are manifold, and lie too deep down in our nature for human eyes to follow them. To give their merits or demerits — nay, those of any one among them — with an absolute exactitude, as they will be fixed in the scales of the Almighty Judge, is a process transcending the powers of any or of all human intellects. And it would be, not indeed a definition but a true indication of the science of morals, as it lies opened out before us in the Butlerian field, if we were to call it the science of the indeterminate. I have already spoken of his chief works as an intellectual exercise; but let us also consider them as a guide to belief and to conduct. The mental habit which he forms in us is that mental habit which, in all questions lying within the scope of Butler's arguments, suits and adapts itself with gradually increasing precision to the degree of evidence adapted to the subject-matter; where that is much, thankfully rejoices in the abundance; where it is scanty, recognizes the absolute duty of accepting the limitation; backed by the consciousness that, in each and every case, it is sufficient. For in each and every case it is an award of supreme wisdom, adjusted to that case by a sure if a hidden process; and we are enjoined to entertain and follow it upon rules which, if they are magisterially those of religion, are also those of reason, and of the common sense which we rightly accept as our guide in all the interests and incidents of life.

The student of Butler will, unless it be his own fault, learn candour in all its breadth, and not to tamper with the truth; will neither grudge admissions nor fret under even cumbrous reserves. But to know what kinds and degrees of evidence to expect or to ask in matters of belief and conduct, and to be in possession of an habitual presence of mind built upon that knowledge, is, in my view, the master gift which the works of Butler are calculated to impart. It can, however, only be imparted to those who approach the study of them as in itself an undertaking; who know that it requires them to pursue it with a whole heart and mind, if they would pursue it profitably; that it demands of them collectedness, concentration, and the cheerful resolve not to be abashed or deterred by difficulty.

To conclude; if it be true that this mental habit is produced in that field of thought which above all others is occupied by the science of the indeterminate, the study receives an important though secondary recommendation from the applicability of that habit to those other pursuits, in which also the indeterminate largely prevails. When Lord Bacon said that of all sciences that of politics was the most deeply immersed in matter, this was, I conceive, his meaning, that it was the branch of knowledge in which it was hardest to sever the true idea from environments not properly belonging to it, and necessary therefore to be detached in order that, relieved thus in mere dimension, but refined and consolidated in its essence, it might be brought as near to the truth as our weakness, our passions, and the urgency of circumstances will allow. Undoubtedly, if my counsel were asked, I should advise the intending politician, if of masculine and serious mind, to give to Butler's works, and especially to the *Analogy*, a high place among the apparatus of his mental training.

But the scope of these remarks on the method of Butler requires to be yet further widened. When Bacon said that politics were the most deeply immersed in matter, he meant that they were the most closely kneaded up with human action. Let us set out from this point to consider where is the real breadth of subject-matter involved in Butler's argument, and therefore contributory to the habit of mind which the study of his works is calculated to foster. I proceed by reference to his own text. When he has made his profuse admissions as to the insufficient character of his own argument, he turns from the sphere of speculation to that of life; and says with pathetic correctness :

'Indeed the unsatisfactory nature of the evidence, with which we are obliged to take up, in the daily course of life, is scarce to be expressed[1].'

He institutes this reference as a bulwark of his argument: it proves, as has been elsewhere observed, that what is given us as the guide to belief, is already, and has ever been, the guide of practice. As though he said to us, this argument of mine, which I am offering to you on behalf of belief, ought not to startle you as a novelty; for it is the staff on which, whether you have observed the fact or not, you are leaning morn, noon, and night, in the course of your daily life. Let us now consider whether this undeniable statement has not another aspect and one relevant to the present contention. If Butler's argument on his own subject of belief fosters a particular habit of mind, most precious in its nature; and if the evidence which he gathers is evidence of the same nature with the evidence on which we act, and that not occasionally, but habitually, nay incessantly, in the daily course of life, a most important inference must be drawn, and to the following effect: Since the evidences, or experience, of life, and the evidences of belief, are the same in character, He, who forms in us a habit of mind engendered by the study of the first, is, *ex vi terminorum*, also forming in us a habit of mind equally appropriate to the evidences, that is to say the experience of life: a habit well broken into all forms of difficulty; not easily inflated, not easily abashed; able to encounter every contingency, to extract from it the solution of which it may be capable; or if it yields none, then to accept the inevitable, and to live and act accordingly. The supreme excellence of this habit does not lie in its intellectual triumphs, but in its radical hostility to exaggeration, in its generating a profound and invincible σωφροσύνη. For, as probability is the guide, so exaggeration is the mental bane of conduct. When we err in thought, word, or act, it is not usually that there is nothing to be said for the alternative to which we incline, but it is that we so exaggerate as to transform it, and by transforming it we bewilder and befool ourselves. To my eye, the several stages of this reasoning are continuous and

[1] *Analogy*, II. viii. 17.

inseparable. If it be sound, it at once disposes of every cavil, of every misgiving which may have beset some with the idea that Butler's philosophy was great in his day and for his purpose, but is now antiquated and obsolete. For in this view he is no longer, in a particular form, the philosopher of belief; he is also, and that apart from all form, the philosopher of life. For probability is its guide, and here we have the *archididaskalos* of probability. While he professes, and while at first sight he seems, to be dealing with the sceptic, he is really dealing with us all. The man of weak faith, or of strong; the man of the most questioning, or of the most docile temperament; the man of the most determinate, or the most indeterminate, pursuit; all are alike his scholars, and in modes far beyond the immediate purpose of the *Analogy*, great as that purpose is, should turn his lessons to account.

The reader, therefore, will not be surprised at the large proportionate weight and moment which I have assigned to the method of Butler.

In the upshot, I think it may be fairly said that Butler achieves more than he promises. For his engagement is only to show that the truth of the Christian religion is so well worthy of inquiry as to impose a moral obligation to inquire. But he does more than he professes to do. For only let a man be a genuine student of Butler, and, like every genuine student in every case, he will try to contract a sympathy with his author, which means in the case of Butler a sympathy with candour, courage, faith, a deference to the Eternal, a sense of the largeness of the unseen, and a reverential sentiment always healthful for the soul towards the majestic shadows with which it is encompassed. In these there is no small gain.

Although this is not a controversial work, yet I feel it incumbent upon me, bearing, in my advanced old age, my latest testimonies to the world upon matter that touches the deepest interests, to add a few words for the purpose of bringing home what I have thus written respecting the method of Bishop Butler.

The argument of the *Analogy* is an argument perhaps even greater than Butler himself was aware. In its first aspect it was an argument for religion at large, drawn from the course of natural government at large. But in opening up this argument, which in my judgement stands among the masterpieces of the human mind, Butler has unfolded to us the entire method of God's dealings with His creatures; and in this way the argument which he offers is as wide as those dealings themselves.

Our Almighty Father is continually, aye every day and hour, calling upon us, almost compelling us, to act. Now acting is not the mere discharge of an outward function. It is a continuing process, in which we are responsible throughout. What is meant by being responsible ? It is meant that we expose ourselves to consequences flowing from our actions. These are (say) of two kinds. First, there is alteration of environment: which implies that in the future actings, which cannot be escaped, we shall have to cast our account anew with circumstances. The second cuts deeper still. It is that our action modifies, that is to say progressively but silently alters, from time to time, and eventually shapes, our own mind and character.

These being the weighty, and from one point of view the terrible, consequences of action, they impart a piercing force to the question, how has the Almighty Father equipped us that we may encounter it ? And this question really involves the entire issue of His Government; His Fatherhood; His essential Character, as we cannot help judging it when He condescends (and He does condescend) to plead with us. The first step towards answering it is taken when we note, as we cannot help noting, that He equips us for action by supplying us with evidence to throw light upon the issues which it raises ; which, be it borne in mind, it raises continually, every day and every hour of our lives. Next comes a more searching inquiry. What is the law or rule which the Almighty has prescribed to Himself for meting out this evidence to us, and thereby, in the last resort, determining our destinies ?

The answer is supplied by Butler — 'Probability is the guide of life.' And life is divisible into two great departments, those of thought and of action. Butler has had occasion to show that the provision of evidence for each is one and the same. When he has made his confession that the evidence supplied by his argument for belief is far from satisfactory, he turns in vindication of it to the region of life, and is not afraid to impress upon us that the evidence on which we have to act in the course of life is very far indeed from giving us satisfaction [1], and when he comes to practical applications he points out, that in this graduation and this imperfection of the evidence may lie a part, and even a large part, first of our trial, and then of our reward, when 'this tyranny is overpast.'

Now these propositions, be they demonstrative or not, are certainly comprehensive. They are comprehensive in the same sense as the rules of arithmetic are comprehensive. When we say twice one makes two, we propound a law which governs and (as far as it goes) disposes of every quantitative relation, whether it be of miles, or pounds, or acres, or worlds.

And so the conclusions of Butler, if they be sound, override and rule the entire range of human life in the twin spheres of thought and action. If conduct is in twilight, can we suppose that belief is in the blaze of midday? Belief indeed is important; but is it more important than conduct? Nay, does it not derive its importance, some would even say its whole importance, from its influence on conduct?

Now what is the law, by which the Almighty rules Himself, in furnishing us with evidence to govern conduct? It is the law of graduation: of variety, not capricious but doubtless adjusted by the all-seeing Eye to every variation and every need of circumstance. It is, above all, the law not of perfection, but of sufficiency. How different are these from one another! Perfection is self-attested : sufficiency is ascertained upon examination. Perfection dispenses with labour: sufficiency requires, nay depends upon it. In labour there is effort, growth, development, advance : in the absence of labour there is remission, poverty, stagnation. The first is the making of that great and noble product, which we term manhood : with the second it

---

[1] *Analogy,* II. viii. 17.

languishes, dwindles, dies; or remains only in outward form, like those functional organs, which are smitten by atrophy when they have no office to discharge.

I say then that this relation, which Butler has once for all unfolded, between natural and Providential government, is an universal relation. We have to trace it backwards, if we enter upon the great controversy, which Butler was allowed by the conditions of his times to waive, respecting the being of a God; as to which, however, it is interesting to remember that he has put upon record the admission that he had not succeeded in finding a demonstrative proof of the affirmative proposition. If on the other hand we travel downwards, and find ourselves, on the field of religious controversy, called to determine, for our own guidance, between the claims of conflicting religious professions, are we not subjected to this comprehensive law of sufficiency in the evidence, of probability in the conclusion?

I know that this idea of guidance by probability is revolting to human pride; is truly a stumbling-stone and a rock of offence. But is it the law of life? Only the most superficial minds can dream that probability means only fluctuation and wavering, together with the weakness which results from them. For lo! the courage, the indefatigable and even too absorbing energy, with which in common matters of business, with only temporal advantages in view, men labour for their end. Is it then, I say again, the law of life, of life including both action and belief? Or is it our duty to partition off one selected part of life from the rest, and to hold that within this consecrated precinct all is knowledge, light, and certitude, in their most absolute forms, while outside the paling all is the reverse? So that upon this theory our life is cut in two, and the two parts (both alike due to God and responsible to God) are governed by laws radically different. For the being of God, the basis of all religion, no demonstrative proof has been supplied; but the convert from (say) the Anglican Church to the Roman Church, as modelled by Pope Pius IX and his coadjutors, is taught to believe that he possesses one.

In the remarkable and profoundly interesting *Life of Cardinal Manning*, by Mr. Purcell, I find the following passage [1], extracted from a sermon preached by Manning while he was moving down the slope:

'Is it possible to believe that this scheme of probabilities (that is, of uncertainty) in doctrine, and imperfection (that is, of doubt) in evidence, is a part of the probation of the regenerate within the revelation of the faith?'

Now it seems quite plain that this passage never could have been written by a follower of Butler, or by any one into whom his teaching had entered more than skin deep. I say nothing of the passage or passages [2] in which Butler glances, it might almost be said rails, at 'Popery'; or of any form of Latin belief except that which the modern Roman Church seems to have adopted in its despair of finding a *modus vivendi* between the Syllabus and the thought of mankind. These are meant to be words of help and duty. If the spirit of insolence, of wrath, of insubordination, have crept into them, I lament the error, and would gladly see it exorcised.

In sum: all duty, then, is to be regarded from a religious point of view, and all human life is charged with duty. Every movement which takes place in this unmeasured universe, from the least to the greatest, from the falling of the sparrow to the eclipses of the sun and the precipitation into space of the fragments of some shattered world, have the Ruler of this universe behind them. It is Butler who, more than any other writer, opens to us the one pervading scheme, upon which He deals with His creatures. Of their existence this method is a governing, daily, and indeed never-ceasing law. In all its occasions, both great and small, life is ever presenting to us problems of duty. In his *Sermons* Butler has exhibited to us that equipment of faculty with which we have been endowed in order that we may face these problems. In the *Analogy* he presents to us the general character of the problems themselves. It is, then, no exaggeration to say that if there be the power of truth in its lessons, they provide us with the key of life.

And now one word as to the alleged superannuation of Butler in respect to the direct argument of the *Analogy*.

---

[1] Purcell's *Manning*, i. 702.

[2] See *Sermons*, V. 8. In some other cases the reference, if it exist, is inferential only, and open to question.

The contention of the present essay is that the highest importance of Bishop Butler's works, and of the *Analogy* in particular, is to be found, not in his argument, but in his method; which is so comprehensive as to embrace every question belonging to the relations between the Deity and man, including therefore every question of conduct.

Those, who make such an admission as against the argument, are not thereby driven to the conclusion that the reasoning of this great writer has become useless for the needs of the present day and of the coming time. It has great value through the robust exercise derivable by the human intellect from thorough acquaintance with the most powerfully constructed among the models which that intellect has from time to time produced, since this is a mode of acquiring power that is not to be had in other ways, and since the works I have referred to are entitled as models to the praise of extraordinary cohesiveness in their tissue, be it from powerfulness in the mason's hand, or be it from tenacity, like that of the old Neronian brick, in the mortar he employs.

But is there no claim in advance of this which the followers of Butler are entitled to urge on behalf of his argument? Yes: for first they may plainly press this point, that there is and can be no superannuation in the *Sermons*, which deal with human nature as it is, and the most important parts of which might evidently have been written, to a large extent, independently of that belief in God which Butler everywhere presupposes. From this point of view it may be doubted whether the atheistical reasoner has ever done as much for himself, as Butler has done for him, not in abetting his denials, but in constructing on his behalf something in the nature of a religion founded upon the constitution of man.

The principal step in advance, for the present stage of our inquiry, has, however, still to be made. The contention of those, who maintain that Butler is antiquated, seems to be of this kind. They allow that in his day there were two champions in the lists, of whom he was one, and that he overthrew and disabled his adversary, who appeared there no more. But, if the adversary is virtually extinct like the dodo, what is Butler's title still to parade the arena? Since the *issues* of the present day go to the root of the matter, and bring directly into question that belief in an intelligent Author of nature, which Butler's antagonists are found to have compromised themselves by admitting, the cause, it may be said, is disposed of, and the next step simply is to remove it, with the winner's as well as the loser's pleadings, from the list.

The reply seems to be this. The cause is not disposed of: only the issue has been widened. Not only the righteous character of our Governor, not only His special communication with His creatures by Divine Revelation, but His existence is in question; and, unless and until it can be placed beyond question, it is waste of time to discuss other issues, which can only be legitimately raised after it has been affirmed.

So far so good. But what if the arguments of Butler for a moral and righteous, and for a self-revealing Governor, are also, in their essence, arguments which, so far as they are good, go to prove that such a Governor exists? Now this is exactly what we may and ought to hold concerning the reasonings by which the *Analogy* is built up. Of course there is here involved the assumption that they are good and sound for their immediate aim; and the contention, now advanced as an outgrowth from that assumption, is that, being good and sound for their immediate aim, they are good and sound for an ulterior (but logically antecedent) aim in addition. That is to say, he has not simply dealt with the case of the Deist, but has, in dealing with that case, furnished materials available in the controversies now in hand against the several opposing systems which seek to abolish the idea of a personal and righteous Governor of the universe.

As the subject now placed before the reader is important I shall endeavour to make it clear by pointing, more definitely than Butler required to do, to the difference between the arguments of the Deist, or Theist, and those of the *Analogy*.

The Theist may, we will suppose, claim a *locus standi* for such pleas as the following: the physical order established among the heavenly bodies; the tendency, and indeed ability, of reason to acquire superiority over brute force; the climatic arrangements in the world, which suggest that exchange of material commodities, between countries, which so manifestly aims at social no less than physical advantages; even the wonderful monetary system of civilized countries, which exhibits the balance of forces in a manner more curious and striking than any merely physical ponderation can do it; and again, in connexion with these, the whole intelligent quality of man, as distinguished from those qualities which are moral. These, and other such pleas, may be set down among the πίστεις, or arguments of belief, for an intelligent Author of nature.

Now we come to the argument of the *Analogy* that the intelligent Author of nature is also moral, for He takes sides in that conflict between virtue and vice, which incessantly prevails in the world [1]. But a Being who, besides establishing wonderful counterpoises, both physical and social, for the advantage of His creatures, thus takes sides in such a conflict, not only as against the Deist gives evidence on behalf of the probability that He is a moral Governor: He also applies a fresh and additional supply of argument to show that He is an intelligent Governor, or a Governor at large.

So again, if Butler has adduced good evidence towards proving that the Intelligent Governor has acted wisely and justly in meeting a manifest need of His creatures by Divine Revelation, then in the very act of doing this he has furnished a new element of evidence in support of the purely theistic argument.

In other words, speaking of the *Analogy* as a whole, he has superadded to all the purely rational, but not moral, arguments for the existence of God, a mass of truly moral arguments, available for that purpose exactly in the same measure as that in which they were available for Butler's avowed and immediate aim. Without doubt they are no more than probable reasonings; but then we must remember that, from Butler's point of view, the whole theistic argument lies within, and not beyond, the precinct of probability.

[1] *Analogy*, I. iii. 21, 34.

CHAPTER II

THE supreme value of Butler will probably be found in the future, as it has been in the past, to lie in this; that the works of the Bishop are singularly adapted to produce that mental attitude required for treating the questions which concern the dealings of God with man. But, as it seems to me, there is much that we here inclusively assert with regard to a variety of questions which have sprung into great prominence and activity since his time. I propose now to touch upon one of them. It is the manner of God's dealing with man through the Holy Scriptures.

On the one hand, it is probable that a greater number of copies of the Sacred Volume have been circulated among the different nations during the nineteenth century than in all the preceding centuries put together. On the other hand, is it not also probably true that the assaults upon the inspiration, authority, and historical trustworthiness of that volume have within the same period exceeded in number, in breadth of scope, in currency, and in some sort of acceptance or tolerance among Christians, those of all previous ages combined?

The old, and what may be called the stereotyped, method of treating this subject, within the orthodox precinct, was to assume what is called the verbal inspiration of the Bible. The prevalence of this theory shows how unsafe it is to place implicit reliance upon any authority, which has acquired its title simply through its having been allowed to remain undisturbed through long periods of time. Of what avail is the verbal inspiration, if such there were, of the original books of Scripture available for us, unless, by a perpetual miracle, provision has been made against the errors of copyists, printers, commentators, whose notes may find their way into the text, and of translators into hundreds of languages? But the existence of such a miraculous provision is, I suppose, asserted by none.

The chief mischief resulting from these usurpations of right, and this facile adoption of controversial positions which in the day of conflict prove untenable, is great and manifold. Reaction one day comes; and such reactions are commonly vindictive. The discovery of error is formidable not only in proportion as the error is grave, but also in proportion as the interests involved in the subject are weighty. And the discredit of any one favourite argument, however small its intrinsic importance, infects all the other arguments legitimately available to support the same contention. For argument is propelled by impetus as well as weight.

Again, it seems undeniable that the indolence of human nature would be greatly flattered by a scheme such as that of the verbal inspiration of Holy Scripture. In this view it might be a great convenience that there should be put into the hands of each of us, as we grow up in succession, a volume which should operate as an Act of Parliament operates, to the last and farthest extremity of its letter. It is essential to such an idea of the Bible that it should be alike applicable to every portion of the volume. If any development of Divine Revelation be acknowledged, if any distinction of authority between different portions of the text be allowed, then, in order to deal with subjects so vast and difficult, we are at once compelled to assume so large a liberty as will enable us to meet all the consequences which follow from abandoning the theory of a purely verbal inspiration.

But the issue raised is not one of convenience or inconvenience; it is strictly one of fact. Has the Almighty given us, or has He not, a volume verbally inspired? And that question is sufficiently answered by two brief observations: first, there is no absolute security for identity with the original record; and, secondly, there is no verbal inspiration of translators.

Now the teaching of Butler has the most direct bearing upon everything that is fundamental in the great inquiry, What is the character of the Holy Scriptures as a Divine

c

record ? Let us try a little to develop the argument he quotes from Origen. If nature and Scripture have the same source, then we may expect to find in Scripture somewhat of the same difficulties that we find in the constitution of nature. It seems obvious this rule applies not only to this and that detail in the system of natural government, but to any characteristics which we may find attaching to the scheme of nature as a whole. Now there is one such characteristic which overrides and is antecedent to every other : it is that of the general method in which the evidence supplied by it is conveyed to us. And here we find it is not conveyed by precise and easy rules ; we cannot lay hold of it in rough and ready forms. It requires observation and watchfulness at every step, to pick out from the mass of material which life places before us, what is available for our purpose, and carefully to put aside the rest. We know, indeed, that the whole of life is providentially ordered on our behalf ; and yet we also know how readily we may be misled when we attempt to read the will of God in the particular facts of life. His hand is in them all ; but it does not follow that that hand and its working is at every point to be made visible to us. On the contrary, while we can clearly discern the general rules of divine government in nature, as Butler gives them, we find that these rules are neither absolute, nor to our eyes uniform ; that they are attended all along with qualification and exception, and that liberal interpretations are rarely given. Most of the judgements we can safely form upon them are after the fact, and are not therefore available in definite form for the determination off-hand of the issues of conduct.

The statutes of the realm may admit any amount of contest on the meaning of their text, but the text itself is of absolute authority throughout. If this were the case with Scripture, it would in the first place be not a little difficult to account for its fragmentary, unsystematic form, and for the informal and incomplete manner in which it most commonly deals with its subjects. A further and most formidable difficulty arises from the fact that it gives no definition of itself, and that the canon has been formed by agency not inspired, and by judgements which were unrecorded. But, when we turn to Butler, we find that as to the whole of these characteristics the work of God in Scripture corresponds with the work of God in nature. The moral law, and its application to justice, veracity, fortitude, benevolence, and the like, do not rest upon determinate and formal judgements that can be quoted in a court or controversy, and all the instruction which we receive on these great subjects is fragmentary, occasional, and incomplete in its particulars. The instruction it conveys is also mixed : it requires secretion and severance of material, that we may not be misled by premature or unwarrantable inference, and may by the removal of what is inappropriate turn all that is available to account. If therefore we had in Scripture, as we have in the statutes of the realm, an uniform code, absolute and inflexible down to its last letter, should we not be obliged to say that the Author of Scripture had in the delivery of His revealed word followed a method somewhat broadly severed from that which he had pursued as the Author also of nature, in the method of communicating His will ?

Let us not, however, allow ourselves to be driven too far by logic. We seem to verge towards certain propositions that God's methods of conveying His will are not absolute but variously conditioned, and that this rule of supply for us, in faculty, in knowledge, in the adjustment of life, and in all beside, is not perfection, but sufficiency. But in matters of moral action, if we have not mathematical assurance, we may have, and we very commonly have, such conviction as dispenses with all need of doubt. In the government of life, occasions of doubt, and even of doubt that refuses to bend, will arise from time to time ; but the everyday life of right-minded people is not troubled with them as regards conduct. If they speculate on the constitution of nature, they find themselves in a region of labyrinthine difficulties ; but the mass of mankind may well be content with their mental food from day to day, and this, by the merciful ordinance of God, is ready to hand. Nature indeed offers us with profusion at every point of her surface a combination of knowledge, delight, and mental training, which we do not sufficiently appreciate. All these are to be had by a kind and degree of mental application which are open to multitudes of men; and they will encounter little or no provocation to entangle themselves in the many and unsolved problems, which are opened by a philosophical contemplation of this comprehensive subject. And so with regard to the Holy Scriptures, which are appointed to be the daily food of the people of God. Those who with simplicity of mind accept them in that character, will surely find in them an increasing instruction as well as comfort, but need fear little perplexity, however grave the scientific questions concerning the Bible (so to call them) which, in another order of thought and experience, have to be dealt with only by a few.

There is in this great matter, as in the whole adjustment of the supply divinely ordained for our mental aliment, a pervading application of the rule which adapts the back to the burden, the ordinary human soul to its environment. The teaching supplied by the words and actions of the great Exemplar, as it comes to the common eye, is in the highest degree simple, effective, and majestic, and finds its way with penetrating force to the mind and heart of man. Each dispensation of the Almighty works in alliance with His other dispensations; and we must look at them, as Butler teaches, not in isolation, but as a whole. If we are told that the apparatus for setting forth the Divine Word in Scripture, and for conveying it to our minds, is not one of mathematical precision, we have to bear in mind that it does not stand alone. The art, history, institutions, and life of Christendom are all based upon that, the record and the propagation of which were solemnly entrusted by our Lord at the close of His earthly career to human hands. In the period when there was no written Word beyond that of the older covenant, and when Christians as a scattered few scarcely dotted the surface of a hostile world, the abundance of miracle and of extraordinary gifts came in aid of the weakness inherent in the individual mind. As the canon was gradually constructed, and the world so far at least reclaimed as to bear historic witness to Christ with ever-increasing force, miracles and extraordinary gifts ceased by degrees to form part of the stated sustenance of the Church, and the central verities enshrined in the creeds became axioms, from infancy

onwards, for us all. It is in his method of gathering and
combining evidence that Butler supplies us with an instru-
mentality most valuable for the safe handling of this and of
many other questions; and, being dead, yet speaks upon
matters of which there was not a whisper in his day, but
which are now echoing so loudly through the world.

CHAPTER III

THE CENSORS OF BISHOP BUTLER [1]

I. Mr. BAGEHOT.
II. Miss HENNELL.
III. Mr. LESLIE STEPHEN.
IV. Mr. MATTHEW ARNOLD.
V. MINOR STRICTURES: Mr. MAURICE, Mr. PATTISON, Mr. GOLDWIN SMITH.

Until the present century, and indeed until more than half of it had passed away, Butler, as represented in his most conspicuous production, had no censors; that is to say, none of any note, none who were themselves entitled to be noticed. His works, both before and after they had been published collectively in Oxford and in London, were received, as they issued in successive editions from the press, with an almost unbroken concert of applause. During the second portion of the century, while it does not appear that their circulation has declined, and we cannot affirm that their hold on the confidence of the Christian world has diminished, various writers of ability and even eminence have pointed out what they considered to be flaws in these remarkable productions; while some among them, without denying the great powers and high moral as well as philosophic rank of the author, have taken objection — mostly, but not exclusively, in the case of the *Analogy* — to some of his main positions, or even to the general scope of his argument.

I propose to undertake a close examination of the criticisms of four writers who form or belong to the last-named class, and to take them in their chronological order. These are Mr. Bagehot (1854), Miss S. S. Hennell [2] (1859), Mr.

[1] This chapter (now slightly changed) was printed in the *Nineteenth Century*, for November and December, 1895.

[2] A member of a family of distinguished talents, which is known to have exercised a powerful influence on the mind and career of George

Leslie Stephen (1876), and Mr. Matthew Arnold (1877). Of these, one — namely Miss Hennell — incorporates an important criticism by Dr. Martineau, which was first published about 1840, and which may in no vulgar sense be said to have been in the van of the attack.

There have been other comments in the nature of censure, sometimes accompanied by preponderating praise. Among these are Mr. Maurice, Mr. Mark Pattison, and Mr. Goldwin Smith. But these comments are on specific points, and have not been carried into detail.

Among the censures passed upon Butler, we may include the comments of a class of writers who, adopting uniformly a kindly tone, have expressed their regret that the works of Bishop Butler should, as in their judgement they do, fall, in sentiment or phraseology, beneath the true evangelical standard. I have offered, in discussing the theology of Butler, a vindication which appears to me to be sufficient.

I. Mr. BAGEHOT.

In his essay [1] on Butler, which I do not regard as one of the best specimens of his literary handiwork, Mr. Bagehot refers, in terms which appear to be far too disparaging, to the subject of style. 'In some places the mode of statement is even stupid'; and 'it is curious that so great a thinker should be so poor a writer.' Again, in graver matter, he thinks that Plato saw the truth; but Butler only groped for it. It was not difficult for Plato to see a truth, which in the main he moulded at his pleasure; but if Butler did but grope, his case was not wholly different from that of St. Paul, who only saw through a glass darkly. Plato's *assiette* was of and on the earth; Butler had all along to bind together earth and heaven. Mr. Bagehot's criticism [2] strikes also at Aristotle, who, like Butler, worked in rigid subserviency to facts, and not as master over them. The style of Butler, too, has been made largely responsible for

Eliot. See Mr. R. H. Hutton on 'George Eliot's Life and Writings' in his *Modern Guides of English Thought in Matters of Faith*, p. 270.

[1] *Literary Studies*, vol. ii. essay ii. pp. 74, 75.
[2] *Ibid.* p. 76.

the difficulties of his subject [1]; but those who might rewrite one of his pages would find it more difficult than they may suppose to improve the style without impairing the substance. In his illustrations Butler is particularly happy; and, upon the whole, in his case, and also in that of Aristotle, it may be that the style and the substance cannot be parted.

Taking it at large, I think the following passage, extracted from the very able preface of the late Bishop Steere to his edition of the *Analogy*, presents no unjust view of the question of Bishop Butler's style:

In truth, the greatest beauty of an author's style consists in its appropriateness to express his meaning. There is a rough likeness between the style of the *Analogy* and that of a legal document; and it goes deeper than might have been expected. For what makes a deed obscure to the uninitiated? Chiefly the attempt on the part of the framer to exclude all ambiguity. It looks like irony, but it is true, that no written thing, when examined, is clearer than a legal document; and the object, the attained object, of all those obscure phrases is to avoid the possibility of being misunderstood. Therefore it is that, the more one examines into possible meanings of what seemed clearer (*sic*) expressions, the more we shall realise and admire the sound judgement which has preferred what we, at first sight, thought ill-chosen and obscure. Thus it is that careful students of Butler's works generally come, in the end, to have a sort of relish for his peculiar style [2].

Granted fully that Butler's style is difficult. But it does not in any degree follow that it is, properly speaking, obscure.

It is needless to dwell on the judgement of Mr. Bagehot concerning the great argument of Conscience in the Sermons; for it is in a strain of nearly unbroken approval. But, when we come to the *Analogy*, Mr. Bagehot propounds grave objections to its reasoning.

---

[1] One, however, of Butler's editors has had the courage to undertake the reformation of his style. See *Bishop Butler's Treatise on the Analogy of Religion to the Constitution and Course of Nature: with a Summary of the Argument, and the Style in some parts simplified.* By the Rev. Edward Bushby, D. D., Fellow and Tutor of St. John's College, Cambridge. London, 1842.

[2] *Butler's Analogy,* with analytical preface and index, by the late Right Rev. Edward Steere, LL.D., Bishop in Central Africa. London, Bell, 1886, page v.

Firstly, he denies it to have been 'probable' that Revelation would contain difficulties of a like kind with nature, and subjoins, 'we should have expected that it would explain those difficulties [1].' The rational likelihood was that the Revelation 'would be one affecting our daily life and welfare; would communicate truths either on the one hand conducing to our temporal happiness in the present world, or removing the many doubts and difficulties, which surround the general plan of Providence, the entire universe, and our particular destiny.'

There is no doubt that this objection strikes at the very heart of the *Analogy*. If the objection stands, the Treatise must fall. On the other hand, every reviewer of Mr. Bagehot's criticisms must feel how cautiously he ought to deal with the views and arguments of a writer who is not less modest than he is able and acute, and who himself deals so tenderly with all that appertains to the religious belief of his fellow-Christians, and regards it with so deep and genuine an interest.

I must nevertheless express a conviction that Mr. Bagehot mistakes the seat of that evil, which he does not fail to see. No doubt we are entitled, and indeed bound, to anticipate that a Divine Revelation will be aimed at the heart of a great mischief, and will be designed and adapted to remove it. But the case of human nature is not a case of mere difficulty; it is a case of disease; and the mischief lies not in the darkness of the understanding, but in the perversion of the Will. Darkened without doubt the understanding is, but darkened by those fumes of passion, which rise so densely from the furnace of our desires. These cloud the atmosphere within us, and thicken what ought to be a translucent medium to convey in their purity the authoritative sentences of conscience. Had want of knowledge been the capital difficulty of our state, fishermen would not have been the chief ministers of the Gospel, nor would babes and sucklings have perfected its praise. Not from an upper chamber in Jerusalem, not from the stable, offering to the Redeemer of the world the shelter denied Him by the inn, but rather from Pnyx and Theatre, from Portico and Aca-

[1] *Literary Studies*, vol. ii. essay ii. pp. 86, 87.

deme of Athens, would the notes of salvation have been sounded forth.

If we proceed upon the narrative of Genesis, it was not for want of knowledge that mankind fell from a peaceful into a troubled existence, but from the unauthorized and premature pursuit of it. If Butler is right in referring for the origin of what he terms natural religion to a primitive revelation, yet the historic traces of that revelation became with the lapse of years faint and imperceptible. There were indeed times, such for instance as the Achaian period described by Homer, when belief in a Divine government of the world was still sustained, and the foundations of right and duty still remained visible, in virtue of the law written in the heart. Generations passed away, and knowledge increased in the world; and, together with this increase of knowledge, the conditions of social order came to be better understood; but in other respects virtue diminished, and the idea of sin, except among the Jews, was virtually lost.

Mr. Bagehot rightly observes that the argument of Butler is one dealing with our religious difficulties: and 'this is the exact class of difficulty which it is most likely a revelation if given would explain[1].' But the view of Butler is so different that his critic will be found here to challenge one of his main and deliberately assumed positions. As his teaching runs, there is no absurdity in supposing that the speculative difficulties, in which the evidence of religion is involved, may constitute even the principal and most fruitful part of the trial of some among us. The generality have to contend with more vulgar temptations; but 'there are persons of a higher stamp, without this shallowness of temper, persons endowed with a deeper sense of what is invisible and future.' Had such persons no doubts to contend with, the practice of religion would be to them, as Butler thinks, unavoidable; and at least it seems clear that they would stand in no such need of effort as to brace the mind and train the character in the manner of what we term a discipline; which discipline nevertheless may be very needful for their perfection[2]. Objections to the truths of Christianity, apart from its evidence, Butler holds to be

---

[1] *Literary Studies*, vol. ii. essay ii. p. 87.   [2] *Analogy*, II. vi. 18.

mostly frivolous : and it may be presumed that, had he thought them worthy of more consideration, he would have treated them as he has treated objections to the evidence.

With his habitual sincerity, Mr. Bagehot falls back upon first principles ; and holds that 'the supposition and idea of a miraculous revelation rest on the ignorance of man' : and that God, if He should speak, 'would shed abundant light on all doubts, would take the weight from our minds, would remove the gnawing anguish from our hearts.[1]' He anticipates, however, a form of reply to his argument. It is that there may be facts impossible for us at present to appreciate, but most important for us to know. His answer is that there is no advantage in the revelation of an inexplicable fact : that such a revelation is extremely improbable : that the revelation we might properly expect is one throwing light on the world in which we live ; and in which 'poverty and sin, pain and sorrow, fear and anger, press on us with a heavy weight[2].' But this, as Butler truly teaches, is asking to be acquainted with the whole counsel of Providence : a task which he renounces, finding that he undertakes enough in endeavouring, not to explain the conduct of the Almighty, but to point out to man his duty[8].

Mr. Bagehot thinks also that a revelation of rites and ordinances, as compared with duties, is antecedently most improbable. But, in this large and sweeping proposition, does he not forget the exigencies of our complex and compound nature ? It would be strange, without doubt, if external prescriptions were to form the substance or main bulk of a revelation. But it may seem that a revelation may naturally comprehend what provides for the discipline of the body ; what corresponds with the large office of the senses in the business of human life ; and even what satisfies the imagination. The lofty doctrine of the Gospel, which consecrates the body as an inseparable portion of our nature, and at the same time propounds our reunion with the Divine Nature in the person of the Redeemer, as the one thing needful, shows that there is here an unfilled gap in the teaching of Mr. Bagehot which deals with us as pure

---

[1] *Literary Studies*, vol. ii. essay ii. p. 88.   [2] *Ibid.* pp. 88, 89.
[8] *Analogy*, II. viii. 10.

intelligences ; and may well justify Bishop Butler when he teaches that the exterior part of Christianity belongs to its essence [1].

Mr. Bagehot contends [2] that the argument of the *Analogy* 'may be used in the defence of any revelation, the Mahometan as well as the Christian'; and it has appeared to some that herein lies an objection to the Treatise. But let us suppose, though the supposition may be an extreme one, the case of a Mahometan philosopher arguing, as Butler has argued in his first Part, and substituting in a second Part the Koran for the Gospel, each of them as illustrated by the course of history ; suppose that he could establish the claim of his religion to a serious examination : such a claim, on such a basis, constitutes no objection to the argument of Butler. The Koran then presents itself, according to Butler's method, at the bar of reason for scrutiny : inasmuch as reason is the judge both of the proofs of the religion, and even of its character. When the proofs of the Gospel are opened, we find that it alleges, taken roughly : (1) Prophecy, (2) Miracle, (3) History, (4) Moral adaptation. And of these the first two appear especially to have been vital to its first acceptance. But when we turn to Mahometanism, these two great subjects are presented to us as an absolute blank. If we come to the third, we find anterior history in the narrative of the Old Testament leading up to Christianity, but having no point of contact whatever with Mahometanism. If we pass to posterior records, we find that the history of Christianity, down to the time when it had conclusively established its hold on the greatest races and ruling intellects of the world, was a history of suasion. But the history of Mahometanism, as a religion systematically propagated by violence and bloodshed, seems to renounce the appeal to reasoning altogether, and to make the whole inquiry ridiculous. It is hardly necessary, after this, to enter on the question of moral adaptation, or an efficacious remedy for the disease of human nature. Perhaps from this brief review we may sufficiently judge what is the practical upshot of Butler's argument, when applied to religions other than the Gospel. And this without our

---

[1] *Analogy*, II. i. 19.   [2] *Literary Studies*, vol. ii. essay ii. p. 90.

being bound to deny that the Mahometan and other religions may, in virtue of such elements of truth as they
contain, have acted for special purposes, and may still operate upon humble and simple souls, in conjunction with
purely natural affections, for purposes of real good. It is
but too easy to show, on the one hand, how the results of
Christianity are intercepted and marred by our corruption
of nature: and we should not really mend our own case by
grudging to those, who live under other systems, every
acknowledgement that truth demands. If it be the fact,
then, that Butler's argument is available for religions other
than our own, it can only be made available for them in so
far as they are true; just as, in the case of Christianity, it
does nothing to accredit those corruptions which he admits
and deplores. In so far as it tends to support such elements of truth as may not have been stifled in other religions, this surely is not a defect, but a recommendation of
the reasoning he has employed.

Mr. Bagehot sums up the first chapter of his argument by
declaring it to be monstrous that there should be a Divine
revelation which enumerates the difficulties of natural government and yet casts no light upon them; and so, instead
of relieving doubt or anxiety, should 'proclaim every fact
which can give a base to them both [1].' As regards the first
of these, it is simply a misconception to suppose that γνῶσις
and not πρᾶξις was the purpose for which our necessities
demanded a provision. As regards the second, it will be
more conveniently considered in connexion with the objection as it has been taken by another of the censors of
Bishop Butler.

Thus far Mr. Bagehot has been clear and explicit in urging his exceptions against the Treatise of Butler. But now
he announces [2] that he has a second objection to the argument of the *Analogy* on which he is inclined to lay nearly
equal stress. I must own that I have failed, in this portion
of his Essay, to gather his meaning. He nowhere cites a
passage from the work; he nowhere even describes one.
Instead of this, he cites passages from Professor Rogers [3],

---

[1] *Literary Studies*, vol. ii. essay ii. p. 90.   [2] *Ibid.* p. 90.
[3] *Ibid.* p. 98.

and perhaps makes good certain points against them; but for Professor Rogers, Butler certainly cannot be held responsible. At one moment[1] he seems to admit Butler's argument within certain limits, and allows that the 'style of Providence' would probably be the same in revelation as in nature; but neither here nor elsewhere does he collect evidence from the text. And he somewhat strangely winds up his article by tracing to deficiencies in Butler's mental constitution faults in the Treatise, as to which he does not supply a particle of evidence to exhibit or make good their existence. Those who would either condemn Butler or defend him with effect must be prepared to deal with their subject at much closer quarters.

II. Miss HENNELL.

In 1859, Miss S. S. Hennell widened the ground of the attack by publishing her essay 'On the Sceptical Tendency of Butler's Analogy.' Without doubt she begs a very large question in her title; but no critic can surpass her either in reverence or in candour; and she records this judgement upon Butler's position as it has been generally estimated: 'By the main body of Christian believers he is still considered unanswered and unanswerable, strong as a giant against all the puny attacks of infidelity[2].'

She considers, indeed, that the Treatise 'engenders a deep spirit of scepticism,' and supplies no principle capable of effectually combating it. But of this anon.

Following many others, but quite innocently, she quotes a reported remark of Mr. Pitt on Butler's *Analogy*, to the effect that it suggested to him more doubts than it solved. From the eminence of the names concerned, this remark may have circulated widely; but I have never had the means of verifying the statement until within a few days ago, when I found Wilberforce's Diary quoted as the source.

The *Life of Wilberforce* was published nearly sixty years ago, and was allowed to run to the inordinate length of five volumes. The public has avenged itself by suffering the book to pass into literary oblivion. I have, however, an

---

[1] *Literary Studies*, vol. ii. essay ii. pp. 95, 96.   [2] *Essay*, p. 2.

original copy, and I will give from it first the statements, and then the authority on which they rest.

In November, 1785, Mr. Wilberforce was much agitated by deep religious convictions, leading to a great elevation in his tone of life. He was in a correspondence with Mr. Pitt, to whom he had not, at the date I have first cited, opened his whole mind. Still it must have contained references to his serious course of thought, for he records under the date of November 24, the following : —

' Pitt called, and commended Butler's *Analogy* : resolved to write to him, and discover to him what I am occupied about.'

And accordingly on Sunday, the 27th, he read Butler for three-quarters of an hour [1]. He fulfilled his resolution to write to Pitt in very explicit terms. Pitt promptly announced to him his intention to call on the following day [2]. He came accordingly and pressed on the discussion. As Wilberforce says : —

' He tried to reason me out of my convictions. . . . The fact is that he was so absorbed in politics, that he had never given himself time for due reflection on religion. But amongst other things he declared to me, that Bishop Butler's work raised in his mind more doubts than it had answered [3].'

Considering Butler's extreme candour, nay scrupulosity, in stating the objections to his own case, there is nothing wonderful in this passage, taken by itself : for, if Pitt's mind was not fully prepared, he might be struck with the difficulties of the case more vividly than by the solutions of those difficulties. But we have these curious facts before us. On the 3rd of December (which appears to have been the date), in a conversation controversial though friendly, he condemns the tendency of the very book which he had spontaneously, and not in disputation, recommended to Wilberforce nine days before. This really amounts to a contradiction. But Pitt was a man not likely to contradict himself. How are we to reconcile the two passages ? and are they of equal authority ?

The answer is that they are not of equal, but indeed of

---

[1] *Life of Wilberforce* (Murray, 1838), i. pp. 89, 90.
[2] *Ibid.* p. 94.   [3] *Ibid.* p. 95.

most unequal authority. In their Preface, the editors of the Life carefully explain the different sources of the material which they have woven into one continuous narrative ; and they have for the most part, in the body of the work, noticed them at the foot of the page.

The first of these sources was from manuscript books, or detached sheets, in which Mr. Wilberforce was accustomed himself to note down daily occurrences. These will be found referred to under the head of 'Diary.'

The commendation of Butler is quoted from a series of extracts reaching continuously from the 24th of November, day by day, to the 30th; and these are apparently among the first fruits of his private 'Diary,' which he began now, 'whilst this struggle was at its height,' with a view to spiritual uses. So the commendation of Butler by Mr. Pitt comes to us (1) at first hand, (2) in a contemporary record.

But the sources of materials are five[1], and the fifth is neither contemporary, nor first hand. It represented partly conversations of this venerable man; some of them taken down when uttered, but at times never specified, by members of his family. At the dates we have been dealing with, Mr. Wilberforce was twenty-five and a bachelor ; so that all the materials of this class, if written at all, were written (say) at periods later by from twenty to forty-eight years (he died in 1833), when he had sons full-grown. Another portion was supplied by the editors from their own vivid recollections, apparently after his death, when they came to execute their task as biographers. And a third portion was furnished by certain friends. It is to this last class of material that the condemnation of Butler belongs ; or, as we are informed by a footnote, to 'conversational memoranda[2].'

It appears, then, that the condemnation, on which a good deal of stress has been laid, stands in a category of information which is at best only doubtful ; but in this case it comes at once into conflict with another account of a directly opposite tenor, and recorded under circumstances which give it the highest degree of authenticity. In other words, it is not, as it stands, entitled to credit.

The reader will, I am sure, excuse the minuteness of this

---

[1] Preface, pp. v, ix.   [2] *Ibid.* p. x.

detail. [I must now add to it my own conjectural, but I think not irrational interpretation. Once only, as it appears upon the evidence, was Wilberforce tempted, even by the recommendation of Pitt, to spend less than one hour in reading the *Analogy*. He also had it read to him for two hours! a proof I think that he never girded up his loins to it at all, or gave it more than a perfunctory attention. Any one, who thus trifles with the work, is likely enough to be struck with the objections raised rather than with the answers to them. Upon the whole, seeing that the remark assigned to Pitt cannot well be true, it seems possible, if not probable, that Wilberforce (if the reporting friends have made no mistake), a generation after the facts, put into the mouth of Pitt a distant and shadowy recollection of an impression of his own [1].]

It would be unwarrantable to resort to any such plea with a view to excluding Miss Hennell from this arena. Her thoughts on Butler are palpably serious and earnest; and side by side with her ingenuous statement as to the ruling Christian opinion on the subject, we must register the admission that, in one, and possibly in more than one, intelligent and upright critic, Butler leaves a 'permanent feeling of unsatisfactoriness rankling in the mind,' and transfers from himself to his reader 'a sympathetic gloom,' which the great 'intellectual and moral power' of the work heightens into 'a kind of paralyzing awe [2].' Into the recesses of emotion we cannot penetrate; but it is permitted to deal with arguments; and it is a task of something better than a combative interest to inquire into their reality and weight in the case of Miss Hennell.

Butler, in every instance without exception, reduces his demands upon the antagonist whom he always sees before him to their minimum. There is not in the *Analogy*, from beginning to end, a word of rhetoric, of declamation, of either wilful or neglectful over-statement. It is a purely dry light which he seeks to cast upon his theme. He opens a path before us, and the whole purpose of his book is summed up in the word 'ought'; while to this 'ought' there is no other sequel than the words 'to inquire.' For all those

---

[1] Added to the text, March 17, 1896.   [2] *Essay*, p. 5.

whose temperament is warm, whose imagination is lively, this seems but a jejune result; they have spent much labour and much patience in toiling up the steep road of the Treatise itself, and then they find themselves simply introduced into a new field of arduous investigation. They are tired, and demand refreshment; he offers them only a recommencement of work. After a hot and hard day, it seems a scanty wage. It is no wonder if some are disappointed; it is well that so many are not. To my mind, there is no preparation for a satisfactory study of Butler so good as to have been widely conversant with the disappointing character of human affairs. With touching simplicity he says:

'Indeed the unsatisfactory nature of the evidence, with which we are obliged to take up, in the daily course of life, is scarce to be expressed[1].'

Yet such evidence suffices for those whose one habitual endeavour it is to discern and follow the way of duty. So it comes to this; that the method of guidance given us for practice is one with the method of guidance given us for belief. And of these two, the first is perhaps the very best προπαίδευσις for what is to follow it in the *palaestra* to which Butler introduces us. So viewing the matter, are we entitled at once to complain of a 'sceptical tendency' in the *Analogy?*

I proceed to consider Miss Hennell's arguments.

Some twenty years before the Essay of Miss Hennell, Dr. Martineau had published a Sermon, in which he was, I believe, the first to object broadly [2] to Butler's mode of using the argument from analogy. Miss Hennell adopts and presses the criticism of Dr. Martineau. I sum up the passage as follows. Vicarious suffering is admitted to be found in nature. But it is the exception, not the rule. If we make it the rule, if it be a key to unlock the whole problem of Divine Government, then we place creation under a tyrant's sway. Again: 'We pass through the great infirmary of God's creation'; and Butler is said to say that 'it is all the same in the other world, and wherever the same rule extends.' And so the question arises whether this victory is won in favour of Revelation, or against Natural Religion.

---

[1] *Analogy*, II. viii. 17.   [2] *Essay*, p. 11.

The argument is alike intelligible and forcible. If we represent disease and wrong as the characteristic features of creation, we clearly administer a terrible persuasive to Atheism. But is this a true representation of the language of Butler? I know of no other case in which a great author has been so largely misapprehended, and consequently misstated, and that by critics who cordially respected him. Butler has nowhere drawn for us such a picture. He has, indeed, said that the difficulties which are alleged against religion are found in nature, and yet do not displace belief in an Author of nature. But he is so far from representing this as a normal state of things, that he takes his stand throughout upon the proposition that this world, in which our lot is cast, is in a state of apostasy and ruin. For this condition, religion professes to supply remedial provisions. The question is then raised upon the credibility of the scheme it offers. And Butler supports it, as to credibility, by showing that it presents to view no difficulties, unless such as have their counterpart in nature, and as, when urged against believing in a supreme Author of nature, have been found not to warrant that negation. They cannot, therefore, be more effective when urged against religion. He first marks our entire condition here as exceptional by showing us to be in a state of apostasy and ruin. He then points out that, even in this disordered and impaired position of things, virtue or good makes a partial but intelligible assertion of its prerogatives, and visibly promises one more unequivocal and complete. He urges that even here the bad man has small satisfaction in what he enjoys, and the good man large compensations for what he suffers ; that in indirect forms — for example, in those of civil government — a law of right is to some extent proclaimed : that God even here and now takes part in the controversy, and proclaims Himself to be on the side of virtue. In anticipation of criticism, Butler has girt himself about with precautions which ought to have shielded him against these serious and strange mistakes of the reasoning he actually uses. But I proceed.

Miss Hennell next supposes the case of an inquirer into the truth of Christianity who finds himself[1] brought face to

---

[1] *Essay*, p. 6.

face in Scripture with representations of the actions of
Deity that shock his moral sense. Repairing to Butler for
aid, he is instructed that like infractions of right occur in
nature, and that as we nevertheless believe in a supreme
Author of nature, so we may still believe in the authenticity
of Revelation. But as Revelation, she thinks, gives a sanction to such infractions, her inquirer is in a painful dilemma.

Now I am not considering objections to religion founded
on any moral anomaly which may seem to be presented by
the Old Testament histories, but am dealing simply with
objections to the argument of Butler. Butler has nowhere
so much as touched in detail any of these moral difficulties.
They did not lie in the main line of his argument. To consider how far a Revelation, because Divine, is tied to conditions of absolute perfection in the manner of its communication, is a subject at once large, and distinct from that of
Butler. It is true that this may be held to be included in
the parent-suggestion of Origen, which presents to us the
Scriptures as the groundwork of the proposed comparison
with nature. But, probably for the purpose of avoiding an
extension of his field which would have made his subject
unmanageable, Butler in his title alters the description, and
takes not the Scriptures, but religion, as the subject which
he is to compare with nature. He was surely entitled to
hold that the subjects of discussion which he thus escaped
are not directly presented to us by the religion which he
teaches, and which relies on the Scriptures of the Old Testament in proof of the Advent, but does not directly or
essentially associate itself with every particular of government over men; any more than the arguments of our Lord
and of Saint Paul from providential action in the world bind
them to account for all the difficulties which may offer to
our view. How true this is we may the better perceive if
we bear in mind that, in the centuries immediately succeeding the age of our Lord, the general contents of the Old
Testament were far from being either formally or largely
presented to the acceptance or to the eyes of converts to
Christianity.

It is true, however, that while Butler avoids the discussion in detail on the difficulties of Old Testament history,

he lays down principles applicable to them; and this, too, in one of the most assailable passages of the *Analogy*, which, if it allows of defence, may fairly be said to invite and tempt attack. Miss Hennell here finds him guilty of sophistry, and of open defiance of natural principles. She conceives that the best apology which can be made for him lies in the 'noble straightforward candour with which, casting aside all disguises, he lays bare to every reader the nature of his contentions.'

What he contends for is as· follows: He lays it down in the first place[1] that reason is a judge, not indeed of things contained in Scripture and at variance with our expectations of what a Revelation would convey to us, but yet (first) of the evidence, and (secondly) of the morality of what is offered for our acceptance. It is to judge whether the matter propounded to us is 'plainly contradictory to wisdom, justice or goodness; to what the light of nature teaches us of God,' or, again, it cannot accept what is contrary to 'immutable morality[2]'; or 'the principles and spirit of treachery, ingratitude, cruelty.'

But, as he contends, the case is different with external action; 'for instance, taking away the property or life of any'; the title to hold these proceeding from the Divine Will, and being revocable by those who gave them. In these cases, actions, which without command would be immoral, cease to bear that character when commanded. They are indeed 'offences' — *that is to say*, they are liable to be perverted 'to serve the most horrid purposes,' and possibly they may mislead the weak[3]. They belong also to a course of things liable to create an immoral habit: but this will not follow if the occasions of them be only few and detached.

Upon this passage at least three questions appear to arise. (1) Is it consistent with itself? (2) Can it be defended in all its parts? (3) What was the probable intention of the author, and what is the equitable interpretation to be placed upon it as a whole?

First, if reason is to judge whether matter propounded to us in the name of religion is, or is not, plainly contradictory

---

[1] *Analogy*, II. iii. 26.   [2] *Ibid.* 27.   [3] *Ibid.* 28.

to wisdom, justice, and goodness — is, or is not, tainted with
'treachery, ingratitude, cruelty' — it seems impossible to exclude from the province of judgement by reason 'the whole
of external action': such as the cruel murder of Abel by
Cain, or the treachery of Rachel and Jacob against Esau.
Yet such exclusion seems to be conveyed in the words which
here describe external action; and therefore the language
of the passage does not appear to be consistent throughout.

Nor is it possible, secondly, to defend a statement which,
taken in its letter, asserts by implication that no breach of
wisdom, justice, or goodness can be involved in an external
act. Nor can I undertake to support the assertion that in
cases where 'a course' of acts would create an immoral
habit, a few detached instances have no 'natural tendency'
in the same direction.

So far Butler seems to lie open to the animadversions of
the severer critics: and, without doubt, every shortcoming
in point of accuracy in a Treatise dealing with subjects of
the first moment is to be lamented.

But the third question is the most weighty. Suppose, for
argument's sake, it were the intention of Butler, not to lay
down an universal proposition denying that an essential
morality or the reverse may attach to external action, but
only to assert this, that there are large provinces of external
action, within which the character of the things done essentially depends on the authority under which they are done,
not upon the nature of the action as it stands apart from
such authority: this, I think, we may defend both as clearly
true and also as important.

It seems to me probable that Butler, whose age was not
an age of minute Scripture criticism, had before his mind
nothing more than the general severity of punishments recorded in the Old Testament, such as the large, though by
no means universal, extirpation of the Canaanitish nations,
or the summary judgement executed upon the partakers in
the schism of Korah, where, however, no human agency was
employed.

And again with reference to the formation of habits in
the individual mind. The Bible presents to us the case of
Samuel, who conveys to us the idea of a character alike wise

and gentle; but who was the appointed instrument for
destroying with his own hand King Agag, in requital for
his cruelties [1]. To be the mere minister of lawful but bloody
sentences is an occupation tending to form some kinds of
immoral habit. But surely all must so far agree with
Butler as to say that there is a wide difference between the
habitual performance of such acts, and such a performance
on a single and separate occasion. It is such a difference
as we may recognize between the effect on the character of
a soldier who has, once or upon rare occasions, wounded or
slain in battle the enemies of his country, and the case of a
public executioner, addicted, before the recent mitigation of
manners, to the constant launching of his fellow-creatures
into eternity; one marked in the tradition of the Christian
nations as having been placed, by the public instinct of the
community, under a kind of moral proscription, which lays
the office under a sort of traditional discredit. Confining
ourselves to the assertion of a difference, and that a wide
one, we stand on ground that is unassailable. It must
indeed be acknowledged that the single act, such as that of
Samuel, is the first step towards the formation of a habit;
but is it not like the first step of the foot over a series of
stepping-stones, which may be drawn back? Even so the
deed, remaining without sequel of any kind, is as if it were
retracted; for in the course of nature the habitual tone and
bias of the character resume their sway.

The question is, are we, with Miss Hennell, utterly to
condemn the whole doctrine conveyed by Butler in this
passage, or are we, while admitting that his language at
one or two points falls short of his usual accuracy, and
requires qualification, to accord to him the benefit of such
qualification, and admit that he in no degree intentionally
tampered with the moral law? It seems to me that the
latter is not only the more equitable, but the more rational,
process; and for the reason which, plain as it appears to be,
Miss Hennell has entirely overlooked. It is this. Butler
has laid down emphatically in this very passage that there
is an immutable morality, which no positive command can
change; and has made a strict adherence to wisdom, justice,

[1] 1 Sam. xv. 33.

goodness, and the inflexible rejection of treachery, ingratitude, and cruelty, the governing idea of the entire passage. With this he combines the unquestionable truth, that a multitude of acts, such (say) as the levying of taxes, the invasion of liberty by incarceration, and executing the forfeiture of life for crime, which would be immoral if the agent be unauthorized, are habitually made moral, and even obligatory, by public authority. Even more, then, in an age and under a dispensation of more direct and palpable relations between the Almighty and His creatures, might devolution, similar in principle, but of yet higher authority, lead to acts, such as the terrible penalty upon Canaan, which may not in their whole grounds be comprehensible by us, but which it would be the extreme of audacity on our part to condemn.

In no case can Miss Hennell be warranted, as it seems to me, in drawing inferences from the passages to support the general doctrine that the *Analogy* favours scepticism ; because any corrections or limitations which the writer's phraseology in this instance may require can in no way interfere with the general course of his argument, or impair its force. If the system under which the world is actually governed inspires the conviction that it has a righteous aim, while presenting incidents for which that righteousness of aim does not always give account to us, the very same rule must serve us in our dealings with moral anomalies in the Scriptures of the Old Testament.

But Miss Hennell is occasionally so carried off her balance by emotion that she too deviates into inaccurate representation of Butler. She says Butler charges us 'not to be disturbed by exceptional interruption of the law of morality [1].' It is no wonder that she has no citation in proof of this grave statement; for none can be found. Butler treats morality as immutable, and emphatically holds that it is not based upon the mere consequences of acts [2], that moral fitness resides in them of themselves, and that the will of God is thereby determined [3]. There can be no interruption, then, of the moral law in the Divine government. Instances there may be which we cannot demonstrate to be

1 *Essay*, p. 18.   2 *Analogy*, I. vii. 21.   3 *Ibid.* vi. 16 n.

in conformity with it; but on these we are to suspend our judgement for the very sufficient reason that our ignorance prevents us from giving a full and perfect account of any one thing whatever [1], and especially of such things as give no explanation of themselves. With this misconception of Butler, Miss Hennell's declamation against orthodoxy of itself falls to the ground.

Miss Hennell states with moderation [2], that the work of Butler, faithfully adjusted as it was to the needs of his own day, is inadequate to the needs of ours. This is indeed indisputable. His argument does not of itself confute the Agnostic, the Positivist, the Materialist; and it is also true that, the argument against miracles not having been fully developed when he wrote, his observations upon the point, as they stand, are incomplete. But these facts in no way sustain the purpose or the title of Miss Hennell's tract. Butler cannot minister to scepticism merely because he does not conclusively dispose of questions that were not before him. To supply the missing link between them, Miss Hennell resorts to assumption. She assumes that he had examined what she called the positive question, meaning apparently the argument on the being and attributes of God handled by Clarke, and had found it wanting. This assumption is in the first place altogether gratuitous; in the second highly improbable. The works of Butler are limited in bulk, but the immense amount of substance they contain furnishes a very adequate outcome in the philosophical region for a life like his, not over long, and for a mind so circumspect and profound that, upon subjects of such difficulty, its operations may of necessity have been slow. But also upon moral grounds the supposition is one dishonouring to Butler. He had, as we know, solemnly devoted his life to the search for truth. Yet Miss Hennell can suppose that in theology he accepted and argued from the important concessions of Deists, without being within himself persuaded of their truth. This too although she has herself warmly eulogized his high mental integrity. But in truth he has on his own behalf settled and *de jure* if not *de facto* closed this question. For he tells us in the correspondence with Clarke

---

[1] *Analogy*, I. vii. 6.   [2] *Essay*, pp. 20, 21.

that he had long hoped and looked for a demonstrative proof of the being and attributes of God, but had felt himself obliged to recede from this extreme demand and to rest content with ' very probable arguments,' which, as we know, in his mind carried with them the full weight of practical assent, and also imposed all the stringency of high moral obligation.

Why Miss Hennell should term Butler's method negative, while it consists simply in the search for facts and in positive deduction from them; or why she should describe it as of that 'metaphysical kind' which is 'very fruitful in delusion [1],' while it is purely experimental throughout, it may be hardly worth while to inquire. But she now proceeds to a ground of argument both broad and relevant. Butler alleges that there is a scheme of Providence. But we know only 'a most insignificant portion of the whole order of things.' How, then, can he be justified in attempting to make it into a system, and put it forward for acceptance? The answer is plain from Butler's point of view. It is just because the known facts, though their amount be insignificant in comparison with the facts unknown, yet afford sufficient proof that there is a scheme, and that it is righteous, though the evidence of it, like almost all the evidence on which we have to found our conduct, is far from giving 'satisfaction': that is, from being what we could desire [2]. Confute him on his facts if you can: but his reasoning is perfectly consecutive; and, being based on human experience at large, is as durable now as in his own day.

Miss Hennell proposes to make Butler responsible for setting up a conflict between reason and faith. Reason is purposely checked by obstacles arbitrarily interposed, in order that faith may have space for cultivation [3].

There is no other ground for saying reason is checked, than the fact that our knowledge is limited. Our bounded powers have a bounded field for their exercise and development. This is not to check but to train them. Reason is only checked, in any proper sense of the word, when it is forbidden to judge, according to the nature and degree of the evidence supplied, upon matters presented for its acceptance.

---

[1] *Essay*, p. 22. [2] *Analogy*, II. viii. 18. [3] *Essay*, p. 25.

But this prerogative of reason is one which Butler has been beyond most other writers solicitous to enforce. And as for the doctrine that our struggles with obstacles may be good and fruitful provided we do not believe that God designed them [1], it neither admits of support, nor deserves confutation. Again, in making war on the idea that Duty is 'conformity to the will of a Divine Moral Governor,' our critic is not showing the sceptical tendency of Butler's *Analogy*, but simply putting in question both the method and the basis of instruction under the Gospel.

Miss Hennell proceeds to ascribe to Butler all the following propositions [2]; which she holds to be false:

1. That exceptions to a supposed moral rule are better not regarded. There is not a word in Butler's *Analogy* to this effect.

2. That it is desirable for man to content himself with probabilities. What Butler says is, that the provision with which we are furnished in order to the guidance of life is a provision of probabilities. But the spirit alike of his life and of his works is a spirit which must, on the one hand, stimulate every sympathizing student to obtain in every case the best evidence he can before forming his judgement, and, on the other hand, warn him against mistaking the character or overstating the value of that evidence.

3. That the effect of this reliance upon probabilities should be little different from that of acting upon ascertained truth. Now, Butler places the obligation to act, imposed by probable evidence, very near that which ascertained truth would impose. But he nowhere states or implies that the action is to be the same. The possibilities of error, which remain in the one case and not in the other, may have to be carefully watched for, and therefore entail an important difference in the mode of action.

4. That nature suggests a Governor who commands strict obedience; 'a Father best pleased with uninquiring filial love.' There is not a word to this effect in the works of Butler. They do not contain a single highly-coloured passage in favour of authority, and their spirit throughout is surely favourable to intelligent and unflinching scrutiny.

[1] *Essay*, p. 26.   [2] *Ibid.* p. 31.

5. That perplexities have been contrived for us by the Creator in order to prevent our reason from mastering our faith. Not a word is, or can be, cited to support this 'averment.' The purpose suggested by Butler for these perplexities is the training and hardening of faith as a moral principle, without the smallest inkling of an aggression upon reason, which Butler never places in conflict with faith. Criticism of this kind can only be met by a challenge for proof; and, till proof is forthcoming, it is null and void. Miss Hennell herself happens to agree with Butler in his main contention that there is proof of a natural and moral government with a 'preponderating tendency towards good [1]'; and it is difficult to understand why she should labour to set up a factitious opposition between the Bishop and herself, by imputing to him, without a shadow of evidence, and really in contradiction to the whole groundwork of his Treatise, that he encourages a 'forced attempt to believe that *all* is good!' Again, it is not a little singular that here [2] he should be censured for efforts to produce a forced content with his case, while we shall find Mr. Arnold making it his capital boast against the *Analogy* that Butler himself has so loudly expressed his own discontent with it [3].

I have now gone through all the material allegations which Miss Hennell sets forth in fulfilment of the great promise conveyed in her title-page, and have endeavoured to exhibit them in their fullest breadth. In the large portion of it, from p. 35 to the close, she abandons the attempt to prove her thesis from his text, or from vague descriptions of it, or even through the strange expedient of quotations from Professor Rogers [4] and of holding Butler responsible for his language.

She now launches into pure speculation on his interior state, and into theories, evidently dictated by prepossession, on the tendencies of his works, which she conceives to be, without doubt, on paper, towards unbelief, and in religious practice towards the Church of Rome; while she retains for him a reverent and even affectionate admiration. She calls him 'our great ecclesiastical thinker'; she plainly intends to crown him with honour when she places him in company

[1] *Essay*, p. 32.   [2] *Ibid*. p. 34.   [3] See *inf*. p. 70.   [4] As in pp. 27, 28.

with Locke, and declares the two to be the 'legitimate precursors of the positive philosophers of the present day.' But I pass onward from some amiable inconsistencies, to observe that it still remains to notice one more topic directly connected with the announcement of the title-page, and indeed the most important of them all, which has not been developed in the tract, but which is glanced at by Dr. Martineau, when he asks whether consummation of Butler's argument is indeed a triumph for Revelation, or against Natural Religion.

It is alleged with truth that, when Butler defends Religion, Natural and Revealed, by the contention that they only reproduce difficulties with which we are already familiar in 'the constitution and course of nature,' he casts a weight upon the back of nature itself, and raises the question whether nature is adequate to sustain it. At the date of the *Analogy*, and in dealing with the Deists, it might have sufficed as a defence for controversial purposes, though it hardly would have satisfied a mind like that of Butler, to reply 'that is a closed question ; it is already disposed of by your own admissions.' But their admissions bound only themselves : and it would indeed be a heavy blow to the general argument for belief, if Butler had left us in doubt on the vital question whether the argument suggested by these difficulties against the constitution and course of nature themselves had any validity.

But upon this subject Butler is perfectly explicit. Pursuing his usual method, he himself puts [1] the objection to his argument as strongly as it could be put by the most adverse critic. He knows the gravity of the demand which he makes upon the system of nature, and he asserts plainly that in his judgement it can adequately meet that demand. In his concluding chapter he declares that the general objections against the moral system of nature have been obviated [2]. So, upon the threshold of the work, he had declared that the objections against religion were those similarly alleged against nature, 'where they are found in fact to be inconclusive [3].' Again : that a more distinct observation of certain things 'contained in God's scheme of natural gov-

1 *Analogy*, II. viii. 2.   2 *Ibid.* II. ix. 7.   3 *Ibid.* Introduction.

ernment' 'will further show how little weight is to be laid upon these objections[1].' And further still, in a very bold passage, Butler declares it has been proved (meaning, proved by himself), as to the things which have been objected to in nature, that it is not only possible but credible that they may be consistent with wisdom, justice, and goodness; that they may be instances of them; and that the constitution and government of nature may be perfect in the highest possible degree[2]. He does not, therefore, refer us to the constitution and course of nature as our *fulcrum*, without having first ascertained, in his own conviction at least, that the ground is, and will remain firm under our feet.

III. MR. LESLIE STEPHEN.

Mr. Stephen introduces Butler to our notice as 'the most patient, original, and candid of philosophical theologians[8].' His special claim lies in moral earnestness. I must not pass by in silence his ascription to Butler of a 'strangely cautious understanding[4].' Like the other censors, he does not withhold his admiration. The bulk of his remarks, however, are adverse. Not unfrequently the censures are those of a skirmisher rather than a combatant at close quarters. In some cases, vague and general statements occur, which slide unawares into unfairness. For example, 'That is the last effort to represent doubt as a ground for action[5].' Butler nowhere represents doubt as a ground for action. Only it may not be a sufficient reason against it; there may be good ground for action, doubt notwithstanding. These remarks are offered to the reader by way of *caveat*. With all Mr. Stephen's main contentions I shall attempt to deal; passing by what is remote or secondary, or what has been answered already[6]. What I may call the licence of misapprehension is once[7], if not more than once, carried to heights hardly credible in serious literature. Yet Mr. Stephen also abounds in generous admissions; and

---

[1] *Analogy*, I. vii. 3.
[2] *Ibid.* II. iv. 1.
[8] *English Thought in the Eighteenth Century*, ch. ii. 11.
[4] *Ibid.* v. 9.
[5] *Ibid.* v. 25.
[6] For example, the objections taken in his ch. v. 24.
[7] *English Thought, &c.*, at the close of ch. v. 26.

seems to feel, as an opponent, not without discomfort, that, even for him, there are two sides to the critical case. I proceed to particulars.

Mr. Stephen states in an ingenious form an objection, which he applies first to the chapter on a Future Life [1], and then to the whole method. Butler, he says, avails himself of the absence of contradiction, and passes by the absence of confirmation ; and so converts absolute ignorance into the likeness of some degree of positive knowledge. As a foundation for this censure, he states that Butler, in his first Chapter, leaves it to be inferred that, because parts of the human organism are not essential to life, therefore the whole organism is superfluous. Had Butler done what Mr. Stephen imputes to him, he would in truth have circumvented and trepanned his reader : would have obtained from him an assent, or some portion of an assent, without his knowledge. There is no charge to which he is less open. He seems continually to be warning us to keep our eyes open, to be always on our guard. And, in the case before us, he is not advancing an argument, but rebutting an objection [2]. His positions are these : (1) Our gross organized bodies are no part of ourselves ; (2) for large portions of them may be lost, while (the *ego*), the self, remains exactly the same ; (3) as they are not part of ourselves, you cannot from their dissolution infer ours. But the question of dispensing with the whole organism is in no way raised or touched ; and the stratagem ascribed to Butler, which if proved would shake our confidence, forms no part of his tactics. Of two processes essentially distinct, he is following the one. He is rebutting, not proving ; and he really leaves no shadow of excuse for those who confound the one with the other, and charge on him a confusion which is their own exclusive property.

Mr. Stephen [3] truly describes Butler as teaching that, according to his view, virtue is 'a plant intended to flourish more vigorously in another world.' He allows that if we could prove that the discipline of this life tended to develop qualities fitted for another life, Butler's 'argument

---

[1] *English Thought in the Eighteenth Century*, v. 3.
[2] *Analogy*, I. i. 12.   [3] *English Thought, &c.*, v. 15.

would be forcible.' What does Mr. Stephen mean by proving? Butler professes no more than to show that his contentions are credible or probable; and we must not ask him
for a kind of proof which he does not profess to give. But,
in his fifth chapter, he shows from observation that our
condition here is intended to be progressive; one intended
for our improvement in virtue and piety; and it is from
the progressive character, which our experience exhibits to
us in the various stages of the present life, and the capacity
of virtue for further development [1], that he draws a probable proof of a further existence beyond the grave. Our life
is a process; and it is also an incomplete process. The
qualities fitted for this life will, it is probable, be fitted for
the same creatures in another life, and it is likely that the
environment which corresponds here will correspond there
also. What is the flaw in this argument? Mr. Stephen
sets up his own contention on the matter at issue.

'If he could point to some quality, encouraged by the
existing conditions, and yet not useful under present conditions, his case would have a certain support.'

But as it is, continues Mr. Stephen, he is in a hopeless
dilemma. Now, what colour of justice is there in the demand, which alone places him in this dilemma? He is said
to fail in one of Mr. Stephen's conditions: he does not show
that the qualities, which are being formed in us, are useless
in the present life. Nor is there any reason why he should.
What his argument requires is to show a state of progress
through discipline. This he shows from experience as to
this life, and from likelihood as to the life to come. It is
not that we are busied with things useless here and useful
there; but we are busied with things useful here and more
useful there; more useful, because they will have grown by
training, and because the environment may be more favourable to their expansion. If there be a flaw in this reasoning, Mr. Stephen does not succeed in showing it.

Mr. Stephen next proceeds [2] to give what he says is Butler's account of the scheme of redemption. In a single
portion of one of his chapters, Butler, who usually speaks

---

1 *Analogy*, I. v. 1, 2.
2 *English Thought in the Eighteenth Century*, v. 23.

of mediation as causing the suffering of one man for another,
uses the phrase 'vicarious punishment[1],' and observes that
it is a providential appointment of every day's experience.
This appears to me to be one of the very rare instances, in
which Butler's language comes short of exact adaptation to
his thought; for his 'vicarious punishment' seems really
to mean no more than vicarious suffering. He, who suffers
for another, may himself receive in that suffering the very
best means of progress, so that it may be a sign not of
God's wrath but of his favour. Punishment, on the other
hand, involves the element of some judicial condemnation.
Mr. Stephen adroitly avails himself of this slip, and builds
his statement upon it. But what right have we to regard it
as a slip? First, because it does not harmonize with Butler's usual phraseology; for vicarious suffering is his ordi-
dary phrase. But secondly and principally because he
nowhere employs it when treating of its central subject,
namely, the mediation of our Lord. Mr. Stephen, however,
in order to bring his argument to bear in full force against
Divine government, puts into Butler's mouth, as if part of
the mediatory scheme, the words 'Divine punishments
sometimes strike the virtuous person on account of his virtue; they often miss (striking?) the vicious person on
account of his vice.' But it seems that here Butler could
only be saddled with an assailable argument by making him
use words which are in direct contradiction to his actual
teaching. Listen to his own language[2].

'Good actions are never punished, considered as beneficial
to society, nor ill actions rewarded under the view of their
being hurtful to it. . . .

'In the natural course of things, virtue *as such* is actually
rewarded, and vice *as such* punished.'

So the critic readily and safely contends that punishment
inflicted in his manner is no punishment at all. But, inflicted in Butler's manner, it is punishment, and is both
perceptible and righteous, though not perfect nor uniform.
To sum up, then, on this particular objection; in a particular case, where Butler's usual language is careful and accurate, but he has in a particular passage twice used a lax

---

[1] *Analogy*, II. v. 22.   [2] *Ibid*. I. iii. 12, 13.

expression, that lax expression is treated as if it had been the normal exposition of his doctrine; and then the doctrine itself is set out in terms not only varying from but contradictory of what Butler has emphatically stated to be the law of punishment and reward, as it now subsists in living experience.

Mr. Stephen does not omit to reproduce the charge that the real tendency of Butler's work is to unbelief; and this in a form apparently more crude and more shallow, than that which it elsewhere assumes.

'No evasion can blind us to the true bearing of Butler's statements: God made men liable to sin. He placed them where they were certain to sin. He damns them everlastingly for sinning. This is the road by which the *Analogy* leads to Atheism [1].'

This charge acquires a momentary colour of plausibility, when we allow ourselves to dwell in a manner exceeding due measure on the many and complex difficulties, which press upon us as we contemplate the natural government of the world. By gazing on them they multiply, like the stars to the eye of one contemplating them by night; and we may thus come so to enlarge their number and exaggerate their intricacy as to blind ourselves to the preponderating evidences of righteous government, and to forget that of the huge mass of evil in the world an overwhelming proportion is due to our abuse of that free agency with which we have been entrusted. But it is not from this point of view that Mr. Stephen is censuring the *Analogy*. The recitals which introduce the passage cited above simply exhibit Butler as a teacher of free will and of probation. In construing Mr. Stephen's passage, for 'Butler' we may reasonably read 'Belief.' The charge of opening a road to Atheism is not shown to lie against anything in the *Analogy*, but (if at all) presumably to lie against the dispensation and the world of which the *Analogy* undertakes to treat. If the Almighty be chargeable with the offences here laid at His door, it is not upon evidence drawn from any matter peculiar to the works of Butler. Not a word has any specific application to him. The application is to the

1 *English Thought in the Eighteenth Century*, v. 22.

whole body of Christian theology, and to the Holy Scriptures from their first page to their last. Nor may we stop here. It strikes at the whole body of theistic belief. Both the charge and the answer are recorded with childlike simplicity in the Odyssey. 'Mortals,' says Zeus in the Olympian Assembly[1], 'hold us responsible for the prevailing evils : but it is themselves, apart from destiny, who by their sins afflict themselves' :

$$\text{οἱ δὲ καὶ αὐτοὶ}$$
$$\text{σφῆσιν ἀτασθαλίῃσιν ὑπέρμορον ἄλγε᾽ ἔχουσιν.}$$

Mr. Stephen appropriates a section to Butler's 'Chapter on Necessity[2]'; which he thinks 'probably the weakest part of his argument,' and gives proof that in pure metaphysics he is but a child when compared with Hume, Hobbes, or Jonathan Edwards. For Butler, he says, confounds two theories, which are 'really contradictory.' One of these is a fate, 'which determines certain points in the chain of events, and does not determine the intermediate points'; whereas Necessity, a doctrine of which Mr. Stephen speaks with much appearance of sympathy, determines all things alike. This confusion of the two things is the sole ground on which Butler is condemned as no adept in pure metaphysics; which it appears to me that he may have mistrusted as a somewhat barren study. But the ground of Mr. Stephen's verdict is no better than a quicksand, and the supposed confusion is a pure misapprehension, unaccountably engendered in the mind of Mr. Stephen. For the first paragraph of Butler's sixth Chapter says a fatalist must, as such, assert 'that the opinion of *universal* Necessity' is reconcileable with the facts of human experience[3]. So that the fatalist as defined by Butler is one who as such believes that necessity is universal, and the eclectic necessitarian, who holds only an intermittent necessity, is nowhere to be found in Butler's treatise. It is hard to comprehend how an acute critic and conscientious reporter of his author, such as Mr. Stephen, can have fallen into so palpable an

[1] *Odyssey*, i. 33, 34.
[2] *English Thought in the Eighteenth Century*, v. 18.
[3] *Analogy*, I. vi. 1.

error. As to Butler, his real offence seems to lie in the curt severity with which he, without confuting it, casts aside as 'absurd[1]' the opinion apparently rather favoured by Mr. Stephen. The whole of his argument in the Chapter, which is clear and consecutive, would be marred by the introduction of a dualism in the theory he is exposing.

But Mr. Stephen deals with the subject of Necessity more at large, and draws from it the reasons of his fundamental objection to the argument of the *Analogy*. Butler's Necessity he says[2] is an external entity, coercing God and man alike. He does not impeach the conclusiveness of Butler's argument as it stands ; but he alleges that there is a 'more profound theology,' which teaches that Necessity dwells within the will of God. He justly lays on Butler the responsibility of teaching moral desert, and punishment for sin[3]. This holds with Butler's representation of a Deity 'who leaves us a certain sphere of independent action.' But then there is a God 'proved by ontological reasoning,' evidently identical with the God of the 'more profound theology' to whom we have already been introduced. This Being is Himself the fountain-head of Necessity ; and, as it appears that this Will, which is also Necessity, governs all our acts, the doctrine of the penal character of suffering (naturally enough) becomes 'monstrous.' We can all the more readily tolerate objections to Butler's argument, when we thoroughly comprehend the standing-point of the objector. In this instance, his ποῦ στῶ appears to be supplied by the philosophical system which effaces from the universe free agency, responsibility, and moral desert, and simply introduces us to an internecine war upon first principles, with which the *Analogy* had here nothing to do. Butler ceases to be the true object of the critic's activity. He really aims his darts at the doctrine of free-will, 'the device by which most theologians justify God's wrath with the work of His own hands.'

In his account of Hume's Essay on Providence and a future state[4], Mr. Stephen treats the Essay as destroying Butler's argument for a moral government in the world.

---

[1] *Analogy*, I. vi. 1, 8.   [2] *English Thought in the Eighteenth Century*, v. 19.
[3] *Ibid.* v. 20-22.   [4] *Ibid.* vi. 29.

Hume asks if there are marks of distributive justice in the world. If you reply that there are, then, he contends, you have nothing more to expect. If there are not, you have no groundwork of Divine justice to argue from. But further, 'If you say that the justice of the gods, at present, exerts itself in part but not in its full intent, I answer that you have no reason to give it any particular extent, but only so far as you see it at present exert itself.' This argument, apparently quoted by Mr. Stephen as conclusive, seems rather to deserve the epithet awarded by Beattie, who calls the Essay flimsy. We shall see directly that from the meshes of so poor a dilemma the weakest fly might escape. What Hume tells us is, that the distributive justice, which we are supposed to see in the world, begins and ends with itself, and is unalterable. A strange exaggeration indeed of the doctrine of continuance, which Butler has perhaps over-stated, but which Hume, the Hume of Mr. Stephen, absolutely caricatures. Our case is this. We have a life, not uniform and homogeneous throughout, but progressive. The several parts of this life exhibit to us a development; and this development represents to us a plan and a purpose. But, whilst it is governed by a scheme, imperfectly developed it is true but still a scheme, of distributive justice combined with intelligence, the plan is seen to be incomplete. Now, given an intelligent Author of nature, who will say, with these data before him, that there is no presumption in favour of the idea that this incomplete scheme is on its way to completion? Let us suppose a case of commonplace occurrence. A maker of engines is engaged in constructing a complicated machine. While he is at work, the dinner hour has struck, and he departs for his meal. During his absence a visitor arrives, sees the work in its unfinished state, and recognizes its plan and purpose. Will not this visitor presume, will not nature and reason oblige him to presume, that the workman means to return, and to finish the task he has in hand? Childhood and boyhood raise a presumption of youth and manhood to complete them. And as the earlier stages of life raise a presumption of the later stages to complete them, so life as a whole, by virtue of the constructive features it presents, raises a presumption of its continuance hereafter in order that the work, which has been visibly begun, may be proceeded with, and may reach its integration.

In his ninth chapter, Mr. Stephen proceeds to deal with the *Sermons* of Butler. He rightly connects them with the *Analogy* by observing that, as there he comes at the existence of God through the facts of the universe, so here he reaches the same great doctrine through the facts of human nature. In that nature he finds the law of virtue written, with conscience at hand, as God's vicegerent, to enforce it. But in setting out the facts of the case, Butler also finds that 'duty and interest are perfectly coincident; for the most part in this world, but entirely and in every instance if we take in the future[1].' Hereupon Mr. Stephen observes, 'Butler is bowing the knee in the house of Rimmon; and . . . is consenting to make virtue a question of profit and loss[2]'; and thus 'is endangering the very core of his teaching.' Now Butler nowhere makes the authority of virtue dependent on its utility. He goes so far as to teach that our obligation to follow virtue remains, even if we are not convinced of its utility. Is not, then, this criticism pointless? Nay, might it not be called captious? But the critic proceeds to a 'more vital' objection. For, as Butler has taught that, in disobeying conscience, we act wrongly, this, says Mr. Stephen, means that those who disobey conscience, 'disobey conscience.' This is not a correct representation of the *Sermons*. 'Conscience must in some way derive its credentials from some other authority than itself[3].' True: but this is the very demand which Butler satisfies. Our nature comes from God; and it is God, who has given to conscience its place of supremacy in our nature. These are propositions sometimes asserted, always implied, throughout the *Sermons*. And Mr. Stephen himself closes by limiting his charge to this, that Butler referred the promptings of conscience to a supernatural source. A charge not hard for him to bear.

The remaining exceptions taken to the *Sermons* are meta-

---

[1] *Sermons*, iii. 13.
[2] *English Thought in the Eighteenth Century*, ix. 51.
[3] *Ibid.* ix. 51.

physical, and need not therefore be noticed in this place. Mr. Stephen winds up his review with a disinterested and truly noble acknowledgement of Butler's moral grandeur.

'With all his faults, Butler remains in a practical sense the greatest moralist of this century. . . . Theology, in him, seems to utter an expiring protest against the meanness and the flimsiness of the rival theories, by which men attempted to replace it [1].'

The passage, from which these few words are extracted, may serve to strengthen the hope that, over and above the conviction which they carry to a large class of minds, the works of Butler will always render valuable service in the mitigation of controversy; both by good example, and in assisting men of upright minds, though of differing opinions, to regard each other with mutual sympathy and respect. And thus much is unquestionable. As Johnson said of Goldsmith in his admirable epitaph, *Nihil tetigit quod non ornavit*, so it may be safely averred of Butler, *Nemo impugnavit qui non laudavit*.

[In the Number of the *Nineteenth Century* for January, 1896, Mr. Leslie Stephen referred to the remarks relating to him in this chapter. His paper, entitled 'Bishop Butler's Apologist,' refers but slightly to me. It reasons upon the argument of the *Analogy* at large in a manner which, as it appears to me, would have been possible had Butler's position been what it supposes. Butler, however, nowhere proposes to offer a complete affirmative justification of the subsisting scheme for the moral government of the world. He admits the difficulties presented by it, and only contends that we should examine it as a scheme; and that, when so examined, it warrants his conclusions and demands.

He cites James Mill as having been led, 'according to his son,' 'to Atheism by reading the *Analogy*.' But Mr. Stephen's memory has here strangely misled him. The testimony of the son, in a most interesting passage [2], is this. His father, bred as a Presbyterian, was on the point of giving up all belief in religion, Natural and Revealed, when the *Analogy* came into his hands, and arrested for a time the down-

---

[1] *English Thought in the Eighteenth Century*, ix. 54.
[2] *Autobiography of J. S. Mill*, p. 38.

ward progress of his mind, by the proof it gave that the difficulties alleged against religion were also met with in nature. He eventually, however, concluded, 'doubtless after many struggles,' that 'concerning the origin of things nothing whatever could be known.' All that can be alleged against Butler is that, though the *Analogy* did much in sustaining Mr. Mill's belief, it did not do all.

As it is one of the capital claims of Butler to draw his reasonings from experience, I must notice Mr. Stephen's allegation [1] that Butler 'stipulates beforehand that experience in general is to be regarded as exceptional.' Now, except in recording the admission of the Deists with respect to a Supreme Being, Butler has no such thing as a 'stipulation beforehand.' He takes the facts of experience in a body and unconditionally, and draws from them all his inferences.

With regard to Mr. Stephen's argument on the Atonement [2], I am content to refer to my own reasoning in the *Nineteenth Century* for September, 1894, as furnishing a reply.

And with regard to the closing part of his paper on 'the fallacy of Free-will [3],' I need do no more than present as my answer the chapter in this volume in which I have treated of Determinism, with a brief addition which I have now made.]

IV. Mr. MATTHEW ARNOLD.

If, among the more full reviews of Bishop Butler's works, Miss Hennell's was from its tone the most attractive, the review by Mr. Matthew Arnold, in his *Last Essays on Church and Religion*, is the most thoroughgoing. It consists of two parts: the one attacking the *Sermons*, the other the *Analogy*; and it would be difficult to say which of the two is the more condemnatory. He admits, indeed, that there are 'many precious things' contained in the works of this great man [4], and he sets forth at times with truth and force some of his doctrines [5]. Further, he introduces his hostile

[1] *Nineteenth Century*, Jan. 1896, p. 113.
[2] *Ibid.* pp. 119, 120.
[3] *Ibid.* p. 117.
[4] *Last Essays on Church and Religion*, pp. 121, 147.
[5] E. g. *ibid.* p. 144.

review with an admiring and sympathizing account of Butler, which is of the highest interest. There is nothing petty
in the matter or spirit of his charges. His friends need not
fear that his character as a man will suffer from the publication of his (I think) unfortunate essay on 'Bishop Butler
and the Zeitgeist'; a *Zeitgeist* of which we read from page
to page in the title, but hear very little in the text. This
perhaps may be accounted for by the supposition that, in
the critic's own view, the term is but a synonym for 'Matthew Arnold,' for whom it is perhaps well that the fame of
his performances in other fields cannot be justly disparaged
on account of his failure — if, indeed, he has failed — in this
portion of his indubitably high-minded searches after truth.

Mr. Arnold was placed by his own peculiar opinions in
a position far from auspicious with respect to this particular
undertaking. He combined a fervent zeal for the Christian
religion with a not less boldly avowed determination to
transform it beyond the possibility of recognition by friend
or foe. He was thus placed under a sort of necessity to condemn the handiwork of Bishop Butler, who in a certain
sense gives it a new charter. For he not only accepts that
religion *talis qualis*, but secures for it, in the opinion of his
eulogists, a high and secure, as well as to some extent a new,
place in the region of philosophy. The critic does not recognize this radical difference as in any degree the cause of
his hostility to Butler; but, whatever view we may take of
the merits, there can be no doubt that the system of Butler,
and the system of Matthew Arnold, cannot stand together.

So that we have little occasion for surprise when we are
introduced to an attack along the whole line, alike minute
in its details and broad in its general scope. After reciting
no less than five out of the multitude of the glowing panegyrics on Butler, which have been pronounced by various
writers, who think he has 'firmly and impregnably established his doctrine,' Mr. Arnold proposes to ascertain 'how
far the claim is solid [1].'

While I am very desirous that this examination of Mr.
Arnold's objections should in no degree exhibit a spirit
of retaliation, I must frankly own that some of them seem

---

[1] *Last Essays on Church and Religion*, pp. 67, 68.

to me to be such as could only have been suggested by what I must term the spirit of objection. Nor is extremism the only fault which it seems necessary at once to allege against Mr. Arnold's censures. There are others, which cannot be overlooked. One of these is that he thinks it quite enough, on various occasions, to bestow hard condemnatory epithets upon some of Butler's best considered and most careful statements, and then to treat them as sufficiently disposed of. He censures in these cases *de haut en bas*. His *ipse dixit*, his ἀναπόδεικται φάσεις, are to be accepted by his reader as self-attested. He ascends the magisterial chair, and delivers the doom which we have only to register. Another fault, more elementary, and still less pardonable, is the not unfrequent occurrence of palpable inaccuracy in representing the doctrine which he is about to arraign.

It may be convenient at once to present some illustrations of the magisterial method, which I have imputed to Mr. Arnold.

Butler teaches that reason alone is not for man in his present condition a sufficient motive to virtue; and that affections, of a mixed character, indeed, but which work upon the whole for good, have been joined to it, in order to supply what was lacking. And, again, Butler teaches that we have a more lively sympathy with distress than with prosperity, and finds the reason herein, that distress calls for our intervention, while prosperity does not. The first of these positions is pelted by Mr. Arnold with hard words; it is ' fanciful,' is an 'immense hypothesis.' is not 'based upon observation,' cannot 'satisfy the mind[1].' The second is simply dismissed as 'fantastic[2].' To take a third instance, Butler regards anger in its twofold form, as sudden and as deliberate. The first of these, he thinks, is given to avert pain or loss; the second, to further justice, by preventing or reducing injury. And as pity is often too weak for its purpose if single-handed, we are furnished with indignation against wrong to reinforce it. But the Bishop's teaching on anger is set forth with extreme care and fulness[3]. Mr. Arnold disposes of it by saying that it will be found to be

---

[1] *Last Essays on Church and Religion*, pp. 100-2.
[2] *Ibid.* p. 103.   [3] *Sermons*, viii. 4-11.

arbitrary, fantastic, and unavailing, at times when facts are felt to be necessary, though it may pass for being New-tonian in times when everything is conventional and no man looks closely into himself[1]. To hard epithets are here joined some bald generalities; but to grapple with Butler's full and closely reasoned statement there is in these cases no attempt whatever.

We are next arrested by another of our critic's character-istic faults, his want of accuracy. He complains of Butler for teaching that compassion is given us 'in order to lead us to public spirit,' and, again, to 'a settled, reasonable principle of benevolence to mankind[2].' But, so far as I find, Butler has taught neither the one nor the other. He connects public spirit[3] with the love of our neighbour, and thus with charity, benevolence, and good will. It is not compassion, but a form of what is now called Altruism. Nor is compassion the basis of benevolence: that is an original, distinct, particular affection[4].

Mr. Arnold may not stand alone in complaining of the manner in which Butler separates self-love from the par-ticular affections. Among these he places benevolence; and self-love appears to be towards ourselves what benevo-lence is towards others. On the other hand, there is a practical consideration, which may have led Butler to this mode of classification. Benevolence, it may be said, is oc-casional, but self-love has in each of us a continuous occu-pation; and so largely and variously does it employ the particular affections in the prosecution of its aim, that there is some convenience in ordinarily viewing it as apart from them. There is no equivalent reason for removing benevo-lence from the list of particular affections.

Butler has observed that, were it not for the calls of hunger, thirst, and weariness, we should often neglect the proper means of cherishing our life, although self-love steadily recommends them. Mr. Arnold replies that this supposition is unsatisfactory, and absurd[5]. But he should

---

[1] *Last Essays on Church and Reli-gion*, pp. 104, 105.
[2] *Ibid.* pp. 106, 107.
[3] *Sermons*, vii. 1, 2.

[4] *Ibid.* v. 2.
[5] *Last Essays on Church and Reli-gion*, pp. 106, 107.

surely condescend a little to the weakness of such readers
as see in Butler's observation nothing but very plain good
sense, and inform them of the ground on which he launches
this anathema.

Butler is next arraigned for having taught that it is as
unnatural to suppress compassion by turning away from
the wretched as it would be to attempt suppressing hunger
'by keeping from the sight of food[1].' 'Can there be anything more strange,' says Mr. Arnold, 'than to pronounce
compassion to be a call, a demand of nature to relieve the
unhappy; *precisely in the same manner* as hunger is a
natural call for food, and to say that to neglect one call is
just as much a violation of nature as the other[2]?' But the
Bishop has not said that it is a violation of nature 'precisely in the same manner.' On the contrary, he has said
expressly that, though the violation of nature is equally
present in both cases, yet the incidents are different; we
can do one with greater success than we can do the other[3].
The manner, then, is far from being 'precisely the same.'
But, after all, the Bishop's sin in this matter is that he
compares the two as being, both of them, violations of
nature. In the case of hunger, the idea of its being such is
near and familiar. In the case of compassion, the idea is
remote and probably never may have occurred to us. Butler, acting according to a method of sound philosophy,
employs the familiar to illustrate the unknown. But he
does more. The unknown is here closely associated with
a practical and urgent duty; a duty which involves more or
less of self-sacrifice. He is now in the pulpit; where it is
his right and obligation to appeal to feeling. By his comparison between hunger and compassion he at once conveys
knowledge and arouses right emotion. In so doing he uses
the hortatory method; yet, strange to say, he is taken to
task by Mr. Arnold for generally avoiding it. Yes; it was
Mr. Arnold who, at the outset of his article[4], found the
gravest fault with Butler because his method was totally
unlike that adopted by true Christianity; and because,

---

[1] *Sermons*, vi. 6.
[2] *Last Essays on Church and Religion*, p. 108.

[3] *Sermons*, vi. 6.
[4] *Last Essays on Church and Religion*, pp. 67, 68.

instead of aiming directly at the heart and will, he trusted everything to 'fair logic and fair reason.' But here, as heretofore, Butler's contention stands on solid ground; the demand of compassion is as natural, in the highest sense, as the demand of hunger, though compassion may not be armed with equally coercive means for its enforcement.

The next charge against him is more plausible. It is his teaching that man's proper aim is to escape from misery rather than to pursue positive happiness. Against this rather saddening doctrine, our censor quotes a French moralist, who writes thus : 'The aim for man is, to augment the feeling of joy.' But, further, Butler is here found guilty by Mr. Arnold of contravening 'the clear voice of our religion[1]. "*Rejoice and give thanks,*" exhorts the Old Testament, *rejoice evermore*, exhorts the New.'

A more careful writer than Mr. Arnold would deserve to be smartly handled for extracting words from a Psalm composed for a joyful occasion, and representing them as a standing maxim or precept of the Old Testament in general. But he is only acting in his too usual manner. The subject he raises gives him, perhaps, a better standing-ground than is supplied by most of his ill-conceived and infelicitous attempts. There may be in Butler's words somewhat of a melancholic strain, drawn from within himself. But they are not to be met aright by simply turning them topsy-turvy, as seems to be proposed. Mr. Arnold can hardly have imagined that in the two words he cites from Saint Paul the Apostle intended to do more than supply a much-needed solace, a reactive and bracing incitement, in effect a moral tonic, to enable those whom he was addressing to bear up against their trials and their burdens. Butler might perhaps have said, I am not speaking of the temper in which we are to live. I am speaking of the objects we are to pursue. And then his position may be stated thus; that labour in avoidance is on the whole more fruitfully bestowed than labour in appetence.

The charge of contravening religion ought not to have been brought. The picture of the actual face of the world presented in the New Testament is not a joyous one. It is

---

[1] *Last Essays on Church and Religion*, p. 110.

rest, and not felicity, which our Saviour promises to the weary and heavy-laden. The world is represented as under the dominion of the Evil One. Saint Paul points to consolation elsewhere when he describes life as 'this light affliction, which is but for a moment.' True, the 'present distress' lay harder and heavier upon him than upon us. But the great, the enduring, the fundamental sorrow of life is the conflict of the soul with sin, which endures, and must endure now, even as it did then. The Greek more than any other perhaps enjoyed his joy, and was of all men the least pessimistic : yet we find in Homer that no creature creeps upon the earth more lamentable than man ; and of the two caskets, which lie before the throne of Zeus, and are charged with the destinies of the race, the better can only boast of mixed contents, while the other is filled with unmitigated woe [1]. It is probable, indeed, that from the reconstructed Christianity and Scripture of Mr. Arnold there had disappeared, together with (or as involved in) the 'anthropomorphic and miraculous,' everything that belongs to what may be called the evangelical sadness of the Gospel. In his light-hearted citation from his French moralist, and his misapprehended Scripture, Mr. Arnold followed too summary a method : and he probably omitted to take into account that a scheme of religion such as his had no room for the idea of sin in its full force and virulence, and that such a scheme really disabled him from passing an impartial judgement on the difficult questions raised by Butler's observations [2].

It is not surprising that Butler's account of self-love should have become an object of criticism : and it is perhaps to be wished that he could have found occasion to gather together into one *conspectus* all the important and leading propositions on the subject of it, which are scattered about his Works. But, though some difficulty arises from this sporadic method of treatment, and from the want of facile reference and comparison between one part of the Works and another, it is not easy to excuse Mr.

---

[1] *Il.* xvii. 446, xxiv. 527.

[2] From a different point of view, but one entirely just, Mr. R. H. Hutton, in his *Modern Guides of English Thought*, pp. 119-21, demolishes the criticism of Mr. Arnold relating to joy.

Arnold for the account [1] he has given of Butler's doctrine of self-love. He speaks of Butler's 'arbitrary definition' of self-love. He says Butler describes it 'occasionally' (should he not have said habitually?) as 'a general desire of one's own happiness.' But his 'constant notion of the pursuit of our interest is, that it is the pursuit of our temporal good, as he calls it; the cool consideration of our own temporal advantage.' Now, there are various passages, in which Butler deals somewhat at large with the subject of self-love. One of these is in the fifth chapter of the first part of the *Analogy* [2]. Another is in the eleventh of the Fifteen sermons [8]. In neither of these does he connect self-love in any way with the present world. Nowhere does he associate it with our 'temporal' good, which Mr. Arnold seems to put forward as the favourite appellation. The passages which name self-love may be reckoned in the *Analogy* by the score; but in one only of these, or possibly two [4] (so far as I know), does the phrase appear in any expressed relation to our worldly interest. And here Mr. Arnold may be to a certain extent upheld, but only if we content ourselves with a miserably garbled quotation. For Butler names 'that reasonable self-love, the end of which is our worldly interest [5].' But the sentence, taken as a whole, entirely overthrows him. Butler is speaking of the way in which 'habits and passions' lead us into vice, apart from external temptations. And yet, he says, this error is doubly forbidden: for 'particular passions are no more coincident with prudence, or that reasonable self-love, the end of which is our worldly interest, than they are with the principle of virtue and religion.'

Now Butler is not here treating of our nature at large, or of self-love as such. He is simply treating of a matter of worldly conduct, and of the motives which ought in reason to guide it. One of these is drawn from 'virtue and religion'; the other is from interest, or 'that reasonable self-love the end of which is our worldly interest.' Indicat-

---

[1] *Last Essays on Church and Religion*, pp. 111, 114.
[2] *Analogy*, I. v. 24 n.   [8] *Sermons*, xi. 4, 5.   [4] *Analogy*, I. iv. 4.
[5] There is also a passage in the *Sermons* where self-love is placed in association with present interest.

ing in one branch of the sentence the loftier motive for
doing right, he points out, in the other, the lower one. He
is not defining self-love. He is speaking of self-love not
at large, but in relation to worldly interest, when it ought
undoubtedly to act as an *adminiculum* to virtue and religion. Is it not rather too bad on the part of a censor,
and one, as he has touchingly noted, 'past fifty years of
age,' first to take this particular and limited reference to
self-love where it is placed in a particular light, and to
exalt it into a definition; and then, in still more reckless
disregard of his author's text, to describe this isolated use
of the phrase amidst a number of utterly adverse instances,
as Butler's 'constant notion' of self-love?

Then, shifting the ground of his assault, Mr. Arnold complains that Butler 'sophisticated things' by saying [1] that
love of our neighbour is no more distant from (Butlerian)
self-love than hatred of our neighbour; a mode of reasoning which, he holds, will never convince or carry a serious
student. It is most unfortunate that, in many of his
charges, Mr. Arnold, probably feeling, as we have all felt,
the difficulties of reference to particular passages, so often
fails to cite what he censures. The language of Butler is
this — that:

'Benevolence is not in any respect more at variance with
self-love than any other particular affection whatever; but
it is, in every respect, at least as friendly to it [2].'

And again [3], more at large, the Bishop says that there is
'no peculiar inconsistence and contrariety' between benevolence and self-love. The whole idea of self-love being affection to ourselves, it cannot exclude affection to others, otherwise than by not including it. Thus we are carefully led
up to the broader proposition that love of our neighbour is
'no more distant from self-love than hatred of our neighbour.' For Butler holds all things which are distinct to be
'equally distinct.' What Mr. Arnold deems sophistication
appears to be an accurate and studiously careful statement.

And why should we set up a factitious opposition between
benevolence and self-love? The duty of doing good to

---

[1] *Last Essays on Church and Reli-*   [2] Preface to the *Sermons*, 32.
gion, p. 112.   [3] *Sermons*, xi. 2, 8, 9.

others, and the duty of doing good to ourselves, rest on the same authority, and form in harmony portions of the work which the Almighty has appointed for us to do during our sojourn upon earth. True, there is a perverted and over-grown self-love, which is at odds with benevolence; but it is just as much at odds with sound and reasonable self-love. And to shift the terms of Butler's equation by substituting another self-love for his, and then making him responsible for the conflict between this self-love and benevolence, would not be philosophy, but quackery.

But again, perhaps from feeling uneasy on the ground he has chosen, our critic alters it; and makes it his capital charge that Butler gives no account, or a fantastic account, of the genesis of conscience, benevolence, compassion, and the rest. 'Into this vast, dimly-lighted, primordial region [1]' Butler never enters. Now, his so-called fantastic account is this: By observation he finds these powers set in human nature as essential parts of it, planted there by its Author. So he treats them as ultimate facts, and uses them as points of departure. And it may be that the student will prefer this eminently rational mode of handling to a cruise with Mr. Arnold in his 'dimly-lighted and primordial regions.'

Into those regions Mr. Arnold now proceeds to introduce us, by setting up a counter-philosophy [2]. Its references to Bishop Butler are here for the most part inaccurate. His picture is, indeed, so different in tone and colour from that of his Author, as in a great degree to account for the sever-ity of his judgements. As compared with the system and method of Butler, it is indeed a philosophy upon stilts. And it provokes the repetition of the old dictum that what is true in it is not new, and what is new is not true. He begins by substituting for Butler's 'self-love' the desire of happiness, or effort to live. For the planting of conscience and affections in us by the Author of nature, he substitutes a growth of them, and of the practical reason, as arising out of the effort to live. (This is simply putting a non-theistic in the place of a theistic theory.) Such an effort, or instinct, becomes the strongest, and in virtue of strength gains the right to rule. But learning from experience that men are

---

[1] *Last Essays on Church and Religion*, p. 113.   [2] *Ibid.* pp. 113–21.

'solidary,' it also learns, by a process not explained, that
private ought to give way to public good. Man likewise
finds in himself a higher and a lower life, and Mr. Arnold
unduly charges Butler with saying that they are alike the
voice of God. Experience gradually established the higher
life, and conscience is the recognition of that experience.
If we abstract the unhappily numerous points in which,
from want of care, he misstates Butler, there does not appear to be any point in which the critic makes good his hostile position. The doctrine of conscience, enthroned amidst
the various impelling powers of our nature, and calling
them to account with authority, remains unshaken; and
Mr. Arnold's contention that the earnest inquirer will give
no heed to a rational account of human nature, until he
has been supplied with a theory as to the genesis of all our
faculties, appears as reasonable as if it were contended that
a traveller, terribly in earnest from a sharpened appetite,
arriving at his home, and finding an excellent dinner prepared for him, would not dream of sitting down to partake
of it until he had been informed of all the processes which
the cook had employed to make it ready.

We have now reached the close of the criticism on the
Sermons.

Butler published the *Analogy* at forty-four, and was still,
as Mr. Arnold thinks, too young. To read it is, however,
'a very valuable mental exercise [1].' But it is of no value to
us, unless we hold the positions of the Deists, with whom
it dealt; 'and we do not.' Surely a strange doctrine. Few
readers of the present day hold either the opinions of Mr.
Burke, as given in his *Reflections on the French Revolution*,
or the opinions of the revolutionists. Does it, therefore,
follow that we have nothing to learn from the book, and
need not care 'two straws' about it? Nor should any man
(it seems) read the *Provincial Letters*, unless he holds the
same opinions which Pascal exposed.

The argument of the *Analogy*, says Mr. Arnold, is an
argument to prove, from the reality of the laws of moral
government in this world, a like reality of moral government in the world to come [2]. But the grave inaccuracy of

---

[1] *Last Essays on Church and Religion*, p. 122.   [2] *Ibid.* p. 125.

this statement is shown by the very title-page of Butler's
work, which is inscribed *The Analogy of Religion, Natural
and Revealed, to the constitution and course of Nature.* According to Mr. Arnold, it ought to have been 'Moral Government in the next world inferred by Analogy from Moral
Government in this.' A great subject without doubt, but
not the subject chosen by Butler. For moral government
in this world is one of the matters which Butler does not
assume, but sets himself to prove. Such want of care, as
is here shown, in laying the very foundation stones of an
argument is hardly conceivable; and, after such a specimen,
we can hardly expect to establish either the perpendicular
or the square in the structure which the censor is about
to raise. It is 'the constitution and course of nature' on
which Butler builds, and not the reality of moral government in this world, which he has got to prove, and spends
the first part of the *Analogy* in proving.

Butler is next found guilty of failure to satisfy the demands, not of his own argument, but of Mr. Arnold's; who
naturally observes that before moral government in the
hereafter can be proved from moral government here, it
must be shown that there is an hereafter. Of this, he proceeds to observe, Butler has supplied no probability whatever [1]. Let us see how he supports his contention.

The differences, says Butler, between different states of
life, all known to us by experience, are almost as great as
can be mentally conceived. Therefore an existence hereafter, differing from the present, but only within the measure of those known differences, would not be beyond the
analogy of nature [2]. Since our terrestrial existence is so
elastic as to allow of difference x, and since we have no
proof that our existence hereafter would involve a difference from the present exceeding x, the supposition of future
existence, so conditioned, is within the analogy of nature.
No, replies Mr. Arnold, for you have not proved that there
will be such an existence. He does not perceive that his
arrow passes by the mark, and lands in a vacuum. Butler
does not here pretend that his argument proves a future

[1] *Last Essays on Church and Religion*, p. 127.
[2] *Analogy*, I. i. 3.

existence. He has only rebutted an objection to it. by showing that it need not transcend the present and known analogies of nature.

Again, Butler has observed [1] thus: (dreamless) sleep, and swoons, prove that our living powers may exist when there is no capacity for exercising them. *As we know not on what their existence depends, it may depend on something quite out of the reach of death.* Therefore there is no sign of any connexion between death and the destruction of living agents.

My last paragraph is an abbreviation from Butler, and gives his argument. In lieu of it Mr. Arnold prints, and prints in the form of a quotation, a passage which entirely omits the middle portion, while he gives the first and last. That is to say, he gives Butler's conclusion, but omits the reason for it, and presents this to his reader as if it were a citation from the *Analogy*: with a want of care even more gross than that which has marked some previous errors. The presumption raised by Butler's argument, thus overleapt, of course remains untouched. And to say, as Mr. Arnold here says, that experience alone constitutes the reason of the thing is to strike at the very heart of all arguments founded on analogy. For it amounts to saying that there never can be any argument for the existence of anything, except experience of its actually existing.

He next contends that the presumption of extinction at death 'goes upon the unbroken experience that living powers then cease [2].' There cannot be a more complete misconception. Our experience is not of their ceasing to exist, but of their ceasing to afford us sensible and constant evidence of their continued existence.

Mr. Arnold appears habitually or incurably to overlook the distinction between the rebuttal of an objection, and advancing an affirmative argument. Thus when he finds that Butler alleges our remaining the same living agents after the loss of limbs, he observes [3] that our so remaining after the loss of some limbs gives no proof that we can dis-

---

[1] *Analogy*, I. i. 6.
[2] *Last Essays on Church and Religion*, p. 128.
[3] *Ibid.*

pense with all, and thinks that he has made a reply. But the Bishop has never used so futile an argument. On referring to his text[1], we find that he is arguing only to show that our 'gross organized bodies' are no part of ourselves because we can lose parts of them without losing any part of ourselves. The body has become different: while the self remains the same. Here as elsewhere Mr. Arnold wastes his sword-stroke upon a ghost.

Mr. Arnold then proceeds[2] to admit the existence of a system under which we have experience of reward and punishment. But he says we have no experience to show that they are administered by a 'quasi-human agent' called the Author of nature. True; Bishop Butler fails to substitute for God 'a stream of tendency, not ourselves, that makes for righteousness.' This valuable discovery of a substitution for Deity was almost made by Aristophanes[3]:

Δῖνος βασιλεύει, τὸν Δί᾽ ἐξεληλακώς.

But the critic does not perceive that the Bishop might reply as follows. Your admission is all I want. Call the agent an agency, or call him what you please. Let us part with *he* and have recourse to *it*. *It* may, if you like, be nothing nobler than a treadmill, which awakens by a blow those who neglect to keep the proper pace. But *it* rewards and punishes, and this according to righteousness. Therefore my argument holds, and men are bound, by the rules which in common life are held binding, to govern themselves accordingly. And this is not 'abstraction or speculation[4],' but is in the strictest sense an argument from experience. 'Religion must be built on ideas, about which there is no puzzle[5].' The idea of a personal God, we are told, is a puzzle. A 'stream of tendency' then, is none!

The long catalogue of detailed objections draws near its close: but the end is not quite reached. Dealing with the sad question of the apparent waste of human existences, Butler refers to the profuse waste exhibited in other orders of nature; which he says does not destroy the argument of

---

[1] *Analogy*, I. i. 12.
[2] *Last Essays on Church and Religion*, pp. 128-31.
[3] Aristoph. Νεφ. 828.
[4] *Last Essays, &c.*, p. 131.
[5] *Ibid*. p. 132.

design as to those seeds and bodies which come to their perfection [1]. Mr. Arnold's comment is that the difficulties in argument, arising from the existence of waste, are due to our assuming that nature means 'an Infinite Almighty moral being'; and his very simple proposal is to get rid of the difficulty by getting rid of reference to such a being. Yet it is really most difficult to imagine that Mr. Arnold could think we disposed of the difficulties of the case (such as they are) by holding that nobody but Δῖνος is accountable [2]. I call in Δῖνος as a fair equivalent for Mr. Arnold's favourite 'stream of tendency.'

I pass over Mr. Arnold's remarks on Butler's treatment of miracles, as the question is rather too large for succinct treatment; and I will not follow him into the field of Bible history, for I have already overtaxed my reader's patience. But I must say a few words on his summing up.

The most wonderful thing about the *Analogy* is, he thinks, the poverty of its result, as estimated by Butler himself [3]. He then rends from their context various brief sayings from different parts of the text, some of them hard to identify, in which Butler has stated, with perhaps even more than his accustomed modesty and fearless candour, his admissions as to the defects of the evidence he presents. These phrases our critic represents as truly embodying the upshot of the *Analogy*. He gives us the weights that are in one scale, but he forgets to take account of those in the other. It mounts accordingly, and leaves him exultingly to conceive that he has proved his case. He has overlooked the fact that they are balanced by other statements; and that a joint consideration of what is said on the two sides is especially necessary in the case of a writer like Butler in order to get at any true appreciation of his real judgement. Perhaps the strongest of the passages in which he disparages his own performance is the sentence in which he says 'the foregoing treatise is by no means satisfactory; very far indeed from it.' But he presently explains : ' Those who object against it (the evidence of religion) as not satisfactory, i. e. *as not being*

---

[1] *Analogy*, I. v. 35.
[2] *Last Essays on Church and Religion*, p. 134.
[3] *Ibid.* p. 138.

what they wish it, plainly forget the very condition of our
being ; for *satisfaction, in this sense, does not belong to such
a creature as man*[1].' He further observes that he has
argued upon the principles of others, not his own ; and that
he has waived all reference to arguments which he deems
of the highest importance, the two principles of liberty, and
of moral fitness[2]. A fairer summing up of his judgement
than Mr. Arnold's seems to be given in the following words
concerning his treatise :

'Those who believe, will here find the scheme of Christianity cleared of objections, and the evidence of it in a
peculiar manner strengthened : those who do not believe,
will at least be shown the absurdity of all attempts to prove
Christianity false, the plain undoubted credibility of it;
and, I hope, a good deal more[3].'

But Mr. Arnold does not conclude without a parting kick.
Butler has laid it down that, in such a matter we ought 'to
act upon evidence much lower than what is commonly called
probable.' He may mean, in the language of chances, when
the adverse chance is say two or three to one. No, says Mr.
Arnold ; I take fearlessly a given road, though a menagerie
is travelling it, and a tiger may break out of his van and
destroy me. In other words, a chance of two or three to
one, and a chance of two or three thousand to one, the
chance of an accident in rope dancing and of one in railway
travelling, are for the purposes of his argument one and the
same. The *Analogy* is 'for all real intents and purposes now
a failure[4].' And we return from it to the 'boundless certitude and exhilaration of the Bible' ; a certitude and exhilaration which do not restrain Mr. Arnold from cutting out
of the Scripture, as anthropomorphic and legendary, what
nearly all its readers believe to be the heart and centre of
its vital force.

Various objections have been taken from various quarters to this point and that in the argument of Butler ;
but Mr. Arnold's criticisms, as a whole, remain wholly isolated and unsupported. It is impossible to acquit him of
the charge of a carelessness implying levity, and of an ungovernable bias towards finding fault. The homely fare, on

[1] *Analogy*, II. viii. 17, 18.   [2] *Ibid.* 23, 24.   [3] *Ibid.* 27.
[4] *Last Essays on Church and Religion*, pp. 140, 141.

which Butler feeds us, cannot be so gratifying to the palate
as turtle, venison, and champagne. But it has been found
wholesome by experience: it leads to no doctors' bills; and
a perusal of this ' failure ' is admitted to be 'a most valuable
exercise for the mind.' Mr. Arnold himself will probably
suffer more from his own censures than the great Christian
philosopher who is the object of them. And it is well for
him that all they can do is to effect some deduction from the
fame which has been earned by him in other fields, as a true
man, a searching and sagacious literary critic, and a poet of
genuine creative genius.

Upon the whole, I conceive that these four censures [1], the
only censures in detail upon Butler which are known to me,
inspire respect for their authors, as well as other sentiments
directly due to their conspicuous talents. I trust that this
sentiment of respect has not disappeared from my own
examination of their criticisms. On the other hand, speaking for myself, after careful endeavours to weigh each and
all of the objections which they have taken, I confess to a
sense of satisfaction upon finding that after a century and
a half, the latter portion of the time distinguished by an
unusual activity of the questioning spirit, no more formidable grounds of exception should have been discovered.
The catapult has beaten on the walls of the fortress ; it has
stood the shock. The tempest has roared around the stately
tree; and scarcely a leaf or twig has fallen to the ground.
My confidence is strengthened not only in the permanence
of Butler's fame, but much more in the permanence and
abundance of the services he has yet to render to his country,
to its kindred, and perhaps to Christendom, as a classic of
thought in the greatest of all its domains, the domain of
religious philosophy.

V. MINOR STRICTURES.

I proceed to the criticisms on particular points which
have been passed by some distinguished writers not to be
reckoned as objectors to the general argument either of the

---

[1] I have not thought it necessary to
defend Butler against the exceptions
taken by Tholuck, which are little
known in this country, and which
have been sufficiently dealt with by
Bishop Fitzgerald in his *Life of Butler*, prefixed to his edition of 1749,
p. xlvii.

Analogy or the *Sermons* of Butler. But I first offer a preliminary observation. While, on the one hand, no writer
within my knowledge who has been so largely called to account has obtained, from all objectors and questioners alike,
so sustained a strain of eulogy and admiration, alike on intellectual and on moral grounds, none I think has been so
unfortunate in the amount and gravity of misapprehension
with which his contentions have been stated when put upon
their trial. This circumstance I cannot but ascribe to the
difficulty incidental to the extraction of particulars from so
continuous and so wonderfully close a tissue of argument as
he presents ; and yet more to the want of proper means of
discharging the duty of reference and cross-reference (as it
has been called) to his works [1].

In his *Moral and Metaphysical Philosophy* [2], Mr. Maurice
not only assigns to Butler an honoured place in Christian
literature, but shows that he had studied the philosopher
deeply, and had so drunk in his fundamental conceptions
that it might almost appear that he had drawn the very blood
of Butler into his own veins. And yet Mr. Maurice falls into
most serious inaccuracies in the account he gives of Butler's
religious opinions. The idea of human nature presented in
the Sermons on Human Nature is according to him the exact
opposite of that presented by Mr. Wesley. It raises the question, what provision does human nature supply as a remedy
for the disorder admitted to have invaded it ? Still more
does the *Analogy* create a necessity for an answer to this
question. Mr. Maurice then imagines a challenge from John
Wesley to Butler, on the ground that he, Wesley, held a supernatural operation to be necessary for the regeneration of
man [3]. Mr. Maurice evidently believes that on this great subject the theologies of Wesley and of Butler were at issue.
As regards Wesley, the fact, doubtless unknown to Maurice,
is that he uses the most commendatory epithets concerning

---

[1] The Delegates of the Clarendon
Press have recently published a new
edition of Butler's Works, prepared
by me, in which both the *Analogy*
and the other principal compositions
are broken up into short sections for
greater convenience of reference. I
have availed myself of these sectional
divisions in the notes to the present
volume.

[2] London, 1862, 2 vols.; republished
with a preface, 1873.

[3] *Moral and Metaphysical Philosophy*, vol. ii. pp. 466–468 (ed. 1873).

the *Analogy*, and gives no hint of dissatisfaction on any point. But what says Butler himself? No recognized theologian has presented more strongly than Butler the corruption and degradation of man through sin. In the Introduction, he tells us that this world is in a state of 'apostasy, wickedness, and ruin[1].' And as respects the remedy he is not less unequivocal. The doctrine of the new birth is that which most absolutely involves a supernatural operation. The corruption of our moral character, and the necessity of the assistance of the Holy Spirit for the renewal of our nature, are implied, says the *Analogy*, 'in the express though figurative declaration, *Except a man be born of the Spirit, he cannot enter into the kingdom of God*[2].' It is difficult to understand how so single-hearted a student as Mr. Maurice could have overlooked so conspicuous a declaration. I am driven to suppose that it must have been owing to the extreme difficulties in the way of reference to particular passages of his author, which I have already noticed. This alone can explain the palpable mistakes of critics, whose good faith is as unquestionable as their ability[3].

Mr. Goldwin Smith, in a criticism on Mansel's Bampton Lectures[4], has occasion to refer to Butler as follows:

'One word more on the authority of Butler. . . . In dry intellect he was mighty. . . . But he was wanting in feel-

---

[1] *Analogy*, Introd. § 16.

[2] *Ibid.* II. i. 24.

[3] In his Essay on Regeneration (*Theological Essays*, 1853, p. 236) Maurice laments the language used by Butler as seeming to confound probabilities with chances, and otherwise to deal in an unsatisfactory manner with the process to be followed in the acceptance of religious truth. Mr. Maurice does not quote words or refer us to passages, and in the expression of these regrets it would be well always to include, when we are dealing with a great teacher, and especially if we are teachers ourselves, the means of verification. It may be admitted that (1) the argument from probabilities lends itself to the gibes of the scoffer, and provokes the sensi-

tiveness of over-fastidious intellects; and (2) that Butler has in a single passage confounded probabilities with chances (*Analogy*, II. ii. 11, 12). But, as regards the first, it constitutes no sufficient reason for eschewing a line of reasoning, which can never be dispensed with when we are challenged to undertake the defence of our own cause. As regards the second, Butler stumbled into his error, if any, not by lowering probabilities to chances, but rather by exalting chances to the rank of probabilities, when, by this undue promotion, they were to do duty in the service of the religious argument. His mistake has long ago been pointed out by Bishop Fitzgerald *in loc.* See his *Analogy*, 1849, p. 184.

[4] *Rational Religion*, 1861.

ing, the power of sympathy; and his religious philosophy
is grievously marked with this defect.'

The tributes of admiration which Mr. Goldwin Smith
pays to Butler in this passage show plainly that the animadversion was extorted from him by a sense of duty to
truth, such as he conceived it to be. But is it just?

With regard to dry light, it may be, not conceded, but
avowed and proclaimed, that the atmosphere of the *Analogy*
is one of dry light, and only dry light, throughout. Nor
does it seem doubtful that Butler acted with intention; or
that he judged wisely in excluding from this philosophic
treatise anything which would have deviated from the line
of strict reasoning by an appeal to emotion. Even feeling,
and the power of sympathy, these glories of our nature, are
only good in their place; and this was not their place;
because, if Butler had allowed such elements to be mixed
with his argument, every word of the matter so intruded
would have served to harden and to arm the cold indifference, and the hotter prejudices, of his adversaries against
the appeal which he made to their reasoning faculties, and
to their judicial integrity.

But surely, when Mr. Goldwin Smith penned these words,
he had forgotten the proof in our possession that the philosophy of Butler reserves for the affections their proper
place. We find his estimate of them on every appropriate
occasion with which the subjects of his *Sermons* supply him.
It is known that he was given to religious retirement and
to reading the biographies of holy persons : a circumstance
which, perhaps, might suitably have arrested the pen of the
critic. But we have also the direct evidence afforded by
the Sermons on the Love of God. He notes with care the
ascending stages of this love. It should pass beyond all
servile fear, and should attain to 'resignation,' a phrase by
which Butler means not the merely passive sentiment, but
an entire concurrence with the Divine Will. All earthly
objects, he observes, leave a void in us, which only God
Himself can adequately supply [1]. He believes that heaven
will provide a happiness coming directly from God Himself,
and not merely as now from the intermediate objects which

[1] *Sermons*, xiv. 10, 11.

He presents to our view. Butler's religion undoubtedly was marked with that reserve which is a marked characteristic of English piety, which may sometimes be carried into excess, but which is so far from implying a deficiency in fervour, that it rather indicates a dread lest the emotions of holy devotion should come to be mixed with inferior elements, and should be chilled by exposure to the rude climate of the world. He therefore takes refuge, at the close of these Sermons, in those expressions of the Psalms which are consecrated by the use of so many generations, and raised to so high a level that no irreverence can touch them. I feel persuaded that a perusal of the closing portion of the two Sermons would lead Mr. Smith to withdraw or modify the judgement he has given.

The writings of Mark Pattison, which touch at various points upon those of Butler, bear what may be termed an unbroken testimony to their power. His Essay on 'Religious Thought in England' includes a series of excellent reflections respecting the *Analogy* [1], on which he appears to have bestowed much hard study. In his *Memoirs* [2] he bears witness to 'the solid structure of logical argument, in which it surpasses any other book that I know in the English language.' He follows up this weighty judgement with a passage for which it by no means prepares us.

'But it is not a book adapted for an educational instrument, as it diverts the mind from the great outlines of scientific and philosophical thought, and fastens it upon petty considerations, being in this respect the converse of Bacon's *Novum Organon*.'

In a later portion of the same work he records with evident satisfaction that, as one of a board of liberal examiners, he shared (from his great ability it may be that he largely shared, or even led the way) in striking Butler off the list of books which might be taken up in the Oxford schools [3]. Mr. Pattison's condemnatory proceeding would have carried great weight, had he not, with so singular a frankness, informed us of the reason by which it was governed. He has just before given us one reason which went

---

[1] Pattison's *Essays*, edited by Nettleship, vol. ii. p. 74 sqq.

[2] Pattison's *Memoirs*, p. 134.

[3] *Ibid.* p. 324.

to show that the *Analogy* was admirably suited for an educational instrument, for it was the most solid structure of
logical argument known to him in the English language.
It is indeed unlucky, to say the least, for scientific and
philosophical thought, if its outlines are so tightly drawn,
that they cannot include ' the most solid structure of logical
argument' in the English language known to this learned,
able, and accomplished man. But then this great performance fastened the mind upon petty considerations. The
issue is plainly stated, and it remains only to ascertain
what are the petty considerations in question. They are
those which form the subject of the *Analogy*. Now the
subject of the *Analogy* may be succinctly described. It is
the dealings of God with man in the kingdoms of Nature,
Providence, and Grace, which it handles in a structure of
logical argument more solid than is to be readily found in
any English work of ' scientific and philosophical thought.'
Of these three kingdoms, Bacon's *Novum Organon* introduces us only to that commonly regarded as the lowest;
but if we are to interpret Mr. Pattison strictly, the one
alone capable of supplying us with philosophical and scientific thought. We seem here to be in the face of a strange
dilemma. A treatise consummate in logical structure is
proscribed as an instrument of education, by reason of the
unworthiness of its subject. For those who think it worthy,
Mr. Pattison has supplied a perfect demonstration that the
Analogy is admirably fitted to be an instrument of the most
masculine training. If, on the other hand, Mr. Pattison's
dictum be sound, Butler's *Analogy* may justly disappear
from among the instruments of education. But the thorough and impartial application of his principle will require
that much else should disappear along with it: perhaps not
least, that the Scriptures themselves should abdicate their
position as the final rule and the staple food of Christendom,
and should remain among us to be only an object of exhibition as the greatest and the strangest among the archæo-
logical curiosities of the world.

CHAPTER IV

ON ITEMS WHICH OUGHT TO BE TAKEN INTO ACCOUNT WHEN COMPARING BUTLER WITH THE ANCIENTS

TURNING now to the drawbacks which may seem to encumber, and to discourage the study of Butler, it seems to be felt that, besides the difficulties of expression which they present to us, we cannot but be deeply, perhaps painfully, impressed with the higher difficulties that presented themselves to him, and with the deep marks which they have impressed upon the whole course of his writings. As if his tread were less firm than that of many philosophers, both ancient and modern, he not only does not claim the authority, which even the ordinary teacher as such habitually inclines to assume, but he seems to remove that claim to the greatest possible distance from the path he traverses. Here, then, was probably a happy adaptation of his nature to the purpose of his work. The absence of such a claim tended to disarm suspicion, and to procure an easier access for his arguments. Yet it will be felt that this is not saying enough. It may be right to deal more at large with the remark of one among his kindly critics, who says that Plato sees the truth, while Butler gropes for it. The nature and conditions of the work which they respectively had to do were broadly different. The truth, which presented itself to the mind of Plato four centuries before the Advent, was not the same truth which lay before the mind of Butler, seventeen centuries after it.

It is a well-known characteristic of Butler, particularly in the *Analogy*, that after pursuing his aim through preliminary argument and observation of close texture and possibly not of facile comprehension, he lands his readers in conclusions which are limited and reserved, and which may sometimes appear clouded and indefinite. It is plain that

Butler abounds in reserves, such as we rarely meet with in the ancient schools of philosophy. Indeed all he offers as the reward of close attention and no inconsiderable mental effort, is that the matter he has adduced appears to go part of the way towards a solution; or has so much at least of weight that it cannot without levity be put aside before careful examination; or that it will command attention from considerate men. These guarded and (as against himself) niggardly conclusions are offered us; and they are exactly the reverse of what is required to satisfy the indolence and carelessness, or the intemperance and coarse perceptions, of the ordinary reader. His desire is to please the taste, not to be nourished; to be excited, not to be educated; to have what is called loudness in colouring presented to his eye, with a stimulating diet provided for his palate, which shall leave the health to take care of itself. To give delight to the average unsophisticated man was what Homer could venture to prescribe to himself as the proper office of the bard. Butler is not a bard, but a philosopher. He does not conform to this condition; and man at large has in these last three thousand years travelled far from the early simplicity of his nature.

Nor is it only that nature has become less simple. It has also become more profound. Christianity has penetrated more deeply into the essence of man than any agency previously offered to his mind; has opened up in him new depths; has added to him a new intensity. Those, who believe in a Divine Incarnation, will readily believe that a nature which has once had such an inhabitant as the Saviour, and has even been subjected to all the resulting influences, cannot in its facts, and still more in its capabilities, remain just what it was before. It must, as the character of man unfolds under continued, varied, and ever-enlarging experience, undergo searching modifications, the aggregate of which it is impossible to measure, but of which some characteristics may be observed. The whole world, both of duty and of love, has been opened out to a far wider horizon. The action of man is brought into more close and constant relation with the Divine dispensations. God is ever nearer us in the still small voice. The thought of man too has become habituated to the clearer and nearer contemplation of Deity, and a new relation, mental as well as spiritual, and highly fertile in results, has been established between the Creator and the creature.

And if we compare the developments of character in practice, as known in the ancient pre-Christian world, and that which Christianity has so insufficiently but yet marvellously permeated, we shall be astonished at the difference. Every vice and every virtue has altered in its character, is a larger and a deeper thing. The ancients lived more on the surface; we have dug deep into the subsoil. The cruelty of Christians is more cruel. Of this fact, at first sight so startling, we have recently had a very striking illustration in the singular elaboration of those horrible instruments of torture, of which there was a remarkable exhibition in London a few years ago. To the ancients, the arts of torture were little known; and the legend of Regulus holds a solitary place in their popular literature. The lust of Christians is more lustful, and carries with it, as to acts which may be the same, the consciousness of a much deeper sinfulness; for, as Butler is careful to instruct us, moral acts can only be estimated aright when taken in conjunction with the nature and capacity of the agent. Antiquity has displayed for us in its records all the worst that it had to say of itself, in this painful chapter of the experience of the race, and has done it with a certain *naïveté*. It has been of a surety entirely outstripped in the performances of the Satanic schools, under the earlier and the later conditions respectively. The animal greed of Christians is tenfold more greedy; and the pre-Christian times afford us no panorama of Mammon worship to compare for a moment with our own. The systematic, or, if the expression may be used, the scientific use of the apparatus of life to build up a godless existence, an atheism of act, which by the mere extinction of all thought avoids the name, has so developed as to seem different, not in degree only, but in kind. The luxury and the worldliness of old were but child's play in relation to those of modern times.

There is another subject, the further mention of which is odious, but it cannot be avoided. The lust of Christians is more intense, and on that as well as other grounds far more wicked than was the lust of the heathen. It is indeed the fact that they practised largely the worship of obscene symbols; and it is certain that this worship cannot possibly revive in conjunction with that social standard of idea and common judgement which has been established (but, be it observed, as a social rule only) by the Christian tradition. It is also clear from the plays of Aristophanes, the Roman spectacles indicated by Martial, and such ideas as those proclaimed by Heliogabalus, that the sense of shame as a public sense, which had been at the epoch of Homer at once delicate and strong, had wellnigh ceased to exist. All this is of the past; and a real, and even perhaps a rigorous, standard of public decency has been established. And the private sense of shame given us, as Butler truly says, to prevent shameful actions, is doubtless of a far greater average power, than in those heathen days. But when the question is as to what is done, and contrived to be done, far from the public eye, and when that barrier of personal shame has once been overleapt, I fear the verdict upon any such comparison as may conjecturally be made must be that, while the acts may continue in great part the same, their intensity and the pestilent devices and contrivances associated with them, have been enhanced and multiplied; and that we have here a new and crying confirmation of the profound observation of an ancient philosopher, that if the worst is sought for, it is to be found in the corruption of the best[1].

And why is all this? The explanation lies in few words. If they had not had the law, they had not had sin. For the heathen, the mental and practical process of obliterating the law, without thought or effort carried on through so many generations, came wellnigh up to its perfection. The idea of sin, except in Judea, was obliterated. The practice of sensual sin (if we properly understand the word) became matter of course, and prevailed largely among the best. Growing to be matter of course, it was, naturally enough, more nearly universal; but in the individual it

---

[1] Plato, *Rep.* vi. (p. 491, Stephens). 'The most gifted minds, when they are ill educated, become pre-eminently bad.' Jowett's Translation.

required and hastened less of obliquity, of obtusity, of hardihood, of true and obstinate demoralization.

And so with regard to the virtues, and to the energies of our nature capable of moral or of immoral use, and appertaining to its manhood. With the multiplied forms of torture there has been developed a more tenacious and unyielding product; the faculty of endurance. A nobler cause has here been at work. The heavens became open to the spiritual eye through the operation of faith, which was not only the substance of things hoped for, but also the evidence of things unseen. The greatness and loftiness of the interests, and of the entire destinies thus opened to mankind, developed new powers both of action and of suffering in respect to them. The resolution of Regulus was indeed sublime; but the records of antiquity afford no historic proofs of resolution equal, as a whole, to that of the martyrs, even if allowance be made for possible exaggerations. There has in this, as in many cases, been an action not only upon this or that individual, but upon the race, and new developments of its character. The daring of our navigators some centuries ago, and their hardihood in encountering the extremities of difficulty and danger, form a feature of Christian times which compares in marked advantage with the energy and bravery of the Phoenicians, who mainly crept along the coasts, and this greatly in congenial latitudes. Let any one peruse in detail the wonderful account given by General Greely of the sufferings entailed by his Polar expedition, and of the heroic courage with which they were borne by an assemblage of men not perhaps greatly differing in physical or in moral force from the average of their countrymen. Such occurrences were beyond the pale of possibility even in the great days of Greece and of Rome.

There is, however, another case, collective not individual, which appears to exhibit in a still more vivid light that intensity of heroic endurance, up to which human character may be trained under the influence of the Christian tradition. Of this fortitude abundant instances may be gathered from the narratives of religious persecutions. But there is no parallel known to me, in records either ancient or modern, to the history of the people of Montenegro. In the end of the fifteenth century, when the awful curse of Turkish invasion had spread like a deluge of flame over Eastern Europe, this small people, numbering a very few tens of thousands, abandoned their lands and homes to save their faith and their freedom, and made for themselves a Noah's ark of the Black Mountain. And here they maintained, with diversity of fortune, but without ever succumbing, a war of four hundred years against that Ottoman power which overwhelmed everything else in the Levant. All the brightest examples of courage, animated in olden times by the enthusiasm of freedom, grow pale by the side of this unequalled experience. To the enthusiasm of freedom there had been added the twin enthusiasm of religion.

As it is of the force engendered in our human nature, without direct application to the spiritual element, that I now speak, I will at once turn to the case of the man whose sufferings probably exceeded any that are known ever to have been inflicted by human hands. I mean the appalling case of Damiens, who attempted the life of Louis XV of France. Goldsmith has commemorated

Luke's iron crown, and Damiens' bed of steel.

But the bed of steel conveys only a stinted idea of the tortures to which Damiens was subjected for having endeavoured to rid the world of a much worse man than himself. All the science of Paris was taxed by royal command to determine by what processes vital power could be so husbanded under torture as to secure that Damiens should pass out of this world with the greatest amount and intensity of suffering that could possibly be devised. It may seem strange to cite this fiendish contrivance of Louis XV or his advisers in connexion with the operation of Christianity upon human nature. Yet it could never, as I conceive, have entered into the mind of antiquity to conceive the idea, or to construct the machinery, of this terrible occasion, the characteristics of which appear in truth to belong to hell more properly than to earth.

It may also seem strange to some that I should introduce the case of Damiens in this connexion, as if his rules of action had been those of an intelligent Christian. In that respect, let us leave him to his Judge: my reference is to his powers of energetic endurance, as being powers not to be found among mankind in the ages anterior to the Christian dispensation. His environment was Christian; he lived in the atmosphere of Christian tradition. In his case, as in that of others, the effects of tradition and environment may have been developed in character, apart altogether from personal convictions [1].

I do not enter into consideration of the cases of self-torture among the devotees of the East, which belong to another chapter of human nature, and are hardly relevant to the present remarks.

Nor do I enter upon the question how far the comparison between Christian and pre-Christian periods, here partially set forth, can be extended to the department of intellectual or imaginative power. The province of the present discussion is that of character, not of intellect. To this I do not extend my affirmations as they stand.

Indeed, what I ask is to bring the whole of these considerations to bear upon our appreciation of the work of Butler, and upon such comparisons as we may be tempted to make between his work, with his method of performing it, and the work and method of the ancient philosophers.

My position is that he had a different human nature to deal with, and a different relation between that human nature and the Almighty Maker; that they speculated freely and at will, while he moved with a nobleness of object indeed that was unknown to them, but with a burden of responsibility upon him at every step, which almost bore him down to the ground. Even of common duty, what seems to some men light, to others is a sense almost oppressive: how much greater was the pressure on a quickened conscience labouring under the belief of being charged with that argument, on which the whole ultimate welfare of the world depends!

After familiarizing ourselves with the secure and steady steps of Aristotle, and the rarity of his resorts to doubt and reservation, or even with the questionings of Socrates in the

---

[1] The particulars of this proceeding have recently been published in a painfully interesting volume entitled *Le Procès de Damiens.*

Platonic Dialogue, which almost habitually lead us up to a prepared conclusion, we may be tempted to feel some impatience in the first stages of our acquaintance with a philosophic writer who so carefully clips his own propositions, who loads us, as his sentences make way, with qualifications, and then so often ends with what may seem lean and stunted affirmations. But no ancient philosopher had to face the difficulties which beset the path of Butler. Two such representatives of Christian and pre-Christian thought as Butler and Aristotle are not unlike two soldiers marching along the same road, the one heavily laden with his kit and military equipment, the other rid of encumbrances and prepared for action. But the first carries material which, though it may augment his burden, means also enlarged resources and a graver destiny.

None of the ancients could endeavor to exhibit in systematic detail the methods of God's dealing with the individual Greek or Roman. None of them took the world as a school, and life as a discipline, in the close and searching sense, which has been brought within arm's length of every competent inquirer by the Christian Revelation. Only in limited portions of the Old Testament are we introduced to a fully constituted personal relationship between the human soul and its Almighty Maker, Governor, and Judge. And as on the one side it was permitted to Butler to treat of a heaven unveiled, so on the other side he had perforce to contemplate the human being in that more extended and diversified moral development, which he has undergone through the long and slow experience of Christianity, and which has so largely enhanced his perils, his privileges, and his hopes.

CHAPTER V

i. *His Quality of Measure.*

ALTHOUGH no one would charge Butler with egotism, yet he is evidently, like Dante, a self-revealing writer. As a man governed by one dominant influence, he wears his heart upon his sleeve. The master passion with him is the love of truth: and it is never leavened, never traversed by any other feeling. He is, without doubt, a singularly circumspect writer. He has even been described by Mr. Stephen as having 'a strangely cautious understanding.' Few indeed are the instances in which he can on this score be called in question. But, while the caution of many is largely based on fear of detection, it seems to have been in Butler simply a steady as well as an intense desire to be in exact correspondence with the truth. Following in the train of this love of truth, as an outgrowth or a satellite, there is an unceasing desire to keep faith with his readers, a fear of committing a grave offence against the student (who may be considered as in some degree giving over himself to his author, as we obey a guide) by carrying his mind one inch beyond what the facts of the case will warrant. If there are over-statements in Butler, they are commonly against himself. They are, in truth, under-statements of the case on his own side, as when he says that the evidence he presents is not indeed satisfactory — very far from it [1]. It thus appears that, if the insect can take colour from what it feeds upon, our minds can derive no colour but what is genuine from assimilation with Butler. He sees the proportion of things, and not only the things themselves; and does not thrust forward the small as if it were great, nor

[1] *Analogy,* II. viii. 17.

shuffle away the great as if it were small. The one word which best describes his carefulness, and its result as to breadth of statement, is *measure*.

ii. *His Strength of Tissue.*

It seems quite safe to assert that Butler is among the least commonplace of writers. He is always dealing with the heart, never with the surface of his question. There is, if it may be permitted so to speak, no outside, no mere skin, to his writings. It would be difficult to name any other writer on kindred subjects who altogether resembles him in the closeness of the contact between the author and the argument. Had he, like the ancient philosophers, been unfurnished with a strong view of providential government in the world as a law of universal application, I cannot but think he would have had a style like that of Aristotle, who, like Butler, is solitary in his class as to the mode of conveying his thoughts.

In the march of a battalion, every forward step is itself a separate exercise, with a relation to what precedes and what follows it. The rambling thought of many authors may seem to have no more continuity than a rope of sand: or it thins itself away like a river lost in the desert. One of the greatest properties of a human composition is to present to us continuity of tissue; and the greatness rises in proportion as the tissue, besides being continuous, is close and strong. The subject of the composition will not always admit it; but the mind of the writer is more commonly in defect. This continuity is eminently observable in the highest works of art: in a truly great statue, for example, every part is in close kindred with every other part, and the union between them is not merely mechanical but vital.

Pattison's account of the *Analogy* [1] is a just acknowledgement of its character as a compacted logical structure from end to end. Butler may in a measure be said to stand by the side of Aristotle, and is perhaps excelled by no writer, unless it be Euclid. But in Euclid, while the certainty of the connexion between point and point is greater, the effort required for grasping firmly the connexion between them is

[1] *Memoirs*, p. 134.

less. When Pitt had recommended the perusal of Butler to
Wilberforce, he in his turn records in his diary [1] that he had
the *Analogy* read aloud to him for two hours : it is not, I
think, too much to say that we might run through many
thousands of educated minds before lighting upon one
which could take real benefit from such an exercise; and
the strength of Wilberforce, not small in its own line, was
mainly dependent upon susceptibility and pious emotion,
warm but without extravagance. Butler assuredly was not
made for butterflies to flutter about. He demands the surrender, not to him but to his subject, of the entire man. It
has been well said of him that he is as much in earnest, as
if he were a gamester. Still better, perhaps, Fitzgerald
supplies us with the remark of ' an ingenious person ' who
said that each single sentence is, with Butler, ·like a well-
considered move in chess [2]; a most felicitous illustration
of its proper subject, which may well dispense with all
others, but need not exclude that able writer's description
of many a compressed clause or single word of his author,
as σφυρήλατος νοῦς ἐν ὀλίγῳ ὄγκῳ.

iii. *His Courage.*

With the circumspection which is one of his most marked
characteristics, Butler appears to unite a great boldness upon
occasion ; sometimes he even makes the occasion. As examples of this boldness, I would refer to the following heads :

1. The possible development of the brute creation and its
elevation to a higher stage of existence [3].

From the frequency and gravity of his references to the
lower animals, it plainly appears that Butler had thought
much, and with adequate care, about them. Even in our own
day there are many who resent any attempt to draw closer
the ties of relationship to our humble kindred [4]. But in those
times, when a lady of rank reproached Lady Huntingdon for
applying the same doctrines concerning sin to the case of

---

[1] *Life of Wilberforce*, i. pp. 89, 90.

[2] *Fitzgerald*, preface, p. xci.

[3] *Analogy*, I. i. 21.

[4] I seem to recollect a speech of Lord Beaconsfield, in which he was reported to have said that there were two theories of our descent. Some would have it that we were descended from the apes; others derived us from the angels. For his part he preferred the descent from the angels.

her own equals as were applicable to the common people in the street, it is probable that such ideas concerning the brutes would be yet more repulsive than, outside the scientific domain, they may still be. But he was not a man to be bound by mere prepossessions, nor did he estimate opinion according to the breadth of its prevalence. And besides the courage which in this instance he exhibited, I cannot but admire the insight of anticipation which, without a manuduction (if the term may be allowed) by natural science, enabled him to forecast what is now, though not a scientific truth, yet at least an agreeable and widely accepted opinion. At least it cannot be denied that the flint and bone discoveries, and the remains of the geologic man, have been narrowing the interval between the orders of creation; for it must be borne in mind that the effect of these discoveries may be to exhibit our race, not at its present and known standard of faculty, but in the possession of inferior powers, and only on the way upwards to the more elevated plane.

2. Not less boldness did Butler exhibit when he propounded that the whole scheme of Scripture is not yet understood; and that (apart from miracle) if progress was to be made in understanding it, such progress must be effected in the same way as natural knowledge is come at. It may contain many truths as yet undiscovered[1]. This is surely a very remarkable declaration, especially as coming from Butler. For his early training could hardly have been altogether discharged from the narrow ideas of Scripture interpretation which must have been most unfavourable to such progress; and, again, he had a most vivid sense of the corruptions which, under the mask of development, and through enlarged interpretations, had made their way into the Christian Church. Yet he was not to be deterred, when he saw his way, from enunciating ideas on this topic which seem to be of considerable breadth.

3. Still more striking, perhaps, are the original conceptions which Butler applied to the great subject of eschatology. He nowhere dogmatizes beyond the language of the Apostles' and the Nicene Creeds. He has unfolded no theory which disposes of the final condition of all souls

[1] *Analogy*, II. iii. 21.

hereafter; and his subject did not require it. But his subject did suggest to him the glorification of virtue; and, with this end in view, he considered not only what virtue does, but what under favouring circumstances it might do. He found the prevailing tradition, due to the biassing circumstances of the Reformation, too narrow; and he conceives that the power of virtue, rising upwards in distant scenes with less of hindrance, may then newly amend those who are capable of amendment. I reserve for another place a fuller statement on this subject [1].

4. Butler has also achieved an important work with regard to the respective departments of reason and faith, a favourite subject for the sneers of some sceptical writers. No one charges Butler with having robbed faith of its due prerogatives. Yet surely none could on the other hand desire a greater boldness in defining the office of reason. ' I express myself with caution, lest I should be mistaken to vilify reason; which is indeed the only faculty we have wherewith to judge concerning any thing, even revelation itself: or be misunderstood to assert, that a supposed revelation cannot be proved false, from internal characters [2].' And Butler may embolden many to maintain, as he does, that there is not only no contradiction, but no opposition, between faith and reason; the intellectual element in faith being reason employed upon a special subject-matter.

All these are instances in which Butler's prescient courage had a tendency to place him at issue with friends of his own cause, less sagacious than himself. There are other cases worthy of notice, in which no such likelihood was before him.

5. Such is the treatment of the word 'natural' in ch. i, a treatment which may involve the solution of many difficulties. There is no absurdity, he tells us, in supposing that there may be beings in the universe so enlarged in capacity and experience, as that the whole Christian dispensation may to them appear natural, i. e. conformable to God's dealings with other parts of His creation; as natural, as the visible known course of things appears to us [3].

---

[1] *Analogy*, II. iii. 3. *Inf.* Part II. Chap. iii.   [2] *Analogy*, II. iii. 3.
[3] *Ibid.*, I. i. 31.

6. Again, when confronting the objector who dwelt on difficulties apparent in the scheme of providential government, he is not content with defence, but betakes himself also to retaliation in argument. The things to which objection is commonly taken in the scheme of providential government may be things good in themselves, and even indispensable [1]; and the entire scheme may prove to have been the best that it could be.

7. And again, outside the contentious portion of his teaching, he goes far beyond the ordinary stream of Christian instruction in his suggestions respecting future bliss, which, as he thinks, may include the opening up of kinds of vision altogether strange to the human soul. For what we now see of the goodness of God is by seeing Him in His works ; but we may come to see Him, and His glorious attributes, as they are in themselves [2].

iv. *His Questionable Theses.*

It may seem as if eulogy of this kind stood in ill-assorted companionship with the admission that in very rare instances his critics appear to catch him tripping; as when Miss Hennell arraigns him for saying that one or two actions of a particular character have no aptitude, if few and detached, to create a bad mental habit. But the fact seems to be this. Circumspection is easy or difficult according to the subject-matter. It is easy in copying a letter ; it is most difficult in a philosophical treatise such as Butler's. And from the effort required to maintain continuously such a circumspection as this it is inseparable from humanity that the mind should occasionally and for moments recoil. Take the case of two horses ; one travelling on a road absolutely smooth, the other happening to tread a mountain path, its surface almost made of broken stones. The last may stumble once in a day's work, where the first does not; and yet may be by far the more sure-footed of the two.

Even in Butler, then, we may expect to find scattered about cases of inconsistency, or of deviation from absolute precision. Among them, not wholly without misgiving, I should reckon the following instances.

---

[1] *Analogy*, viii. 15.   [2] *Sermons*, xiv. 15, 18.

1. He seems to deviate from his own doctrine when in a particular passage he couples self-love with conscience; seeing that he has never ascribed to self-love a judicial or magisterial faculty [1].

2. In twice using the phrase 'vicarious punishment,' he departs from his customary use of the better phrase 'vicarious sufferings,' without any apparent recollection that he is introducing a new and important element into his argument, and indeed so as to create presumptions that this is done simply through inadvertence [2].

3. He sometimes expressly distinguishes between passion and affections; but at other times, without expressly identifying them, he seems not to exclude the supposition that the terms are interchangeable.

He makes also a different and relaxed use of the term 'affections,' so as to let it include 'appetites, passions, senses.'

And just afterwards he restrains the sense, without noticing the change; but again returns to the wider sense soon after [3].

4. Again, he says that 'any disposition, prevailing beyond a certain degree, becomes somewhat wrong': yet the love of God is a disposition, and to this he (most justly) affixes no limit [4].

5. The language of one of the Sermons seems wholly to exclude self-love from the category of affections; but can this in strictness be maintained [5]?

6. It seems difficult to sustain the proposition that our bodies consist of foreign matter [6], if the word 'body' be taken in its most comprehensive sense.

7. Or the proposition that 'a few detached commands' have no 'natural tendency to the formation of a habit' which is surely in keeping with their subject-matter.

8. The term 'imagination' in the first chapter would appear to be a misnomer [7].

9. We have also the well-known passage where the name

---

[1] *Sermons*, iii. 13.
[2] *Analogy*, II. v. 22.
[3] *Sermons*, v. 6–9.
[4] *Ibid.* 8.
[5] *Ibid.* 10.
[6] *Analogy*, I. i. 11.
[7] *Ibid.* I. i. 9.

of Caesar occurs, and where probabilities appear to be con-
fused with chances [1].

10. Does not it appear questionable whether Butler does
not venture upon hazardous ground, when he says that the
ideas of happiness and misery are more important to us than
those of virtue and religion [2]?   Some qualification appears
to be here required.

Unless, however, this list of seriously questionable propositions could be largely extended, we need not fear that the
fame of Butler's circumspection will seriously dwindle.

v.   *His Supposed Defect in Imagination.*

It is sometimes said that Butler is deficient in imagination. I am aware of no plausible ground for this imputation,
except that supplied by the passage in which, employing the
actual word, he has made imagination, 'that forward delusive faculty,' the subject of warning and censure. 'It ever
obtrudes beyond its sphere.' It is 'the author of all error.'
It is singular that what he denounces is not ' the imagination,' but ' imagination,' as if he were dealing with a process
rather than a faculty. But we can hardly dwell upon this,
since he proceeds to describe it as a faculty, and, moreover,
assigns to it a 'sphere.' The mischievous products of this
abusive practice were, we must suppose, those of which Butler was cognizant, and with which he deals so largely in his
work. But these, mentioned almost in every page, are not,
in truth, errors of the imagination, but of unbridled fancy
and caprice; of unbalanced, ill-regulated judgement. It
seems probable that this is one of the rare instances in
which Butler, relaxing the firmness of his hold, forgets himself and assumes licence in the use of words. Sometimes,
though rarely, he deals with schemes purely metaphysical;
but these, if erroneous, are not errors of the imagination
properly so called.

If the question be only verbal, all reason for maiming the
mind of Butler in this particular disappears. But it does
not seem hard to assign some positive reasons for asserting
that Butler was duly — indeed, as I think, somewhat more
than commonly — endowed with his share of this faculty.

---

[1] *Analogy*, II. ii. 11, 12.   [2] *Sermons*, xi. 21.

I should assign in proof of this the felicity of his illustra-tions, which, though less copious (as being indeed less germane to his subject), may remind us of Macaulay. As another indication of the same kind, I notice the fact that Butler is a believer in beauty. He believes in it not merely as, like colour, an impression on the brain; not merely as a fashion or a whim; but as a true entity. No one would describe Burke as a man void of imagination; but Butler masters the conception of beauty in a way more effective than Burke, when he classes it with other ideas such as all admit to be definite and substantive. The ideas of happi-ness and misery, he says, will and ought to prevail over those of order *and beauty,* and harmony, and proportion, if they could clash, which he thinks they cannot[1]. Yet more strongly does he mark his sense of the self-consistent and substantive character of beauty in his ascription of it to the character of the Almighty. This, he says, possesses in perfection 'everything of grace and beauty' which is variously distributed in degree among the orders of crea-tion[2].

vi. *His Originality.*

It is perhaps right to introduce the present section with the inquiry, What is originality? Can nothing be original which has already been said or suggested by another? Ruskin[3] has taught us that originality 'is only genuine-ness.' I understand this to mean that, while a mechanical appropriation is plagiarism, there is also such a thing as a vital appropriation, both intellectual and moral, which is of an order essentially different. Moreover, the man who creates a thought, deposits a seed, which carries in it life, and which is to be sown in the minds of others. It may there germinate and bear fruit: and, if the second mind supplies a soil richer than the first, the thought primarily borrowed may spring up anew, endowed with a deeper life, with a greater force of nutritive quality, than it drew from the earlier source where it first received its form. Again, the hot light of the sun, transfused through coloured glass,

---

[1] *Sermons,* xi. 21.　　　　　　　　　　　[2] *Ibid.* xiv. 14.
[3] Quoted in Morley's *Diderot,* vol. i. p. 303.

may in its disintegration supply tints of beauty sought in vain from the outward glare. Or we may once more turn to another side of the subject, and say that, as many seeds spring from one parent seed, so it may be given to an author, who begins with being no more than a borrower, to embody this single thought in vast and varied combinations, to which its relation may eventually become to be that of the individual to the community in which he moves. Such is the work of Butler in its relation to the parent suggestion of Origen. May it not have been also such in relation to the anticipatory productions of Cumberland ?

It is not, however, necessary to dwell at great length on the originality of Bishop Butler.

The highest form of originality is ' discovery '; and this is the phrase of eulogy which Macintosh has applied to the *Sermons* of Butler. But it is with regard to the *Analogy* that the question of originality has been principally raised.

This subject was opened by Hallam, the historian. His *History of European Literature* terminates with the seventeenth century. The works of Butler, therefore, were not within his subject. But he has noticed at length, and greatly commended in certain portions of its argument, the treatise of Bishop Cumberland, *de Legibus Naturae*, which was published in 1679. In a brief note he takes occasion to observe that the second and third chapters of the first part of the *Analogy* are in great part to be found in it [1].

But he also shows in his text how much, in using the work of Cumberland, Butler had to avoid. Indeed, he had not only to avoid particular arguments, but to adopt a different method of reasoning ; for Cumberland had an ambition to put his processes of reasoning into mathematical form. But he gave to ethics a basis independently of revelation, and, as Butler did after him, he resorted to experience as the source from which to draw his supplies of argument [2].

Again. In the preface to his edition of the *Analogy* [3], Bishop Fitzgerald has the following observation :

---

[1] Hallam's *History of European Literature*, vol. iv. p. 317 *n.*
[2] *History of European Literature*, vol. iii. p. 301, *et seq.*
[3] Fitzgerald's *Analogy*, preface, p. xxxviii.

'The second chapter of Foster's Reply to Tindal, for instance, is a remarkable anticipation of Butler's reasoning, in P. ii. c. vi. upon the want of universality in revelation [1]; while the following passage in Bishop Berkeley's *Minute Philosopher* clearly contains the germ of the whole argument.'

Then follows a long extract, of which the pith is contained in a single sentence :

'It will be sufficient, if such analogy appears between the dispensations of grace and nature, as may make it probable (although much should be unaccountable in both) to suppose them derived from the same author, and the workmanship of one and the same hand.'

This is indeed a remarkable passage. It corresponds, not with the declaration of Origen, on which Butler founds himself, but more nearly with Butler's own amendment of that declaration [2]. It was published in the year 1732, and it contains a summary of the entire argument. For that very reason, although it sets forth a grand anticipation of Butler, yet we cannot suppose Butler to have been indebted to it. The *Analogy* bears the date of 1736. It must have been published early in the year, for a second and amended edition appeared before the year expired. The *Sermons* had been published in 1726. Viewing the distribution of Butler's works over his life, as well as the character of his mind, we can hardly doubt that he had been working out his great argument from a date considerably antecedent to 1732, and not improbably prior even to 1726. The germ must have been deposited, and begun to develop, long before Berkeley gave his work to the world.

Once more, Dr. Bernard, a Professor of Divinity in Dublin University, has printed a noteworthy paper entitled 'The Predecessors of Bishop Butler [3].' He gives a list of writers to whom he thinks that Butler was variously indebted.

---

[1] See *Defence of the Usefulness, Truth, and Excellency of the Christian Religion.* London, 1731.

[2] The analogy suggested by Origen (see *Analogy,* Introd. § 8) is between nature and Scripture. The analogy exhibited by Butler is between nature in its ordinary course and constitution, on the one side, and religion, natural and revealed, on the other. Butler widens the field both of Origen and of Berkeley.

[3] 'The Predecessors of Bishop Butler,' *Hermathena,* vol. xi. No. xx. 1894.

The first is Wilkins, Bishop of Chester, the author of *The Principles and Duties of Natural Religion*. In his third chapter he pointed out that in common life men are to guide their actions by probable evidence when they cannot attain to certainty.

Wilkins has also cited from Grotius the passage cited by Butler in the *Analogy*, II. vi. 19. Butler's debt is, I think (if any), to Grotius, rather than to Wilkins, as the terms of the citation would seem to me to imply.

The gratification of a passion, according to Butler, would not please, but for 'a prior suitableness between the object and the passion.' This doctrine had been previously laid down by Wilkins.

Wilkins has very clearly defined superstition. Butler has not, and Dr. Bernard thinks the sense he puts upon it is not immediately apparent.

Butler and Wilkins have both referred to the Jews as a standing memorial and example. They both regard the correspondence between conscience and self-love as indications of the wisdom and power of God.

Dr. Bernard points out some heads under which the philosophy of Butler coincides with that of Shaftesbury; and also thinks that Colliber's work on *Natural and Revealed Religion* might have suggested some of the arguments used in the *Analogy*.

It may perhaps be held that coincidences at certain points in two philosophical systems cannot always be regarded as proofs that the one later in date is indebted to the earlier. Upon all subjects that have undergone open and repeated discussion, there is gradually accumulated a common stock of materials which cannot be regarded as exclusive properties, but remain open to the use of all. Much of what the acuteness and research of Dr. Bernard have drawn from Bishop Wilkins may fall within the scope of this remark. It is only when there is something decidedly peculiar in the matter, or in the form given to it, that we can safely predicate derivation by the later author as probable or certain. The passages from Wilkins, who was a very considerable person, on probable evidence, and of the harmony between a passion and its objects, appear to me to be probably of this character.

Or again, we may say the case is like that of a young man beginning his career in the world of business, who receives from some friend a gift or loan of capital comparatively small, which by skill, courage, and assiduity he develops into a magnificent fortune.

It seems to me far from unlikely that the colossal character of Achilles may have been suggested to Homer by the great martial figure of Rameses the Second, a figure not less exceptional than that of the Achaian hero; but that, even if this should be the fact, it in no way detracts from the paramount conception presented to us in the *Iliad*. It may indeed be a specific gift of genius to appropriate elementary material for the purposes of its grand combinations, and to give them an execution of which their original author had never dreamed. We may, then, securely say that Butler has a stock of originality amply sufficient to maintain his literary credit; and the question which has been raised, though worthy of discussion on its own grounds, is not one of great moment in reference to the claims of Butler and of his main works on the attention of the world.

As I own, it appears to me that if a student of Butler, after perusing and intelligently apprehending the *Analogy*, were to be told that it was not a work of originality, his nature, from its inmost depths, would cry out against the assertion. It matters not that particular thoughts, or even that some portions of the argument may have been promulgated before him by others; even if we are to suppose, and the supposition might be somewhat violent if universally applied, that he was in every case cognizant of the passage cited against him. Surely if all this be granted, and be taken at the highest value which can be assigned to it, the originality of Butler's work remains indisputable. Are not these thoughts of other writers, scattered and uncombined, in the main like the bricks lying here and there, and from which a building may be constructed? But the original mind in this case is not that which moulded the bricks; it is that which raised the building. Or if we go further and admit that we find here and there the embryo of substantive portions of the Treatise, as Origen has supplied the embryo of the entire Treatise, will not the truly great work, though both may be original, be that of him who discerns and develops the capacities of what is still essentially inorganic, and gives to it once for all a fully moulded and imperishable form? Till their hour comes, the mere rudiments await the hand and eye of the master-builder.

CHAPTER VI

SOME POINTS OF BUTLER'S POSITIVE TEACHING

THE influence of Butler's works upon opinion; the value of the ethical qualities they display; the applicability of his arguments in forms never suggested, perhaps never dreamed of by himself, to controversies posterior to his time; all these are topics of importance, and worthy severally of independent prosecution, but they are distinct from the positive teaching conveyed by his writings; a few points of which I will now proceed to consider.

i. *His Elevated View of Human Nature.*

The relations of man, in which his duty and his training are involved, are threefold. They are relations to God, to other men, and to himself. He may exercise.manual arts; he may be given to civil affairs; he may be a philosopher, or a divine, or a fisher of men, or a student of the visible creation in one or other of its kingdoms. But all that he does in any such or any other department, falls into the triad of relations which has been named; as indeed whatever he does in any of those relations, is, when traced up to the sources of action, comprehended in his over-reaching, all-comprehending, relations to God.

His relations to man may subdivide themselves as follows. He has duties to his kind at large, which in certain cases may be active, in other cases may be mental only, as, for example, in the injunction to make supplication for all men [1]. He has duties to his country, to its ruling authority, to his neighbourhood, to his friends, to his family. But he has also duties to himself. These duties to himself are directly associated with his maintenance, with his security, with his tranquillity; it may be with his advancement,

[1] 1 Tim. ii. 1.

inward as well as outward. But he has a further and perpetual duty to himself. For covering all these, pervading every action of his life, and coincident with, though distinguishable from, his duty and love to God, is his duty to his own nature, the nature in which God constituted and constructed him. It is largely in his own nature that he sees God. Not in those faults and weaknesses of his nature with which he was born into the world, or which he himself has imported into it; but according to the noble scheme on which God projected it, apart from the ravages of sin, and with all the vital development which training and experience can give it.

This respect for our nature is a principle most of all exhibited in his disquisition on the supremacy of conscience; but it is one with which the whole works of Butler are profoundly imbued. It is a sentiment which is to accompany every act of our lives, and to give to them a tacit assent and sanction. The moral law comes to us in various forms. The nearest of them all, for which its own proper mental habit has to be formed, is the sense of reverence for our nature, and the desire of conformity to it. These, duly matured and assimilated, come to operate with the directness and certainty of an instinct; and violations of nature and its laws are put aside as an unclean thing, as importing not only sin but shame.

Butler is sometimes thought to connect too closely his idea of virtue with happiness. But then we must recollect what is his idea of happiness. Happiness he holds to consist only in the enjoyment of those objects which are 'by nature adapted to our several faculties[1].' Virtue lies in a rightly conceived following of nature, vice in departing from it[2]. The force of Butler's teaching on this subject cannot be sufficiently estimated from this or that single passage : it pervades the tissue of his thought. And there is no part perhaps of his teaching which, as he has developed it, is so peculiarly and originally his own. But our best security against misunderstanding him is probably to be found in the passage which sets forth that the obligation to follow virtue still subsists, even for a man, if such there

---

[1] *Sermons*, xi. 6-13.   [2] *Ibid.* Preface, § 8.

be, who is not convinced that his interest will be served thereby [1].

It seems to me probable that the high place accorded by Butler to what he terms self-love, and the favourable view he has taken of it, may have been in a measure due to his lofty estimate of our human nature. Not that I can find solid ground for dissent from his doctrine, though it may seem to grate a little upon the ear. As to the substance, I only regret that self-love is not more sharply marked off by his text from selfishness, which, of course, he nowhere commends, and very rarely mentions. But an object so precious as is the idea of humanity in Butler's conception, requires or justifies the existence of an apparatus for its conservation, of a powerful faculty dedicated to the steady prosecution of its welfare. In fact, the ideal concept of human nature, and the practical power of self-love, almost seem to coalesce. Butler's mind was incapable of harbouring an ignoble conception. And surely there is nothing ignoble in conceiving of the Christian world as a garden divided into plots, each of which represents an individual soul, and is committed by the supreme Gardener [2], to the special care of that same soul. Self-love, then, in the only commendable sense, is our view, taken with the eye well purged from disturbance and obstruction, of what God has committed to every one of us as our principal work in life.

It is idle, as I conceive, to dispute Butler's doctrine of human nature on account of that other doctrine of ruin through sin, which he has not less emphatically set forth. The gamut or register, in musical phrase, of humanity, is of enormous range. Capable of contracting into littleness and meanness, and of sinking into unfathomable depths of depravity, it has the correlative capacity of rising to supreme heights of excellence; to moral heights bordering upon perfection, as well as to lofty planes of genius. The contemplation of it in its littleness sickens heart and mind. But the contemplation of it in its greatness, a greatness not

---

[1] *Sermons*, Preface, §§ 20, 21.   a profound and elevating passage.—
[2] Dante has employed this figure in   *Paradiso*, xxvi. 64–6.

> 'Le fronde onde s' infronda tutto l' orto
> Dell' ortolano eterno, am' io cotanto,
> **Quanto da lui a lor di bene è porto.'**

measured by rank or intellect, seems at times to give us a glimpse of those profoundest counsels, which took effect in the Incarnation of our Lord.

ii. *His Doctrine of Habits.*

This lesson, then, of human nature, if it be a true one, is one of cardinal moment; and, for a Christian country, Butler may perhaps be deemed to hold the first place among those by whom it has been taught.

The present notice of the positive teaching of Butler aims at placing especially in clear view what is most distinctive in that teaching. The *Analogy* is not a treatise upon education; but what treatises are there which as faithfully and profoundly impress upon us the place and function of training, and especially of self-training, in the destinies of the human soul? The portion of the work most fully developed in this respect is his doctrine of habits in the first part of the *Analogy*[1]; and in its whole compass it might be hard to find anything either more valuable or more truly his own.

Habits (after the Greek ἕξις) are not in Butler's view mere θέσεις, states or dispositions, but growths, and growths which are ever growing. Every growth is an acquisition as well as a growth. If we could conceive of a machine, instinct with mind and gifted with the power of self-development, we might call habits a 'going machinery.' They include the acting as well as the being of the mind, and cannot, like their Greek counterpart in Aristotle, be sharply distinguished from, and put in antithesis to, energies[2]. They form a primary factor in the human life; and upon them hangs an immense responsibility, for there can hardly be one of our waking moments in which we are not contributing something to the constitution of one or other among them; that is to say, to the eventual constitution of ourselves.

Such being their ground-idea, habits are divided between perception and action; perception, indeed, often being itself mental action. And, again, they are divided between the body and the mind. They are the product of use, or single

---

[1] *Analogy*, I. v. 6–17.   [2] Aristotle, *Eth. Nic.* II. i. 7.

acts over and over again repeated. Thoughts which have
no proper regard to action, and impressions which are
purely passive, lose force by this repetition ; but active
habits, mental processes which contemplate or take effect
in action, gain it. It is not easy to trace the formation of
habit from point to point. Yet the reality of the formation is matter of certain experience. It is also to be observed, on the one hand, that the augmentation of true
force in active habits may be accompanied with a loss of
force merely emotional ; and, on the other, that a process,
which in its inception was passive, consisting of impressions on the mind, say, from admonition, experience, example, may in its advance become active by impelling us to
a course of action. [It has been well shown by Doctor
John Brown that the right-minded man, on becoming a
surgeon, loses in passive humanity, for he becomes inured
to the contemplation of suffering, and is better able to regard it steadily ; but he advances in active humanity, for
he acquires a desire to relieve the pain he witnesses, and to
exert his care and energy for that purpose.]

From habit we derive, when in action, supplies of readiness, ease, satisfaction. It is by habit that we attain to
maturity, which could not be attained by mere duration.
For nature casts us forth into the world unfurnished, yet
with a capacity for furnishing. Habits may have their
place in a future state ; but meanwhile they provide us
with a security *ab intra* against mischiefs assailing us from
without, and form the fitting antidote and guarantee
against our liability to lapse. The evil habit is produced by
repeated or continuing disobedience, but positive advance
in virtue is achieved by victories over temptation, and by
forming that wariness of mind which baffles it. This is
doctrine generally sound ; whether its application is limited
by the law of a mean in nature, or otherwise, is uncertain, and need not now be inquired into[1]. Upon the whole,
here lies a great instrument for the bettering of our character; and to the use of this instrument our nature is
adapted[2].

We may find the germ of this remarkable exposition in

[1] *Analogy*, I. v. 33.   [2] *Ibid.* 20.

the Ethics of Aristotle. They teach that the consummation of energies is in the habits imparted [1]. It is by action that, in our intercourse with men, we grow to be
righteous or unrighteous ; and habits are a gradual growth
from energies [2]. Seminally these declarations are of great
weight. But he seems to limit the formation of habits
to acts done in our communications with others. He does
not enter on the field of self-education. There is not a
glance at the profound distinction between active and passive habits ; the idea of mental habits is radically distinct
in the two writers ; and the full development of the subject, with the great lessons it conveys, seems to be due to
the thought of Butler.

iii. His View of Human Ignorance.

A corner-stone of Butler's mental system is certainly
to be found in his strong but carefully bounded view of
human ignorance. There is no part of his teaching more
urgently required at the present day, when not only are
the large recent accessions to human knowledge apt to be
over-valued by some of those who at least have laboured
hard to learn and perhaps to add to them ; but when many
who are totally ignorant of what they are, vaingloriously
boast of them as if sciolism approximated to omniscience.

Butler was not a man indifferent, as some are, to knowledge outside his profession. He attached a high value to
natural knowledge. He thought some parts of it were ' of
the greatest consequence to the ease and convenience of
life [3].' He was deeply impressed with those enlargements
of 'the plan of Providence,' which 'late discoveries' had
supplied [4]. From these enlargements, indeed, he seems to
have drawn the suggestions he has made bold to make as
to what may take place after death with regard to the
souls of men. For it seems to him that, as the material
world appears to be in a manner boundless, 'there must
be some scheme of Providence vast in proportion to it [5].'
With this radically sensible disposition to take account of

---

[1] Aristotle, *Eth. Nic.* I. viii. 9, 11.
[2] *Ibid.* III. vii. 6.
[3] *Analogy*, II. iii. 22.
[4] *Ibid.* I. iii. 28.
[5] *Ibid.* I. iii. 28.

every real gain, Butler pointed out, in his admirable sermon on Human Ignorance, that what we know is of effects only, not causes. We know nothing of the real essence of beings, next to nothing of ourselves, of our creation, and conservation; he showed that all knowledge served to raise a curiosity which it could not satisfy. Every opened secret, discovery, effect, 'convinces us of numberless more which remain concealed, and which we had before no suspicion of[1].'

Yes, some things are plain, and many of them tend to show the multitude and vastness of those which are impenetrably obscure. Sometimes we have to confess that knowledge once possessed by mankind has been lost by them[2]; sometimes that the knowledge possessed by savages is inferior to our own; sometimes that, in matters open to observation, and which we have a great interest in observing — such as the weather — the race of man has, or had up to an exceedingly recent period, accumulated nothing. But these observations are of limited scope; and it may seem both vague and trite to remark on the vastness of the unknown compared with the known. Let us, then, take the point suggested by Butler. Every extension of our knowledge is an extension, often a far wider extension, of our ignorance. When we knew of only one world we also knew a good deal about its circumstances, its condition, its progress. Now we are surrounded by worlds innumerable, spread over spaces hardly conceivable for their extent; and yet those, who may be rapt in their wonder at the grand discoveries of the spectroscope, may also be the first to admit that as to the condition, purposes, and destinies of all these worlds we are absolutely in the dark. Consider the conditions of our civilization : disease in its multiplied forms is more rife among us than in savage life, while the problems of the social kind seem to gain upon us continually in the multitude of puzzles which they offer to our bewildered minds. Then, in the moral world, we must be still more conscious of our limita-

---

[1] *Sermons*, xv.

[2] For instance, the hardening of copper among the ancients ; the loss of the knowledge of the steam-plough, invented in Scotland, and lost during many years, until it was re-imported.

tions ; for, while we are continually required to pass judgement for practical purposes on actions, every right-minded
person will incessantly feel that to form any perfect judgement on any action whatever is a task wholly beyond our
power. When Butler pronounced his severe sentence on the
claims of the Popes, his horror was not the result of theological bigotry, but, without doubt, he was shocked (with
his strong, just, and humble sense of our limitations in capacity) at the daring and presumption of the claims set up
by some on their behalf.   Yet he keenly saw the obligation
that knowledge imposes to act when we know, not less than
to abstain when we do not.

On this great and critical subject, he seems never to have
let fall a faulty word, and of all the topics he has handled
there is not one on which we may more safely accept him as
a guide.

CHAPTER VII

THE THEOLOGY OF BUTLER AND CHARGES RELATING TO IT

IT would appear as though the most characteristic employment of Butler's mind lay in the exercise of reflection rather than in the acquisition of learning. And, further, it may perhaps be not very hazardous to suppose that the knowledge which he coveted was philosophical more largely than theological, if we take theology in its proper sense as the science of religion. All the theology of the *Analogy* (and it contains much theological matter) is derived straight from the Holy Scriptures, and ends as well as begins with them. The philosophy, however, which he affected, was philosophy on its moral side. He rarely dwells on the metaphysical side of philosophy. The famous youthful correspondence with Clarke leaves on my mind the impression that when the unbending integrity of his mind, by actually throwing certain questions of metaphysics in his way, led him to notice them, his desire was to get clear of them as soon as possible. Not once in all his other works does he argue a question properly metaphysical.

It may perhaps be truly said that Butler's mind turned little to theology, as such, considering theology in what I have already described as its true sense. Butler never but once quotes a theologian, and that only in one of the notes[1], which he appends to his text with a just parsimony. With regard to the exclusiveness of his habit of quoting from Holy Scripture, it seems probable that his education as a Presbyterian dissenter may have done much to form the habit of his mind. His theology was made up, so to speak, with raw material drawn straight from the fountain-head. He had the deep insight given by true piety; and it was

---

[1] *Analogy*, II. i. 18 *n.*

guarded not only by his habitual circumspection, but by a
striking soundness, so to speak, of this instinct. The process might have been a dangerous one for men of inferior
scope if employed on the same arduous work; but his
theological statements, properly so called, have never been
impugned, and have appeared to be in a singular degree
measured and exact. He shows no sign of familiarity, or
even of acquaintance, with the Anglican divines of the
seventeenth century.

No teacher has laid more firmly than Butler the foun-
dation-stones of external religion, or has more clearly set
forth the place of the Church in the Christian system as
dating from the closing charges of our Lord, and from the
first inception of the Apostolic mission. He has therefore
done a great work for churchmen as such, and the work is
perhaps of all the greater value because it is not, to all
appearance, accepted from Anglican tradition, but drawn by
him out of the treasures of his own thought upon the Scriptures, and upon the subject which he may from time to time
be bringing under philosophic treatment. Indeed, medita-
tion appears to have been his special office, rather than
breadth and abundance of acquisition from the works of
others.

The imputations of having favoured Popery, and even of
having died in the Roman communion, are charges which
may justly be reckoned as among the most damnatory signs
of the religious character of the period in which he lived.
It was probably the very worst period, which can be noted
in our whole religious history during the four centuries
which have now nearly completed their course since the
days of Wolsey and of Warham. And the fashion of defence offered by his friend, Bishop Halifax, is not a highly
redeeming feature of the case. Bishop Butler shared this
imputation with Johnson, Burke, and other men alike eminent and excellent. The reader of the present day will
regard it as crushed by the weight of its own absurdity.
Were we engaged in the consideration of his life at large,
it might not be improper to enter upon a detailed notice
of the subject, since it attained the undeserved honour of
being treated as a matter of serious importance at the time

when it was made. Indeed, it led Secker, a respected Archbishop of Canterbury, for the first, and I trust the last, time in the history of his illustrious See, to figure as an anonymous correspondent in the columns of a newspaper for the purpose of defending his friend. But it cannot be necessary any longer to present the details of this paltry controversy to the world in connexion with the publication of his works, and I have felt no hesitation in dismissing it from a place of honour which it has, for a considerable time, rather unworthily usurped in the best known editions of the Works.

Still, the charge that the tone of his writings has a tendency to promote the Roman Catholic religion [1], unjust and indeterminate as it is, can hardly be met with summary dismissal. But it seems mainly referable to the mental frame of those who make it. The works certainly do not encourage a negative habit of mind; and on this account, since the Latin Church is the largest and the least restrained in affirmation, all persons who from nature or habit are, in matters of religion, given to negation, may be readily led to impute to Butler this Romanizing tendency. No less a person than the historian Hallam was, I think, of opinion that any one who admitted our Lord to have been the founder of a polity upon earth was in the last resort bound to the admission of the Roman claims. If this were so, it would be plain that the Anglican divines as a body hold a very slippery position.

I offer one or two remarks. The first is that no one within my knowledge has ever been stated to have been led into the Church of Rome by the teaching of Butler; and the second is, that he has been studied and eulogized by men such as Wesley, Chalmers, Angus, and others, whose position would have made them quick to detect any such tendency, but none of whom have found it. The study of him is much favoured in Ireland among the members of the disestablished Church, who are as a body pre-eminently anti-Roman; and his celebrity in America appears, much to their honour, to lie very largely among the same religious communities which in this country pass by the general name of Nonconformists.

[1] Miss Hennell's *Essay*, pp. 50-2.

Finally, we cannot properly pass by without notice the remarkable passage in which, so far from showing any inclination to 'Popery,' Butler condemns it in terms which seem at first sight to involve a departure from his habitual moderation. He denounces it as 'that great corruption of Christianity, Popery [1].' It may well be called an exceptional passage, for it is not Butler's usual manner to deal out his judgements of men or things in terms so broad and unqualified. Also, in some passages of the *Analogy*, though he does not name the Church of Rome, he speaks of the corruptions of religion in terms which suggest that he may have had it in his mind [2]. If we try to come at his more definite meaning, we do not find that he appears to have had in view this or that particular doctrine or usage of the Latin Church, but partly its incessant aggression, and mainly the claim of the Popedom, as it was even then pushed 'at Rome' to a 'plenitude of power,' which he regards as a 'manifest, open, usurpation of all human and divine authority.' Plainly he is not employing the term 'Popery,' as has been common, in order to vent controversial heat, but with reference to those assumptions of the court of Rome, which, though strongly opposed in, and long after, his day, were resolutely pushed at headquarters. While, then, we need not regard Butler as tinged with any form of ultraism in religion, we surely must acknowledge, in the case of a man so honest and so bold, the great force of his declaration in showing his mental attitude to have been one removed as far as possible from any disposition to accept the Roman system. His mind, essentially estranged from any and every form of unlimited power, probably found in such a feature of the Roman scheme its central force, and hence was led to use such terms of severity concerning it as require careful notice in order to secure our placing upon them a just interpretation.

It now only remains to take notice of his alleged failure to treat subjects of religion in a manner duly evangelical. And here I offer a preliminary observation on the associations belonging to his extraction. Persons familiar with the methods of the more modern Nonconformity might feel

[1] Sermon before the Lords, 1747, § 8.   [2] *Analogy*, II. i. 13; vi. 5.

inclined, from his having been bred as a Dissenter, to be specially exacting with him on this account. But, from piecing together the threads of circumstance, I think it most probable that his connexion was with that portion of the contemporary Dissenters who, during the period of his boyhood and youth, were rapidly moving away from the older standard of Puritanism, and towards the system afterwards known as Unitarian. There are perhaps some grounds for surmising that the Tewkesbury Academy, where he was trained, was passing towards the more latitudinarian side of Nonconformity. His relations with Clarke, who passes for an Arian, look in the same direction. The writers whom he quotes do not include any among either the Nonjurors, or those champions of Anglican divinity who had given it form and body during the seventeenth century. If Waterland be thought an exception, it must be borne in mind that Waterland's commendations of preachers included the sermons of Hoadly. In dealing with external religion, and with the historical institution of the Church, Butler makes good positions markedly conducive to the constructive process which had been advancing from the time of Hooker to that of Beveridge; but these positions carry no mark of Anglican tradition, and seem to have been taken up as the result of his own independent thought.

The charge itself, if it were well founded, would be a serious one. But I confess that it appears to me to be wholly wanting in foundation. It may even have been a duty laid upon Butler by the origin and purpose of the *Analogy* to avoid, as a general rule, the warmer religious phraseology. For, firstly, it is a scientific treatise on the basis of belief in the Divine Government of the world; and, in such a treatise, the doctrines of grace find but a narrow place. But, further, he was in part arguing against Deists, and in part dealing with a state of society divided in the main between indifference and unbelief. He has himself acquainted us that, doubtless with a view to the furtherance of his cause, he argued 'upon the principles of others, not his own[1]'; and, if he argued upon their principles, it was a matter of course that he should not stand in marked

[1] *Analogy,* II. viii. 32.

contrast with the strain of their language. Half a century later, the excellent work of Mr. Wilberforce adopted a different tone; but Mr. Wilberforce's work was a treatise *d'occasion*, and he sought not so much to lay the foundations of belief, as to stir men up to the practice of what they already professed. It is true there is an absence of what may be termed evangelical flavour, or unction, from Butler's general strain. But his plan was surely the plan best calculated to secure for him that which was the farthest limit of his modest wishes, an impartial hearing, accorded by educated men. All colouring given, beyond what necessity demanded, to the handling of his topics would have seemed to them a surreptitious method of drawing attention away from the merits of the case, and, as I have already urged, would have supplied a plea at least plausible for shutting a book which did not give them fair play.

But it undoubtedly lay within the necessity of the case that Butler should convey to his readers, in outline, a true idea of that gospel which he was commending to them under the name of Revealed Religion. He was bound in his sphere to 'reprove the world of sin, of righteousness, and of judgement [1],' by presenting to it a true picture of human nature, of its actual fall, and of the means divinely provided for its recovery. He depicted human nature as a thing beautiful and noble, as the work of God, not of the devil: and those who may be startled at his attitude might do well to note what St. Augustine says on the same subject in his writings against the Manicheans. Has he, then, been stinted in his acknowledgement of the havoc wrought in that nature by the introduction of sin into the world? On the contrary, he is alike distinct and copious, not in merely acknowledging, but in enforcing, this melancholy truth. Before we have read many pages of his Introduction, we learn that this world is in a state of 'apostasy, wickedness, and ruin [2].' If training be generally required for the imperfect, how much more for those who have 'corrupted their natures,' for 'depraved creatures who want to be renewed [3].' The present state was intended to be a

---

[1] John xvi. 8.
[2] *Analogy*, Introd. § 16; also II. i. 16; iii. 23.
[3] *Ibid.* I. v. 30.

I

discipline of virtue; but the 'generality of men' 'seem to make a discipline of vice[1].' Mankind are 'corrupted and depraved,' and thus unfit for the state which Christ has prepared for His disciples[2]. We are in a condition of 'vice, and misery, and darkness[3].' That the world is in a condition of ruin 'seems the very ground of the Christian dispensation[4].'

In a very full and striking passage he sums up the case[5]; and here he does not stop short of avowing that 'the generality grow more profligate and corrupt with age.' In truth, if there be any one topic on which repetition may plausibly be made a charge against Butler, it is the sad and solemn topic of the misery, debasement, and corruption which virulent and inveterate sin has brought about in the world. The numerous passages afford abundant proof of his anxiety not only to promulgate this unhappy truth, but to stamp it on the minds of his readers.

The recovery of this race, to all appearance hopelessly lost, is by a Priest-Victim, foreshadowed in ancient predictions, who is also our Prophet or Teacher, and our King, and who has made on our behalf an atonement or expiation, the mode whereof is not revealed to us, but as to which we know that it has an efficacy beyond that of instruction, example, or government. By this Atonement we are enabled to escape wrath and obtain life[6]. And He has founded a church or kingdom, as the home within which this process is to be carried on. But inasmuch as we are enfeebled and incapacitated by sin, there is also a provision for rectifying the perverted will, and making good the energies so sadly exhausted as concerns the pursuit of good. This is the assistance of God's Spirit to effect the needful renovation, which is implied in the declaration, 'figurative but express, *Except a man be born of the Spirit, he cannot enter into the kingdom of God*[7].'

The exception taken to Butler, which I have thus endeavoured to obviate, has been taken by men both sincere

---

1 *Analogy*. I. v. 34.
2 *Ibid*. II. i. 24.
3 *Ibid*. II. v. 5.
4 *Ibid*. II. v. 23.

5 *Ibid*. II. v. 12.
6 *Ibid*. II. v. 13-21.
7 *Ibid*. II. i. 24.

and eminent, and in terms of regretful sympathy and admiration, such as show a reluctance to find faults in one whom they admit to have been a great benefactor to the Christian world.   Still I am fain to hope it will be admitted, not only that his belief is sound and strong, but that, when we sufficiently consider both the purpose with which, and the circumstances in which, the works themselves were composed, it will be felt that the cast of his phraseology is capable of an effectual defence.

CHAPTER VIII

ON SOME POINTS OF METAPHYSICS RAISED BY THE TEXT OF BUTLER

WHEN we are led to speak of metaphysics in relation to Butler, we find ourselves obliged to draw a great distinction at the outset. Butler found a body of ideas truly metaphysical in possession of the philosophic field. The head and front of these was the abstract argument for the being of a God, which purported to be demonstrative, but which Butler avowed himself unable wholly to accept in that character : though his statement to this effect in his correspondence with Clarke [1] is accompanied with acknowledgements that the abstract arguments reached a high degree of probability, so that in this sense they amounted to proofs.

Butler was not born nor bound to question all opinions on all subjects. He set before himself a great purpose, which was to establish the essential groundwork of an ethical system, which included God together with ourselves, and what lay between Him and ourselves. He sought to rectify the current ideas respecting God, ourselves, and the relations between God and ourselves ; and, in doing this, to establish their due limitations. He conceived that these ideas, so rectified, were calculated to uphold a great fabric of belief ; and he rationally justified and demanded, on principles acknowledged as irrefragable before the impartial tribunal of common experience, the adoption of a supernatural creed. In the prosecution of his great purpose, he applied himself not only with earnestness, but with the most vigilant circumspection, to gathering into his net whatever seemed to belong to it, lest anything should be lost. But metaphysics, as a whole, did not seem to belong to it ; that is to say, did not seem either to promote or to cross and traverse his purpose

[1] See First Letter, and Introd. § 10.

in such a way as to compromise his principles or method. It was only at certain points that he found himself brought into contact with them.

I am far from asserting that either his methods or his principles were in conflict with the metaphysical opinions which he found, and left in circulation. And I do not deny that he may have largely accepted them, so that they have *prima facie* the sanction of his authority. But I submit that they are not entitled to the real weight carried by that authority. It is sufficiently remarkable, considering his modesty, that he struck out for himself 'a more excellent way.' They did not command what I venture to call his intellectual sympathies: they come over to us, his followers, as unexamined opinions, traditions in some cases of recent and local philosophy, lying outside his province and his subject-matter, though having points of contact with them. I am so bold as to think it most probable that, if Butler had applied to these opinions the same patient and searching insight, which he employed with much mastery in his public work, he would have seen cause to withhold at certain points such countenance as he may seem to have given them.

I proceed to indicate the points I have in view.

1. In a note to the first Chapter of Part I of the *Analogy*, he explains the meaning of his phrase 'destruction of living powers' when taken in its widest sense. Stopping short of any term such as extinction or annihilation, he treats it as meaning that the being in whom they reside 'shall be incapable of ever perceiving or acting again at all[1].' And he goes on to say, ' We have no reason to think the destruction of living powers in (this) the former sense to be possible.'

Thus, he is seemingly committed to the opinion, that to extinguish or annihilate a substance not material is beyond the power of God.

On this I observe :

a. We are dealing with possibility only, not with likelihood, in the present remarks.

b. It may be difficult, if this opinion be admitted, to prevent its extension to material existences. This would bring us to the old heathen sentiment concerning the eternity of the universe.

[1] I. i. 4 *n.*

c. It is easy to understand how the ancients, who regarded matter as uncreated and indestructible, might readily regard the soul as incapable of annihilation.

d. But can it be seriously asserted that the power to destroy is a greater power than the power to create ? And unless this assertion can be made good, surely we, who believe in the creation of soul as well as body, are bound to admit the power of annihilating that which has been created.

e. It seems probable that this notion, belonging to the philosophic schools, had, like some other notions of kindred origin, made its way unperceived within the precinct of religion. Unperceived, not in the sense that notice was never taken of it by individual minds, but that it never was made the subject of prolonged and separate consideration by the Church at large; which, in the formation of the Creeds, appears carefully to have eschewed the subject.

2. The next metaphysical argument I have to notice is set out in the same chapter [1].

' All presumption of death's being the destruction of living beings, must go upon supposition that they are compounded; and so, discerptible.'

But the conscious being, so he proceeds, ' is one and indiscerptible; and the organized body is simply so much foreign matter set apart for its service.'

There may be much force as well as ingenuity in the proposition that death, which seems to proceed by severance of parts and dissolution, thereby seems to be an instrument of no natural aptitude for putting an end to a form of conscience like consciousness, which appears to be at once complete and bound in an absolute unity within itself.

Admitting the inappropriateness of death, which proceeds by discerption, to deal with the soul, which supplies no evidence to show that it is liable to such a process, we cannot, I think, with safety rely upon indiscerptibility as a substantive argument for immortality. In a portion of the long and wearisome controversy between Clarke and Dodwell, we find a statement by Clarke on the argument from

[1] *Analogy*, I. i. 10.

indiscerptibility, which may enable us to appreciate the value of that argument[1]. He writes as follows:

'As evidently as the known properties of matter prove it to be certainly a discerpible (*sic*) substance, whatever other unknown properties it may be endued with; so evidently the known and confessed properties of immaterial beings prove them to be indiscerpible, whatever other unknown properties they likewise may be indued with.'

Now the state of the case appears to be this. Discerptibility is and must be an operation in space. It is a thing essentially related to space, and also to matter in space. But immaterial beings have, so far as we know, no relation to space; and cannot be described or indicated in terms of it, any more than questions of ethics can be indicated in terms of numbers. If, then, we have no right to declare the soul (which is presumed to be immaterial) discerptible, so neither have we any right to declare it to be indiscerptible; neither the one term nor the other touching in any material its real character. So that an argument for or about the immortality of the soul, founded on indiscerptibility, is wholly out of place.

But is it not assuming much to place human bodies so far from our true being as to hold that they 'are no more ourselves, or part of ourselves, than any other matter around us[2]'? For our bodies do what no other foreign matter does: they enter habitually, nay unceasingly, and most intimately into association with our mental and moral action, have a large influence upon it, and even seem to determine what are at least appreciable parts of it.

Moreover, we have to consider that religion has something to say to this matter. In the Apostles' Creed we declare our belief in the resurrection of the body. St. Paul beseeches the Romans to present their bodies unto God as their reasonable service[3]; travelling herein immeasurably far from the heathenism around him, which had never conceived the dedication of the body to be a part of general religion. And to the Thessalonians he writes, 'I pray God

---

[1] Clarke's *Defence of an Argument made use of in a Letter to Mr. Dodwell*, p. 101 (ed. 1731).

[2] *Analogy*, I. i. 11.

[3] Rom. xii. 1.

your whole spirit and soul and body be preserved blameless
unto the coming of our Lord Jesus Christ[1].' So that the
body is not an appendage but a portion, though a separate
portion, of ourselves. And that spiritual body[2] in which
the righteous will be presented at the resurrection is a
product sprung from the seed of the natural body. So that,
while the established relations between soul and body are at
the critical point placed wholly beyond the compass of our
knowledge, it seems impossible to treat the body, except in
connexion with its grosser accidents, as 'foreign matter,' a
character incompatible with such relations.

3. In his chapter on the Future Life, Butler attaches a
great importance to the doctrine of continuance. In § 4 of
this chapter he alleges that our possession of certain powers
and capacities before death 'is a presumption that we shall
retain them through and after death,' unless death supplies
some positive reason to the contrary. He thinks there is
always a probability that things will continue just as they
are except as to points 'in which we have some reason to
think they will be altered.' And further, he conceives that
the continuance of the world until to-day is our only reason
for expecting that it will subsist to-morrow; and that the
same may be justly affirmed as to all substances, except the
self-existent. And in a cautionary summation of his arguments near the end of the Chapter[3] he seemingly gives us
to understand, by the reintroduction of this argument, that
he largely relies upon it as a positive argument for the support of his claim[4], to have brought up to a 'very considerable degree of probability' his contention, on behalf of the
living being, for a future state of existence. In popular
phrase, everything may be expected to continue except
those things as to which cause can be shown to anticipate
their cessation.

This is an idea which must, I suppose, be termed metaphysical. It is quite distinct from that of continuing existence allied with, or depending upon, the fulfilment of purpose; and is in truth continuance as such, apart from any
associated idea of waste or change on the one side, of an

[1] 1 Thess. v. 23.   [3] *Analogy,* I. i. 30.
[2] 1 Cor. xv.   [4] *Ibid.* I. i. 32.

end to be gained or a reason to be alleged on the other. It appears to be a conception not easy to grasp. Nor can I see that, when it has been grasped, we can readily attach to it any presumption either in favour of or against the prolongation of the existence in question.

In truth, if we regard the question as believers in God — and such were both Butler and his assumed antagonists — we must surely find it hard to entertain, even for a moment, the idea of any existence whatever without simultaneously entertaining an idea of the use to which it is appointed. If it is subserving that use, then *caeteris paribus* a presumption will arise in favour of continuance; if it is not performing its proper work, there may be some faint presumption of the reverse, but this is not of itself enough to build upon.

Another element of the case will be found in the two opposite conditions of exposure to change, or exemption from it — the former suggesting, though not proving, the approach of termination, and the latter leaning to the opposite expectation.

Butler refers to the physical conditions in which we are placed, and says the idea of their further continuance grows out of their having thus far continued. Here we seem to be drawn upon slippery ground. However it may have been in Butler's time, the scientific opinion of to-day anticipates an end of the world; which seems difficult to reconcile with the argument of what may be called neutral continuance, as Butler presents it.

Is there not much to be said for another conception of the matter, viz. that continuance cannot be duly considered at all in the abstract, and apart from purpose? If our world has the appearance of half-grown corn or of unripe fruit, we may suggest that there is a likelihood that it is destined, and will be allowed time, to bring its processes to maturity, to establish a clear issue, and, in the event of failure, to place that failure visibly on record.

4. In the Butler-Clarke correspondence some points of metaphysics have been raised, which are not in any immediate way connected with the *Analogy* or the *Sermons.*

In his first letter Butler appears to follow Clarke in considering place to be a condition or incident of Divine existence. It is possible that this idea may have been encouraged by the declarations of Scripture and that article of the Creeds, which speak of our Lord as sitting at the right hand of God; and it probably did something in the sixteenth century towards perplexing Eucharistic doctrine. I suppose, however, that there is nothing of presumption in treating the declaration as a figure designed, like all other figures of Holy Scripture, to transcend the merely symbolical reality and to elevate the conception involved. We may conceive the Deity to be exempt from all the limitations of space, and may take His omnipresence to mean that the plenitude of Deity is alike operative in each part of the entire sphere through which locality extends.

In his fourth letter Butler, still submitting to the yoke of a system which appears to impose physical and finite conditions on the unseen and infinite, assumes that spirits, as well as bodies, 'exist in space,' and conceives that space is 'absolutely self-existent, and antecedently necessary to all existences, including even the self-existent.' But I presume there are many who reject all physical limitations of this sort as attempted to be imposed upon a nature immeasurably above them. In this proposition I include limitations of time.

What may be said for Butler is that, even at this early period of his life, he was less magisterial than Clarke, as we see from his suspending his judgement on the Clarkian figment that space and duration are properties of the Divine substance; a specimen, as I conceive, of over-bold adventure into regions where it is not given to us, under the conditions of present existence, to obtain a foothold. Perhaps it is not too much to say of our author, that, both from original inclination and from experience in thinking, he was disposed to view abstract or metaphysical disquisition with a latent mistrust.

BUTLER, when a youth of twenty-one, peruses the work of Dr. Clarke on the Being and Attributes of God, and would desire to acknowledge in it not merely a probable, but a demonstrative proof of what it seeks to establish. Some part of the argument he finds himself unable to accept, and he seeks from the author, with studied deference, elucidation and satisfaction. The topics are abstruse; and they require to be stated in the simplest grammatical form.

No finite being, says Clarke, can be self-existent.

For a finite being may, without 'a contradiction,' be conceived not to exist.

Whereas what is self-existent must of necessity exist: and to say it does not exist involves 'a contradiction.'

But the form in which Clarke embodied the idea of non-existence is 'absence': and this must mean absence from some particular place: for if absent from one place at one time, it may conceivably (he says) be absent from every place at every time. This Butler questions. He does not admit that the possibility of the particular absence proves the possibility of the universal absence.

Both Butler and Clarke, it will be observed, agree in holding that existence means existence in place: and this not only for a finite, but for an infinite Being. It will be needful to revert to this point. If there can be existence, which is not existence in place, the whole matter thus far in dispute between these champions vanishes by the withdrawal of a vital condition.

There is a second issue raised. Clarke has argued that the self-existent Being can be only one. It involves (he says) a contradiction that there should be two Beings, both necessary (or self-existent) and both independent. For if one be independent of the other, that other may be conceived not to exist, that is to say, not to be necessary. No, says Butler. It does not follow because Being *A* is independent of Being *B*, that therefore Being *B* may be conceived not to exist. [I pass by a comparison, introduced by Butler, with the case of ' the angles below the base in an isosceles triangle ': for it does not appear easy to see what angles there can be that shall be subject to such a definition.]

Here the phrase used by Clarke is that, on the hypothesis in question, either of the Beings may be supposed ' to exist alone.' Butler points out that this phrase is ambiguous. It may mean, to exist by its own resources only, to have a self-sufficing existence : or it may mean, to have an existence such that nothing shall exist along with it. Clearly, if independence involves this kind of existing alone, the independence of *A* is incompatible with the self-existence of *B*, and *vice versa*; but as no proof has been given that self-existence involves this kind of independence, the question has simply been begged, and no proof has yet been given against a possible plurality of self-existences.

Dr. Clarke replies first upon the first argument, by the contention that existence by necessity in space meant existence by necessity in all space and at all times. Were it a question of existence not necessary but by command, such merely commanded existence might conceivably be absent from certain spaces at certain times.

On the second point, Clarke holds that any one existence whatever presupposes all other necessary existences; for example, presupposes space and time.

Butler, in a rejoinder, denies that 'absolutely necessary' means necessary always and everywhere. Self-existence means existence somewhere, not existence everywhere. So much for the first head.

On the second head, he canvasses the doctrine that for a particular existence all necessary existences are ' needed.' He allows that space and time are thus needful, because the particular existences come of course into relation with them ; but he sees no universal relation between a necessary existence, as such, and all particular existences. And, in passing, he lays down the following proposition :

'Space and duration are very abstruse in their natures,

and I think cannot properly be called things, but are considered rather as affections which belong, and in the order
of our thoughts are antecedently necessary, to the existence
of all things.'

Clarke, in his second reply, exhibits an unbroken front.
Self-existence, he declares, implies ubiquity ; necessity, antecedent in the order of nature to all existence, *must exist
everywhere for the same reason that it is anywhere.* And
on the second field of battle, by the needfulness of a thing
self-existent for the existence of any other thing, he means
only needfulness as a *sine qua non.* In this sense he might
have added, the equality of the three angles of a triangle
to two right angles is needful for the equidistance of all the
parts of the circumference of a circle from the centre, and
vice versa.

Butler, hoping against hope, resumes his pen, and admits
that a necessary Being can only exist in space : but denies
that he need therefore be finite.

And on the second head he charges upon Clarke that
his propositions come to this. Space is a property of all
substance ; if so, every substance must be self-existent, as
space is : but this cannot be. *Ergo.*

In his third reply, Clarke restates his doctrine as to the
universal application of necessity ; and, on the second head,
declares that space is a property or mode of the self-existent
substance, but not of any other. In this surely most arbitrary and totally unproven proposition, he finds a refuge
from the clenching objection Butler had put before him.

In his fourth letter, Butler concedes that an absolutely
necessary Being must exist everywhere. He likewise admits
that he had been rash in assimilating the mode of the self-
existent Being's existence in space, to that which holds good
for other existences. He also admits the difficulty of forming an idea of the relation between spirit and space. He
thinks it plain that space is ' manifestly necessary ' and
' antecedently needful to the existence of all other things, not
excepting (as I think) even the self-existent substance.'

In his fourth reply, Clarke lays it down that space is not
substance, but necessarily infers substance : as for a blind
man hardness, though it is not body, necessarily infers the
idea of body.

The fifth pair of letters add nothing material to this singular correspondence, except Butler's admission that he is really 'at a loss about the nature of space and duration,' and is conscious that the correspondence has turned upon the question whether our ideas of them are partial, and whether they presuppose the existence of something else.

Do we not in this last-named suggestion come near to the truth, namely that the entire discussion hangs upon ideas incapable of being treated in a satisfactory manner? Butler, who writes all through as a simple seeker after truth, and Clarke who, with a magisterial air, defends the substance of every proposition he has advanced, are agreed in this one proposition: that all which exists must exist in space and time. Therefore space and time are uncreated, and have an existence independent of the Creator.

To me it would appear an elementary proposition that the universum has to be bisected or divided into two entities which between them absolutely exhaust it: Creator and creature. But now we are introduced to a category altogether new. Space and time are not the Creator, but neither are they creatures, for they exist independently of the Creator, and are conditions antecedent to His existence.

It is no sufficient answer to contend that we can form no idea of existence outside of space and time: that is to say of any given mode or fashion of existence thus ejected out of these two conditions. For there are other existences, with regard to which we can form no conception whatever as to their manner, and yet by which we firmly hold. We believe in the existence of pure spirit; but the moment we begin to connect it with a manner of existence, we find that we annex it in one form or another to body, that is to matter. But if we say spirit cannot exist except in space, we ought also to say spirit cannot exist except in body. But as we hold that spirit can exist apart from body, so we ought to say, spirit can exist apart from space.

I have said that Butler and Clarke were both entangled in this untrue proposition, that space attaches of necessity to all existence. The difference between them is that Clarke appears to rest in it as an absolute and comfortable certainty: Butler, on the other hand, only with an unquiet mind. He finds them to be unmanageable conceptions. 'I

am really at a loss about the nature of space and duration'
(Letter V). He cannot commit himself to the doctrine
that the self-existent Being is the *substratum* of time and
duration, for this would make them dependent upon it; and
yet he seems drawn and tempted towards this doctrine. He
might have worked his way out of the thicket, had it been a
distinct and professed portion of his inquiry.

And surely it is very important to get free of this doctrine, for it involves strange consequences. It involves the
consequence that space and time are uncreated, and inher-
ing in the idea of things that are eternal, so that they are
also themselves eternal. Therefore the Creator is not the
Creator of all things, but only of some. Space and time
are exceptions: but why should they be the only exceptions? Why should not matter at large be an exception,
as the ancients, with a rare unanimity, thought it was?
Why should not force be also an exception? How, in fact,
is any full, any real, doctrine of creation to be reconciled
with the doctrine that space and time are outside of it?

Then there arises the curious question, How came these
philosophers to be involved in the meshes of this theory?
Can we say that they were bound down to it by an immemorial tradition? No, for in the case of matter, where such
a tradition existed, they did not accept it. Is it then possible that their acceptance can have been due to the influence
of an opinion belonging to a local and occasional theology?
It seems clear that the controversies of the Reformation
respecting the Holy Eucharist helped to lead men upon this
slippery ground. According to the extreme Protestant contention in those controversies, it was absolute and fundamental to provide against the supposition of a real presence
of the Body of the Lord upon the Christian altar. The
proof of its not being there was sought and found in the
theory that it was already elsewhere: and that Body as such
could not be present in two places at one and the same time.
It was subject to local or space-conditions. But an escape
might be attempted through the contention that the Body
of our Lord in the Sacrament of the altar is glorified and
Divine: and it could be pointed out that, by appearing in
the closed chamber, where the disciples were assembled for

fear of the Jews [1], that Body, by transferring itself through a solid obstacle, emancipated itself from space-conditions. An all-covering reply was fashioned: Divine or not Divine, even the essence of the self-existent could not subsist, except in space and under its laws. Nothing, however, can be more dangerous than a philosophical answer to a theological proposition, until it has been shown that the two are *in pari materia.*

It was, however, only by Butler's youthful and soon-abandoned contention, which placed the self-existent not in space at large but in some particular part of space, that he could be said to satisfy the Zuinglian, or extreme Protestant, contention. When he admitted, as he promptly came to admit, that the omnipresence of the self-existent in space essentially followed from its presence in any part of space, he by implication lost hold of the doctrine that a Real Presence in more than some one portion of space was impossible. We have no proof, however, from the correspondence that either of the authors had consciously in view any connexion between it and the true doctrine of the Eucharistic Presence.

If we efface from the correspondence the futile conception that the self-existent must of necessity exist in space, I conceive that nothing substantial remains. Consequently that no profit, except it be incidental, can be extracted from it as it stands.

I confess that, in the way of conjecture, further notions present themselves to my mind. Butler's works in general are very far removed from the region in which this correspondence moves. His touching deference led him rapidly enough to concessions, but did not relieve him from a sense of embarrassment, in a discussion where Clarke's easy self-confidence must have been taken to imply the assurance that all was plain sailing. And this embarrassment, together with the cause of it, may have helped permanently to disincline him to traversing these rather barren heights, and may happily have been among the causes which brought him to apply his whole intellectual and moral force both to matters and to methods severely practical and disengaged from all waste appendages.

[1] John xx. 19.

CHAPTER X

THERE were numerous editions of Butler's *Analogy* in the eighteenth century, but I have not been able to trace them all with precision. The work appeared in a quarto volume in 1736, and an edition in octavo was published before the year had expired [1], a circumstance which appears to show that it at once attracted much attention. Another edition, with some account of the author, appeared in 1738. The work was not directly challenged by any author of that century; and there is abundant evidence that this absence of contention respecting it in the higher regions of literature was not due to its falling into oblivion or insignificance. Indeed, the publication of the collected works at the Clarendon Press in 1807 ought to be regarded as a sign of their progressive advance in public estimation. The same may be said of their still earlier publication in the Scottish metropolis in 1804 [2].

He appears to have laid hold in various quarters of the more hard-headed members of the labouring population. In an account of a congregation of Scottish Seceders, formed in 1745, at Logiealmond in Perthshire, and without doubt largely composed of the labouring community, it is recorded that in the early part of the present century the *Analogy* formed one of the subjects of their study [3]. It is still more remarkable that an edition of the *Analogy* was published at Aberdeen in 1775. It bore the title of the seventh edi-

---

[1] See Watt's *Bibliotheca*, and the catalogue of the British Museum Library.
[2] Edinburgh: Constable, 1804.
[3] *At the Edge of the Heather*, by the Rev. D. M. Forrester, p. 36. Edinburgh, 1895.

K

tion [1]. Thus proceeding from a press local and remote, it could hardly be due to any other cause than a demand for it among the students of the universities of that city. It is the glory of the Scottish universities to represent the mass of the people, and this glory has belonged to those of Aberdeen [2] even in a higher degree than to their sisters; while the people of the city and county are especially distinguished for force of mind and character. Over and above the contemptible charges of Romanizing, which were alleged against Butler through the press, seven works of animadversion or comment, dated between 1737 and 1794, are mentioned by Dr. Hanna in his prefatory notice published with Chalmers's *Praelections on the Analogy*, none of which, however, attained to any sort of celebrity. Lord Kames [3] noticed Butler with praise and with general criticisms, which do not require notice; and Hume seems plainly to have had some of Butler's arguments in view, but without naming him.

He may be thought to have attained the climax of his power, in his own country, when, between sixty and seventy years back, he took his place by the side of Aristotle, among the standard books for the final examinations in the University of Oxford. After about a quarter of a century, he was removed from it [4]. The removal was not due to any lowered estimate of his power. This is clear from the language of Mr. Mark Pattison, who was a main agent in procuring it. It was probably due to the circumstances of the powerful religious movement of which the University had been the seat, and of the reaction, for the moment hardly less powerful, by which it was followed. There is no sign at the present moment that a smaller aggregate of thought is employed upon Butler in this country at the present day, than in the preceding generations. It is, moreover, pretty plain from the editions and relative works produced in Ireland and America, that the circle of his influence has been materially extended. In the United States there have been nine editions of the *Analogy* [5], and scarcely fewer of the

[1] Catalogue of the Museum Library.
[2] Now amalgamated (1895).
[3] Edinburgh, 1849.
[4] See *supra*, p. 76.
[5] Bearing on the title-page the words 'A New Edition,' so that they had appeared collectively at an earlier date, at some place which is unknown.

Sermons. Their influence, and the influence of Butler at large, was specially imported into Cambridge by Dr. Whewell, a leading spirit of the University. In speaking of the *Sermons*, it must be understood that the reference is chiefly made to the three on Human Nature, and to such of the others as most resemble them in the subjects of which they treat. It may probably be said of these that their influence and their circulation has been only second to those of the *Analogy.*

But criticism is a test of influence as well as circulation. Criticism includes eulogy if based upon examination. And of the eulogists of Butler it may be truly said that they are alike remarkable for number, for eminence, and for diversity of colour. The later half of the century has indeed brought into view a number of critics who deal, some of them largely or systematically, in animadversion. Every one of these has accompanied his adverse judgements with panegyrics, often of a striking kind. Of the value of their hostile criticisms, and the amount of deduction which they will warrant from our estimate of Butler, I have spoken elsewhere [1].

But there is an inner and more subtle sense in which I have not yet touched upon the influence of Butler. What power did he exercise over British thought? Had he a share, and, if any, what share, in causing that reaction in favour of belief which marked the second half of the eighteenth century?

I say upon British thought, because it cannot be pretended that he then became, or that he has yet become, an appreciable factor in forming the thought of Continental Europe. In this respect he stands in the most marked contrast with Locke. Among his works, only the *Analogy* has been translated. A German version of it appeared at Leipzig in 1756, and at Tübingen in 1779. A second translation was published at Leipzig in 1787. It has received notice and commendation from various writers, somewhat recently from Lotze; but there has been no call for any further edition. In France a translation has gone forth from the press, but it was the work of an Englishman or executed under English influence, and appears to have been still-

[1] *Supra,* Ch. iii.

born [1]. Down to the present day experience has assured us only of his hold upon communities of British blood. The elaborate recital by Zart [2] of those forty-eight British workers who influenced German thought in the seventeenth and eighteenth centuries does not include his name. This failure to lay hold on Europe is the more remarkable, because the chief part of the works of Butler appears to be as clearly available for the European mind at large as for that of the English-speaking countries. It has however been translated into Hindoostanee, in connexion with missionary purposes; and into Welsh. The most important part of the answer to that question in relation to his moral influence on the eighteenth century has not yet been given. And as it is the most important, so also it is the part most difficult to deal with.

As a general rule, it is but rarely that we can trace the influence exercised by particular books upon particular minds through the medium of actual record, any more than we can trace by formal evidence of cause and effect the powerful influences of climate upon individual health. Hooker's great work on Ecclesiastical Polity first gave systematic expression to what is termed Anglican thought in theology, and we are told of an emphatic eulogy pronounced upon it by the contemporary reigning pontiff [3]. But it would be difficult to trace even this influence in the testimonies of subsequent writers, or in the moulding given to their forms of expression. Thought has been powerfully affected in England within the last sixty years by the successive influences of Coleridge, of Mill, and (in a somewhat different sphere) of Carlyle; and it is safe to say that our country underwent great elevating influences from Scott and from Tennyson. But, excepting that Newman had occasion for a personal purpose to bear strong witness in the case of Scott, how far could any of these influences be adequately verified by direct evidence drawn from our general literature, or from any positive record?

---

[1] See appendix to *An Academic Sketch*. Oxford: Clarendon Press, 1892.

[2] *Einfluss der Englischen philosophie seit Bacon auf die Deutsche philosophie des 18 jahrhunderts*. Berlin, 1881.

[3] Walton's *Life of Hooker*.

We may show that Butler early attained to a position in which he could not fail to share in the current influences of the day. And the whole inquiry relating to the ebb of the sceptical tide in 1750–1800 is so full of interest as to justify illustrative remark and any attempt to gather together such fragments of evidence as we possess. So early as in 1742, when Hume published his *Political Essays*, he wrote [1] as follows to Lord Kames, who had on an earlier occasion advised him to consult with Butler:

'I am told that Dr. Butler has everywhere recommended them, so that I hope they will have some success.'

But we must endeavour to come closer to the question. What share, if any, is to be claimed for Butler with regard to the religious and affirmative reaction which marked the second half of the century? That the deistical movement had been one of great power is sufficiently proved from the single fact that Butler made it the occasion of the great argument he developed in the *Analogy*. But the force with which a stone falls into the water may not unimpressively be measured by the distance which may be reached by the outermost of the resulting circles on the surface. Now I have before me a pamphlet printed at Perth in the year 1715, and conceived in the interest of the Jacobite party, which aims at promoting the views of that party by discrediting the Legislative Union then recently formed with England, and still partially unpopular among the Scotch. It is termed *Scotland's Lament*; and Scotland, dramatically impersonated, is made to say, 'All I have got by the bargain is Slavery, Poverty, and Deism.' This spread of Deism in England must have been a very conspicuous fact in order to make it worth the while of the pamphleteer thus to employ it as an instrument for working on the popular imagination in Scotland.

We have before us the remarkable fact that, whereas in the time of Hobbes, Lord Herbert, and the Deists, England had exercised an influence upon France in the negative direction, yet, as the century advanced, and as France travelled with rapid strides towards negation under the influence of Voltaire and the Encyclopaedists, England not only refused

[1] Fitzgerald's *Memoirs*, p. 56.

to follow but moved perceptibly along the old paths in the opposite direction, so that no intelligent person could have written towards the close of the century, as Butler had written at the dates of 1736 and 1751, as to the currents of opinion during its earlier moiety.

It must be borne in mind, as to both these movements of affirmation and negation respectively, that they had their seat in the upper classes of society, and were wholly exterior to the mass of the community. There is evidence that, at the date of Butler's complaints, the profession of religion, and the clergy, still kept that hold upon the people, which was so strong at the period of Sacheverell's condemnation. The operations of Wesley belonged to the wider circle of the masses, and were little felt, except sporadically by individuals, within the narrower one ; though even there they may have done something. The most active social influence of the period was that with which the name of Johnson, and also that of Burke, is associated ; and it is probable that this influence had more than a trivial share in the work. The influence of books, however, has also to be considered, and it was probably a large one, first in the destructive, and then in the reconstructive portion of the process. But that influence is a silent one, and in its first stages it is formless, only taking shape, and finding its way into consciousness, by reflection. I have here spoken of books : but there was one among them which far transcended, and almost eclipsed, all others ; for its only rival in the sphere of the higher literature was Law's *Serious Call*, and the ground taken in that remarkable work [1] is wholly separate from that occupied by Butler.

The effect which is thus produced is real, but its visible signs may be no more than the track of some great vessel in the sea, with the waters closing in behind it. The field of evidence, however, is not absolutely blank.

Lord Chesterfield was a man of extraordinary talents, for his own day the veritable king among men of the world, of

---

[1] Lately recalled to public notice by the comments of Mr. Stephen (*English Thought*), Mr. Lecky (*History of England*), and especially by the able and striking *Life of William Law*, which we owe to the pen of the Rev. Canon Overton.

whom life is built up with an infinity of care and skill upon well-organized, though worldly, self-love and consummate enjoyment of the world; with no negation of religion, but with no interest in it; with a toleration of it, conditional upon its abiding peaceably in its own place, as a hat abides in the hall until it is wanted for going out of doors. Such is his habitual strain.

And yet when he was becoming not an old, but, according to the ideas of those days, an elderly man, we find him writing from Bath, under date of November 11, 1752, with regard to benefit which his physician promised him from the waters, in the following terms: 'As I do not expect it, if I receive it, it will be the more welcome. If not, I have both philosophy and religion enough to submit to my fate without either melancholy or murmur. For though I can by no means account why there is either moral or physical evil in the world, yet, conscious of the narrow bounds of human understanding, and convinced of the wisdom and justice of the Eternal Divine Being who placed them here, I am persuaded that it is fit and right that they should be here.'

If Chesterfield, who was a great reader, had read Butler, and deliberately conformed to all his conditions, he could not have given a more conclusive account of the process than in the terms of this passage, which represents the dominant ideas of Butler's work brought together into the shortest compass, stated with the terseness, closeness, and seriousness of the great original, and if coming a little short in point of strict accuracy, yet representing a real influence exercised upon a mind of extraordinary insight into all matters to which it seriously addressed itself. Such a passage I think could hardly have been written in England, unless by an expert, before the appearance of Butler's work.

The religious reaction in England, which marked the later half of the eighteenth century, I have said, was two-fold. Its most patent features were popular, and are associated, above every other name, with the name of Wesley. It soon established itself as a salient fact in the public eyes. Contemporary with it, subsisting on a much smaller scale, principally in connexion with other classes of society, yet eventually of a kindred character, was the Evangelical movement in the Church of England; and it is probable that the nonconforming bodies were also affected by a sympathetic action. So far as the upper classes of society were concerned, the Evangelical teachers exercised on them as a whole no attractive influence whatever, and possibly may have repelled them. But a select and very limited number of individuals, chiefly ladies, embraced their opinions by an operation not wholly dissimilar to the conversions of the early Christians from the world to the Church. These changes of individual lives were important in themselves; but they had no influence (unless a repulsive one) on the general mind of what is termed society. I speak of a state of things which continued to prevail as late as in the period of my own youth. The Evangelical party had wrought hard, and had deservedly and usefully thriven; but its members were still a small minority, extraneous to the general body of society in the upper class, and not very largely felt in the lower.

Quite apart from this reaction on behalf of religious character and life, there had been another, a more tranquil and less visible reaction. The descriptions given by Bishop Butler in 1736, and again in 1752, were no longer applicable in 1790 or in 1800. Of indifference, doubtless there remained enough, but in those who were neither indifferent nor fervent Christians there had been substituted for a rampant scepticism a decorous acknowledgement of the general truths of Christianity. This was something, though not all that could be desired; and it is with this reinstatement of Christianity in the receipt of a general homage, that the name of Butler has probably a vital connexion. If it be true that his argument is in the main a defence of outworks, still they are outworks, whose security is absolutely vital to the defence of the central fortress. But it would be more correct to call them foundation courses; which, although out of sight, sustain the building: for he deals in the *Analogy* with the very basis of those relations between God and man which, as he truly tells us, are anterior to Christianity, and but for which Christianity would be without a standing-ground.

A misunderstood episode in the life of Wilberforce gave rise to a confident supposition, hardly deserving the name of a belief, that Mr. Pitt, in conversation with his friend, had alleged against the *Analogy* that it had suggested to him more doubts than it removed. But it now appears from the account recorded by Mr. Wilberforce himself at the time, that Mr. Pitt, knowing his mind to be occupied with serious thoughts, had spontaneously recommended to him the perusal of the *Analogy*. It is a remarkable fact that, absorbed as Mr. Pitt was in politics, he should have read the *Analogy*, and his recommendation and favourable judgement upon the work, whether the offspring of his own thought or a reflection of the public opinion, throws a happy light on its influence.

We might, perhaps, have anticipated from Johnson notices of Butler. But none are to be found in Boswell. It would appear, indeed, as if Johnson had no disposition to revive even for a moment the extinct volcano of the deistical controversy ; for the elaborate index appended to Dr. Birkbeck Hill's classical edition of the great biography, takes no notice of the works of Tindal, Collins, or Chubb. Boswell himself, however, in one passage, notices Butler's argument in terms which harmonize with the idea that his reasoning was generally accepted [1]. Wesley has, in more than one place, spoken in praise of the *Analogy*.

I regret to have no adequate means of exhibiting, by direct personal acknowledgement, the action of Butler on behalf of belief in individual minds during the eighteenth century. Warburton's statement of his eminence is not without value, but it does not appear to own any personal obligation on his own part. This negative state of things is in remarkable contrast with the glowing attestations of Macintosh, Chalmers, and a host of eminent writers belonging to the present century. It throws us back, in the main, upon the internal and statistical proofs supplied by frequency of editions. Yet these are sufficient for their purpose. When we embrace in our conspectus the entire period of 160 years since the publication of the *Analogy*, we may, as I conceive, safely lay it down that his works have

[1] Birkbeck Hill's *Boswell's Life of Johnson*, vol. v. p. 47.

fastened upon themselves, in the English-speaking countries, a larger amount of serious and permanent attention
than those of any other writer on moral and mental philosophy who has lived during the same period.

If the amount of attention which has been bestowed upon
Butler be great, we are safe in asserting that the mental
effort which it implied was greater still. The careless
reader is a being towards whom, as such, Butler seems to
have felt as great an antipathy as his gentle and considerate
nature was capable of entertaining[1]. Such a reader is
effectually warned off the writings of Butler by their character. To read them with levity is impossible. The eye may
indeed run down the pages, the images of the letters may be
formed upon the retina; but the living being that dwells
within the brain is unapproached, and either dormant or
elsewhere employed. The works of Butler are in this
respect like the works of Dante; we must make some kind
of preliminary preparation, we must gird up the loins of
the mind for the study.

[1] See preface to the *Sermons*, §§ 1, 2, 5.

CHAPTER XI

Upon the whole I am content to sum up the argument for the study of Butler under the following heads:

1. In the study of his works, the student finds himself in an intellectual *palaestra*, where his best exertions are required throughout to grapple with his teacher, and thus become master of that teacher's thought. Any remission of exertion will promptly convince him that, if he be content with anything less than this, the hours he spends on Butler are likely to be found pure waste of time. Manly education is a process of wrestling; and it is best to wrestle with the highest masters.

2. In following the steps of Butler, which are as carefully measured out as if he had been climbing the hill of the *Purgatorio*, we breathe all along the bracing atmosphere of a singularly high morality. There is this further great advantage, that the *Analogy* is not didactic: it is morality in action. The virtues, both natural and Christian, have so saturated the character of our teacher, that their perfume is exhaled in every line.

3. Butler deals with the Deist; and the Deist is one who has already travelled one stage on the road of full Theism. Butler produces a multitude of reasonings to show him that he ought in consistency at least to consider whether he shall also travel all the other stages. It should be borne in mind that the whole of these, besides being effective as against the Deist, also form, on independent grounds, available portions of the general theistic argument.

4. By his argument he has set forth to us with remarkable closeness and precision, in the *Analogy* the method of the government of God, and in the *Sermons* the provision supplied to us for the discharge of our several offices under

that government; taking the two together, he has here supplied us with the main substance of a philosophy of life. The difference between them is, however, this: that while the *Analogy* purports to exhibit God's method in one department only, that which deals with religion, it is equally applicable to the whole of our moral experience; first, in every study, in philosophy, history and the rest; and secondly, in conduct, in the entire weaving of that web, whereof our life is made up.

PART II

CHAPTER I

A FUTURE LIFE

THE teaching of Bishop Butler with respect to a life beyond the grave, which supplies me with a point of departure, divides itself under two heads. The first of them embraces the likelihoods which can be collected out of the 'course of nature' with regard to the effect of death upon our existence as a whole. This is a physical or metaphysical, and in neither aspect a moral, discussion; it occupies the first chapter of the *Analogy*. From its position on the threshold of the Treatise, as well as from the nature of its topics, it has attracted much attention, and, it is fair to add, much criticism.

There is, however, a general strain of teaching on the future life, which pervades the work, and which for the most part is scattered piecemeal through it, as the opening up of the general argument into wider spaces gives occasion for introducing the topic. This relates not to the question whether we are barred by death from passing into another world, but to the prospects of man in that other world. In a certain part of the Treatise[1], it opens in a pointed way a discussion not metaphysical but moral; which is also one of extreme interest. With these two widely separated branches of the subject it will be appropriate to deal quite separately.

And now as regards the first.

At the outset certain remarks are to be made.

In the first place, the Chapter 'On a Future Life' contains

---

[1] I. iii. 28.

a disquisition, not upon immortality but upon survival. The inquiry is simply whether we can pass the bourn into the undiscovered land, and has no relation to our condition, or the duration of our existence, after we have arrived there.

In the second place, as the Chapter is a plea not for immortality, properly so called, but for persistence of life as against the special occasion of death, so it is a plea not for the survival of the whole man, but only of the spiritual or immaterial part of man. The body of man takes no benefit from the argument of this Chapter. Butler was well aware that, from the only sources open to him at the first inception of his work, he could offer no effectual argument on its behalf: and it was enough for his purpose if he could obtain an admission of some reappearance of the rational and responsible human being in a future world.

In the third place, the condition of our author in this first Chapter is that of a man who has to fight with one of his hands tied up. His general discussion is upon analogies. Analogies, considered as resemblances of ratios, require four terms to complete them. Butler has before him facts of nature, exhibited in our present life, and admitted to stand in a certain relation to an Author of nature. He has a third term in certain facts of moral government or of revealed religion also placed before our eyes; and from these three he has to infer the fourth. But in his argument on a future life, the third term, on which he has to build the fourth, is entirely wanting; for, being precluded from referring to any Divine authority, he has no supply of experimental facts to adduce, which might cast a light on the condition of the soul after death.

There are those who say these two things, survival and immortality, are but one : and who seem to suppose that the case of surmounting death is like that of obtaining a passport which will carry us over the frontier of some foreign country ; where, this once done, we have no other impediment to apprehend. But, on such an assumption of the identity of survival with immortality, it is to be observed that it is a pure assumption, and nothing more. We have no title to postulate *in limine* that powers, which may be so adjusted or equipped as to face the contingency of death, must therefore be in all respects such as to be certain of facing with a like impunity every other contingency which, for aught we know, the dimness of the future may enfold in its ample bosom. Such questions may remain open, and without prejudice, for independent discussion.

There is a fourth observation to be borne in mind, when we set about the consideration of Butler's Chapter. It does not form a necessary part of his general argument. He might, without this Chapter, put in array all the facts experimentally ascertained which prove the existence in this world of a government by rewards and punishments, and the righteous character of that government; and might, with this apparatus of moral considerations, now made ready for use, build upon them the usual and irresistible arguments for a future state. But this must have been at a later stage. From the opening sentences of this Chapter, he seems to enter upon it with reluctance, and only because he thinks it practicable and needful to clear the subject from certain metaphysical difficulties as to personal identity with which it had been darkened, and which, unless removed, might have barred his access to the great moral argument he desired to introduce.

Addressing himself to his task under these circumstances, his argument is partly negative, and partly affirmative. The first goes to show the futility or insufficiency of the presumptions against survival, which are drawn from the character of death. The second and more limited part goes to show substantive likelihoods, drawn from nature or experience, that the soul may survive death. In the first he is eminently successful. In the second we become sensible how scanty is the supply of material at his command. Much of the depreciation lavished on the Chapter has arisen from the careless supposition that he is advancing as substantive arguments what in reality he only propounds as rebuttals of adverse presumptions, and with the limited view of removing out of his way a preliminary bar.

Let us now begin by taking note of his manner of supporting his first contention, namely, that death and the incidents of death afford no presumption that we are extinguished by it.

1. It is not proved by the immense change which death undoubtedly makes in us. For we know by experience that vast amounts of change in ourselves, and in inferior creatures, are compatible with a continuity of identical existence. We have no absolute knowledge that the change effected by death is greater than these changes; and, until we do know it, the presumption of our extinction by death does not arise. (True, none of these changes is marked by severance of essential parts: but we cannot say whether such severance constitutes a greater change than the change from the state of embryo to that of manhood, or from the egg, through the larva or caterpillar, to the moth or butterfly [1].)

2. There is no ground, 'from the reason of the thing,' to suppose that death can destroy our 'living powers'; that is to say, disable them from perception and action [2]. For of death in itself we know nothing, but only in certain effects of it. And as we know not on what our living powers depend for their exercise, it is possible that they may depend on something wholly beyond the reach of death [3]. Death gives no evidence of destroying the living powers, but only cancels the sensible proof of their exercise [4].

3. Nor is any such ground furnished by the 'analogy of nature.' For in no case do we know what, at death, becomes of these living powers. They simply pass from our view [5].

4. The power of death to destroy living beings is conditioned by their being compounded, and therefore discerptible. For as consciousness is indivisible, so it should seem is the conscious being in which it resides [6]. And, if this be so, it follows that, the body being extraneous and foreign to the true self, no presumption can arise out of the dissolution of the body against the continued existence of the true self.

5. As we may lose limbs, organs of sense, large portions of the body, and yet the true self continues entire; and as animal bodies are always in a state of flux and succession of parts, with no corresponding loss or gain of the true self, we again infer the distinctness of that true self from the body, and its independence at the time of death [7].

---

[1] *Analogy*, I. i. 2, 3.　　[2] *Ibid*. 4.　　[3] *Ibid*. 6.　　[4] *Ibid*. 7.
[5] *Ibid*.　　[6] *Ibid*. 10, 11.　　[7] *Ibid*. 12, 13, 15.

6. Even supposing the 'living being' to be material, we know not its bulk; and, unless it be bigger than one of the elementary particles which are indissoluble, and which represent the minimum, no presumption arises against its surviving death [1].

7. Much less have we to fear extinction from anything happening from any system of matter other than our bodies, and not so near to us as they are [2].

8. Inasmuch as our senses do not perceive, but are carriers only to the perceiving organ, as is proved by cases of losing them, and by dreams, we again infer the distinctness of the living powers [3].

9. Once more we so infer, because our limbs are only servants and instruments to the 'living person' within [4]: and have a relation to us like in kind to that of a staff.

10. If this argument comprehend brutes, and imply that they may become rational and moral, it will still hold. But it need not comprehend them. The objection taken under this head rests wholly on our ignorance [5].

11. If, even as to his state of sensation, the true self of man indicate an independence of the body, much more is he independent as to his state of reflection, and its accompanying pains and pleasures: on which we see no effect from death [6].

12. Certain mortal diseases, up to death, do not affect our intellectual powers. Is it likely that *in* death they will kill these powers? or that, in death, anything else will do it [7]?

13. We cannot infer from anything we know about death even the suspension of our reflective condition and action. Nay, it may be the continuation thereof, with enlargement [8]; all this in a course which may then be found strictly natural [9].

14. The case of vegetables is irrelevant to a question on the survival of faculties of perception and action; since they have none [10].

In sum; there is sufficient proof of independence to bar any presumption of simultaneous or allied destruction. All

---

[1] *Analogy*, I. i. 14, 16.　　[2] *Ibid.* 15, 20.　　[3] *Ibid.* 18.　　[4] *Ibid.* 19.
[5] *Ibid.* 21, 22.　　[6] *Ibid.* 24.　　[7] *Ibid.* 25.　　[8] *Ibid.* 26-28.
[9] *Ibid.* 31.　　[10] *Ibid.* 29.

L

such presumptions have now been rebutted: and a 'credibility,' sufficient for the purposes of religion, indeed 'a very considerable degree of probability,' has been shown [1].

Having thus summed up the negative arguments of Butler, let us proceed to the positive, which indeed are few.

1. The fact of existence carries with it a presumption of its continuance; which presumption holds until rebutted by adverse presumption or proof [2].

2. From the fact of swoons, if not also from dreams, we know that our living powers exist at times when there is no capacity of exercising them in the usual way [3].

3. From the fact that in certain mortal diseases the reflective powers remain wholly unaffected, he seems to infer such an independence as supplies a positive presumption of future existence [4].

It may be worth while to ask why Butler did not employ among the presumptions of a future life one from resort to which it seems plain that he was not precluded by its dependence upon religion, either natural or revealed. I mean that desire for it which, altogether apart from belief, has prevailed in the higher mind of man, and which may be thought to have prompted the Platonic speculations. It seems possible that he may have anticipated the reply which was offered by D'Holbach to this argument after he was dead. D'Holbach does not deny the existence of the desire; but he says, pertinently enough, '*nous désirons la vie du corps, et cependant ce désir est frustré*; pourquoi le désir de la vie de nôtre âme ne seroit-il pas frustré comme le premier [5] ?'

I shall presently refer to Butler's treatment of the question concerning the natural immortality of the soul; at this moment it is enough to say what is indubitable, that he does not make use of it as an argument.

When we put the question, What is the force, in the aggregate, of the arguments which have been adduced in this Chapter, and what was the author's own estimate of that force? it will not be found altogether easy to reply: and perhaps we have here felt the consequences of his having dealt with a subject extraneous to his main argument, in its

[1] *Analogy*, I. i. 32.　　　[2] *Ibid.* 4, 8, 30.　　　[3] *Ibid.* 6.　　　[4] *Ibid.* 25.
[5] *Système de la Nature*, Part I. ch. xiii.

not being handled with the same extraordinary exactitude and continuity. I will refer to two points in particular.

With respect to the argument of indiscerptibility, much favoured by preceding writers from a very ancient date, it ought not to escape remark that Butler does not appear to place reliance upon it; as, in his summing up, he makes no allusion to it, but puts forward other topics in its stead. And yet it is an argument which, if it were sound, would dispense with every other, and would at once prove the whole of his case, so far as the soul, apart from the body, is concerned. But is it sound? To me it appears wholly valueless.

For what is discerptibility? Can it be defined otherwise than as the severance in space of the portions of some whole, which were previously united in space? so that the parts of a material substance, which necessarily exists in space, are said to be discerptible. But the soul is not, according to the ordinary acceptance of the term, material. It does not then (as far as our knowledge goes) exist in space, and is not subject to its conditions. So that the idea of discerptibility is wholly foreign to it, and can have no concern in proving either its mortality or its immortality.

Yet Clarke has advanced a very high doctrine of indiscerptibility. 'As evidently as the known properties of matter prove it to be certainly a discerpible (*sic*) substance, whatever other unknown properties it may be endued with; so evidently the known and confessed properties of immaterial beings prove them to be indiscerpible, whatever other unknown properties they likewise may be indued with [1].'

Again, Butler is evidently led to his conditional argument on behalf of the immortality of brutes by the palpable fact that they give evidence of living powers, some living agent, some true self, within and above their corporeal organs. It has been feared by some that this may lead to an inversion of the argument, and a contention that if our 'living being' be like theirs, little can be inferred from it as to a likelihood of independent survival. The absolute finality of death for brutes ought not, I suppose, to be taken for

---

[1] Clarke's *Defence of an Argument made use of in a Letter to Mr. Dodwell*, p. 101.

granted. But we must carefully eschew the recognition of
any full parallelism in the application of the argument from
living powers as between the two orders respectively. And
this on more grounds than one. The living being in brutes
may suffice to warrant our presuming it to be possibly independent of death : but it is contracted in scope, and insignificant in function, when they are compared with man ;
who has not only perception and action, but reflection ; and
not only reflection, but conscience ; and with conscience a
sense of moral right and wrong, together with an array of
moral powers, as to which it is to be observed that, unlike
the powers merely intellectual, they as a general rule lose
nothing with the lapse of years, but often ripen down to the
very hour of death.

And again, that great argument for human survival,
which arises from the palpable incompleteness of the work
of discipline for which men came into the world, not universally, but still in a great multitude of cases, has little or
no application to the case of brutes, whose life and death
are not similarly associated with growth, and do not suggest
in the same way the idea of unfulfilled purpose. Much
of this, however, is not within the scope of Butler's first
Chapter.

In the beginning of § 32, he states that he has shown the
credibility of a future life : and truly may it be said that
a thing, against which no adverse presumption has been,
or presumably can be, made good, is credible. But at the
close of the section he says that he has proved it up ' to
a very considerable degree of probability ' ; which is a different matter.

He seems to have been perfectly successful in the business of pure rebuttal. The instrument, by which he has
achieved it, is giving proof of our possession of living
powers, and of their high character, apart from, and above,
the corporeal organs : and, on the whole, it seems to be his
view that the nature of these powers, together with the
likelihood of their continuance (which, in the absence of any
proved power of death to destroy us, he estimates highly),
amounts to ' a very considerable degree of probability.'

It may perhaps be thought that a rebuttal of objections,

not only successful, but so comprehensive and complete, as that supplied by Butler, has an importance, real though indeterminate, which reaches somewhat beyond its immediate aim. It may leave behind it, on a view of the whole case, some amount of impression in favour of that affirmative which, though not demonstrated, has been so well defended against assault.

Credibility, however, as he holds, is sufficient for all the purposes of religion, and this is reasonable; for, in a matter which may profoundly concern us, such credibility binds us to move onwards, and to weigh all the elements of the case, such as the argument of the *Analogy*, in the course of its development, may present them.

Again, the argument of continuance based upon existence is made by Butler to play a capital part. Is it strong enough to sustain the whole weight so laid upon it?

This question, as it seems to me, can hardly be answered without introducing other considerations. May it not be held that the likelihood of this or that entity's continuance cannot be measured until after first measuring the arguments for its present existence? We may presume (always proceeding upon the postulate that there is an Author of nature) upon the continuance of a rosebud in one way, but upon the continuance of a decaying rose only in a different and much more limited way. If things exist only for an end, the strength of the argument for their continuance will surely depend, in each case, upon the condition they have reached with regard to the attainment of that end. If they have upon them the mark of a design, together with marks that it is not yet fulfilled, the argument of likelihood for their continuance is strong. Such is the case with man. But then Butler's evolution of his subject has not reached a point at which he can make use of this argument. And it seems open to doubt whether simple continuance, apart from purpose, affords a solid standing-ground from which to project this or that existence into the future. Butler may be right in throwing the burden of proof upon those who refuse to admit as probable the continuance in the future of that which now exists; but this burden need not in every case be a very heavy burden.

The establishment of the apparent independence of the 'living being' upon death is, however, of itself a great result; and its greatness grows upon us in proportion as that living being is richly equipped with faculty. Every attentive reader, in considering Butler's management of this subject, must remark how slightly, in presenting to us his 'living agent,' he puts forward the ethic and pathetic, or shall I say the moral and affectional, sides of our nature. Here we have an army of faculties, which greatly enhance the force of his reasonings from the nature of the living agent. And Dr. Eagar, a recent commentator on Butler, has well observed that our moral feelings and emotions are not subject to deterioration or abatement with the lapse of years, down to the latest, in the same manner and degree as are the powers of memory, perception, and reflection. Once only, in discussing this subject, does Butler name, in connexion with reason and memory, 'the affections which they excite [1].'

A question may, I think, reasonably be put whether we ought or ought not to reckon, among the presumptions in favour of the survival of the soul, those preternatural or extraordinary manifestations, immensely varied in form and in the manner of their appeal to our percipient faculties, which from time immemorial have made their appearance among the records of human life and experience? During the nineteenth century they have occupied a larger space in the public view than perhaps at any other period, and have without doubt been subjected to more systematic, prolonged, and dispassionate examination. The Society incorporated for Psychical Research has been actively at work for a series of years in Cambridge, probably the greatest mathematical University of the world. The Society has now a branch in the United States. It is almost needless to observe that, in connexion with the name of Spiritualism (for which I should much desire to substitute the title of Spiritism), these phenomena have obtained very great notoriety, with large and in some cases weighty adhesion, in our own country and still more in America. There is, and ever has been, a popular impression more or less favourable to the idea of such manifestations. Among the wealthier classes there is a large

[1] *Analogy*, I. i. 26.

amount of determined negation, which is also shared by many men of scientific attainments. Those who are thus armed with a resolute and universal preconception, have their answer ready made to the question I have above propounded. The body of believers whose names carry authority is probably small. But there is an intermediate class of those who have neither generally nor in any particular case accepted the alleged occurrences as established facts, yet who, upon a view of the whole case, think it hardly reasonable to consign them in mass to a limbo of non-entities; and who lean to the idea that they have probably some amount of real, though as yet undetermined, basis in realities. If they have any basis at all, they so far testify to the reality of the immaterial and spiritual world. If any portion of that basis is supplied by manifestations, which are connected with our future existence, they must, I suppose, be held to supply, as far as they go, available evidence on its behalf. There are also those who think that the antiquity and wide extension of a belief of this kind may of itself reckon among the secondary evidences in its favour.

Let us now turn to the argument from natural immortality, which includes *a fortiori* the question of survival, and with regard to which we may be naturally led to inquire how it is that Butler, having said so much, has not said still more.

His references to natural immortality are found in the twenty-first and thirty-first sections of his first Chapter. In the first of these he speaks of a natural immortality of brutes, and observes that it does not imply their being endowed with any capacities of a rational or moral description. In the second, he propounds to us that there may, in the future or unseen world, be a state of existence for us new and yet natural; and he conceives in general that this cannot reasonably be denied. He then proceeds to designate persons, or circumstances, such as in a particular manner exclude the denial: speaking thus — 'especially whilst the probability of a future life, or the natural immortality of the soul, is admitted upon the evidence of reason.' What idea, if any, does he wish to convey to his reader on the important doctrine of natural immortality?

With regard to the first of these passages, touching the immortality of brutes, Butler does not admit it to be a consequence of his teaching with respect to the living powers, or living being, as existing in man. With regard to the second, it is to be observed that when he has occasion to refer to immortality as it stands under the Christian dispensation, he says that 'life and immortality are eminently brought to light by the Gospel,' and that 'the great doctrine of a future state' is confirmed by the Gospel[1]. The whole argument of the first Chapter is an argument for the survival of the soul, in which no distinction is drawn between simple survival and immortality. Certainly it may have been meant to serve as an argument for immortality. And yet, in the passage which I have quoted from the first Chapter (in § 31), his language as it stands is ambiguous. It may signify only that the denial cannot take place compatibly with the dogma of natural immortality, and therefore not among such persons as happen to hold it. Or it may mean to take for granted a natural immortality, and to urge that, as this is an established principle, his proposition cannot possibly be contested. Which of the two is his meaning? I have arrived at the conclusion that it is the first. If this is so, he makes no assertion of natural immortality. My conclusion is that he does not intend to make any positive assertion either for or against it, but to hold his judgement in reserve. He may have leant to it in his inner mind: he may have felt reluctant to oppose himself to an opinion which may be taken to have been nearly universal in his time, and for long ages before. But it is plain to me, that he has stopped short of an absolute categorical assertion of it: and he could, as I conceive. have had no reason for stopping short of such an assertion, except an unwillingness to be committed to it, either from his general mistrust of propositions founded only on abstract reasoning, or from his believing this particular proposition to have been insufficiently established.

Had he been prepared to propound it, he would surely have altered the whole argument of his first Chapter; for, if the natural immortality of the soul be an established

[1] *Analogy,* II. i. 9.

truth, it must at once take precedence of all those elaborate presumptions, which he has adopted for the basis of his reasoning in favour of a future life. He argues for a future life as hope, as credibility, as likelihood; but he does not venture to propound it as a thing of dogma or as a certainty. Had he felt himself in a condition to propound it as an established truth, his whole attitude in the first Chapter must apparently have been changed. That dogma would have been the head and front of the discussion; and all his rebuttals of adverse presumption, and his modest pleas for favourable inference, needed at most only to appear as an army of auxiliaries, preparing and making straight the way for the acceptance of that doctrine.

Now, if Butler has not bound himself hand and foot to the metaphysical principle of the soul's essential immortality, of an immortality for the soul inherent in its nature as soul, plainly it was not because he lived in a world to which that doctrine was in any manner new or strange. On the contrary, it was, and it had been for many ages, a standing doctrine of popular, and, within certain limits it may even be said, also of authoritative, theology. Nor was recognized philosophy in disaccord with theology. I will quote one instance which may serve to show how deeply the persuasion has been rooted in the general sentiment at least of Western Christendom. At the Reformation, when so much of teaching long unassailed was shaken down to its foundation, and Michael Servetus was prosecuted in Geneva, under the inspiration of Calvin, for heresy in respect to the Trinity, this question also was brought upon the carpet. Servetus was, or supposed himself to be, accused of denying the natural immortality of the soul. His reply was given thus:

'If ever I said that, and not only said it but published it, and infected the whole world, I would condemn myself to death [1].'

At a period when there was a disposition [2] in philosophy to exalt time and space almost to the dignity of the uncreated, it was little likely that the natural immortality of

---

[1] Guizot, *Great Christians of France*, chap. xix.
[2] See the volume of correspondence between Clarke and Leibnitz.

the soul, supported as to a wide extent it was by the authority of tradition, would be repellent to the general mind. It had indeed received in England, at the epoch of Butler's activity, new and weighty consecration. First, this had come from the Cambridge Platonists, who set the argument very high. Before proceeding to adduce proofs of the doctrine, John Smith writes as follows:

· The immortality of the soul doth not absolutely need any demonstration to clear it; but might be assumed rather as a principle or *postulatum*, seeing the notion of it is apt naturally to insinuate itself into the being of the most vulgar sort of men. . . .

'All nations have consented in this belief, which hath almost been as vulgarly received as the belief of a Deity [1].'

It has been more questioned by · unskilful philosophers' than by the unsophisticated mind of man: and has such a *consensus gentium* as Cicero rightly holds 'enough to conclude a law and maxim of nature by.' This stress John Smith lays on the consent of the general mind, though he thinks it includes an idea of the soul's materiality, and, it may be, its traduction too, as wide as the belief itself. And he takes as his common basis or principle this hypothesis, '*that no substantial and indivisible thing ever perisheth*.' For a moment only, as it seems, he declares himself indeed content with that idea of Plato which, in the *Timaeus*, introduces the Deity addressing the angels (or νέοι θεοί) in these words, 'You shall hold your immortality by a patent of mere grace from myself'; yet he remembers that Plato also falls back upon the dictum of Plotinus, 'that no substance shall ever perish.' Even mathematical considerations are pressed into the argument for the soul's immortality, which is enforced [2] with great persistence, and in a fashion not much according to the cautious and measured mind of Butler.

The doctrine of indivisibility, as precluding death and entailing immortality, was commended to Butler for acceptance by an authority nearer to him alike in time and in association than Smith, namely, by Dr. Samuel Clarke. The acceptance is, however, qualified, not absolute. The claim

---

[1] Smith's *Select Discourses*, IV. ii.   [2] In chapters iii-vii.

for immortality from indivisibility, he says, has been argued, 'and for anything appearing to the contrary, justly.' This is, at most, no more than a provisional assent. His ultimate judgement on the question seems to be held in reserve. For this reserve, as for all the notable inflections of his thought, he must, without doubt, have had grave reasons. If Butler really held himself back from the full adoption of the popular and established opinion, such an abstention presents to us an instance both of circumspection, and of a mental courage founded on solid originality, which may be said to form a landmark in the history of opinion. It may warrant an attempt to map out the position of the question, as it would present itself to Butler's eye.

It may, perhaps, be well to begin by reminding the reader that the idea involved in the term immortality is not single, but manifold. I have already referred to two of the distinctions which we have to keep before the mind.

1. A vitality surmounting the particular crisis of death is one thing : an existence without end is another.

2. We may speak of an immortality of the disembodied spirit, and may combine it with, or disjoin it from, a survival or resurrection of the body. In the second case, it is of the entire man ; in the first, it is of part only of the man, although it be the chief part.

3. The new life to which death is to introduce the human being, may be active, intelligent, moral, spiritual, and may be placed in an environment accordant with all these. Or it may conceivably be divested of any one of these characteristics, or even of them all.

4. The life of the unseen world may be conceived as projected into the future only, as it is presented to us by Divine Revelation : or it may be projected also into the past, and viewed there in association with a past eternity.

5. It was when Butler saw personal identity, as he thought, in danger, that he undertook to deal with the question of our existence in the unseen world [1]. This identity is in truth the very core of the whole subject. An immortality without identity is of no concern to us ; and the transmigration of souls is an effective denial of the doctrine.

[1] *Analogy*, I. i. 1.

6. We have to distinguish between a condition of death-lessness into which we grow by degrees, and an immortality which, ingrained (so to speak) from birth, is already our absolute possession. This distinction is a vital one for one class, namely, those who do not accept any dogma of immortality belonging to nature, but who look upon it as a gift resulting from union with Christ and with God.

With these diversities before us as to the nature of immortality, let us now consider the various ideas of the tenure on which it is to be held.

We are not to suppose that those who maintain the natural immortality of the human soul, of necessity intend thereby a life so conditioned that it is beyond the power of the Almighty to put an end to it. Clarke, in answer to Collins, points out that God may have more ways of disposing of His creatures after death 'than we are let into the secret of.'

He may indeed, if He please, annihilate them at the dissolution of their bodies (and so He might, if He thought fit, annihilate the disembodied souls of men; and yet it would be nevertheless true that they are in their own nature immortal)[1].'

When we speak, then, of the natural immortality of the soul, what is the idea that we have in view ? Is it an immortality like that of God Himself, and is it such that the soul, having been introduced into the universe, becomes inseparable from it, or must under all conditions continue to form part of it ? It is scarcely possible to suppose this to be seriously held.

There is another conception, which Clarke includes under the phrase of natural immortality, and which is radically different from this. It is that the soul is framed (so to speak) upon the lines of immortality, as the destination alone appropriate to its nature, and to the consummation of that nature ; and, further, that it will, as matter of fact, continue to exist unless it shall please God to impose upon it a doom which will put an end to that existence. As the body is framed to die, so the soul is framed to live. This would seem to be Clarke's conception.

[1] Clarke's *Defence of an Argument made use of in a Letter to Mr. Dodwell,* p. 103.

Then there is a third conception which in so far agrees with the second that it regards the soul as qualified by its nature to attain to immortality; but varies from it in so much as it does not hold the soul to be endowed with that gift at birth, but conceives of it as a gift derived from the Incarnation of our Lord, and the renovating powers which it provided, to be put in exercise on behalf of our fallen nature. It inverts a portion of the last-named idea. The one says, 'the soul may live, but it will be by the reception of a special gift.' The other says, 'the soul may die, but it will be by the infliction of a special doom'; and if that doom shall prove to be the natural consequence of inveterate sin, spread like a canker over and within its entire substance, the question which remains is practical rather than merely theoretical. It is whether God will allow sin, as a deadly disease, to accomplish its perfect work in the destruction or cessation of the sinner; or whether, sin in the person of the wicked, will continue, under all conditions, to deface the aspect of creation, as indefeasibly as the immortality of the righteous shall adorn it.

Then there remains the further question: what portion of His counsels, on this mysterious and solemn question, has the Almighty Wisdom deemed it meet to reveal to us?

There is, of course, a fourth mode of dealing with the subject. It simply regards the soul as subject, like the body, to dissolution at death, which is for both of them without hope of revocation. But with this view, that of the pure negationist, and the converse of the first-named conception, we have here nothing to do.

The difference between the second and the third of these schemes does not appear to be great in the abstract, for the first of them allows that the soul may be smitten by a doom of annihilation, while the second involves the belief that it may receive immortality by gift, and that it is appointed so to do in the normal course of its existence. Yet room is left for practical differences of the most important kind. For if, while the doom of annihilation is admitted to be possible in the abstract, it is also held that the idea of such a doom is excluded from the counsels of Providence, then the immortality of all human souls, whether it be in the abstract indefeasible or not, is absolute for every practical purpose ; whereas, under the other hypothesis, it remains an entirely open question except for such as attain to immortality through union with the Divine nature.

So much with respect to the subject itself. Now with regard to the evidence which seemingly caused Butler to stop short of positively affirming for himself the tenet of natural immortality. We may consider that tenet as derivable from reasoning, from consent, or from authority.

With regard to the first head, Butler had before him all the remarkable achievements of those among the ancient philosophers who contended for the immortality of the human soul. This conception rose to its climax with Pindar among the poets, and with Plato in the ' Groves of Academe.' We habitually suppose, and with reason, that this great performance of the philosopher was achieved mainly by reasoning in the abstract and of a metaphysical character. But in a remarkable passage of the *Timaeus* [1], Plato represents the Supreme God as charging the inferior gods, whom he had produced, to undertake the construction of men in imitation of his example. And he will himself sow the seed in these beings of the part which is worthy of the name immortal, and will hand it over to them for completion [2]. Plato may have founded this ascription to the Deity on the conviction which he had worked out for himself by his abstract argument. He was, however, not well supported by the rival schools of philosophy. The powerful mind of Aristotle did not embrace the conception of a personal and practical immortality for man [3]. ' The really human in the soul, that which has come into being, must also pass away.' This is taken by Döllinger as the sum of the Aristotelian doctrine. And the Stoics ' viewed the soul as destined to immediate reabsorption into the great world-soul after death,' or, as surviving only for a time [4]. Then came the school of deliberate extinctionists, headed by Epicurus ; and it seems

---

[1] Plat. *Tim.* 10. 1. The words describing the productive operation of the Supreme God are rendered by Jowett 'the Creator of the Universe.'

[2] See Salmond, *Christian Doctrine of Immortality*, p. 151.

[3] See Döllinger, *Heidenthum und Judenthum.*

[4] Salmond, p. 151 ; and Grote's *Plato*, ii. 204.

probable that his following among men of the world was
greater than among philosophers. The doctrine of immortality has impressed but slight footprints upon the Roman
literature. The letters and poetry of consolation, which
antiquity has bequeathed to us, are especially instructive
in this respect. They are miserably pale and thin, although
in various cases singularly touching. Nor did matters improve with the lapse of time. Lucretius rebukes the folly of
those who quail before the idea of punishments after death,
and bends the whole force of his great genius to constructing
a magnificent apology for the doctrine of extinction : and the
grave Juvenal informs us that none in his day believed in
the survival of the soul, unless such as had not yet emerged
from boyhood [1]. The language of Cicero, partially quoted by
John Smith, is highly inconsistent. Grote declares that
Plato settled nothing, and agrees with Lord Macaulay that
the philosophers, from Plato to Franklin, who attempted to
prove immortality without the aid of revelation, failed de-
plorably [2].

And Butler could not but be well aware that the question
of the soul's immortality, open to so much abstract discussion, had been incurably apt to wander into entanglement
with the pre-existence and transmigration of souls, and that
desperate battles had to be fought, both against terminability
and on behalf of individuality. Nor was the abstract argument altogether on one side. ' Is it not contrary to all the
analogies of present experience,' we are asked, ' to suppose
that I, who lately began to be, shall never cease to be, or
that I shall not be refunded into unconscious existence as
in the centuries before I was born ? Whatever is generable
must surely be perishable. My soul, if immortal, must have
existed before my birth : and if its existence then no way
concerns me now, as little will its existence after death [3].'

This portion of the field, the portion depending upon
argument in the abstract, was open, I conceive, to Bishop
Butler as it is to us. On the argument from the general
consent of mankind, he had not all the sources of information that we possess. The religions of Egypt, China, Per-

[1] Juv. *Sat.* ii. 149.
[2] Grote's *Plato*, ii. 203–5.
[3] Campbell Fraser, *Philosophic Theism*, p. 16 (Gifford Lectures for 1894–5).

sia, India, Chaldea, with Assyria, had not been laid open to the world. The religions of the uncivilized races had not been so largely elucidated by knowledge obtained upon the paths of travel. The roads, open to him among mankind at large, were principally those which led to an acquaintance with the sentiments of two races, the Greek and the Roman, the most powerful ever known among mankind, one in the world of thought, and the other in the world of action.

The first and also the fullest record supplied to us on the thought of the Greeks concerning an unseen and future world is that which we find in the poems of Homer. The largest mass of such information continuously given is that contained in the great Nekuïa, the eleventh Book of the *Odyssey*; but much is also to be gathered from notices dispersed throughout both the Poems. The most important of the affirmative propositions which the evidence will warrant is that everywhere there seems to be a protest of nature, an instinctive shrinking from the idea of simple extinction at death; nowhere is it mentioned, or in any manner entertained, as fixed for any particular date. The life or soul is as distinct from the bodily organization as is the body of one man from the body of another. The entire man is at death severed into parts, but the nature of the division made, the question where lay the true self, is open to dispute. Twice Homer speaks of what has happened to the αὐτός, or *ego*, after that last earthly crisis. Once at the beginning of the *Iliad*, where he says the wrath of Achilles prematurely dispatched many souls of heroes to the Underworld, but they, the αὐτούς, remain to be the prey of dogs and birds [1]. The other where, at the close of the eleventh Book of the *Odyssey*, we are introduced to Heracles in Hades as a shade or εἴδωλον only, for he himself (αὐτός) has been admitted to the banquets of the Immortals, and there has Hebe for his mate [2]. But Heracles was a favoured mortal. The glimpses of future happiness are so rare, as hardly to enter into the general account. The aspect of the future life is indefinite, except in one respect, that it is profoundly overcast with gloom.

---

[1] *Il.* i. 2.   [2] *Od.* xi. 601-3.

Again ; the whole apparatus, so to speak, of the Homeric Under-world is foreign : as much so as the framework and picture of the terrestrial world is Hellenic. Olympus is within Achaian limits; the entrance to Hades is by the Ocean River, at the remotest border of the earth. The Egyptian Amenti reappears in the name of Rhadamanthos, but this name is not placed in connexion with any judicial function. True, we have Minos introduced as a judge in Hades, but he has nothing to do with awarding destinies based upon earthly conduct: he is a police magistrate, hearing the complaints, and ordering the controversies, of the ghostly community [1]. The questions of pre-existence and transmigration are nowhere touched in Homer, for whose use the ψυχή is indeed not so much the soul in its proper sense as the living being or living agent treated of in Butler's work. If we are asked whether the Shades of the Homeric Poems were immortal, we have no means of providing a full answer to the question. Except in a single passage, where he refers to the rapidity with which thought (νόος) traverses or neutralizes space in dealing with its proper subjects [2], he never seems to have speculated upon the human spirit apart from its experiences in the flesh. Much less would he, whose grasp of numbers, except within narrow limits, was totally indeterminate, endeavour to realize to himself the idea of absolutely deathless and endless existence. Indeed, that idea in its full extent is altogether beyond the reach of human faculty, and even now is only and very faintly approached by the largest use of enumeration. I reserve the further consideration of it for another place, in connexion with all that relates to the condition of man in another world. We are here concerned only with duration: and as to duration, we may safely say that the early or Achaian Greeks believed in survival; that their detailed embodiment of it was not indigenous, but imported; and that the conception is not either broad or definite enough to comprise the idea implied by natural immortality, either for affirmation or denial.

In the great historic ages of Greece, the old Achaian or Homeric conception of the future life tended rather to

[1] *Od.* xi. 568-71. [2] *Il.* xv. 80.

dwindle than to grow. It nowhere assumed the character
of a force operative, through personal expectations, upon
conduct in this life. Yet the idea of extinction and death,
while it was argued for and against in the philosophic
schools, had no place in the mind or heart of humanity
at large. Grote, who has formed so low an estimate of the
upshot of the great labours of Plato, nevertheless writes as
follows : ‘ The popular orthodoxy recognized some sort of
posthumous existence as a part of its creed, and the uninquiring multitude continued in the teaching and traditions
of their youth [1].’ If, however, we wish to appreciate the
practical attitude of the public mind with reference to the
world of shadows, we must look, not so much to tragedians
who had to deal with archaic traditions and the ideals of
life, as to Aristophanes, who bodied forth the true form and
pressure of his own time, and who leaves upon us the
impression that the prevailing conception of the future life
had been effectually stripped of all that could make it either
venerable in theory, or operative upon conduct. The early
part of the *Frogs* of this extraordinary writer appears to
supply conclusive evidence that the Under-world and the
future life could, in his day, with safety be made the theme
of pure ridicule before the most cultivated and popular audi-
ences in Greece or in the world.

The practical thought of Greece was, indeed, directed to
affirming the sufficiency of the earthly life ; while its freedom left ample room for speculation on the future. The
Latins were little disposed to formulate either in the one
direction or the other, and practically made little or no
addition to the materials which Butler had before him.

The most important part of those materials has still to be
considered, the part, namely, which could claim the authority of a Divine Revelation. Butler could not admit such a
claim into the argument of his first Chapter. But neither
could he fail to consider for himself what bearing the state
of ideas disclosed in the Old Testament might have on the
question of the natural immortality of the soul. In Gen. i.
26, we read thus : ‘And God said, Let us make man in our
image after our likeness’ ; and much thought has been

[1] Grote's *Plato*, ii. 204.

bestowed on the great inquiry, wherein did this image of God consist? We are guided up to the meaning in part by the place which the passage holds in the narrative of the great First Chapter. It is a narrative of ascension; and thus we see at once that the being, introduced by this majestic announcement, was differentiated from the last previously-named order of creation by a higher intelligence. So much, however, we should have inferred from the general arrangement, even in the absence of the very marked introduction, and of the descriptive phrase. So that interpreters have reasonably looked for meanings which would convey the conception of a true likeness to God, though not one commensurable with God, nor pushing us into His province. These they have found in purity and integrity of the moral nature; in wealth of intellectual capability; in freedom of the will; and in immortality. All this not perfect, yet in training for perfection, and put in a probation which was guarded by the penalties that were to follow upon sin.

St. Augustine has dealt largely with the case of Adam. He appears to have felt the subject to be difficult; for he says of his own work: ' plura quaesita quam inventa sunt; et eorum quae inventa, pauciora firmata; caetera, non · ita posita, quasi adhuc requirenda sint[1].' In his work on Genesis, he says that the body of Adam in his innocence was mortal, because it might die; immortal, because it might escape death. It was not an immortal nature like some others, ' ut quasdam naturas immortales creavit Deus '; but it had a capacity of immortality through the tree of life; ' quod ei de ligno vitae, non de constitutione naturae.' For nothing is immortal except the spiritual (body), which is only promised to us at the resurrection. · ' Neque enim immortale, quod mori omnino non posset, erit, nisi spiritale, quod nobis futurum in resurrectione promittitur.' But, by the Fall, this nature of ours became no longer mortal only but dead. ' Factum est propter peccatum non mortale . . . sed mortuum [2].'

Besides the tree of knowledge, which was forbidden to

---

[1] Lib. ii., *Retractationum*, c. 24.
[2] *De Genesi ad literam*, bk. vi. c. 36.

Adam, there was set in the garden the tree of life, on which, in his state of innocence, he was permitted to feed. According to the plain reading of the text, this tree (as the other would have given knowledge) was so endowed as to give immortality. 'And now, lest he put forth his hand, and take also of the tree of life, and eat, and live for ever: therefore the Lord God sent him forth from the Garden of Eden [1].' It is said that this may be an allegory. But, allegory or no allegory, in this view it is all the same. By the tree of life is signified something which had lain open to the access and use of man, and which would, by the ordinance of God, have enabled him to live for ever. St. Augustine accepts this teaching in all its breadth, and elsewhere he says man was created an *anima vivens ;* his body was a *corpus animale,* a body with an *anima.* He was not immortal by the necessity of nature, but would have become immortal by the tree of life, had he not sinned ; ' nisi in Dei praedicentis minantisque sententiam delinquendo corruisset [2].' There is nothing in these passages to show a natural survival of the *anima* after the death of the body, which was a *corpus animale.*

Elsewhere, however, St. Augustine teaches explicitly the immortality of the soul. After having variously felt his way upon the subject, he wrote a treatise, *De Immortalitate Animae,* and with this doctrine his name is prominently associated. To the last-named work is subjoined another, *De Animae Quantitate,* the argument of which, as might be expected from its title, is far more of a metaphysical than of a theological character. But he did not estimate highly what had been achieved on this subject by human means. The immortality of the soul was an arduous matter which had been penetrated only by a very few, under the most favourable circumstances ('vix pauci, magno praediti ingenio, abundantes otio, dictionibusque subtilissimis eruditi '). And even these either thought that the souls would after a term return to the miseries of this life, or else believed in the eternity of the world *a parte ante,* that is to say, disbelieved in creation [8]. For the present I pass lightly over the succeeding centuries. When we come down to the time of St. Thomas Aquinas, we find the principle of natural immortality laid

[1] Genesis iii. 22, 23.   [2] *De Civ. Dei,* xiii. 23.   [8] *De Trinitate,* xiii. 12.

down broadly and without hesitation. 'Forma autem hominis est anima rationalis, quae est de se immortalis:' meaning, apparently, with a proper and indefeasible immortality ordained of God [1]. This appears to indicate a great clearing and hardening of opinion since the time of St. Augustine. But there was as yet no declaration proceeding from an authority competent in any degree to bind either the Universal or the Western Church; and it may be that Butler did not take great account of what may be regarded as no more than a current of ecclesiastical opinion, philosophical rather than theological in its ultimate grounds. But, without doubt, he would take account of the facts presented to him by the Scriptures of the Old Testament. In his mind a future state was an article of natural religion; and natural religion was due to primitive revelation, for the traces of which he might consistently and reasonably search through both sacred and profane antiquity.

The indications there afforded, when co-ordinated one with another, bear no mark of the idea of natural immortality, either as distinctly revealed, or as prevalent among mankind at large; but are on the other hand as far as possible from giving any direct countenance to the idea of extinction, either at the moment of death or upon the lapse of any assumed period after it. Some see in them a gradual ripening and development of the belief as we pass, from the date of the very earliest records, down the centuries [2]. I have not been able to discover it: the survival of the soul presents itself to me as generally held and in the abstract unquestioned, but without inquiry, from the earliest date; in a form, however, so indeterminate that it sometimes appears to border on, though it never enters, the region of negation. The scriptural tradition offers its contribution to a consent general as against extinction, but refusing submission to any formal statement.

The date of Enoch, the father of Methuselah, is, even according to the Hebrew chronology, as far back as nearly

[1] *Secunda Secundae*, vii. 164, Art. 1.
[2] See Salmond on the Future Life for the Old Testament, *Christian Doctrine of Immortality*, bk. ii : Professor Cheyne, *Indian Church Quarterly Review*, April, 1891, for antiquity in general.

the middle of the fourth millennium before the Advent. The account of his translation is, therefore, by far the oldest of scriptural records indicative of the accepted belief. There can be none more beautiful; and it seems to me as if there could not be a more forcible proof that the idea of survival beyond the grave was both accepted and familiar among the race for whom the Book of Genesis was compiled. Also it seems plain that the happy destinies of the righteous could appropriately be presented to them in terms which, upon any other supposition, could hardly have taken this simple and summary form. But it relates only to a person of distinguished righteousness.

I do not dwell on Deut. xxxii. 22, which threatens that the Divine wrath shall 'burn unto the lowest hell'; for the context appears to connect the sentiment with temporal judgements [1]. The absence of all considerations belonging to a future state from the Mosaic legislation is, however, a fact not less remarkable than any of the notices of that state contained in the Old Testament. It has been common to believe that no scheme of religion, no system of duty and obedience from man towards God, could be constructed on any other system than the belief in a future state. Warburton, in his once famous *Divine Legation*, founded himself on its absence from the Mosaic system to draw a contrast between Moses and other legislators; and argued that, as he was able to dispense with what they had found essential, he must have possessed a mainstay which they had not, namely the revealed authority of God.

Moses had brought the children of Israel out of a land, where religion and life were closely bound up with the expectation of not only prolonged existence, but also retribution, in the unseen world. We may well believe it was essential to keep the Hebrew worship far removed from contact with Egyptian polytheism. On this account we can readily suppose the Hebrew legislator to have avoided a great danger by dispensing with this form of sanction for his laws. But such an avoidance in no way indicates the substantive means which allowed him to draw adequate strength from other quarters, in lieu of that to which he was unable to

[1] So Pool *in loc.*, and references in the *Speaker's Commentary*.

repair. These elements of strength, whatever their nature, were such as empowered him not only to take his place among legislators, but also to construct a scheme of astonishing durability, which, after three thousand years and upward of the most searching and violent experiences, is still alive and at work within our view among many millions of our fellow-men; which is associated in them with many remarkable gifts; and which does not exhibit the smallest present likelihood of disappearance from the face of human things.

These elements of strength are not difficult to discover.

In the first place, the unity of God was a pure and profound conception engrained in the heart and mind of the race; tested, too, by the servitude in Egypt on the one hand, and by the signal events of the great deliverance on the other. It is true that even this race was not always firm in its resistance to temptation; yet many suppose that the worship of the golden calf was not the conscious setting up of a separate and rival power, but only the sign of a lust for the symbolism supplied by a visible form. And the same may, I suppose, be said of Jeroboam [1] with more obvious support from the narrative, since he made not one calf like Aaron but two, and placed them at opposite extremities of the Northern Kingdom with a view to convenience of access. And his motive was quite intelligible. He sought, on political grounds, to supply the people with a substitute for the journey to Jerusalem. How great is the power which this doctrine of the Divine Unity can exercise, even in conjunction with most faulty elements, over man, we may judge from the immense development of force displayed at a later period of history in conjunction with the Mahometan propaganda.

Moreover, this One God, as a covenanted God, was placed in a special relation to the people. 'I have sworn once by my holiness that I will not fail David.' Thus was the Deity brought nearer to them; and this approximation on His side gave them, too, a reciprocal consciousness of nearness to Him. All this was sustained by the powerful threefold combination of a ritual divinely ordered and privileged, of miracle, and of prophecy. And the religious machinery of

[1] Exod. xxxii. 4 ; 1 Kings xii. 28, 29.

the Hebrew system was in its turn enforced by the alternate
experiences of prosperity and misfortune in association with
national conduct, and in accordance with the promises and
threats of the great Law-giver [1].

Yet there is one vital element still to be noted in connexion with this unparalleled case of a religious system
founded exclusively on temporal considerations. The Mosaic revelation was not the oldest in the world; nor had
that older revelation, which had descended along the line
of the patriarchs, become extinct. On the contrary, it was
upheld and transmitted in warm vitality among such of the
community as were of spiritual minds, and it found historical assertion with an extraordinary splendour in the Psalms.
The Mosaic narrative itself gives us glimpses of the Under-
world; for in various passages when our Authorized text
speaks of passing into the grave, this is not the mere earthly
grave, but Sheol, the insatiable, undiscriminating, receptacle
of the dead [2]. The indication of a world beyond the present
one, to be inhabited by man, is perfectly distinct; while
that world is pointed to as something which is wholly extraneous to the Mosaic precinct properly so called. But the
Book of Job, which nowhere refers to the Mosaic law or to
the history of the Israelites, may seem to represent human
tradition beyond the limit of the chosen people, and at a
period, as appears to be generally held, of great though uncertain antiquity. For these reasons, its repeated references
to an unseen world and a future state are of special interest [3]. Most of all, the remarkable anticipation of a great
Messianic day. The translation of Elijah to the heavens
affords a most imposing testimony to the general acceptance of belief in another world; as, from a very different
point of view, does the episode of the witch of Endor [4].
Then we have the marvellous anticipations found in a
variety of Psalms; qualified, it is true, in their recording
evidence by such passages as represent a transitory droop-
ing of the soul in the face of its trials and of the formidable incidents of death. This seems, however, never to be

---

[1] As in Deut. xxx, xxxi.   [2] Gen. xxxvii. 35 ; xl. 38 ; xliv. 31.
[3] Job xviii. 14 ; xxvi. 8, *et al.*, especially xix. 25, 27.
[4] 2 Kings ii. 11 ; 1 Sam. xxviii. 7.

without an upward gaze which always involves the idea
of possible deliverance, as in Ps. lxxxix. 9-12, even though
it is not invariably followed by an instant reappearance
of the sun from behind the clouds. Thus we have in Ps.
xxx. (10, 12), 'Shall the dust give thanks unto thee, or
shall it declare thy truth?' followed and relieved forthwith by, 'Thou hast turned my heaviness into joy; thou
hast put off my sackcloth, and girded me with gladness.'
I will not follow the testimony through Ecclesiastes and
the Prophets. The remarkable picture of the final issue
of Divine government and retribution presented by the
Book of Daniel[1], near its close, seems to stand by itself.
Upon the whole there is a more limited but a nearly consistent witness to a general belief in survival; in Sheol,
or an Under-world shadowy and sad, with no developed
conception of immortality (in the strict sense now attaching
to the word) for the human soul; with no ascription of such
a gift to its nature, but with occasional glimpses of the
blessed condition of the righteous, and their vision of God
after death, to which no idea of further change is anywhere
appended.

Such is a rude but I hope nearly true picture of the evidence derivable from consent in relation to the future state,
as it stood in the middle period of the eighteenth century.

It was conformable to the general tone of Butler's
mind, and sustains our high conception of his judgement,
that on the one hand he should have mistrusted the abstract reasonings by which it had been attempted through
so many ages down to the time of Clarke, to enlarge the
idea of survival into that of true immortality, and to lift
it from the region of hope into that of formulated dogma;
that he should have found the evidence before him, large
and weighty as it was, yet wanting in the precision necessary for a creed; that he should have been content with
the modest presumptions he could draw first from indications attendant upon death, and then from the surer inferences supplied by the experience of moral government in
the world, and above all by the authoritative declarations
of the Christian Revelation.

[1] xii. 2, 3.

Since the time of Butler, there has been a great enlargement of our knowledge on the subject of the traditions of a future life, though nothing has emerged which
goes to alter the fundamental conditions of the problems
they present. This enlargement has been due to three
causes at least: The study of the sacred books of the ancient religions outside the Hebrew pale; the wonderful
revelations obtained by linguistic skill and archaeological
research, mainly in Egypt and Assyria; and the multiplication of the opportunities found by travellers for ascer-
taining the ideas which have prevailed among the outlying
and uncultivated fractions of the human race.

The result, as far as I can collect it, has been as follows : —

1. Greatly to enlarge the proofs of a belief in some existence for man beyond the grave, which may fairly be
called primitive and universal, even if it leave room for
a somewhat feeble doubt with respect to this belief among
a few of the waifs and strays of our race, and for a melancholy exception among a small fraction of educated and
civilized mankind.

2. The conception of the state of the dead in general
was wholly indeterminate as to particulars, but as a whole
was shrouded in melancholy and gloom.

3. The duration of the new existence in the unseen
world came little into view, except, as history evolved
itself, among those capable of speculation; and not only
is there hardly a trace of formulated immortality, but the
whole argument continues all along a matter of controversy among philosophers, and no scheme obtains, even in
the schools, either general concurrence or undisputed ascendency.

4. It was this question of duration which may have led
men to perplex and load their idea of the future life with
the doctrines of transmigration, pre-existence, and absorption. All of these tended to displace the twin corner-stones
of the true doctrine, namely, individuality and responsibility; without which the whole conception wofully abates,
perhaps entirely loses, its dignity and interest.

5. Some think that the idea of a future state exhibited

advance and development with the lapse of time. And those who educe religion out of an original fetishism are in a manner compelled to prop the theory with this sister belief. Apart from Christianity, the evidence of history appears to me to teach an opposite lesson, and to present a picture of religious decline in this order of ideas, with no clear or certain advance in philosophical clearness or consistency. This, as Grote says of the Greeks, was a belief apart from inquiry. Its existence in this form goes to strengthen the argument of those who, with Butler, refer it to a primitive Divine teaching, or revelation. The declarations (*a*) in the case of Enoch, (*b*) in the case of Elijah, (*c*) in the Book of Job, and (*d*) in the public worship of Israel through the Psalter, seem, even if taken alone, to supply a larger mass of evidence as to positive and popular belief than can be gathered from the testimonies available for the period which divided the Exile from the Advent.

6. The state of ideas subsisting among the Jews during, as well as before, the lifetime of our Lord gives no conclusive evidence of advance, and even supplies indications which may seem to tend, to a certain extent, in another direction. Suppose it granted that the Pharisees were the party dominant among educated Jews. Their general belief in a future state is placed beyond dispute by Acts xxiii. 6–8. But we cannot infer from the New Testament their having mastered the resurrection, or embraced the doctrine of a future judgement according to the prophecy of Dan. xii. Let us allow, however, the existence of a large amount of rabbinical belief and tradition. On the other hand, let us observe that in the parable of Dives, which opened to the Jews the idea of future retribution, the subject is not handled as if any such idea were thoroughly planted in the general belief, for the prayer of the suffering spirit is that one may be sent from the dead in order to reveal or enforce it, and the reply of Abraham is not that it is already familiar, but that it might, and ought to be, known from the ancient Scriptures[1]. This tends to limit the received opinion of the Jewish people to that vague and undefined expectation of survival to which we have such redundant testimony at

---

[1] Luke xvi. 27–31.

early dates. There is this also to be remarked: For the first time in Hebrew history, the Sadducees present to us an instance of formulated opinion adverse to survival. Sheltering themselves under a professed, or even real, regard to the Mosaic law, they hold their ground as a recognized or tolerated, sometimes even as a dominant, party; and appear to take common ground with the Pharisees, and to be admitted by them as coadjutors in attempts to oppose or baffle the teaching of our Blessed Lord.

As regards the learned among our Lord's contemporaries, I understand, upon the high authority of Dr. Ginsburg, that the prevailing view may be stated as follows. While the Sadducees denied all continuance of personal existence beyond the grave, the Essenes, who might perhaps be called Ultra-Pharisees, believed in the natural immortality of the soul. According to the Pharisees generally, a first judgement followed upon death, when the righteous entered into Paradise, and the wicked were condemned to an expiatory suffering, with the exception of certain classes, whose sentence had no limit of time. There is a second judgement which precedes resurrection for the righteous, and for the wicked destruction. All this appears to be in the nature of speculation rather than dogma, and the Talmud can be quoted on behalf either of endless punishment, or of universal restoration.

I have dwelt thus at length on the opinion of natural immortality, and on the absence of evidence in its favour as distinguished from simple survival, because the opinion itself seems to have played a most important part in the general evolution of the subject of a future state. It seems, moreover, to have largely contributed towards stirring and fomenting the controversies, which are now so rife, as to the condition of man in the world to come.

CHAPTER II

THE subject of belief in a future state during the pre-historic and early historic ages affords a spectacle of piteous interest. The race of Adam, after the lapse into sin, still yearn for the fulfilment of the hopes, once bright and healthful, now impaired and mangled ; yet shrink back in dread from a future which conscience clothes with terrors, and the prospect beyond the grave is enveloped in such gloom that we cling in preference to the brief but often sunny days of this earthly existence.

But the abstract idea of a future life is the mere skeleton of a great subject, which only becomes clothed in flesh and blood, when we introduce into it all the incidents which do or may belong to the condition of man. 'Unconditioned possibility' is the description which a powerful writer of our own day has given of the unseen world. The total and sudden rending asunder of the portions of our complex nature, now so closely knit into one another, is a transition such that a vast portion of those who have to undergo the change never seriously contemplate or mentally apprehend it. With them, when the vision is at last by compulsion fixed upon it, there is need, in order to face it, either of profound apathy, or of powerful stimulants, or of a great internal strength inherent or acquired. Nature inspires the love of life, cries out against being torn to pieces, and most rarely can be brought to accept the idea of pure extinction. The act of dying, which has to be performed by the least among men, is the greatest act in the entire experience of the greatest. The literature of classical antiquity nowhere makes such piercing calls upon our sympathy as when it laments a beloved object, or mournfully records the inevitable destiny of the race. It is not that the ancients greatly perplexed themselves with the ulterior problems of our state, or what we now call eschatology. It is that death is in itself horrible; and old age comes in for a share of horror, because it is death's next neighbour.

But when the greatest of all events in history launched the Gospel into the sphere of human life, a great change was gradually brought about. In the relative importance of the seen and the unseen, the existing and the coming world, an alteration was wrought which amounted to a revolution, and the mental compromise, which had abated speculation on the future, came spontaneously to an end. On the head and front of the new teaching was written the great doctrine of the Resurrection. Resurrection did not solely point to something about to happen in a future state; it meant also a present change, an union upon earth with the Life of Christ, which was to be perpetuated beyond the grave, and to be consummated by the final resumption of the body. For every redeemed soul a solution of the mystery of death was offered, on the instant powerful, and eventually complete. The aim of the new dispensation was that every soul should be redeemed; that as all had shared in the ruin through sin, so all should share in the redemption through the second Adam. And so, at the very first outset, it seemed to be. Through the first four chapters of the Acts, in the days of the three thousand and the five thousand [1], it appears as though not a single tare had been sown by the hand of the enemy among the wheat. In the New Testament generally, until a cloud of uncertainty envelops the episode of the Seven Churches, the Christian community at large is holy, and the disobedient form the rare exception. The indefeasible beatitude of believers is not only the happiest, but is also by far the largest, object presented to the view. What was in time to become the reverse of the picture was as yet only a speck almost infinitesimal in the spiritual landscape.

From the first, as might have been expected, the happiness without end of man redeemed in Christ, of the very beings such as we see from day to day walking before us, stood as an universal conviction of the Church, and found its place

---

[1] Acts ii. 41; iv. 4.

in all the summaries of her belief. Transmigration of the soul, its pre-existence, and its absorption, did not require to be confuted; for Christians these wild notions had melted away of themselves like mists before the sun. Within given lines of thought, Christianity from the first addressed the world in language which was positive and peremptory.

But so happy a state of things could not indefinitely continue. With the progressive extension of the Church, the proportion of branches that abode not in the Vine was continually raised. So early as at the date of the Apocalypse, there were churches tainted in belief, and other churches paralyzed by the lukewarmness which insults God by owning Him while it disobeys Him. Even while the Christian community had the period of persecution still lying in perspective before it, the world, the flesh, and the devil were actively extending their rule within its borders. During the lengthened period in which the Canon of the New Testament was assuming its form, the sacred books do not appear to have precipitated the mind of the Church into hasty attempts at solving the entire problem of the future state for the wicked in common with the righteous. We shall find that, outside the great revelation of fixed beatitude for holy souls, the question remained more or less an open one for several generations, indeed for some centuries. It would be hazardous to speak with confidence as to the causes which introduced restraint. In such a case as that of the great Trinitarian controversy, it is known that strictness of definition was resorted to as a weapon of defence (and it has proved to be most effectual) against the activity of erratic ideas. In the case of the immortality of the soul, there was no such morbid activity to provoke the general imposition of restraint, and no corresponding danger to guard against.

The conditions under which we approach the consideration of this great subject are widely different from those which were present to the view of the early Christians. For them the question long retained a great simplicity. The positive proof of a future life had indeed received authoritative and final confirmation from the mouth of our Lord. As we see from the writings of the Apostolic Fathers that the redeemed of Christ — that is to say, all Christians who would suffer Christ to redeem them — were thenceforward placed in security from all vicissitude by their vital union with Him. 'He that believeth in me, though he were dead, yet shall he live: and whosoever liveth, and believeth in me, shall never die [1].' He made no declaration whatever as to the origin or nature of the soul. The disquisitions of rabbis, the speculations of philosophers, were quietly set aside. They remained whatever they had been before, in their original impotence or power. Passing by them all as naught, He proclaimed the establishment of His own rule, and He desired that it should not be marvelled at, for did it mean more than the establishment of the rule of righteousness ? 'Marvel not at this : for the hour is coming, in the which all that are in the graves shall hear his voice, and shall come forth ; they that have done good, unto the resurrection of life ; and they that have done evil, unto the resurrection of damnation [2].' Large, in proportion to the small volume of His recorded instructions, was the eschatological teaching of our Lord, but it all went straight to the most central and the simplest truths, His mission to draw all men unto Him, and the beatitude of those consenting to be drawn, in being one with the Father and the Son [3]. For those who refuse, there remains a state of darkness, exclusion, weeping and gnashing of teeth, a scene of misery and affliction, on which the curtain of the Gospel drops. That curtain is never lifted : and all that is behind it would seem to be withheld from us, and reserved for the counsels of the Most High. And surely, if the stony heart of man can be moved, here is enough to move it. On the one hand rescue from all our evils and all our sins, restoration to a partnership with the Divine nature in the image of which we were originally framed, so that human destinies are in a manner linked to those not of the universe at large, but of the universe at its living crown and summit. For this glorious picture, there is of course a painful and shameful opposite ; a Sheol more gloomy than that ancient conception, which so largely sufficed to daunt the mind of man before the Advent. By the general declarations of the Gospel, there

---

[1] John xi. 25, 26.   [2] John v. 28, 29.   [3] John xvii. 21.

is opened to us for persistent sinners in the future state a
wilderness of woe. Yet we cannot say that the fate of the
lost is represented to us as an exact counterpart to that of
the righteous. Such it would have been had the final award
been one of pains and pleasures distributed as reward and
punishment are administered to school-boys, or even as in
a single figure of the Gospels future retribution is represented to us under the figure of stripes few and many[1]. But
this method or presentation would have thrown into the
background the essentially ethical character of Divine government, and especially of its capital exhibition in the
Christian scheme. For the essence of salvation consists
not in any external acquisition of reward, but in vital union
with God, such as that of a creature with his Creator can
be. There is no Ahrimanes in the scheme of our religion,
and no corresponding existence with which the unrighteous
are to be united as the righteous are united with the Deity.
Hence there arises in the eschatology of the New Testament
an almost uniform distinction in the mode of handling for
the two. They are not logical opposites like good and evil.
The consumption of the chaff with unquenchable fire is
not the logical opposite of being gathered into the garner.
Repulsion of the five foolish virgins into a void undescribed
is not the logical opposite of a place in the procession of
the bridegroom, however the one may be in contrast with
the other. The weeping and gnashing of teeth in the outer
darkness represents suffering which has its seat and source
within the person himself, and are not the logical opposite
to that feast, where the master of the house supplies his
chosen ones with food. Union with God is not only a state,
but is also a law, of existence. No corresponding law is
defined for us by the New Testament in relation to the lost.
Whether or how far the duration of their sufferings is described or touched, I do not at this moment inquire; but it
is not merely or mainly in measures of time that the blessedness of the children of God is meted out to them. 'As
thou, Father, art in me, and I in thee, that they also may
be one in us[2].' As they do not marry, so neither need they
take into their reckoning, or deal with, any of the incidents

[1] Luke xii. 47, 48.   [2] John xvii. 21.

of time. Wherever their union with God is named, their
charter is given them anew, and it is couched in other
terms.

'They which shall be accounted worthy to obtain that
world, and the resurrection from the dead, neither marry, nor
are given in marriage: neither can they die any more: for
they are equal unto the angels; and are the children of God,
being the children of the resurrection [1].' With death they
have and can have no more concern, for 'if a man keep my
saying, he shall never see death [2].' But, on the contrary, in
describing the condition of the wicked, death is a familiar
image: The wages of sin is death. The motions of sin bear
fruit unto death. There is a law of sin and death. Sin,
when finished, bringeth forth death [3]. And the only question
which remains is, whether the word death in these and like
passages retains its ordinary sense as the cessation of some
existence, or whether it is here modified to signify a prolongation of existence conditioned by misery. For, do what
we will with that word, we can hardly sever from it that idea
of finality which in one shape or another it is so apt to convey.

The instructions of the Apostles added no new doctrine to
the teaching of the Saviour in respect to death and retribution, to the inalienable beatitude of the just, to the absence
of anything resembling a repeal of the sentence pronounced
upon the wicked. The same, as has been already pointed
out, was the case with those early writers termed the Apostolic Fathers.

It is only with some care that we can realize the value of
this remarkable abstention from all license of speculation,
which indeed continued long after the Apostolic age and its
special inspiration. Even at a first glance it is easy to conceive what difficulties are likely to attend human attempts
to map out the other world, when we consider how imperfectly we succeed in our endeavours to master the conditions
of the world in which we live, ascertained for us though
they be by no small store of experience. First, we have
to deal with the origin and the essence of the soul, and
their relations to those of the body: a subject of itself

---

[1] Luke xx. 35, 36.   [2] John viii. 51.
[3] Rom. vi. 23 ; vii. 5 ; viii. 2 ; Jas. i. 15.

opening a wide field of varied controversies. Then, it is
not one but two future lives with which we have to deal;
the one which precedes the Day of Judgement, and the
other which follows it and reaches out into the infinite.
Then there is the difference of the conditions under which
the great account is to be met by the generation summoned
to it directly from the activities of life, and those other
generations who have passed through the natural dissolution
of the body and the experiences of the intermediate state.
Here the inquirer finds his path crossed by the grave consideration that many have passed into the unseen world
in infancy and childhood without having reached any such
development of the faculties as to attain responsibility, or,
in the·case of infants, even consciousness. On the borders
of this region, lie two others yet more vast: What is the
condition of those who lived and died before the coming
of Christ, and again, of such as dwell beyond the Christian
pale and never hear 'the word of this salvation'? How
are we to encounter the doubts which suggested to the
early Christian mind a division between the *peccatores* who
failed to a greater or less extent in their endeavours after
the true fulfilment of the great Christian law, and the
impii who have not so much as dreamed of endeavouring
to fulfil it, but accomplish the whole work of their earthly
careers in stolid neglect or in audacious defiance? How
are to be adjusted the million-shaded gradations of penalty
and reward, when the books are opened and the dead are
judged according to their works; when the All-seeing Eye
shall take its measure without fail of every act (and words
and thoughts are also acts) done in the body by every
individual human being? What is the place which birth-
sin, the death brought by Adam into the world, will occupy
in fixing the conditions of the dread account? Or again.
The Christian was not redeemed in loneliness: he had been
baptized into a community, and membership in that community established a relation which, under the circumstances
of the early Christian Church, went down to the very roots
of his being, and appeared sometimes to obtain such a command, that the soul, when thoroughly vitalized by Divine
grace, wore such an aspect as if it had experienced an

absorption of all personal cares in the depth and intensity
of its spiritual sympathies? As when St. Paul wrote those
wonderful words: 'I could wish that myself were accursed
from Christ for my brethren, my kinsmen according to the
flesh [1].' In these subjects, and in others such as these, was
opened a field for inquiry and for dispute which might almost
be called infinite. Many portions of it I shall not venture
to touch. But the flights of thought were wider still when
two hundred years after the time of our Lord we find ourselves face to face with the controversies of Origenism.

There was then a wise abstention from feverish inquiries
which could only tend to the premature and inordinate
pursuit of dogma, or the exaltation of mere opinion to
a plane on which it acquires an imposing though false
semblance of authority. A variety of influences favoured
this abstention. First, the early Christian writers were not
generally of a stamp addicted to mere theory, but were
eminently practical. Reality and fervour were then the
rule of Christian life and not as now the exception. The
happy consequence of such a state of things was that in
the contemplation of the coming world, the main object
presented to the view was that blessed and happy one
which had already received from our Lord such fullness
of description as was found amply to satisfy the general
mind, and to throw the sadder portion of the question into
the shade. And further, we must take into view the wide
prevalence among the early Christians of a belief in the
early return of the Saviour to the world for a victorious
reign there, over and with His people, for the term of a
thousand years. It seems evident that, as under the Mosaic
system the prominent place given to temporal inducements
and penalties tended to cast a shade over the entire question
of a future life, so the millennial anticipations of a public
and general triumph of the Lord in person upon earth,
together with His Church, must have operated powerfully
in neutralizing the solicitude of Christians for very large
solutions of the questions associated with eschatology, and
may have caused something approaching to the absorption
of any ideas concerning the particulars of individual destinies

[1] Rom. ix. 3.

in the majestic and imposing imagery of the general expectation thus offered to the spiritual eye. For here it should
be observed that the millenarian or chiliastic expectations
were calculated to exercise a peculiar force of attraction.
The grand anticipation of St. Paul in connexion with the
coming life was 'to be with Christ'; and this was the central
and cardinal idea of chiliasm. Again, it met the weakness
of human nature halfway in abating the magnitude of
changes entailed by death; for many would be altogether
spared; the Christian would still be in his own home, and
if that home was to present an altered, it was also to be a
happier and a nobler aspect. Further, this state adjourned
the sense of that awfulness which it is hard wholly to sever
from the great account; for it preceded the Day of Judgement. Along with that great day, the chiliastic expectation
adjourned what was to follow it; and, by interposing this
subject of adequate and indeed absorbing interest between
the present life and the ultimate determination of the fate
of souls, a powerful means was provided for slackening the
curiosity of the human mind with respect to that ultimate
question. Origen, as we might naturally expect, is found
among the opponents of chiliasm. Upon the whole, and as
regards the early Church at large, I submit that its mental
condition with regard to eschatology was a very happy condition; and distinguished mainly by the union of these three
special notes : a pure faith, a modest self-restraint, and a
large range of freedom for modest and self-restrained opinion.

These ideas were in close conformity with all the best
of our natural conceptions. Through the deviation of man
from his original righteousness, there had been a frightful
rent established in the web of this earthly dispensation.
The teaching of our Lord, and the purpose of His incarnation, both in His person, and in His Church which has been
described as its prolongation [1], aimed at the reparation of
this rent by re-establishing the reign of righteousness ; and
this reign of righteousness was at once fully, clearly, and
simply expressed in the primitive eschatology, which set
aside all the flights of metaphysical abstraction, and simply
assigned to goodness its reward and to wickedness its less

---

[1] *Fortsetzung der Fleischwerdung.* I think the expression is Möhler's.

defined but alarming retribution : with an adequate insistency and precision as to the first, and with a becoming awe, and some consequent reserve, as to all the particulars of the latter.

This description will best apply to the period which extends from the apostolic age down to the time of Origen. With regard to this period, the English-speaking student does not, indeed, receive all the help he might desire (so far as I know) from writers of his own tongue. Dr. Salmond's *Christian Doctrine of Immortality* [1] is an able, truth-loving, and, from many points of view, comprehensive work ; but it does not supply any history of the course and variation of Christian opinion during the centuries since the Advent. The still fuller work of Mr. Alger, which in 1878 had gone through ten editions in the United States, is open to graver exception in this respect, that it propounds a single patristic scheme of eschatology [2], as representing the teachings of the Church from the first to the tenth century ; whereas it is generally recognized, and appears indisputable, that material changes in the tone of principal writers took place during that lengthened period. The ' punishment of the wicked by both physical and spiritual torture ' without any respite, without any end [3], was during the earlier generations denied by many, but was, says Mr. Alger, from the first the orthodox doctrine of the patristic Church. The common representations are different, and, I believe, nearer the truth. According to F. Nitzsch, the immortality of the soul was the subject of free and open discussion among the early Fathers. In Justin Martyr [4] we find it denied; and though the denial be put into the mouth of Trypho, yet Trypho was his instructor, and it is inconceivable that this could have been done if Justin himself had believed that question to be closed in a contrary sense by Divine Revelation. Tatian says in express terms, the soul of man itself is not immortal but mortal ; and Theophilus of Antioch, that Adam was neither mortal nor immortal, but (δεκτικὸς ἀμφοτέρων) capable of either. And, according to Irenaeus, the soul in its own

---

[1] Edinburgh, Clark, 1895.
[2] Alger, *Doctrine of a Future Life*, pp. 395–398.   [3] *Ibid.* p. 402.
[4] See Kaye on Justin Martyr, pp. 99 *seqq.*

nature is not life, but receives its life from God, on whom therefore its continuance depends. It is in itself subject to the law of death, but will owe persistency of life, as a Divine gift, to God its Author. At a later date Lactantius even says that the distinction between the righteous and the wicked would be cancelled if all were immortal [1]: 'Ergo immortalitas non sequela naturae, sed merces praemiumque virtutis est.' On the other hand, Tertullian teaches that the soul is indivisible and imperishable, and has an activity which is not suspended even during sleep. Dodwell, in his work on the Soul, claims Ruffinus, Arnobius, and Athenagoras as supporters of the doctrine of mortality [2]. Clarke's denials of these are bold, but by no means in all cases absolute or satisfactory [3]. Petavel-Olliffe, in his elaborate work [4] on behalf of Conditional Immortality, boldly includes in his claim Barnabas, Clement of Rome, Ignatius, Hermas, Polycarp, and Clement of Alexandria. Flügge, in dealing with the period before Origen, points out that there was as yet no dogma of the Church upon the subject; some affirmed punishments to be eternal [5], others regarded the souls of the wicked as destined to annihilation; in general writers did not go beyond the declarations of the New Testament, nor venture to lift the curtain which hangs over all that follows the Day of Judgement, considering that there is then opened a fresh period in the history of the lost which it is beyond the prerogative of mortal man to examine [6].

Gibbon [7] mentions the menace of eternal tortures, as a great instrument for conversion to the Christian Church; but he does not go into detail, and without doubt employs the epithet in its current sense as implying a period to which no definite limit was assigned.

---

[1] F. Nitzsch, *Grundriss der christlicher Dogmageschichte* (Berlin, 1870), Theil i. pp. 352, 353; quoting respectively Just. *Dial.* c. 4; Tatian, *c. Graec.* 13; Theophilus, *ad Autol.* ii. 27; Iren. ii. 34. 4; Lactantius, *Inst. Div.* vii. 5. See, however, Harvey's *Irenaeus,* ii. 358. And on Lactantius, Gfrörer, *Jahrhundert des Heils,* i. 82.

[2] *The Soul a Principle naturally Mortal,* pp. 55, 67, 76, 79.

[3] *Letter to Mr. Dodwell,* pp. 24-47.

[4] *Problème de l'Immortalité* (Paris, 1842), vol. ii. p. 286.

[5] But the word αἰώνιος cannot safely be assumed to have corresponded with the modern sense of our word eternal. See *inf.*

[6] Flügge, *Geschichte des Glaubens an Unsterblichkeit* (Leipzig, 1799), Theil iii. Abs. i. p. 237.

[7] Chap. xv.

Enough, I think, has now been said to sustain my general proposition that this period was one of faith, of freedom, and of personal moderation and reserve, although I have not yet referred to what is the clearest and most indisputable evidence in its support, namely, the language of the Creeds. That language seems to show that the general characteristics, which I have assigned to the writers before the time of Origen, extended beyond that period, so far as the authoritative standards of the Church at large are concerned.

The secret of this mental freedom, the condition which made it possible, was the absence from the scene of any doctrine of a natural immortality inherent in the soul. Absent, it may be termed, for all practical purposes, until the third century; for, though it was taught by Tertullian in connexion with the Platonic ideas, it was not given forth as belonging to the doctrine of Christ or His Apostles. It was held, too, by Tertullian in alliance with the contention that the soul was material in its nature, an idea very unlikely to recommend it to the Christian mind. And the association of Tertullian with Montanism could hardly be otherwise than detrimental to his influence, as indeed it seems to have left him, through the long course of ages, afloat, so to speak, between the opposite characters of patristic honours and the brand of heresy. It seems to me as if it were from the time of Origen that we are to regard the idea of natural, as opposed to that of Christian, immortality as beginning to gain a firm foothold in the Christian Church.

And now, indeed, in connexion with that great name, it may be thought that we are no longer entitled to speak of moderation and reserve as characteristics of the prevailing tone of Christian thought. The opinion, for which he is now most generally known to have been finally condemned, is that which is called Restorationism or Universalism; an opinion which harmonizes with, and perhaps presupposes, the natural immortality of the soul. But the idea of restoration was only one amidst a crowd of his notions, all of which had the natural immortality of the soul for their common ground.

In the range of his reading, which largely exceeded that of any among his predecessors, Origen became well acquainted with the arguments of Gentile philosophy, and probably with every extant branch of learning. He was a great Apologist of Christianity, and it is supposed that he did not consciously alienate himself from the substance of its traditionary teaching. Yet he himself suspected that his eschatology was one dangerous for the multitude, and it is even suggested that he cherished the notion of having an exoteric theology for the mass of believers, and an esoteric system for the student. A curious passage is cited by Lupus from St. Jerome: 'Ipse Origenes, in epistola quam scribit ad Fabianum, Romanae Ecclesiae Episcopum, paenitentiam agit, cur talia scripserit, et causam temeritatis in Ambrosium refert, quod secreto edita in publicum protulerit [1].' It was indeed the opening of a flood-gate. I think that the importance of the men who took opposite sides in the long period of Origenistic controversy lends great support to my statement I have ventured to propound, that outside the strictly essential there had been a large freedom allowed to eschatological opinion in the early Church. On the other hand, speaking as a remote and ignorant observer, I am struck with astonishment on finding that this great man, so deeply immersed in practical controversy, should have found mental leisure for these far-travelling speculations. They seem, as to many of their subjects, like balloon voyages undertaken into vacant space by one who found the atmospheric ranges contiguous to the earth insufficient for his expatiating energies. Flügge views him [2] as governed by a conviction that he could build out of philosophy, especially out of Platonism, buttresses for the Christian faith and proofs of its solidity; a view in marked contrast with that chosen by the most circumspect minds, and by Butler, a prince among them.

The sceptical temper may frame questions as it will: death sternly refuses to give it any satisfaction. The present is now louder than ever in its imperious demands; but injured nature takes upon her to reply, that the present is the life of animals, and the future is the life of man. The love of money may heap around us mountains of gold; all

---

[1] Lupus, p. 706 ; Jerom. *Epist.* lxv. c. 4.
[2] Flügge's *Geschichte*, Theil iii. Abs. v. (iv. 171).

this is but to lower the ratio of that which a man is to that which he possesses. The fever of self-indulgence may multiply our enjoyments : but each new enjoyment is, for the common run of men, a new want, and each new want is a link in the chain of moral debilitation, a new deduction from our high prerogative of freedom. Schemes of negation may each for a while fret and fume upon the stage of human affairs. It is Death, the great auditor of accounts, that reduces them, one and all, to their natural and small dimensions. In the development of luxury, we are immeasurably ahead of the ancient Greek, and we might have been proportionably more successful in shutting off the questionings of the soul respecting that which is to come, had not a new voice sounded forth in the world to proclaim the word Resurrection : since which it has become impossible, by any process within our resources, to stifle the longings of the human spirit to obtain some command over the instruments for measuring the future which expands before it.

I suppose it to be an acknowledged fact that for the Apostles, and for the first following teachers of Christianity, the doctrine of the resurrection lay at the very threshold of the Gospel. It was a salient proof of matchless force for the new scheme that, whereas the great enemy to be destroyed, according to the ancient promise, was Death, Death was at once and visibly destroyed by the resurrection. Moreover, it was the road toward the solution of that cloud of mysterious problems, which lay spread all round the idea of our own future life. It might have been imagined, then, that as the resurrection was the first word of the Gospel, the handling of these mysteries would be the next. But no. The teaching which at once travelled so far into the darkness before us as the resurrection, forthwith travelled back from it. It came back, in due order, from the resurrection which lay on the farther side of the grave, to the resurrection which lies on the hither side. Under the Christian system, destinies depend upon character ; and it is the character to be formed here and at once, which will shape the destinies that are to be undergone hereafter. It might almost be said without levity that the early Christians set about the work of character, and left destiny to take care of itself. With them, the weight of interest attached to that formation of character immensely exceeded for practical purposes the interest of investigation into the particulars of the future existence, and the Church for some time gave an absorbing attention to the one central duty which lay nearest hand.

Even those, who view with least favour the unbounded speculations of Origen, must regret that, if his works were to be condemned by binding authority, they should not have been brought to judgement until three centuries after his death (from about A. D. 254 to 553). He was a lover of truth; and, if they had been tried in his lifetime, he might in deference to such authority have reconsidered his positions, and have found means of greatly narrowing the interval which separated him from the general mind of the Church. While the question may suggest itself whether his opinions might and ought to have been dealt with sooner, it should be remembered, on the other hand, that during these three hundred years, beginning with the time of Paul of Samosata, the Church had gone through the most perilous and agitated period of its whole existence, and had dealt with and settled once for all the controversies, larger and more vital even than those of eschatology, which concerned the nature of the Object of our worship. The last echoes of those transcendent controversies only died away contemporaneously with the condemnation of Origenism, and in association with the name of the Roman Pope Vigilius. But the point which I desire to press is this. The immortality of the soul had heretofore been a question open and little agitated. The complex group of opinions termed Origenistic had been organically founded on it. The opinions were condemned. Of the immortality of the soul there was neither condemnation nor approval. But as in this way notoriety was given to it without censure, the practical effect may have been largely to accredit it, and this may have operated, in conjunction with other causes, to promote that silent extension of the opinion which became more obvious, perhaps more powerful, from the time of St. Augustine.

It would be out of place were I to present these summaries of Origenistic tenets or hypotheses, which may easily be found on reference [1]. They are set out with authority in the Canons of the Fifth Council from i to ix, in the last of which he is named [2] and anathematized. It is enough to say that, besides speculations of a peculiar kind on the nature and redeeming office of our Lord, they included the pre-existence of the soul, and the universal restitution to righteousness and felicity of all mankind; a proposition which, with inflexible and fearless logic, he carried to its farthest bounds. and included in it Satan and the fallen angels. He was condemned during his lifetime by an Alexandrian synod, and the condemnation was echoed from Rome, but the grounds of it are not known with clear certainty. His defenders, however, were strong in number, character, and influence, so that there were periods when the Church exhibited a divided mind. His vast learning and ability, as well as his elevated reputation for sanctity, may have greatly contributed to the amount and vivacity of the support which he received. For some time after the Council of Chalcedon. there was a lull, but a recrudescence followed, and Origenism became apparently the occasion, as well as one of the main subjects, of the General Council held at Constantinople in A. D. 553.

Even down to and after the time of Gregory the Great. Flügge finds no approach made towards the formation of a Christian dogma of eschatology. There was a disposition to dwell on the immateriality of the soul, but it was (he thinks) still regarded as in its own nature perishable, and as deriving immortality only from the knowledge of God [3]. But yet he considers, and it seems indisputable, that the materials for the opinion that the soul is by nature immortal, whether we call it dogma or hypothesis, were for a long period in course of steady accumulation; though this was not so from the first. After some generations, however, the mental temper and disposition of Christians inclined more

---

[1] For example, in Messrs. Murray's great *Dictionary of Christian Biography*, iv. 150, 154. The article on Origen amounts to a highly developed treatise.

[2] Lupus, *Canones et Decreta*. pp. 671 *seqq.*, 693.

[3] Flügge, *Geschichte*, Theil iii. Abs. v. (iv. 234-236).

and more to its reception. Without these assumptions it would be impossible to account for the wholesale change which has taken place in the mind of Christendom with regard to the subject of natural immortality. It would be difficult, I think, to name any other subject connected with religious belief (though not properly belonging to it) on which we can point to so sweeping and absolute a revolution of opinion: from the period before Origen, when the idea of an immortality properly natural was unknown or nearly hidden, to the centuries of the later Middle Ages and of the modern time, when, at least in the West, it had become practically undisputed and universal. Let us endeavour to obtain so much of light as we may upon the causes which were auxiliary to this extraordinary change.

I have ventured on referring to Origenism, and *nominatim* to its condemnation, as one among them, on the ground that it brought the general mind into familiarity with the idea, previously alien or remote. In the wake of Origen came Platonism, of which he was a zealous champion. At the period when Dante sang, Aristotle had long held that unquestioned sway which is commemorated in the line —

Vidi il Maestro di color che sanno.[1]

But Plato had been supreme in Alexandria; and Alexandria was the parent of Christian philosophism in the persons of Clement and of Origen. He had also a high place in the mind of St. Augustine, and he probably did much more among Christians than he had ever achieved among pagans, in establishing as a natural endowment that immortality of the soul which was already ineradicably fixed as fact for Christian souls (although upon a ground altogether different in the mind of the Church), so far as it touched the destination of the righteous. In all these ages, Christianity was in the West a rapidly growing religion; the extension of the Christian Revelation gave a powerful impetus to what I may term the spirit of affirmation; and with the spirit of affirmation, the arguments and the temper of Platonism intimately coincided. The system of Aristotle, on the other hand, was distinctly negative in the matter of

[1] Dante, *Inf.* iv. 131.

what is now called the Beyond; but the view of immortality congenial to Platonism had, before this rival system became prevalent, so hardened in the Christian mind, that it took no damage from the change brought about in philosophy at large.

By an unwarranted assumption, we are too much wont to antedate the transition of the mass of the population of the Empire from heathenism to Christianity. There is, of course, an utter dearth of sound statistical information on the subject. It is probable that Constantine, when he took the side of Christianity, saw that the balance of the aggregate mental and moral forces had altered in the same direction; but the question of mere numbers is one altogether different. Even in Constantinople, a century after it had been founded 'under the inspiration of anti-pagan ideas,' Beugnot shows that only one-fourth of the population were Christians [1]. The Christian policy of the great emperor was rather an anticipation of the coming time, than an acknowledgement of results already achieved. The world was not yet reconciled to the Church. But that reconciliation was on its way; it travelled fast; and, as it advanced, the powers proper to the world acquired a growing influence within her borders. The proportion of her thoughtless and godless members to those of serious mind continually and rapidly grew. From the reign of Constantine onwards, says Beugnot, we note the disappearance of those simple and frugal manners which for three centuries had been the mark and the glory of the Church [2]. So the warfare of the genuine Christian preacher with large numbers of his hearers waxed hotter and hotter. The question of their destiny in the world to come, which had been but infinitesimal in the first apostolic days, now came to assume grave, and even vast, proportions. And here it was that the new doctrine, as I shall call it, of natural immortality played so material a part. The sinner had to be persuaded. He had also to be threatened; and threatened with what? If the preacher only menaced him with the retribution which was to follow the Day of Judgement, the force of the instrument he em-

[1] Beugnot, *Destruction du Paganisme en Occident*, ii. 195.
[2] *Ibid.* i. 87.

ployed materially depended on what he could say as to the
duration of that penal term, a subject which, in the earliest
teachings of the Church, it had been found unnecessary
minutely to explore. But this war was carried on from the
pulpit at a great advantage; for the age was an affirming
and believing, not a questioning or denying age. At such
a period, the more long-drawn the vista of the impending
punishment, the more effective the menaces with which the
preacher might reckon upon beating down the resistance
of the carnal mind. In an age which has reversed the
tendencies of thought, the doctrine of natural immortality
may have become, for many or some, an impediment or an
incumbrance. But, in what we term the ages of faith, ideas
of a natural immortality, even if rudely and indefinitely
conceived, enhanced the power of the leverage at the
command of the Christian preacher. It seems also indisputable that it enhanced therewith the influence of the
priesthood as a caste. The sharper the edge which could
be given to the configuration (so to speak) of the opinion,
the greater was that enhancement: and the larger was the
increment imparted to a force, which in its first inception
was evidently one calculated for use in the cause of righteousness, although in its ulterior developments, and in its
association with another evolution of ideas concerning the
intermediate state and the power of the Church to act upon
it, the moral action of the tenet may have come to be of
a mixed and questionable character. If, then, the idea of
natural immortality was one thus variously adapted for
promoting, under the circumstances of the time, both the
higher and the more earthy part of the purposes of the
Church, we cannot doubt that this doctrinal interest would
have a large and efficacious operation in promoting the
recognition, acceptance, and habitual popular enforcement,
of that idea.

It seems, however, to be generally felt that the determining epoch in the history of seminal Christian thought upon
this subject was the life of St. Augustine, together with that
period, following closely upon it, when the Western Church
became rapidly imbued with his theology in almost its
entire compass.

It would be difficult, I believe, to frame from the writings of this great teacher — the most powerful, the most evangelical, and also the most comprehensive who has adorned the early annals of the Western Church — an entirely self-consistent system of eschatological opinion. Some questions, such as whether suffering in the future will be physical as well as spiritual, he was content expressly to leave open. It has been shown, by the language already quoted from the *Retractationes*, how he felt the difficulties of the entire theme. The views, which he expressed in connexion with primitive man and with the Fall, seem to be at variance with the endeavours, doubtless due to his acceptance of the Platonic philosophy, which he made to found the immortality of the soul upon abstract and metaphysical considerations. Probably these arguments supplied the basis of his own conviction. His strong conception, however, of the Divine decree, of birth-sin, and (in his later days) of the utter impotence of the will to act rightly, may all have tended to give, in his mind, more and more of fixity and permanence to the conditions of human existence. These views did not pass without some mitigation into the general teaching of the Latin Church. But the conclusion as to the soul's duration by mere nature met with general acceptance, and suffered no abatement in its terms. Not only was there no abatement, but there may even be some reason for saying that in this matter Augustinianism went beyond Augustine. His variations, his queries, his tenderness to opinions of a shade other than his own, were apparently forgotten or dropped out of notice. From this time forward, we cease to look for the appearance of men who, like Gregory of Nyssa in the fourth century, recalled the memory of Origen with regard to the escape in the future of lost spirits from their condemnation[1]. For Augustine, as it was held, in the prevailing tenor of his works, strongly supported the never-ceasing duration of their punishment. This is not surprising; but it may appear singular that he should have recognized such a parallelism between this opinion and the perpetuity of everlasting happiness, as to suggest that the doctrine touching the redeemed would be endangered, unless

---

[1] F. Nitzsch, *Dogmageschichte*, i. p. 404.

the other were propounded as its counterpart. The eternal punishment of the wicked in general for the sins of a life not finite only, but brief, is thought by some to present an aspect of great severity. When this proposition carried with it the notions of inability to escape from sinfulness, and of adverse Divine decrees, and when, further, damnation for original sin was extended to infants, and the heathen were excluded wholesale from salvation, we have before us in very truth an *horribile decretum*, and it may well be said that a theology so fashioned did impose burdens heavy for the human mind to bear. We are now perhaps suffering, in part, from the reaction, which such a scheme might be calculated in the course of time to bring about.

It will not be required to say much more upon the historical growth of this opinion. Flügge regards the ideas of immateriality and immortality of the soul as accepted by St. John of Damascus; but considers that, all along, the Latin Church led the way in this development [1]. The history of the formation of the ecclesiastical dogma (of eschatology), he says, closes with the Schoolmen [2]. To their manipulation of the subject, there is no corresponding process among the divines of the Oriental Church, who remained content with the older methods of presentation. It may have been a sign of this distinction between Western and Eastern doctrine that so late as in the *Decretum pro Graecis* (the words accepted by the Council of Florence as a form of union in 1439), it is declared that those who have died ' in actuali mortali peccato, vel solo originali' pass into punishments of various degrees; but nothing is said, even at so late an epoch, of the duration of those punishments.

We are to regard Peter Lombard, it appears, as the person who gathered together the *disjecta membra ;* and even from him the words are quoted, 'omnibus questionibus quae de hac re moveri solent, satisfacere non valeo [3].' With the Schoolmen the philosophy of Aristotle was established in full authority ; but Peter Lombard found the natural immortality of the soul, in possession of the field of thought,

---

[1] Flügge, *Geschichte*, Theil iii. Abschn. viii. Abth. ii. (iv. 69).
[2] *Ibid.* Abschn. vii. Abth. ii. (iv. 51).
[3] *Ibid.* (iv. 69).

and, perhaps, accepted it simply as part of the common heritage, without minute investigation of the source from which it was derived. Flügge quotes him as content to set out from the resurrection, which he proves by the authority of Scripture. It was his business to give regularity and method to the dispersed utterances of former writers; and this he appears to have done with a certain moderation. Yet, following St. Augustine and Gregory the Great, he described the satisfaction with which the sufferings of the wicked will supply the elect: 'laetitia satiabuntur, agentes gratias de sua liberatione, visâ impiorum ineffabili calamitate [1].' Their utility, therefore, lies in quickening the thankfulness of the blessed for their own relief, though the question remains whether so sad a stimulant can, under the circumstances, be required, as should be gratuitously presumed.

One historical point only remains.

At length, in the year 1513, we have a Bull of Pope Leo X, which purports to be issued with the assent of a Lateran Council. This, however, has been questioned. In the Bull we have the following words : 'Damnamus et reprobamus omnes asserentes animam intellectivam mortalem esse, aut unicam in cunctis hominibus [2].'

I do not know how far this Bull is within the prescriptions of the Council of 1870; but, whether it binds the Latin communion or not, it is of interest as an historical document, and as one which stands in isolation.

But although it was the work of the Schoolmen to supply the Western Church with its formal eschatology, it seems to be generally agreed that the motive force of paramount efficacy in this direction was drawn from the works of St. Augustine. And so we find ourselves brought down in substance to the modern ideas. I mean, however, by this phrase the ideas which prevailed from the Reformation onwards, and reserve for a later stage whatever in the way of shock or change is to be ascribed to the sceptical or negative movement of the present day. So the spectacle which we have before us is in brief outline this : The reserve of

---

[1] Flügge, *Geschichte*, Theil iii. Abschn. vii. Abth. ii. (iv. 69-79).
[2] From the Bullarium of Sixtus V (Romae, 1586), p. 171.

the early Church has been abandoned. Even the recollection of it has faded from the popular mind. Of the immeasurable field of discussion opened by the future life, not indeed the whole, but a considerable part, had been virtually closed against free discussion, not by ecclesiastical authority in its most formal sense, but yet by the general drift of the mind of Christendom, long before the judgement of Leo X was promulgated. An important section of popular beliefs, relating to the intermediate state, had been largely widened. The Western tone had prevailed over the Eastern; and the East had hardly refreshed its theology by reproductions since the time of John of Damascus. With the departure of the ancient reserve there had come a great practical limitation of the liberty of thought possessed by the individual Christian. The doctrine of natural, as distinguished from Christian, immortality had not been subjected to the severer tests of wide publicity and resolute controversy, but had crept into the Church, by a back door as it were; by a silent though effective process; and was in course of obtaining a title by tacit prescription.

The evidence of the change may perhaps be most properly supplemented by the observation of the noteworthy fact that, when arguments are offered for the purely natural immortality of the soul, they are rarely, if ever, derived from Scripture [1]. For it will be borne in mind that, logically viewed, resurrection is one thing, and immortality another. The duration of the sufferings of the wicked was universally assumed to be co-extensive in time with the beatitude of the righteous. But there remained one distinction on which we may have to dwell at a later stage. The human mind had become familiar with the name of eternity, but had dived little into the idea itself. There had not yet been, in conjunction with the acceptance and enforcement of the phrase, any corresponding attempt, by arithmetical calculation or otherwise, to give it with any fullness the character which it bears in recent thought.

It remains to consider with some detail the effect of these great changes, and especially of the substitution in our eschatology, on a larger scale, of widened assertion for reserve.

---

[1] Flügge, *Geschichte*, Theil iii. Abschn. i.

It must not be supposed from what has been said, that
I seek to commit any reader to a sweeping renunciation of
all that has been done since apostolic days in the way of
amplifying statements of Christian doctrine. Such amplification may in many cases have been a natural accompaniment,
or an essential condition, of giving it so much of form as is
necessary for a permanent system of instruction. On the
attributes of the Divine Paternity, on the Divinity of our
Lord, on the personality of the Holy Spirit, the Christian
Church has amplified the express teachings of Holy Scriptures by bringing them into contact, and adjusting them one
to another. The original character of these teachings was
that they were occasional; and it could not but be that, in
order to be suited for linking each successive generation to
those which have preceded it, it should undergo some expansion. Let me not then be interpreted as saying that
because the original teaching as to a future state has been
enlarged, therefore, and on the simple ground of that fact, it
should again be curtailed. We must not disallow in principle
the introduction of method : and it would be most hazardous
to deny without limitation that there are legitimate forces
of development inseparable even from Divine Revelation
when embodied in human institutions, as they prolong their
experience.

So that the person, who recommends restraint in any particular development or amplification, inasmuch as he does not
condemn them universally, may justly be called upon to show
cause for taking a distinction between one which he mistrusts
and another which he accepts. And I admit myself not to
be aware of any criterion, in its nature general and absolute,
by which to separate the genuine from the spurious. It
is true that by their fruits we shall know them. And in
matters such as this we must endeavour to deal with each
case according to its circumstances and merits. I shall, however, refer to two particulars which, if they do not carry us
to a full and summary solution of the problem, yet enable
us to travel some way towards it.

In the first place, it may be well to examine, whether the
amplification of doctrine, to which exception has been taken,
is sustained by the full weight of legitimate authority so as

to be certainly expressive of the mind of the Church of Christ at large. This, to cite an example, is eminently the case with the expositions offered by the Creeds touching the Holy Trinity. In the highest degree they had to sustain the ordeal of discussion; they were submitted to every variety of manipulation; the Church was roused and compelled, so to speak, to a full consciousness of its own action even by the fluctuations which marked it. Its final judgement was deliberate and formal in the highest degree; and the question has been a settled one from that day to this. Very different is the history of the prevailing opinion concerning the future state. The natural immortality of the soul did not become the subject of free and general discussion in the Church. It crept onwards in the dark. I think Dr. Pusey has stated (in his work on Future Punishment) that the denial of natural immortality was condemned by the Fifth General Council; but this seems to be a statement made in error. It appears indisputable that the tenet never was affirmed by the Councils, never by the undivided Church, never by either East or West when separated, until, towards the death of the Middle Age, the denial was anathematized under Leo X on behalf of the Latin Church. Another important distinction is this. In cases like the doctrine of original sin some great mind has been given at the proper time to the Church to meet its needs by a full exposition of the doctrine from the root upwards, such as experience might thereafter show to have been a just interpretation of the true Christian sense upon the subject. But no such work, as St. Augustine performed in the Pelagian controversy, was performed by him, or by any subsequent or preceding writer, with regard to the condition of man in the future state. Nor has there ever been known, with regard to any of the articles defined in the creed, a state of opinion so disorganized as we see now largely prevailing with regard to the subject before us.

Another consideration of the highest importance is that the natural immortality of the soul is a doctrine wholly unknown to the Holy Scriptures, and standing on no higher plane than that of an ingeniously sustained, but gravely and formidably contested, philosophical opinion. And surely there is nothing, as to which we ought to be more on our guard, than the entrance into the precinct of Christian doctrine, either without authority or by an abuse of authority, of philosophical speculations disguised as truths of Divine Revelation. They bring with them a grave restraint on mental liberty; but what is worse is, that their basis is a pretension essentially false, and productive by rational retribution of other falsehoods.

Under these two heads, we may perhaps find that we have ample warrant for declining to accept the tenet of natural immortality as a truth of Divine Revelation.

CHAPTER III

ALTHOUGH Butler supplies important and fruitful suggestions on the condition of man in the future life, which I shall endeavour in some degree to unfold, the observations contained in these papers range over a tract reaching beyond the field he opens. It may be fairly asked of me, Why enter upon a discussion so wide and difficult? My answer shall be explicit. It is not for the satisfaction of speculative curiosity. It is because a portion of Divine truth, which even if secondary is so needful, appears to be silently passing out of view, and because the danger of losing it ought at all costs to be averted; and in the hope that even the feeblest effort in a right direction will not be wholly frustrate, but may, at least in some few minds, operate as a warning.

There is surely a side of the Divine teaching set forth in the Scriptures, which shows that the Christian dispensation, when it fails in its grand purpose of operating as a savour of life unto life, will be a savour of death unto death; and this under no new or arbitrary rule, but under the law, wide as the universe, that guilt deepens according to the knowledge with which it is incurred, and to the opportunities which it despises or neglects. Therefore, the great Apostle of the grace of God sets before us this side of his teaching: 'Knowing the terrors of the Lord, we persuade men.' Menace as well as promise, menace for those whom promise could not melt or move, formed an essential part of the provision for working out the redemption of the world. And I ask myself the question, what place, in the ordinary range of Christian teaching, is now found for 'the terrors of the Lord'? This instrument of persuasion, which St. Paul thought it needful to use with the Church in the stage of its first infancy, and in an environment of

weakness, is it used as boldly now when she is armed with
eighteen centuries of experience, and when social and public power are still largely arrayed on her behalf? If not,
there is danger lest judgement, in a matter of great moment,
should go against her by default. Now the Newtonian law,
that action and reaction are equal, and in opposite directions,
has its application also in the world of thought; and so often
as we truly observe in that world abnormal excess or defect,
it is salutary to inquire whether the excess is in any degree
due to previous deficiencies, or the defect to previous excesses. It is in this spirit that I submit the present observations to review, and, if need be, to correction. If the
'terrors of the Lord' had an indispensable place in the
Apostolic system, it can hardly be that they ought to drop
out of view in this or any later century, unless at the happy
epoch when human thought and action shall present to the
eye of the Judge of all nothing to which terror can attach.

It is now time to carry over our contemplation from the
picture presented by the teaching of the New Testament and
the early Church to the later fashions and later systems; the
first supplying us with ideas which are few, simple, majestic,
and on their human side circumscribed; the second offering
us a more copious presentation of deductions, and in our own
time also of speculations travelling over far wider spaces;
sometimes, perhaps, gratuitous or fanciful, sometimes repulsive, and even irreverent. Is this enlargement of the
repertoire of theological discussion an acquisition of solid
and firm-set territory, and does it represent a real addition
to our wealth in objects of faith? Shall we do well to
cherish for our own minds, and to promote in others, the
hardening of these ideas and speculations or of any selected
from among them, or is it preferable to recommend and
cultivate, after a fashion now antiquated, the earlier spirit
of comparative abstention and reserve?

I shall offer one general remark, which appears to me to
be of weight. There are two compartments, so to speak,
in the vast regions spread out before us, which appertain
to the future of the righteous and the unrighteous respectively. With regard to the first, men have been content to
leave it in the main much as they received it from our Lord

and the Apostles, and have respected the declaration that
'eye hath not seen, nor ear heard.' But there has been an
activity certainly remarkable, perhaps in part feverish and
morbid, in exploring the *domos Ditis vacuas et inania regna,*
and where the New Testament was sparing or silent, it has
been bold, eager, nay even dogmatic. This thirst for information on punishments, as to their nature, the classes who
are to undergo them, and their duration, does not seem to
be founded on the persuasion that there, beyond the grave,
is our home, and that, as if it were an earthly home, we desire
to know all we can about it. Anxiety has taken the same
direction in dogmatic and in anti-dogmatic times, but for
different reasons. It is not now sought to alarm men by
magnifying the power of God and by exhibiting the strictness and severity of the law of righteousness. The anxiety
now is to throw these subjects into the shade, lest the fas-
tidiousness of human judgement and feeling should be so
offended as to rise in rebellion against God for His harsh-
ness and austerity. That this motive is entertained in
good faith, need not be doubted. But the result in practice
is that we seem to call the Almighty to account, and undertake, on the foundation of our own judgement, to determine
what He can or cannot do, because we have concluded that
He ought or ought not. For those who reflect on what God
is and what we are, it will be evident that this is, to say the
least, most dangerous ground to occupy. And propositions
growing out of our own unwarranted assumptions are tendered to us for acceptance with a confidence, which ought
only to be felt when our reason is acting within its own
province, and in the measure of our own powers.

A special temptation to this abusive course has been
placed in our way by lofty assumptions habitually made on
behalf of the doctrine of natural immortality, and by the
presentation of that doctrine in what I will term a doubly
aggravated form. Of necessity and by itself it obtrudes
this change upon the conditions of thought, that whereas,
before the acceptance of natural immortality as a tenet of
religion, the future state of the righteous was the grand
basis of affirmation touching the world to come, it defined
the existence of all human beings in the future world as co-

extensive in duration; indeed, as apparently parallel in all
points except the difference between suffering and enjoyment. Again, when the question of the future life of the
non-Christian world was also dragged within the terms that
the new covenant had laid down, and when, further, the
destinies of all mankind from the very first were included,
it is plain that the subject underwent an enormous and, as
I should urge, a gratuitous extension. The other aggravation of the difficulties of the question is one which requires
to be noticed at greater length.

The word eternal is employed in the parable of the Last
Judgement to describe the duration both of the rewards of
the saved, and the retribution of lost souls. The phrase
employed in the original is *aionios*; and this, in Greek
usage, is applicable according to the context never to brief,
but sometimes to terminable, and sometimes to interminable,
periods. There is, however, another way of getting at the
notion of eternity beyond the limits of fixed period. This
would be to describe it by negation as time without any
time limit, time without end. Such was the conception
which, slightly perhaps from the first, and increasingly in
the course of ages, took possession of the Christian mind.
Indeed we commonly hear of the eternal punishment of the
wicked in the entire literature of the Church. But, while
the word eternal has remained in use, together with the
exclusion as a general rule of a specific time limit, it has
carried very different meanings. It depends upon numeration; and numeration is a faculty possessed in enormously
different degrees not only by the same human person at
different stages of his life, but by the race at different stages
of its development. I have heard a child count upwards
'one, two, three, four, a hundred.' His numeration was
represented by the first four terms; the fifth expressed his
conception of infinity, and infinity applied to time is the
popular sense of eternity. He was not sensible of its faulti-
ness: he knew nothing of the need to establish a defined
agreement between phrase and fact. So it was with the
primitive man; for whom arithmetic was 'fiving[1],' and was
taught by the number of fingers on the hand. The needs

---

[1] *Odyss.* iv. 412.

of the world in its youth do not require the use of largely
extended numeration. When vast numbers have to be
referred to, it is never for any of the ordinary uses of life,
and the purpose is sufficiently served by citing at large the
sand of the seashore, or the stars of heaven. Very long ago
I had occasion to discuss this subject in detail with reference to Homer's faculty of numeration. He never attempts
to give the totals of the Achaian and Trojan armies, or even
the total of the fleet. He derives some assistance from the
revolution of the seasons, and it appears that his idea of
defined number comes to a stop with the days of the year [1].

Beyond doubt, these ideas would gradually open out as
time went on. But the Scriptures nowhere, I think, deal
definitely with very large numbers. In the Apocalypse the
phrase ' Ten thousand times ten thousand ' is plainly figurative, and the total it expresses would seem in modern numeration small. We have now by slow degrees become familiar with hundreds and even thousands of millions, partly
in connexion with money, and much more largely in connexion with astronomical computations. But there is a curious
illustration of the mental capacity of the early Christians
in this department of thought. The millenarian idea embraced an enormous multiplication of fruits and grains upon
the renovated earth. Each corn sown was to produce one
thousand million pounds weight of corn. But this fell far
behind the provision of wine, as recorded by Papias. Each
vine will have ten thousand arms, each arm ten thousand
boughs, each bough ten thousand branches, each branch ten
thousand bunches of grapes, each bunch ten thousand ber-
ries, each berry yielding twenty thousand measures of wine.
Thus, to express the total, the figure 2 has to be followed
by twenty-four noughts, or the fourth power of a million
doubled at the close. But the artificial nature of the process testifies to its entirely fanciful nature. Mathematical
methods, however, have familiarized us up to a point altogether new, if not with the true idea of a boundless duration
in its strictness, yet with a duration so far extended as to
present to us an object alike vast and appalling in connexion
with pain, if not also somewhat stupefying when put in con-

[1] *Studies on Homer*, vol. iii. Chapter on Number.

nexion even with enjoyment. And now, when every one is competent or accustomed to speculate upon everything, it is little or less surprising that the average human mind should instinctively recoil from opening out a volume which beats the roll of Jeremiah in the wofulness of its contents, and which the New Testament seems rather to aim at keeping closed. Again, as to the conception itself of immortality in eternity, where are we? With all our labour to enlarge our conception relatively to its subject, it remains as small as ever. No addition adds to this eternity, no subtraction reduces it. In such imperfect vision of it as by the utmost effort we can entertain, it is so vast as to paralyze, almost to crush, our feeble intellects. Their failure would be more keenly felt, were we duly grounded in the habit of pondering the words we use, and measuring their true weight and force. I will give one final indication of the manner in which the human race has shrunk abashed for so long a time from the microscopic enlargement of this conception. One of the mightiest intellects it has produced was that of Dante; and, in the first division of his great work, he might seem almost to have been driven upon its detailed consideration. And yet he has avoided all attempts at detailed consideration of the nature of eternity. He uses the word eternal in the *Inferno* but twelve times (its derivatives making no sensible addition), and uses it almost exclusively as to the region, hardly ever in relation to a soul, always as a simple epithet without exposition or illustration. From detail and development of duration he altogether abstains; and it is observable that in the *Inferno* of Dante there are no infants.

But how large a space the question of man's condition in a future life occupies on the field of human interests cannot, I think, be more pointedly shown than by reference to a remarkable bibliography lately published which (terminating in the year 1878) contains the titles of over six thousand separate works [1].

It may be, and is even probable that, in the days when the utterance of belief was dominant and often arrogant, not only was the doctrine of eternal pains often publicly

[1] *The Literature of the Doctrine of a Future Life*, by Ezra Abbot, in Al-   ger's *Critical History of the Doctrine*. Tenth edition. New York, 1878.

announced, but perhaps it may have been loaded with extravagant extensions, and with details sometimes unwarranted, sometimes even approaching to the loathsome. This fashion has continued, within narrowing limits, down to the present day, and two remarkable specimens are cited by Mr. Row [1] which may be read with regret. But, before considering excess in an opposite direction, it may be well to dwell for a moment on an extreme form of the provocation which has been given. I therefore copy out of the work of Mr. Alger [2] an extract which he has drawn from the work of Mr. Trapp, an English clergyman :

> Doomed to live death, and never to expire,
> In floods and whirlwinds of tempestuous fire,
> The damned shall groan ; fire of all kinds and forms,
> In rain and hail, in hurricanes and storms :
> Liquid and solid, livid, red, and pale,
> A flaming mountain here, and there a flaming vale ;
> The liquid fire makes seas, the solid, shores ;
> Arched o'er with flames, the horrid concave roars.
> In bubbling eddies rolls the fiery tide,
> And sulphurous surges on each other ride,
> The hollow winding vaults, and dens, and caves,
> Bellow like furnaces with flaming waves,
> Pillars of flame in spiral volumes rise
> Like flaming snakes, and lick the infernal skies.
> Sulphur, the eternal fuel, unconsumed,
> Vomits redounding smoke thick, unillumed.

There is no small talent in the construction of the lines. But it is impossible to avoid seeing that, apart from all other questions, there creeps into this kind of literature a strong element of pure vulgarity. It will be a relief to turn from such an unbridled effusion when we come to the temperate and careful statement of Dr. Pusey [3]. What, however, would be the conclusion, I do not say of any zealous champion of orthodoxy, but of any capable and impartial observer, competently acquainted with the Scriptures and the general conditions of Christianity, upon the weighty question how far

---

[1] *Future Retribution*, by Rev. C. A. Row (London : Isbisters, 1887), p. 16.

[2] Alger, p. 570.

[3] *What is of Faith as to Everlasting Punishment*, 1860.

the present tone of the pulpit and of theological literature assigns to the penal element in the Providential and Christian system of the world a really operative place? I say an operative place, because among believers in the future state there are no denials of the abstract proposition that punishment awaits the wicked after death. But the proposition seems to be relegated at present to the far-off corners of the Christian mind, and there to sleep in deep shadow, as a thing needless in our enlightened and progressive age. So far as my knowledge and experience go, we are in danger even of losing this subject out of sight and out of mind. I am not now speaking of everlasting punishments in particular, but of all and any punishment intelligibly enforced; and can it be right, can it be warrantable, that the pulpit and the press should advisedly fall short of the standard established by the Holy Scriptures, and not less uniformly by the earliest and most artless period of hortatory Christian teaching? Is it not altogether undeniable that these authorities did so handle the subject of this penal element, in the frequency of mention and in the manner of treatment, that in their Christian system it had a place as truly operative, as clear, palpable, and impressive, as the more attractive doctrines of redeeming love? I sometimes fear that we have lived into a period of intimidation in this great matter. That broad and simple promulgation of the new scheme which is known as the Sermon on the Mount was closed with the awful presentation of the house built upon the sand. But as if men were now more easy to be persuaded, and there was no longer any sand to build upon, Christian teachers seem largely to be possessed with an amiable fear lest the delicate ear in the Church, and the still more critical eye in the closet, should find their niceness repelled by any glimpse of hell; and to dwell exclusively on that grace and bounty, which, alas, are as far as ever from being generally comprehended and appropriated. For, if I am right, the effects wrought by this intimidation, not indeed in the distinct consciousness, yet in the language of the great teaching organs, is not confined to popular exhortation, but even finds its way into deliberate and systematic exhibitions of thought. I must not withhold an example. Dr. Salmond, to whose work I have already presumed to refer with honour, dismisses the theory of universalism with decision, and that of conditionalism almost with severity ; and does not shrink from showing that man determines his own immortality for weal or for woe, and determines it finally not for weal only but for woe [1]. When, however, he comes to the closing summation of his teachings, he gives it in the following terms :

'If there be at the decisive point of life, however late it may come, the tremulous inclination of the soul to God, the feeblest presence of that which makes for righteousness and faith in heathen or in Christian, it will be recognized of the Judge, and under the conditions of the new life, it will grow to more, in the power and in the blessedness of good [2].'

But from whence do we derive authority for a proposition so wide? Readers of more insight than myself may more exactly grasp than I do the meaning of these words. If they signify that the determining conditions of a vital conformity to the will of God may subsist, but yet may have escaped the human eye, and may receive their development in a world where virtue or goodness shall expatiate freely and without its terrene obstructions, this, I apprehend, is the doctrine of Butler, to which I shall have occasion further to refer. But if it were signified that in every case where the process of destroying spiritual life, however far advanced, and with however absolute a command of evil over conduct, and however fixed the mental habits may have become, is not yet absolutely completed with every spark of true life extinct, then might it not be difficult to comprehend why Dives was not with Lazarus in Abraham's bosom ; still more difficult to repress the fear that doctrine, hung upon this pivot, would empty Evangelical threatenings of their force, would sorely hinder the rescuing of souls, and would, as Origen feared with regard to his own speculations, be perilous to the common weal. Ought we not in reason to take a distinction between a vital warmth which is ascending, and one which is sinking into the abyss ? In our common experience the candle is not relumed from the dying spark upon the wick ; and the movement of death has oftentimes conclusively set in while its mechanical completion is still delayed ; nor can any doctrine be more at

---

[1] *Doctrine of Immortality*, Bk. VI. ch. iv.   [2] *Ibid*. p. 672.

variance with reason than that which teaches, or implies, that no process is determined until it has been closed.

We seem now to have arrived at the juncture proper for approaching the most practical side of this question ; the side at which we are to consider how our own ideas may most rationally and most dutifully be adjusted. And I wish frankly to express my consciousness that, while I labour to bring real difficulties into view, I have no grand solutions of the kinds now in vogue to offer ; that I must be more forward in recommending the abandonment than the adoption of ideas ; that my prescriptions, so to call them, lie on the lines of reserve, abstention, and thereby of escape from extremes and exaggerations. And this I set about with full cognizance of the fact that no mode of treatment can be more chilling and repellent to the general reader.

Let me, then, endeavour to represent, with as much accuracy as I may, the principal forms of eschatological opinion, which at the present day actively compete for the assent of believers in Christianity. They are, I believe, three in number, and none of them, so far as I am able to judge, altogether corresponds with the sense of the early Christian Church ; while one at least among them not only departs from it, but seems to strike at the root principles of Christian philosophy as they are conceived by Butler.

There has never been any period or condition of the Church in which Christian thought did not associate the future condition of wicked men with suffering. With this suffering there was associated no doctrine or prospect of relief ; if at least we follow a preponderance of writers so enormous as to leave outside their band no more than a remnant hardly appreciable or visible. It is common to use the phrase *aionian*, or eternal, with respect to this suffering. But the idea was not for a long time elaborately formulated, and the word conveyed the sense of a term indefinite, rather than of one properly infinite. Modern usage and experience have effected a great practical change in the sense we attach to the term eternal. And this change in the basis has silently made a profound change also in the doctrine, combined as it has been not only with the tacit yet general, it may almost be said universal, adoption of the doctrine of natural immortality, but with the obtrusion of this philosophical opinion upon the Christian religion as being, in the view of common opinion, an article of faith. Such, indeed, is the popular idea, which now takes it to have been established as an article of faith, first that the wicked will have an endless existence, and, secondly, that this endless existence will be an existence of endless torment. The change seems due to two causes: 1. The adoption from philosophy into theology of the notion of natural immortality. 2. The formulation and distension of the idea of eternity. Let us bear these things in mind while proceeding to bring into nearer view the prevailing schemes of modern thought on this great subject.

The opinion traditionally established respecting eternal punishment has not had in the present generation any more learned or more temperate advocate than Dr. Pusey [1], who also derived advantage from the highflown and unmeasured language of the work on the future life, which he opposed. He does not, I think, enter upon the question of natural immortality, nor upon the gradual unlocking or unfolding of the signification of the word eternal. Nor does he supply a strictly definite answer to the question which is propounded by the title of his work. But he contests the propositions which I have cited from various writers as to the absence of a strict doctrine of eternal punishment even before the time of Origen. He looks upon Origenism as an isolated fact. He does not admit that it was largely or weightily supported, and conceives that it was condemned by the entire Church, through the medium of several local councils taken together; apparently proceeding upon the maxim that a combination of local councils, not contradicted by other councils of larger authority, amounts to an universal acceptance, and in an equal degree binds the entire Church.

He conceives that Origenism was unnecessarily brought up in the Fifth General Council, through the gratuitous desire of Justinian to meddle in controverted theology [2]. He makes but a limited admission, even in the case of St. Gregory of Nyssa, that there was more or less of

---

[1] *What is of Faith as to Everlasting Punishment.* London and Oxford, 1880.
[2] *Ibid.* p. 133.

P

tendency to certain ideas that leaned in the direction of Origen. He says, however, after describing the final hell, that 'no one who can love would be there[1].' He commends (by implication) the language of Cardinal Newman, 'what we cannot accept . . . is . . . that man's *probation* for his eternal destiny . . . continues after this life[2].' And he appears to sum up his judgement on the whole matter in a question evidently involving something of affirmation: 'How do we know that Almighty God has cast into hell a single soul, of which He does not know, in His absolute knowledge, that under any circumstances it would continue to resist the law, and reject the love, of God[3].' And he adds, with tender feeling and wise judgement, 'He can reconcile His own attributes, if we abide His time'; thus evidently implying that there remains somewhat of unsolved difficulty in the scheme of ideas which he has been expounding.

In 1728, Dr. Thomas Burnet gave to the world his *De statu mortuorum ac Resurgentium tractatus*; a work of great ability, published in Latin by him in or before 1728; translated, and so republished, in English, in 1738, after his death. Dr. Thomas Burnet did not possess the wide learning of Dr. Pusey, but he had the advantage of producing his work as an historical treatise, exempt from all immediate concern with controversy.

He propounds, without arguing it, the natural immortality of the soul 'dependentem quidem a Deo, sed vi et principiis suae naturae originariae[4].' His favourite statement is that the pains of the lost in the world to come are neither finite nor infinite, but indefinite[5]. He claims, mostly as not holding the unmitigated doctrine of eternal punishment, or as treating leniently deviation from it, Justin Martyr, Tatian, Irenaeus, Lactantius, the two Gregories of Nyssa and Nazianzus, Jerome, and even Augustine[6]. He cites these words of St. Jerome: 'Sciendum quod judicium Dei non possit scire humana fragilitas, nec de poenarum

---

[1] *What is of Faith as to Everlasting Punishment*. p. 4.

[2] *Ibid.* p. 6.   [3] *Ibid.* p. 281.

[4] *D. statu mortuorum ac Resurgen-* tium *tractatus.* London, Ed. 2, 1728, chap. ii.

[5] *Ibid.* ch. x. p. 301.

[6] *Ibid.* p. 302.

magnitudine atque mensura ferre sententiam quae Domini arbitrio derelicta est.' He cites the phrase which St. Augustine applies to the milder teachers, *doctores misericordes.* He laments the careless incompleteness which many allow themselves in the process of thinking. Few, he says, examine the things themselves; they look only at the images of the things which, in their very selves, we shall see when God removes the veil, 'partim sub occasu hujus mundi, plenius autem in futuro [1].' He taunts the omniscience of large bodies of theologians; that is to say, their ignorance of their ignorance. He recommends teachers to inculcate the immortality of the soul, the resurrection of the dead, reward and penalty according to works and characters in the future world, together with the great conflagration, and the return and Kingdom of Christ. Beyond these limits, he says, let us only study mutual assistance and indulgence. No railing controversy upon matters 'quae nos plane et aperto doceri noluit Deus in hoc statu.' Intolerance in such a matter is the commission of a great offence, none the more pardonable because it is done in the act of correcting a small one [2]. I regret to subjoin that, apparently following Origen, he adds: 'Quicquid apud te statuas, intus et in pectore, de his poenis, aeternis vel non, recepta doctrina verbisque utendum est cum populo, et cum peroratur ad vulgus [3].'

He appears, however, really to have practised within himself the abstinence which he recommends, and he adopts neither of the relaxing theories which have their own respective trains of adherents, those of universalism and of conditional immortality. He severely, however, censures such persons as seem to gloat over pictures of the misery of the greater part of the human race, and thinks it does not well comport with the character of Deity to ascribe to God the formation of a scheme of things wherein so great a part of reasonable nature is entirely cast away [4].

I cannot but look upon the treatise as a noteworthy fact in the history of declared opinions on this difficult subject.

---

[1] *De statu mortuorum ac Resurgentium tractatus.* London, Ed. 2, 1728, chap. ii. p. 310.

[2] *Ibid.* pp. 310–314.
[3] *Ibid.* p. 309.
[4] *Ibid.* p. 307.

Tennyson has said that it is the best, or of the best, in our nature which anxiously desires the restitution of the lost.

> The wish, that of the living whole,
> No life may fail beyond the grave,
> Derives it not from what we have
> The likest God within the soul ?[1]

This great poet adds to his fine and singularly cultivated genius a great philosophical insight, with which the *In Memoriam* is charged throughout. A declaration, then, of this kind, proceeding from such an authority, calls for close consideration.

Justice to him requires that, in the first place, we should dismiss the idea that the thing thus to be desired in compliance with the promptings of our better nature is the prolongation of wicked existence in conjunction with enjoyment. That dispensation, which associates sin with suffering, is a supreme law of the universe, and he that rebels against it rebels against the moral order. To reverse that order, to associate virtue permanently with pain, and wickedness with pleasure or joy, is to establish something worse than moral chaos; it is to establish that which could only be established under the scheme of the Zend, were Ahriman to conquer and extinguish Ormuzd.

Is then the *desiderandum* propounded to us somewhat of this fashion : That we should all long earnestly to see all evil wiped out from the universe ? I suppose there can be no one, whose heart is without a chord responsive to such a desire. But let us observe that it covers a great breadth of ground; that it seems to carry us almost beyond our depth; that hesitation and misgiving may naturally arise if we, so infinitesimally puny as we are, in the face of the Almighty Author, are invited to concentrate our thought and also to concentrate largely our emotion, on this somewhat heroic remedy for the diseases of all creation; when, in the first place, the best exercise of all our powers is called for in the limitation and prevention of evil at our doors and within them, aye, in the very apple of our own eyes; and when, secondly, we have no outlook into the

---

[1] *In Memoriam*, lv.

universe at large, and no knowledge except from one narrow and remote corner, of the conditions under which its immense machinery is arranged and governed.

We seem to know, and to hold with some firmness of grasp the knowledge, that the invasion and activity of sin are not limited in their range to the race of Adam, or to beings who wear the human form. Unhappily, even in the lower orders of creation we perceive what, if it does not fully accomplish the idea of sin, seems to correspond, under the conditions of a lower nature, with what would be sin in a higher one. If we admit the authority of Holy Scripture, we are at once supplied with a cloud of testimonies to the destructive energy of him, or them, whose name is Legion. The temperance of the Christian Church has not laid upon the individual conscience the obligation, as we believe in God, so also to believe in the existence of God's great adversary. But I presume that most Christians, who watch with any care their own mental and inward experience, are but too well convinced that they have to fight against 'principalities, against powers, against the rulers of the darkness of this world, against spiritual wickedness in high places [1]'; that they are beset by a great personal scheme of evil agency, under which method and vigilance, employing whatever bad means, or even good, will serve their purpose, are raised, in their work of seduction and ruin, to what seems a terrible perfection.

Now I must suppose that the words of Tennyson advisedly extend to the reclamation of these unhappy beings. I do not say that their pre-eminence in evil gives them a preferable claim to deliverance, but that what we are bound by the law of our nature to desire for our own race we must also desire for all those invested with a like title to sympathy, as the intelligent, sinning, and suffering creatures of Almighty God. Yet, from the precipitancy, shallowness, and superficiality of thought, with which this most grave subject is often approached, it seems probable that, unlike Tennyson, many of those who have treated it have never faced its broader aspects, or taken any careful measure of the demands that reason inexorably binds up with

[1] Eph. vi. 12.

those principles, on which they found their argument. For meagre indeed would be the scheme of thought which, entertaining a keen sympathy for the fallen of our own flesh and blood, had no room to spare for others, and left to their fate all who beyond those narrow limits had fallen into the same calamity.

The real question is not whether we should desire the recovery of lost souls, for which nature, as it is represented by Tennyson, cries out; but whether this should be the ruling or foremost idea on which we are habitually to dwell, and with which also to contemplate the great subject of the final judgement. The difficulty is that it seems to be like taking into our own hands the tremendous question of the readjustment of a disordered world, with no knowledge except as to a very small part of the case, and without capacity, so far as our experience in matters of moral action and judgement informs us, for the comprehension of the whole plan. Is there no preferable alternative? Is it beyond a hope to find a form of thought which, without shutting the door on any of our sympathies, leaves to the Supreme Governor the ordering of His own government? Those sympathies can require no apology, when we recollect how they swayed the soul of the Redeemer, as He reflected on the calamities that the perverseness of sin was about to bring upon Jerusalem [1]. But have we no faith in His justice, in His goodness, in His power and will to harmonize the two? Have we ever taken measure of our own total incapacity to estimate moral actions with exactitude? an impotence so gross, that no prudent man will, in cases of this kind, ever form any beyond a provisional judgement on the deeds of his fellow-men. The judge on the bench, if he be wise, will not hold it for certain that he himself stands better before God, than the criminal in the dock. Let us remember that the rule for us is 'Judge not'; and we may be helped in the observance of this rule, by recollecting that there is One who judges, and who always judges right.

It may be proper here to offer a few words on the mode now generally adopted of construing the word death in connexion with the lot of the wicked in the future state.

[1] Luke xix. 41-44.

In the first place, we may observe that it does not cover the whole case: for other words, commonly signifying the termination of an existence, are also employed in this connexion; as, for example, when we are enjoined to fear Him, who is able to destroy both body and soul in hell. This double destruction is placed in contrast with a single destruction, that of the body, which is unquestionably absolute, and which therefore must (so it may be argued) have the same meaning.

In the second place, it may be noticed that this method of *hermeneusis* is one never applied to human affairs, unless it be in a sense avowedly figurative, and in cases only such as imply a postponement, not a cancellation, of the final catastrophe.

There is, thirdly, another incident of this method of interpretation, which appears to have received less attention than it deserves. It will not be denied that, in its primary meaning, death is a word that conveys a single idea[1]. It means the conclusion of some existence; it may be an existence integral or partial, but it seems that always something must conclude. It means no less than that one thing, and no more. But when we examine the peculiar process to which the word is submitted in connexion with eschatology, we seem to find not only that the old idea of the word gives place to something new, but that an old idea which was single is succeeded by a new idea which is double. When the souls of the wicked are declared to have destruction or death for their doom, the meaning, as is alleged, is firstly that they will survive, secondly that they will survive for ever, and, thirdly, that they will survive under a double condition: the one, that of continual persistence in wickedness, and, the other that of a co-extensive, and also never-ending, immersion in suffering. There appears to be presented here a good deal of difficulty; so much of difficulty, at least, as may serve to recommend a certain amount of reserve. I do not here venture upon any assertion. If we are told that life in like manner signifies in the future state

[1] The argument on the meaning of the Greek ἀπόλλυμι was very closely and fully examined by Dr. Weymouth, in a letter to the *Independent* newspaper, dated so long ago as March, 1870; which well deserves reprinting.

both the goodness of the righteous and the enjoyment consequent upon that goodness, I demur to the proposition. The life promised is union with God, which is union with goodness. Enjoyment may be its inseparable accident : but it is not the thing signified. Whereas, in the controversy concerning the wicked, everything is made and understood to turn upon their suffering, while the eternity of their vice is little heard of, and certainly is not the idea either primarily or prominently suggested to the mind [1].

We first become acquainted, not with *aionios*, but with *aion*, so far back as in Homer. It is used eight times in the *Iliad*, and five in the *Odyssey* ; most commonly it is the simple equivalent of the Latin *rita*, and the English 'life' relatively to a man. Occasionally it means the heart or flower of life : especially in the address of Andromache to the dead Hector [2]:

$$\text{Ἄνερ, ἀπ᾽ αἰῶνος νέος ὤλεο.}$$

Here the effect of ἀπ᾽ αἰῶνος is that Hector (who was undoubtedly in his early prime) is cut away not only from life, but from the flower of life. The clause in Ps. cii. 24 comes near it, ' Take me not away *in the midst* of my days.' We come next, in classical Greek, to the adjective *aionios*. But the Homeric use of the word shows vividly that the word is essentially relative rather than absolute. It is the *aion* of somebody or something; not abstract, also not an exact counterpart of *mors*, or of the English ' death.' With lapse of time comes a modification of the sense, and varied meanings are given for it [3], *lasting for an age, perpetual, immortal, eternal*. In the Νόμοι of Plato, the Maker forms the human being to be ἀνώλεθρον . . . ἀλλ᾽ οὐκ αἰώνιον, ψυχὴν καὶ σῶμα, καθάπερ οἱ κατὰ νόμον ὄντες θεοί [4]; where the distinction seems to be taken between survival and immortality ; our soul survives the death we know of, but death never comes at all to the publicly acknowledged gods, who have an indefectible existence. But I have not seen in classical Greek any use of either the adjective or the substantive

---

[1] Olshausen, *De significatione vocis* ζωή *in Libris N. T.*, shows that it means not happiness but life ; and observes : ' Verborum notio rarissimo multip'ex est.'

[2] *Il.* xxiv. 725.

[3] Liddell and Scott, *in voc.*

[4] Νόμοι, p. 904.

for eternity in the abstract, if we take the distinction between an expanse of time, to which no particular limit is
attached, and a substantive eternity, consisting of time
ceaselessly prolonged. Mr. De Quincey, who was both
scholar and philosopher, has written a paper on this word,
and he says, apparently with much truth : 'The exact
amount of the duration expressed by our *aeon* depends altogether upon the particular subject which yields the *aeon*.'
It is 'the duration or cycle of existence which belongs to any
object . . . in right of its genus [1].' One approximate rendering of the word *aionios* is perhaps to be found in 'life-
long.' If this be a sense admitted in Scripture, then the
phrase as used in the great parable of Matt. xxv. simply
throws us back upon the question, what is the ordained life
of the soul ? Is it limited, or is it, by its nature, extended
without end ? The adjective will lend itself either way.
That to which it will not bend (unless its meaning have
undergone some vital change in the Greek of the New Testament) is the idea of a period which is affected by any
particular limit, unless it be that of the ordained life of the
subject immediately in question. Some change it certainly
may have undergone : it would be hazardous on my part
to define the amount. Schleusner discusses the word with
care in his Lexicon, but he can only say the meaning is to
be gathered, in each passage where it is used, from the context, the intention of the writer, the things and persons
placed before us. De Quincey conceives that an ambiguous
term is purposely employed in Scripture in order to evade [2],
we may rather say to veil, the question. We have before
us this inevitable consideration ; a punishment which was
itself strictly conformable to the popular conception of
eternity might have been set down in terms which would
have precluded debate upon the meaning ; and a veiling or
reserving, or what may be called an open, phrase, seems to
have been judged more meet for the purpose with which the
Gospel was written. Were the doctrine of natural immortality authoritatively declared in Scripture, then indeed the
sense of the phrase would be one absolutely closed. And,

---

[1] Hogg's *De Quincey and his Friends*, Supposed Scriptural Expression for
pp. 308, 312, in the essay on 'The Eternity.' [2] *Ibid.*

if the intention were to define eternity as lapse of time prolonged beyond the reach of number and without any boundary of duration, would not some other and more explicit language have been employed? This question has for practical purposes been closed by the spread of a doctrine not revealed but philosophic.

There are two theories, which at the present day principally contest the field with the widespread and once almost undisputed theory sustained by an ancient and general, if perhaps not a primitive, tradition. Of these, that which is termed the doctrine of conditional immortality has perhaps the larger number of adherents, and seems to be the better entitled to claim some kindred with that usually called orthodox. It begins by renouncing the opinion of natural immortality, and takes firm ground when denying to it authority or countenance from the Holy Scriptures. On the other hand, it renounces also the conception of an existence prolonged without limit in the endurance of torment. But it neither teaches nor approximates to the notion of an extinction immediately consequent either upon death or upon the Day of Judgement. It does not attempt to find a particular limit for the ordained period of suffering; but holds that it is bounded by the nature of the subject to which it is applied, and that sin is a poison to which the vital forces of the soul must in the end give way, by passing into sheer extinction. It protests against the current method of interpretation, which assigns to death in the New Testament the meaning not of a cessation of existence, but of an existence prolonged without limit in a state of misery. And it insists upon recovering for the word that idea of a termination, which dwells in it as a central essence. Ethically, the destructive nature of sin against God is taken as the basis of this scheme of ideas; and it claims to work according to natural laws, in propounding, as the eventual solution of the problem, not suffering without any end for the wicked, but the disappearance or extinction of their being at such time as the providence of God shall prescribe.

For reasons which I have not been able to discover, this theory of conditionalism (of which I am not recommending the acceptance) is sometimes rejected by writers on the side of traditional opinion with greater emphasis than the far more daring doctrine of Universalism. Quite apart from the comparative merits or demerits of the two schemes, it seems hardly conceivable that, if a theory so clean-cut had been the true mind of the revelation designed to teach and to restore mankind, its discovery should have been withheld until so late a period in the history of the Christian Church. It can hardly be said, even by its advocates, to be clearly revealed in Scripture ; it certainly does not take the benefit of the *quod semper, quod ubique, quod ab omnibus.* It seems to introduce a strange anomaly in a resurrection which is to be effected with a view to extinction : and, most of all, it founds Christian theology upon a tenet of philosophy, though it happens that in a former case the tenet was affirmative, whereas here it happens to be negative.

The speculation of Origen in favour of universal restoration, apparently intended by himself for the schools, has in our day been extensively revived *coram populo.* The revival may have been to a large extent vague and declamatory, or feeble, timid, commonplace; and it has exhibited but little evidence of masculine attempt to grapple with the full conditions of the formidable problem. Yet it presents to us considerable dangers by reason of the fact that it has enlisted, so to speak, a suborned witness on its behalf. That suborned witness is the world of to-day, which, as against the unseen world, has acquired a vast increase of force from the increase of wealth and the multiplication of material and social wants and enjoyments, unaccompanied by any countervailing stimulus to the life of faith. It has also been largely favoured by the carnal spirit of division still largely, though as I trust with some signs of diminution, prevalent among Christians.

This theory, known by the name of Universalism, does not deny that punishment is due as an appropriate consequence to wrongdoing. It does not even define any particular measure of quantity, quality, or duration, as the limit of what justice will allow to be administered. And it concedes the proposition that penalty awaits the wicked after death. But it seems to view retribution rather as a sentence delivered, so to speak, from the bench, and administered *ab extra*, than as an inherent effect of a cause naturally producing it. So regarding the pains of the future, it proceeds to argue that an infinite debt cannot be contracted in a finite, and indeed a very narrowly bounded time. It therefore protests against unlimited penal results from limited offences; and propounds that, when the debt is paid, the goodness of God, finding the sole bar removed, will secure the universal happiness of mankind. And some at least have not failed to discover that the premises of this argument are wider than its conclusion; that, as Origen so thoroughly understood, they include every creature lapsed from righteousness; that 'the devil and his angels[1]' in consequence have a certain prospect of escape from the lot prepared as the reward of their obstinate and ruinous misdoing. And, what may seem strange, it is of necessity included in the scheme of these reasoners that the future fate of fallen angels is thus disclosed in a revelation made to the children of men.

Upon this scheme of Universalism or Restitutionism, although it was at the outset the speculation of a great man, I cannot but regard it as largely, though unconsciously, the offspring of impatience in combination with despair; and I speak on it, as distinguished from those who propound it, in terms of repugnance, on the following grounds.

First, it proceeds with a reckless disregard of the solemn declarations of our Lord, who has supplied us for our greater security with two declarations, which seem intended to close the door upon this discussion. One of these apprises us, that there is a form of sin which is called the sin against the Holy Ghost, and which clearly brings home to us that we have a real capacity of spiritual suicide. The quenching of the Spirit[2], the lying to the Holy Ghost[3], which are *per se* so terrible, lead us step by step to a yet more deadly condemnation. There is a sin that cannot be pardoned. This sin is formally described in each of the three Synoptic Gospels, and plainly referred to by the fourth Evangelist, St. John, when, in his first Epistle, he declares that there is a sin unto death, which he declines to include in the general rule of prayer for the pardon of sin[4]. The

---

[1] Matt. xxv. 41.   [2] 1 Thess. v. 19.   [3] Acts v. 3.   [4] 1 John v. 16.

fullest of the three synoptical notices is that of St. Matthew [1]:
'All manner of sin and blasphemy shall be forgiven unto
men: but the blasphemy against the Holy Ghost shall not be
forgiven unto men. And whosoever speaketh a word against
the Son of Man, it shall be forgiven him: but whosoever
speaketh against the Holy Ghost, it shall not be forgiven
him, neither in this world, neither in the world to come.'
The declaration is, as it were, cased in armour by being
made to reach over our whole existence. That existence
embraces the two worlds; and forgiveness can never be,
neither in this world, neither in the world to come [2]. The
'cannot' here presented to us is by no means, I apprehend,
the fulmination of an arbitrary decree, but rather the announcement of a law of nature. When the last prop is
withdrawn, the fabric falls. The manifestation of the Holy
Spirit is the crowning and most potent means in the Divine
armoury for the recovery of man: and when it is advisedly
repudiated, nothing more remains.

Even more stringent, if possible, is the second declaration:
'Better had it been for that man if he had never been
born [3].' The theory before us is neither more nor less than
a flat contradiction of a Divine utterance clothed with peculiar solemnity. If our existence is measured out in simple
duration, and if the largest conceivable amount and highest
quality of sin is only to be visited with a finite share of
that duration, beyond which lies a stretch of happy existence
reaching into immeasurable distance, then, as the infinite
exceeds the finite, the sinner who commits the sin in view
is not a loser, but a great gainer by having come into the
sphere of living entities. His future life will be a happy
life, though subject to a certain, possibly a large, deduction.
To presume upon overriding the express declarations of the
Lord Himself, delivered upon His own authority, is surely
to break up revealed religion in its very groundwork, and to
substitute for it a flimsy speculation, spun like the spider's
web by the private spirit out of its own jejune resources, and
about as little capable as is that web of bearing the strain
by which the false has, one day, to be severed from the true.

---

[1] Matt. xii. 31, 32; Mark iii. 28 (varied in phrase, but in no way opening a
door of escape); Luke xii. 10.

[2] Matt. x. 28.   [3] Matt. xxvi. 24; Mark xiv. 21.

It is not surprising to find that a scheme, which prefers these crude fancies to the solemn declarations of the Lord, should also prefer them to the lessons of life and fact, and to all true and searching philosophy of human nature. If there be one fact more largely and solidly established by experience than any other, it is, apart from all controversy as to the relative weight of environment and endowment, that conduct is the instrument by which character is formed, and that habit systematically pursued tends, and tends without any known limit, to harden into fixity. This is testified by what is so often said in the case of new ideas and methods, that it is idle to teach such things to the old, and that real progress is only to be made by impressing them upon the elastic and malleable mind of a new generation. The settled laws of our nature are the corner-stones of our education, as well as the landmarks of our Creator's will concerning us. From them we are enabled to comprehend the dispensation under which we live, and to turn it to account. But here there has arisen a tribe, it might perhaps be said, of philosophasters, who tell us that the experience of mankind, tested through so many generations, is an illusion, and that its lessons are henceforth to be read backwards. They rely upon the guidance of an inner sense vouchsafed to them after it has been withheld from all their fellow-creatures; for even the heathen mind, in the extremities of its bewilderment and need, did not catch at a straw as if it were a prop, nor practise upon itself, under the notion of a supreme enlightenment, a superlative trick of self-delusion. I do not deny that there are those who, having appointed themselves to the great enterprise of reforming the universe, may, in the pursuit of their aim, attain even to this height of mental excess ; but I hold that, by destroying the foundations of our belief in the observed facts of human nature, they are destroying the foundations of every other belief, their own favourite scheme included.

But further. Such mental errors cannot be indulged without producing wider consequences than any that their authors have intended. These inventions are revolutionary not only as towards the dispensation we live under, but as towards human nature itself, and all the modes in which it

is rationally impelled to action, or guided in pursuing it.
It is remarkable that this scheme does not present the
prospect of a plan for the reformation of character, with the
cessation of penalty as its natural consequence; but it is
rather a repeal or exhaustion of penalty, with reformation of
character set in the shade, and playing a secondary part : at
the very best a reformation brought about arbitrarily, and in
defiance of all known laws.   And those stern denunciations
of Holy Scripture, which on a long course of trial have been .
found none too strong for their purpose, it is deliberately
sought to relax by promising to every sinner of whatever
inveteracy, audacity, and hardness, an endless period of
immunity from suffering; after a period spent in it, which
they have no means of defining, and which every offender
is therefore left to retrench at his own pleasure, on his own
behalf.   What is this but to emasculate all the sanctions of
religion, and to give wickedness, already under too feeble
restraint, a new range of licence ?   I do not dream of imputing the intention : but good intentions do not suffice to
countervail inexorable laws.   The strong language, which
the subject leads me to employ, is altogether remote from
personal application ; and I use it as treating of what I
understand to be gravely propounded as a great article of
Christian belief.

The appeal to Scripture in support of these ideas seems
to be so ill sustained as to suggest that its chief effect is
to supply the weaker brethren with a handful of material
such as may suffice to suppress lingering scruples.   There
is, indeed, to be a regeneration, a restitution of all things ;
harmony will everywhere prevail, wickedness will disappear
from view.   Christ must reign till He hath put all things
under His feet, and when all things are thus subdued, then
God shall be all in all[1].   But they receive the answer from
one quarter that sin will be effectually put away by being
reduced to impotence ; and from another school of thought,
not perhaps wholly out of sympathy with theirs, they are
reminded that its method is yet more conclusively to dispose
of sin by annihilation.

Upon this scheme as a whole I cannot stop short of owning the impression it makes on my mind to be this.   Its

[1] Cor. xv. 27, 28.

authors, failing to take heed that the entire dealings with impenitent sinners have only in a very small degree been disclosed to us, and impatient of this vacuum which they think, and perhaps rightly think, they have detected in the Divine Revelation, undertake to fill the gap by going outside it altogether, and what, when closely examined, is found to be neither more nor less than constructing a revelation for themselves.

I have still one further observation to make upon this theory. It embraces the other like theories; and it relates to the high ground that appears to be claimed for them by their authors. They are not presented to us in the humble guise of Socratic or Platonic speculations. They seem rather to be regarded as supplemental portions of the Gospel. Finding revelation to be incomplete, a school of thinkers hereupon conclude that it is defective. It being granted that only a portion of the Divine counsels is disclosed to us, the assumption is made that there ought to be a more liberal communication of them. In a very striking tract [1], written in promotion of these views, I find it stated that the dark thoughts of God heretofore prevalent, are becoming unendurable. But instead of showing or contending that the Scriptures and the Creeds disown these dark thoughts, and throw us back upon a filial trust as the just attitude of the believing mind, there is propounded a new philosophy which teaches us to look upon sin as being largely but an incident in the stupendous process of evolution, the working out of the brute, the tiger and the ape from us, 'into an harmonious and beautiful life.' We insist upon raising that curtain which the hand of God let fall. We obtain a view of the scenery beyond it. And this view is really presented to us, less a modest and tremulous human conjecture, than as a Fifth Gospel. It is 'a way of escape,' and a way of escape rather for our Maker than for us; since none, surely, can pretend that it is a moral necessity for us to be informed not only of the result of rejecting salvation, but of the entire destiny of all those who so reject it. But in company with this Fifth Gospel there comes also a Sixth, which is in flat contradiction

---

[1] *Is Salvation possible after Death?* p. 7, by Mr. J. Page Hopps. Williams and Norgate.

to it, and a new battle of life and death is at once set up between two bodies of believers, who seem equally well-intentioned, equally ingenious, equally confident of the truth and sufficiency of the scheme they propound. Nor is this all; they are severally alike determined to propound their scheme as called for by a vital necessity of the case, and as indispensable to the honour and security of the Gospel: alike insensible to the peril of loading the Christian faith with what does not belong to the original deposit; of investing human speculations with the august claims of the Divine Word; of declaring that the current or 'traditional' Christianity is afflicted with a mortal disease, and of proclaiming, within earshot (so to speak) of one another two infallible remedies, each of which is absolutely destructive of the rival specific. Reflective speculation, if it does not forget the modesty and humility that become it, may rightfully claim a wide measure of toleration or of patience: but these claims, marshalled abreast of the articles of the Christian faith, yet loud in their mutual discord, may, it is to be feared, have for their principal result neither the solution of problems nor the mitigation of differences, but a further addition to the diversified forces now at work in the sapping of belief.

It is surely unwise to bind ourselves even to the proposition that the ideas we ought to entertain of the Divine justice unconditionally require us to find or assert a limit of duration for the punishment, or for the state of loss attaching to obstinate and unrepented sin. Before advancing thus far, we ought to know much more than apparently we can know in the compass of this life upon many matters now hidden; what may be all the possible forms of that punishment or loss, whether it is an inflicted penalty or (so to speak) an inborn and inbred result, and what are the essential conditions of that future life into which we are to pass beyond the grave. We should know also much more of the capacity of the soul for change, and of the directions that such change may be capable of taking. I may fare better, and do better, on a lonely and sequestered island, than on a boundless turbid ocean without chart or compass. The subject is large, and many are the avenues of thought which it opens up.

Q

It appears to be an established law of our present condition that under the action of experience, and especially under that of suffering, we have no choice but either to gain ground or to lose it, and to attain or undergo, as the case may be, the consequences of that gain or loss. But if life be for us, according to experience, an onward movement from a beginning to a consummation, and if death, when reasonably contemplated, appears to be much more than a mere accident of that movement, and nothing less than a great crisis, preparatory and auxiliary to a completion, then it follows that in those among departed spirits (if such there be) who are not beneficially affected by the post-mortuary stages of their discipline, a disintegrative power of deterioration may be actively at work; that this habitual power may be then and there even more marked than now and here; and it is even difficult to exclude altogether the possibility, a mere possibility without doubt, that the effect may be great losses and decays of faculty, great reduction and contraction of the scale, and of the sphere, of existence.

Some, who have exercised themselves in suggesting modes whereby the stings of future suffering may be sharpened, have included in their speculations the idea that the power of anticipating the future, and of living over again the past, by which we seem to be so vividly distinguished from the brutes, will hereafter be enhanced, to reset continually, if the expression may be used, the torture of the damned. Such is not my purpose. I do not doubt that such a process is among the resources of Almighty Power and Knowledge should the use of them be deemed meet. But, considering that sin is excess, and that the effect of excess is commonly to depress, weaken, or exhaust, it may seem at least as legitimate to contemplate the possibility that there may be in the class of future existences now under view a change, but in the opposite direction : a change which shall enfeeble faculty, affection, even appetite, and more or less drop them out from the human equipment. If it be so, these losses might, under the laws of our nature, include not an increased but a reduced susceptibility ; a reduction of pain, analogous to that which may be brought about by the amputation of some acutely suffering member. It might be that, in the general depression

and degradation of human nature brought about by proved
incapacity to take profit, here or hereafter, by remedial laws,
we might narrow, if not efface, the interval which severs us
from animals, in these great particulars of realizing recollection and corresponding anticipation, and might, without
having identity, or personality, in any respect impaired,
attain an indefinitely large relief from active penalty, at
the cost of a descent in the rank of being, which perhaps
also may be indefinitely large.

Let me repeat that my object in this strain of remark
is not to suggest the acceptance of doctrines, hardly even to
open possibilities; but to open a view, contracted perhaps,
and yet capable of proving highly important. It is the view
of showing that the issue raised against the Divine character
upon the point of endlessness alone is not legitimately raised :
and that there are several particulars, perhaps even an indefinitely large number of them, which we ought to have the
means of defining before we can form any judgement for
ourselves upon the question whether the quality of endlessness is that upon which, preferably to and independently of
every other quality, judgement is to be solicited and taken. I
open one or two of the doors of mere speculation, to remind
other speculators that they are many ; that the prospect which
they disclose is not inviting to the cautious and thoughtful
mind ; and I suggest again and again the question whether
there is any safer course than to accept the declarations of
Holy Scripture, which award the just doom of suffering to
sin, and leave the sin and the suffering too, where alone
they can be safely left, in the hands of the Divine and un-
erring Judge. I recommend none of these speculations. But
I contend that there is no just title to exclude them from
the view of those, who are not contented with the ancient
reserve : and that they are less dangerous and daring than
some of the ideas which appear to have gained acceptance
of late, and even to have gained it among persons entitled
from other points of view to our high respect [1].

---

[1] Such, for example, as Mr. Erskine of Linlathen. See his recently pub-lished *Remains*. A list might easily be framed (and doubtless it would include Origen) of persons who have favoured these opinions, and have exhibited, along with them, lofty examples of Christian character.

I will not prosecute this line of observation farther; and
I have, indeed, only gone so far on the ground indicated
by Clarke in his wise observation that God may have many
modes of dealing with His creatures which He has not
disclosed to us. It is one thing to open theories with a
covert recommendation of them to surreptitious favour. It
is quite another to support a suggestion of reserve in subjects which may be so justly called transcendental, by showing that there are or may be paths which in the present
state of our knowledge could for us be only quicksands,
but yet which, for all we know, the power of the Almighty
might include within the bounds of possibility [1].

[1] In *Universalism asserted*, by the
Rev. T. Allin (sixth edition, London,
1895), that scheme is represented with
courage, and frequently with modesty.
The work appeals largely to early testimony : and (p. 106) claims, on the
authority of two early, though anonymous, writers, that the last Apology
of Pamphilus, the joint production
(mainly)of Eusebius and himself, 'contained very many testimonies of Fathers earlier than Origen in favour of
restitution.' Mr. Allin quotes as his
authority for this important statement Routh's *Reliquiae Sacrae.* Dr.
Routh has carefully gathered the
information extant respecting the
work. One anonymous author says
that Eusebius used the language cited,
on behalf of restitution *together with
pre-existence.* And Photius quotes a
second writer, as citing on his own
authority Demetrius, Bishop of Alexandria, who subsequently opposed
Origen, Clement, and various others
(ἑτέρους πλείους) ; relying chiefly, however, on Pamphilus and Eusebius, both
subsequent to Origen. The effect of
the citation by Photius is greatly to
reduce the force of the statement
made by the other anonymous author.
Whatever the opinions of Clement,
he did not acquire notoriety in connexion with the Origenian tenets
(Routh, *Rel. Sac.*, vol. iii. pp. 258-69
and 277, ed. Oxon., 1815).

CHAPTER IV

LET us now consider what are the propositions relating to the future life, which have from the first been included in the summaries of our faith, and which, upon the historical principles of the Church at large, are regarded as binding upon all Christians.

If we ask, what are the propositions associated with this subject which ought to be considered as belonging to the essence of the Christian faith, and as obligatory upon our personal belief? the sacred Scriptures do not appear to supply a ready answer to this question. But history informs us at how early a date, how long certainly before the epoch of any Council except that held at Jerusalem under the chief Apostles, the Church, or the general sense of the body of Christian believers, began to build upon the first foundation, and to follow the example supplied with Divine authority by the baptismal formula. It proceeded to incorporate in various forms the substance of the single and brief document which soon, replacing at least one even older version employed in Rome, became supreme throughout the entire West under the name of the Apostles' Creed. In this Creed we declare our belief in 'the resurrection of the body, and the life everlasting.' So far we are clearly dealing with matter of obligatory belief.

The Creed elaborated at Nice and Constantinople represents, even more than any other document, the prolonged, concentrated, and most severely tested action of the mind of the universal Church. In the last of these particulars it stands alone. It was through the agonies of the fourth century, the hardest of all the trials, the noblest of all the victories of the Church of God, that this Creed made its way to a position unrivalled alike in loftiness and in solid-

ity. In the East it may be said to enjoy an exclusive dominance. In the West, through the Eucharistic office, it holds
the grandest of all positions in Christian worship, so that it
is, equally with the Apostles' Creed, incessantly presented
to the mind of the Church. It is not necessary now to
speak of several additions, not relevant to the present subject, which were made to it under Latin authority in much
later times. In this consummate document, mainly as received from Nice and Constantinople, we declare that we
'look for,' and of course therefore believe in, 'the resurrection of the dead, and the life of the world to come.'

The Athanasian Creed, apart from its anathemas, is a
great and wonderful product of substantive theology concerning the Trinity, and, even more, the Incarnation of our
Lord; but it is not (I believe) placed, except in the Anglican Articles of Religion, which do not form a Confession
for the Church of England at large, on a level with the two
preceding Creeds; nor is it, except within the English
Church, presented with an equal degree of familiarity, by
inclusion in the public services, to the general mind of
believers. It declares that men shall rise again with their
bodies; shall render an account for their works; and shall,
if they have done good, 'go into life everlasting'; if they
have done evil, 'into everlasting fire.' The main distinctions
offered by this Creed are not that it penetrates farther, as
modern opinion has done, into the nature of eternity and
the particulars of the Divine counsels, but that it presents
to us expressly what, perhaps, cannot be excluded from the
implications of the other Creeds, namely, the survival and
passage into eternity of the wicked as well as of the righteous. But seeing that the rank given to this Creed is only
(so to speak) sectional, I shall not rely upon it in the examination with which we are immediately concerned. On the
one hand, it repeats words which were solemnly delivered
by our Saviour. But as those words are subject to some
variety of interpretation, while they have a tendency to
widen the demands of faith, which sufficed for the earlier
Creeds, we may reflect with satisfaction that this Creed
does not carry, in the general mind of the Church, an equivalent authority. There is another particular of extension

which may even be thought accidental. For the Athanasian Creed, delivering its propositions in the abstract, applies them to the whole race of men, while the older and more authoritative documents are content to deal, at least by reasonable implication, only with professing Christians.

Concentrating, then, our attention upon the declarations contained in the other two Creeds, and bearing in mind the immeasurable importance of the future state under the Christian dispensation, we cannot but be struck alike with their simplicity and their reserve. Out of four propositions, three, asserting the resurrection, the 'life everlasting,' and 'the life of the world to come,' may be said most rigidly to confine themselves within the limits of elementary Scripture, and to resolve themselves into one, namely, that we, who recite the Creed, are to pass at death into eternity. And here we find that the idea vividly presented to us is the survival of the righteous, whose condition is so properly conveyed under the word 'life.' I do not presume to affirm it for certain that the case of the wicked is excluded. It seems to remain, however, as it were, in the shade. There is here neither declaration nor implication as to the meaning of eternity; as to the relative numbers of those on the right hand or the left; or as to the particular conditions of the doom which awaits the sinner.

And surely it is delightful to contemplate the providential wisdom which guided the mind of the early and undivided Church to establish and enforce for us all the doctrine of a future life, but saved it from the unnecessary and entangling complications, into which more recent opinion seems for a long period to have been betrayed.

But it may be asked, why, if a temper of reserve so largely prevailed, did the Creed of the Apostles declare in express terms the resurrection of the body? It is not difficult to suggest the probable reason. Those schools of ancient philosophy, which had laboured so honestly and well by ingenious speculations to save us from the apprehension of extinction at death, had founded themselves largely on metaphysical arguments associated with the nature of the soul, and had been unable to retain any grasp of the idea of a future corporeal existence. From the time of Homer onwards, great difficulty seems to have been felt in regard to the relation between the several parts of man. Homer was influenced by Egyptian ideas. But the conception of the future life became less and less strong among the Greek race, which supplied the great masters of philosophy; and, whether with or without any definite conception of existence purely immaterial, they lost, as I suppose, the idea of any bodily survival. If, when Christians were few, and the new institutions in their infancy, this was the established tone of thought, we may well conceive that, for a practical fulfilment of the great promise to bring life and immortality to light, it was needful that there should be an express provision, familiar to all the faithful, for securing a complete and not a merely partial conception of the great human survival.

While, then, the sum of authoritative declarations on the future state, by the full action and consent of the Church, is thus carefully limited in the Creeds, I am aware of no other bond which should restrain us from canvassing with greater freedom the assumptions which I have recently enumerated, provided we do not forget the reverence and caution which should encircle the entire subject. It is, indeed, necessary for us to be on our guard against the silent and unwatched intrusion into the religious precinct of conceptions which nowhere bear the sacred stamp, but belong, whether their value be great or small, to the ordinary circle of secular knowledge or opinion. And such we must surely admit to be, among others, the popular conception of time. Be it ever so true that, for us, in our present condition, the idea of time may fairly be regarded as a simple idea, incapable of resolution into parts, it does not therefore follow that we are entitled to pronounce on its always continuing such, or anything like such, in other, and, perhaps, quite differently ordered states of existence.

I confess myself at a loss to see on what just ground there can be constructed any claim upon the ordinary Christian to concern himself with more than the propositions of the Creeds as portions of his necessary faith. It would seem that if he entertain other propositions he is under no obligation, and has no warrant, to elevate them to so high a plane.

Of the limited service, which it is my hope and aim to

render by the present examination to the combined cause of truth and charity, a principal part will consist in my endeavours to remove from the field of controversy a variety of assumptions which, as it appears to me, have no title to a place there, and which have tended both to widen the issue raised, and to perplex and embitter the dispute.

1. It is assumed that the Christian Revelation is designed to convey to us the intentions of the Almighty as to the condition, in the world to come, not of Christians only, but of all mankind.

2. It is assumed that, when the Scriptures speak of things eternal, they convey to us that eternity is a prolongation without measure of what we know as time.

3. It is assumed that punishment is a thing inflicted from without, *flagellum Tisiphone quatit insultans*, and is something additional to or distinct from the pain or dissatisfaction or loss, which under the law of nature stand as the appropriate and inborn consequence of misdoing.

4. It is assumed that the traditional theory propounds, and the teaching of Scripture requires us to believe that, of those who are to be judged as Christians, only a small minority can be saved.

5. It is assumed under the doctrine of natural immortality that every human being has by Divine decree a field of existence commensurate with that of Deity itself.

In all these assumptions there is expressly or tacitly included a claim to be received as portions of our religion; that is to say, of the Divine Revelation to man.

I shall hazard some remarks upon them one by one.

At first as to the supposition that the Christian scheme deals with the future destinies of all mankind.

The New Testament has many references to a future and what seems to be a final judgement, but with one exception they are marked by paucity of detail. Where argument is introduced, and it is found only in one case, the unprofitable servant is manifestly a typical person representative of those with whom the Lord of all has already had open dealings, and who have been placed in a condition to know with whom it is that they have to do, and how they ought to proceed in regard to the trust committed to them; for they were aware that he was an hard man, who would rigidly exact account; while also it is plain that they began their work on a footing of equality with the 'good and faithful servants [1].'

The single instance in the Gospels which penetrates further than this into the case, and exhibits the specific reasons of the future doom, is the majestic recital which immediately follows the parable of the talents [2]. In this profoundly impressive passage, but one description of virtuous action and of its opposite is recorded, that, namely, which includes what are termed in Christian nomenclature the corporal works of mercy. It may be hazardous to do even so much as glance at the reasons which induced our Lord in His wisdom at once to expatiate as He has here done, and also to set bounds to His exposition. Can it have been that He foresaw that the most conspicuous point of failure among nominal believers would be in the law of mutual love, and in discerning the connexion between that law and personal love to Christ, who universally addresses us in the person of the distressed? Be this as it may, we observe that both the righteous, who disclaim all merit, and the unrighteous, who are conscious of no defect, are alike addressed as persons emerging from a temporal dispensation, under which good offices toward man are directly associated with duty to God. This is a conception which not only is markedly Christian, but which had so faded away from, or which lay so little within, heathen knowledge, that it could hardly in their case have formed the basis, or entered into the terms, of an equitable judgement.

What is still more to the purpose, than this noteworthy representation, is the fact that St. Paul [3] has somewhat elaborately expounded the separate case of those who remain under the law of natural righteousness. In the day when God shall judge the hidden things of mankind according to the Gospel revelation, he will also judge the portion of mankind outside the special covenant, according to the law of nature written in their hearts, and according as they have obeyed or disobeyed that law. Let us, therefore, wholly disembarrass ourselves from the idea that those, who have

---

[1] Matt. xviii. 24 ; xxv. 14.   [2] Matt. xxv. 31–46.
[3] Rom. i. xviii. 2-16.

not been supplied with the means of Christian conduct, will be judged according to the demands of the Christian law.

Secondly; it is assumed, that eternity is a prolongation of time, continued without any limit. I ask myself in vain whether there is any governing exposition supplied to us by the Scriptures or the Creeds, or by the authentic tradition of Christendom, which entitles us to make this assumption. Without any suggestion that it should be met with denial, or questioning that it has been much in vogue, and that when indeterminate questions are determined there is a seeming accession to our knowledge which we are readily tempted to accept, I presume to express some hesitation as to both its foundation and its utility. To say that we cannot separate the idea of duration from our common conceptions of future life is saying nothing to the purpose. This may be a subject for metaphysical speculation: but is it a part of the truths declared to us for our guidance? The Scripture goes but a little way on this subject; still, so far as it goes, it does not seem greatly to favour the idea now before us. When it tells us that with God a thousand years are but as one day, it seems as if these words might mean that the being of the Deity is outside the conditions of time, and that this meaning is not only allowable, but may fairly compete with others which can attach to them. And if the grand idea of the future reserved for righteous souls be, according to the Gospel, a re-establishment in the original charter of our nature by reunion with God, and if God have an existence outside of time, who can tell whether or not an independence of time may or may not be included in the conditions of this reunion?

Look for a moment at eternity under the view of its being an immeasurable expansion of time. Consider ever so briefly the very large meaning involved in this proposition. The contemplation even of our own narrow span of life as a whole, when seriously attempted, seems to fill the mind nearly up to the limit of its receptive power. A million is a numerical accumulation which, if regarded at once as a whole and in its units, seriously baffles us. But now we are called to heap together millions, billions and quadrillions without limit, and to recollect that in doing it we do nothing: and that, however often we repeat the process, it is the same *toties quoties:* the score remains undiminished. In dealing with such a conception, we pass wholly beyond our depth. If all this may be so, yet it seems hard to compel every mind into the belief that it must be so; and there is something to be said here also in favour of taking refuge in our ignorance.

This much we may presume to say. Had the Divine Revelation been intended to convey to us that time is an inseparable incident of the future life, and that eternity is no more and no less than the unfolding of an immeasurable roll of time, it seems probable, perhaps it might be said certain, that the Bible could and would have employed some terminology evidently adapted to that purpose. But such is not the terminology actually given us. For, in dealing with the condition of the righteous in the world to come, our Saviour builds not upon terms of time, but upon the reunion with Deity. And, in touching with greater reserve upon the condition of the wicked, the image presented to us is either (1) simply negative, as in the case of the five virgins; or it is (2) one of suffering without any expressed reference to duration, as in the outer darkness, where there will be weeping and gnashing of teeth; or, it is (3) associated with words which etymologically and by use signify the indefinite rather than the infinite. And fourthly, a portion of the passages without doubt introduce the awful image of finality. But such presentations are held by some to indicate a process of extinction and total disappearance, rather than of a miserable existence co-extensive with that of Deity. They may be possibly susceptible of other explanations at present hidden from our view. In any case, we have to take them in connexion with the other passages; and it does not seem extravagant to suggest that this great diversity of delineation may possibly indicate a purpose of reserve.

On the third of the five assumptions, it will not be necessary to dwell at great length. But there is a serious difference between two separate methods of administering justice. This man, let us suppose, has committed manslaughter: let him, according to the circumstances, be imprisoned for one year, or for ten, or for life. This forensic or purely extraneous method, only with a more exact and less coarse adaptation, is the favourite notion under which the opponents of eternal punishment are prone to exhibit it. It is very different from those punishments which lie in the heart of the things themselves, and, in the language of Butler, arrive by way of natural consequence. For, as to these, nature herself is our premonitory teacher. And her lessons cannot be shut out, except by the method, at once stupid and audacious, of refusing to think. The drunkard, for example, knows that, by the repetition of inebriety, he is losing his freedom. And, if he knows this, in the later stages of his downward course, but faintly and dimly, whereas he had known it at the beginning well and clearly, the meaning is, that his punishment 'in the way of natural consequence' has already begun; that its initial stage is a warning mercifully sent, like the first loss at a gambling table, in order that we may be induced to avoid those which are to follow; and that, if the warning be neglected, we shall proceed from bad to worse. As it is on this basis that the teachers of the more rigid doctrine, profiting perhaps by the lessons of experience, commonly build their system, it is surely on this basis that they ought to be met by their opponents.

Fourthly; it is assumed that we are required by the language of Holy Scripture to limit the salvation of professing Christians to a very small minority of their total number.

Fairness constrains me to admit that this has commonly or often been presented as an item of the ordinary teaching on the subject of future punishment. It is now largely used, in the adverse sense, as an aggravation of a dreadful picture. My desire is to offer some considerations which tend so far at least to throw doubt upon the assumption, as to make it expedient and rational to hold this part also of the subject in reserve.

When our Lord delivered in Galilee the Sermon on the Mount, He admonished His audience that the gate of salvation was strait, and the way narrow and found by few; while the gate and way of destruction were broad and easy, and found by many [1]. And all the words of our Blessed

[1] Matt. vii. 13, 14.

Lord are perfect in truth and wisdom. Yet it is our duty to compare them together, and so far as may be to collect their effect as a whole. It seems indisputable that they do not invariably (as, for example, in the parable of the unjust steward) present to us, at each and every point, each and every aspect of the case in hand ; and possibly this is a result, partly inherent in the conditions of human language, and partly incidental to all teaching which takes advantage of occasion. The Gospel of St. Matthew, it is largely agreed, was composed with a special reference to the condition and exigencies of the Jewish race ; that of St. Luke with a wider outlook upon the Gentiles also. In those chapters of St. Luke, which offer many remarkable correspondences with the Sermon on the Mount, and form an echo of it, the image of the strait gate reappears in connexion with the difficulty of entering it, and it becomes the basis of an exhortation not to seek merely, but to strive, that is to seek manfully and with might, to enter it ; while the passage is immediately followed by an impressive contrast between the case of Jews rejected in the great account, and that of Gentiles then admitted [1], which may possibly indicate something of specialty or local colour in what may be called the sister passage. It is also noteworthy that the words of our Lord are a reply to the inquiry, ' Lord, are there few to be saved ? ' In declining a reply to this question, must we not admit that He seems to close the door upon the subject and thereby to mark it for us as one of rather unprofitable speculation ?

In any case, we are bound to have regard to the general effect of our Lord's teaching ; and in this case the more so, because He so frequently deals, not with the present scene and current life, but *ex professo*, with the final upshot of human destinies. In all His teachings, by parable or otherwise, we look in vain for any direct revelation of the relative numbers of the accepted and the lost. It is not in the sheep and the goats. It is not in the tares and the wheat. In the case of the vineyard, a body of rejectors of grace are dealt with exclusively. In the case of the wise and the foolish virgins, where the *poena damni* alone seems to be awarded, the numbers are equal. In the case of the talents,

[1] Luke xiii. 23 30.

two of the entrusted servants are mentioned for acceptance, one only for rejection. In the case of the gathering from highways and hedges to replace those who had refused the invitation to the banquet, there is no specification of numbers or proportions. In the case of the guest-chamber, the wedding-feast is eaten by a number of persons, but only one is detected as not having on the wedding-garment.

It is, I presume, our duty to consider, with humble care and without prepossession, the general effect of these very varied indications in the discourses of our Saviour. For this purpose the foregoing remarks are intended. The conclusion towards which they seem to point is that, as in sundry other matters, so with regard to the comparative numbers of professing Christians saved and lost, Divine Wisdom has, doubtless for the best reasons, veiled its counsels with stringent limitation and reserve.

Lastly, the inclusion in religious teaching of a supposed law of natural immortality has been so largely discussed in prior portions of these papers, and especially in considering the history of Christian opinion, that any return to the subject in this place would be superfluous, except it be with respect to a point properly collateral.

It is admitted that the resurrection of the body as such is an exclusively Christian doctrine; true as it may be that the conception of a future life in the last resort involved an approach at least to corporeal elements, such as figures of some kind. But, according to Christian doctrine (1 Cor. xv. 36–44), the natural or mortal body has in it a seed from which shall spring the spiritual or immortal body. Let us consider how much this implies. The body is now the instrument and servant of the soul, while it reciprocally exercises powerful influences upon it. But this body is not a mere appendage or vestment to the man: it is a part of him. Thus far it seems, then, to be agreed that one part of our immortality is not natural, but is a gift flowing from the Incarnation. This may render it all the more worth our while to examine whether our immortality is likely to be thus divided by the Gospel, and to be natural and indefeasible as to the soul, but only a gift of the Christian system as to the body. One portion of the gap between

the opposite opinions would appear to be bridged over by
these considerations, which lead towards the conclusion that,
with St. Paul for our guide, we shall not readily be persuaded to accept the idea that the Gospel has propounded
to us the natural immortality of all human souls as a portion
of the Christian religion[1].

It remains, however, to consider some larger assumptions
which have been extensively made by writers taking the side
adverse to what they usually call the traditional theology.

1. The experience of life shows on every side that habit
hardens by use, that the gristle passes into the bone, that
under the laws of our nature we travel steadily towards
the unchangeable in cases where bias has been habitually
and permanently indulged by repetition of acts. But all the
lessons of this experience are to be cast aside with respect
to the laws which are to govern character in the world to
come, and we are told that the unchangeable will there
undergo a process of essential transformation and reversion,
by becoming a pliable and docile material, fashioned upon
new laws, which are contradictory of the old.

2. While the justice of punishing wickedness is admitted,
and it is held or not denied, that the measure of our punishment will be found in the amount and character of our
iniquity, and it is moreover felt to be unreasonable for us
to impose limitations of quantity and quality on this effect
without any adequate power of measuring the cause, the single point of duration is picked (so to speak) out of the case,
and it is laid down, without any question raised on severity
and intensity, that the prolongation without limit of suffering in any form, whether forensically inflicted or accruing
by natural laws as the fruit of character acquired in this
life, must be under all circumstances incompatible with the
justice of God.

---

[1] Plato teaches that the body as
well as the soul, though not, like the
gods of popular opinion, eternal, yet
having once come into existence, is
indestructible (*Laws*, x. 904). There
are souls of the sun and stars (*Tim.*
41; *Laws*, x. 899). In man death
(*Laws*, viii. 828) dissolves the union
between them. Impurity (*Phaedo*, 81
seqq.) will prevent the total escape of
the soul. But Socrates hopes to live
wholly apart from the body, and this
seems to represent the summit of the
Greek doctrine concerning the body.
These are simply dreams of speculation. As to the body, we find a metaphysical conception recorded on its
behalf, but a manifest leaning of the
speculative intelligence against it.

3. That the character of the Almighty is rendered liable to charges which cannot be repelled so long as the idea remains that there may by His ordinance be such a thing as never-ending punishment, but that it will have been sufficiently vindicated at the bar of human judgement, so soon as it has been established and allowed that punishment, whatever else it may be, cannot be never-ending.

As regards the first of these features of the new teaching, which has already been touched in part[1], does it not amount to a gratuitous substitution of speculation for experience, and is such a substitution to be properly regarded as an act of courage, or as a desperate venture of mental rashness? To my mind it stands in the latter category.

It would be thought strange to teach a reversal of some great law of the natural universe; for instance, a displacement of the law of gravity in favour of a law of repulsion between material substances. Yet it is conceivable that such a change might be brought about, as to take small effect upon the main work and purpose of our existence, since our relation to them might be susceptible of large adjustments. But the laws of our own constitution and growth, by which our destiny is redeemed from the sport of chance and bound into a whole, supply the standing-ground on and from which we are to confront and act upon the universe. How can the propounders of such a scheme rationally expect that future inquirers will accord to their novel, we might say new-fangled, notions, a respect which they have themselves withheld from the most intimate and universal facts of human experience?

As respects the second and third of these assumptions, it appears that those who make them are, in perfect good faith, impressed with an apprehension, lest the character of the Almighty should suffer in the estimation of a portion of His creatures, from the currency of tenets which they deem to be irreconcilable with His essential attributes.

There is something that is touching, and perhaps also something that is startling, in this enterprise. It was bold on Milton's part, when he undertook

To justify the ways of God to man ;

---

[1] *Sup.* p. 222.

and perhaps his success was not so complete as to commend the further entertainment, without much consideration, of similar designs. And the first condition to be reasonably asked their propounders is that they should measure at the outset the scope and extent of their undertaking. Also that they should weigh the question whether, in our present state of clouded limitation, we are to hold ourselves bound or invited to clear the present dispensation under which we live of all the moral anomalies, disparities, and apparent contradictions lying around us. And if so, whether it would not seem to be in the more natural order that we should begin with the facts and events of the present existence, concerning which we are armed at least with some store of experimental knowledge, rather than launch upon a series of adjustments for the world future and unseen, with our feet planted on ground which we cannot firmly tread, and in an atmosphere which we have no lungs to breathe.

Evil, according to this philosophy, has no right to a place in this world. Its adepts, therefore, set themselves at work to dislodge it, at least in hypothesis, by assuming that, at some uncertain time, there shall be a reign of universal happiness; while, moreover, there is also to be taken for granted the accompaniment of universal goodness. The reply suggests itself: 'Jesus I know, and Paul I know, but who are ye?' When the prophets portended a flood of blessing, when the apostles proclaimed a coming triumph of righteousness and peace, the first referred in vision to, and the last brought into possible and visible action, a scheme of means, adequately equipped with motive power, whereby the results which they predicted were to be obtained. But this new forecast of the future advisedly, or at least manifestly, passes by the remedial system now in action, and steps out into the void that lies beyond it. Not like the cautious Butler, who reckons upon nothing without a foresight of means adequate to the end in view, they make no addition to the 'going machinery' of redemption, but boldly anticipate results without any indication of the means to produce them. Do they not truly stand as men who make bricks without straw, and anticipate the flowers and fruits of their garden without sowing any seed to produce

them? Wickedness and suffering within the bounds of
creation are, as they conceive, disparaging to the Creator,
and inevitably bring into question either His wisdom, His
goodness, or His power. They therefore do not indeed
provide, but suggest, a sweeping scheme for their removal,
thrusting out of the way any established laws of our nature which would hinder the consummation. Evils shall
vanish; suffering shall have an end; the Almighty shall
be vindicated. The thesis is, that evil may not, must not,
always exist in this universe. But is this a real or solid
vindication? Does it not rather include within itself the
materials of a hopeless dilemma, and therefore the doom
of inevitable failure? Evil is to be employed or tolerated
up to a certain date, and then, for the honour of God, it
is to cease. But before that date it has *ex hypothesi* been
employed or tolerated; and where was the honour of God
then? If it was compatible with the honour of God for
a time, why may it not continue similarly compatible, so
as to make use of it hereafter? If employed, or tolerated,
this was either with reason or without. If without reason,
we have no security against its continuance without reason.
If with reason, how can we know that the reason which
operated before may not also operate after? If it is wise,
if there be a vindication at present veiled from our view,
how can we presume to say that there is a date at which
it must cease to be available? If unwise, for the longer
period, how shall we show that it was wise for the shorter?
If wise, for the shorter, how can we tell whether it may
be also wise for the longer? There are special dangers
attending upon labour which is volunteered; and an imperfect vindication may be worse than no vindication at
all; especially in the view of those who see there is
open to us an alternative, in the reservation of our judgement, until the day when the secrets of the Divine Wisdom shall be laid open, or more open, to our view.
Cardinal Newman has well observed that the mystery of
mysteries in regard to the evil now in the world is not
how it is to end, but how it began. And a solution of
the minor mystery, could it be had, would leave us exactly where we now are with respect to the greater one.

Let us endeavour still further to exhibit the perilous, and totally ineffectual, nature of these doubtless well-meant attempts to take into our hands the exculpation of Divine Providence. As we see, the objectors of the present day, to what they term the teaching of the 'traditional theology,' appear to think that, when they have got rid of the single element of endless duration in the matter of future punishments, they have thereby attained to a satisfactory vindication of the Divine character from the charge of inflicting excessive and unnecessary suffering.

As has been said, it is a very serious matter to undertake at all the vindication of the character of the Divine Being. Especially is it so for us, who do so little to maintain, improve, or repair our own. For it even seems in some degree to imply, at least for the moment, the assumption of a kind of superior position ; or to allow that idea, or its results at least, to find their way into the mind. But, apart from any scruple or difficulty on this score, it does not appear to me that this vindication, however honourably sought, is or can be attained by us with our present limited supply of knowledge and means of inquiry. The utmost the vindicator can do seems to be to abate or cancel a single point in the indictment, which it is the practice of negationists to bring against the character of God. It is objected to the doctrine of endless punishment that there is no proportion between offences committed in our narrowly bounded life, and that wide field of an unlimited existence, over the whole of which the expected retribution is to prevail. I do not now speak of the recorded replies to this objection, which may or may not be satisfactory. But let us give the objector all he asks ; and then inquire whether, by expelling the element of endlessness from punishment, we so alter the spectacle presented to us by the conditions of human destiny, that we can then take upon ourselves the burden of bringing them all into harmony (and this is the purpose in view) with the character of an all-wise, all-righteous, and all-powerful God. We have to meet the challenge of the negationist in other and separate lists. Show me the justice, he demands, of placing the responsibility of

existence upon creatures who have no choice given them in
the matter, and then weighing them down with tendencies
to mischief inherited from their ancestors: with pressure
due to adverse and sometimes apparently domineering environment; with suggestion, attraction, menace, danger in
every form; with an evil bias rooted in themselves through
a degeneracy of nature asserted by our highest, that is, by
revealed authority, and but too largely established by cor-
roborating experience ? Is not, he asks, your free will, on
which you so much rely as an argument, frequently placed
under an amount of solicitation or pressure such as, in the
judgement of every equitable observer, comes indefinitely
near to the aspect of coercion ? I go further, and ask
whether the objector may not press us, his respondents,
with a wider question, and take such words as these into
his mouth : You seek shelter behind the free will of the
human being, which you allege enables him to deal with
each action, and with every situation, in detail. But you
cannot deny that there is a broader question, the question
of existence itself. This existence is admitted to be attended with danger ; and yet there was neither a consent
obtained from us as a condition of our entering on it, nor
liberty granted, with a free passage provided, to enable us
to lay it down. What was the All-goodness that called
into existence free beings, with a foreknowledge that the
misuse of this freedom would bring them into misery ?
Why were they to be made examples of the law which annexes misery to a failure to do right, without their first
being freely made parties to a trial upon that issue ? Does
not the title to be free upon each of the parts carry with it
a corresponding claim to be free upon the great question of
existence, which sums up the whole ? To his challenges I
am able to make no fuller reply than this, that, according
to our faith, every man will be judged with full allowances
for every adverse incident of his lot, and that God will
enable all, who sincerely strive for it, to overcome alike the
circumjacent and the indwelling sin, or will in any and
every case deal with them according to the most exact and
largest justice.
    Then he asks me, why were they solicited, and vexed, and

stained with evil in any shape? There is no such thing as an universal right inherent in all who have the power to place people in temptation, because it is hoped, believed, or even known, that with immense effort they will overcome it.

But, I reply, this evil is for them an instrument of good, and, by means of the training they receive, they attain to more and higher good than they could have attained without it.

But I have not yet fully repelled my assailant; he is again upon me, and he says, What then means your sovereignty of a good Power, which in the case of man is dependent upon an evil principle for the best accomplishment of His design? Add to this that I am entitled to ask, how far does the necessity for this ill-assorted aid extend? Does it go beyond the case of man, and is the whole universe tainted with evil as the condition of becoming good? If man is an exception, why is he only placed under this disadvantage, and at the same time told that he is an object of special if not exceptional or exemplary favour in the Divine counsels? At any rate there is one order of beings, made known to us by Scripture, and as many will say, also by experience, with regard to whom the question legitimately arises. These are the fallen angels: are these, too, under discipline, and intended to reap the harvest of the greater good? If not, why not? But, if you reply affirmatively, if good is to become universal, then you contemplate the loss from the universe of the very Power by which this beneficial action through evil is maintained? And this runs up into the final question. Evil is a thing abhorrent to the Divine nature; furnish me with an adequate reason why it came into the world. I am obliged to reply that no such reason is in my actual possession; that I must look for it to the region of Faith or reasonable expectation; and to some province of that region which has not yet been opened, but which is still enveloped in a mantle of clouds and darkness.

So then all that our objector has done is, in his own estimation, to have effected a certain quantitative deduction from the charges advanced by negationists against the character of God. But the matter is one which cannot be disposed of, nor essentially affected, by any merely quantitative process. The vindication of the character of God is a business that ought not to be undertaken by halves. If we are compelled to halt in the operation before placing that character in the light in which it ought to stand to the eye of some high and sinless intelligence, it may after all be better to take refuge in our own humble condition, and to accept the problems of existence under the limited and imperfect forms, in which alone God has permitted us to approach them. So that I make my reply to the opponent in terms like these. Of the injustice you admit to be plausibly charged, you remove but half. But in a scientific vindication of God, half success is in truth total failure ; for what you have to re-establish is the idea of an All-perfect being. But if we have reasonable grounds *aliunde* for belief in such a Being, is it not far better to stand upon those grounds in an unbounded trust, than, by a half-examination of problems not referred to us, to scatter over the field an array of unanswered questions which testify to nothing but our headstrong readiness to charge ourselves with undertakings, for which we have neither commission nor capacity ?

Faith and reason unite to assure us that the world to come will be a world of readjustment ; where the first shall be last, and the last first, and where both good and evil shall uniformly receive their just rewards. This answer covers the whole of the adverse front. It both admits our incapacity together with our ignorance, and points with the finger of Divine hope to the prospect of their removal. But attempts at vindication, unwarranted, precipitate, and mistaking our poor twilight of knowledge for broad day, both fail of their purpose, and recoil upon their projectors.

Let us now revert to another portion of the subject.

I suppose that most of us, if thinking at all upon the coming condition of our companion pilgrims who precede us on their passage into the shadows of death, must think, upon a survey of the field of our experience, that they defy in innumerable cases our feeble powers of estimation. I mean those cases in which some real form of goodness seems to have a real, perhaps a strong and permanent hold,

but where it has not taken conscious and deliberate effect
in full conformity to the Divine will. Take for example
the instances in which, apart from any distinct self-devo-
tion to God, life has been principally or systematically
spent in the endeavour to diminish human suffering; and
this perhaps with the exercise of much active renunciation
and self-denial. Or again, where it has been similarly given
to that improvement of the temporal conditions of human
life, which, in a greater or a less urgent degree, the majority
of our fellow-creatures, or at the very least a large portion
of them, appeared to need. Or again, where men apply
their thought and means not to the indulgence of their appetites, but to the improvement and expansion of their own
powers for purposes of eventual utility. In all these schemes
for bettering God's world, regard to the Lord of that world,
and humble dependence on His power and benediction,
ought to have their proper place; which by the supposition has not, or not in due measure, been given to it. Or
let us turn our view to another and extended category of
those classes who embrace the Divine word with what they
think to be an entire willingness, nay, with a sanguine ex-
ultation. I do not now speak of the modes in which this
state of mind may be contaminated by a self-confidence in
utter antagonism to the true life of the Gospel, but to the
more simple, less entangled case, where the broad propositions of religion are accepted, but accepted too near the surface, without measuring them against the entire thought,
life, and purpose of the man, so that they are but partially
applied, and allow of the retention of this or that habit
which either falls short of, or even is on its own ground in
obvious conflict with, the laws of the Divine life. These
appear to be allowable illustrations of the manner in which
we shall find that certain suppositions of Butler leave un-
impaired all the stringent, as well as all the soothing, life
teachings of the Gospel; but yet supply the mind, in its
permissible excursions beyond the grave, which are so often
suggested by strong motives of nature and affection, with
many ideas such as at once feed us with hope and comfort,
and widen our horizon of thought upon the providential
scheme, and upon the blessings and eventual reach of the

Incarnation, that grand remedial instrument on which we rest all our hopes.

Following in the train of these suggestions, and in comparison and contrast with the three more formal theories or doctrines on the condition of man in the world to come, let us now turn to that larger teaching on the subject, which, though only in an occasional and fragmentary shape, Butler has been led to suggest after he has parted from the formal but limited argumentation of his first Chapter. His suggestions do not, indeed, ostensibly touch the lines of prevailing controversies; but they tend somewhat to modify that idea of an immediate and unconditional finality in the condition of the human soul following upon death, which the Reformation of the sixteenth century, from the particular circumstances of its origin, did so much to foster in the broadest form.

Even in his first Chapter, Butler intimates that death may issue in not only a continuation but an enlargement of existence; in a state where, through the widening of conditions, what we now deem to be above nature, or beyond it, may be found to be thoroughly natural[1]. And here I ask leave to spend a moment in confessing the comparative security and satisfaction with which I follow the steps of Butler, on the rare occasions when he speculates, as comparing him with other speculators. I feel like one resting on the wings of a great and strong bird, when it takes an excursion in mid-air, and is felt to mount as easily as it will descend.

With this notion of death, as leading to enlargement, Butler's very marked views respecting habit, growth, and evolution, as pertaining to our nature, are strongly in accord. It was from or with these views that he was led to question the philosophy, if not the theology, which with such shallow wisdom seems to teach us that with death the book is closed, at any rate until the resurrection and the judgement; by which, indeed, it sets no great store, or at least for which it leaves but little room. Such a man as Butler could not be hasty to assume that, if the interval be one of conscious life and action, it can pass without leaving behind it legible traces of its influence upon character.

[1] *Analogy*, I. i. 31.

Butler, as a sedulous observer of what was going on around him, was struck by the great advances which (probably having Newton in his mind) he conceived to have been recently effected in natural knowledge. The universe is, he finds, in a manner boundless and immense [1]. It is his inference from this grand physical revelation that there must be some scheme of Providence vast in proportion to it. Next, he noticed [2] the essential tendencies of virtue or goodness to acquire for itself augmentation of power. Such tendencies may be expected to operate freely and with energy, so soon as the grievous hindrances which now beset them shall have been removed. These have the signs, what may be termed the air, of belonging to the peculiar conditions of the present life. It is therefore probable that, in the world to come, they may not reappear as now. Should this be so, many souls of creatures, incapable of normal evolution in the inferior state, may be found to be capable of it so soon as a favourable change in the balance between auxiliaries and impediments shall have been effected. This may have no more the character of a paradox than when we say that ten pounds, which will not outweigh twenty, will outweigh five. Powers, the action of which was suspended by the adverse preponderance, will conceivably emerge into the open, and find scope for action, when that preponderance has been removed or reversed.

The discoveries, partly effected in Butler's time, of the vastness of the material universe at once led his profound and searching spirit to inquire whether, under the guidance of his master principle of analogy, he found cause to draw from the fact of those discoveries in the physical order any collateral inferences in respect to the moral and spiritual world. He did not indeed help to mislead his fellow-men by teaching, as is now the fashion in some quarters, that the immense enlargement of the visible kingdom of God proves the insignificance of the world which we inhabit, or discredits the idea that it can be the scene of an exceptional and peculiarly illustrious dispensation, such as is exhibited in the Incarnation of our Lord. His speculation was the very opposite of this precipitate, shallow, and barren sug-

[1] *Analogy*, I. iii. 28.   [2] *Ibid.* 30, *et alibi.*

gestion; a suggestion of which it is enough to say that, when traced home to its principle, it is at once detected in the grave offence of using the weights and measures of the physical universe as the criterion of moral and spiritual magnitudes. On Butler's mind these grand disclosures had the effect of widening his conception of the possible scope of the natural and moral government exhibited to us in nature and revelation. In effect, they suggested to him an enlargement of the purpose and working of the Incarnation itself, beyond the scope of the common conception, both popular and theological. For, says Butler, rising to that highest degree of confidence in which he rarely allows himself to indulge, it is certain that, as the material world appears to be in a manner boundless and immense, there must be some scheme of Providence reaching outside the material world, and vast in proportion to it [1]. With this weighty observation he winds up a course of thought in which he has pointed out that virtue, so sorely restrained and hampered here, might in another state of things be relieved from its impediments, and be placed under conditions favourable to its full development and corroboration. And further, that, being thus in itself enlarged and enhanced, it might be exhibited to, and might form a power of attraction for, others who had not yet been effectually drawn to it. And this might happen 'amongst one or more orders of creatures'; and the benefit might accrue 'in any distant scenes and periods,' to those among 'any orders of vicious creatures' having among them some who were 'capable of amendment, and (of) being recovered to a just sense of virtue [2].'

Thus does Butler appear to have embraced the ideas, first, that the developments of character effected through the Incarnation of Christ might operate upon beings subject to the Creator, but not belonging to the human race; and, secondly, that, also within the limits of the human family itself, persons who had not during this life in any manner perceptible to us actually crossed the line which divides righteousness from its opposite, might make such further advances as would effect that transition, provided their

[1] *Analogy*, I. iii. 27.   [2] *Ibid.* 28.

characters were still in such a state as to leave them capable of effectual amendment.

This limitation is undoubtedly of importance. It secures morality, the religious discipline of life, and the whole scheme of the Christian Revelation, against that general dilution, and indeed virtual dissolution of responsibility in conjunction with the present life, which must result if mankind, so powerfully predisposed to a relaxed belief, were instructed to assume that the exercises of this life might be multiplied in (perhaps) an interminable series of existences, and had no exceptional character, no final and determining effect. It excludes the dangerous notion which would place the central crisis of our probation elsewhere, and not here. We may take it for granted that Butler noticed, in common with every careful observer, the equivocal condition in which so many appear to quit the world. Let me again refer to some of the less difficult among these cases. There may be souls, which have not ceased radically and in their inmost selves to desire good, but they have not brought that desire, sincere yet overweak, to good effect. They perform freely many acts in the service of God; they accept without murmuring every dispensation administered to them from without by His will; they even exhibit much of unselfish devotion to the interests of their fellow-men; and yet they have not conformed to the supreme law which, in God's own world, places the root and centre of all our vital purposes not only in subjection, but in an active conformity, to His sovereign will. For, where positive love and service are due, mere non-resistance forms no legitimate substitute for them. And yet the heart will not desist from asking, Are not such fruits of partial good, such tendencies towards effectual and supreme good, as mark this group, it may be this multitude, of souls, worth preserving; and is it reasonable to suppose they can only be cast away as of none account? It would be still less reasonable to imagine they could be recognized as exhibiting the adequate and normal fruits of the Incarnation of Christ, or represent a spiritual condition which can be permitted to continue, unless in train to what is better, and in vital connexion with the central Life and Light of the universe. It may, then, perhaps appear that Butler has found or approached the true meeting-point of some contrary but not contradictory suggestions, in the noteworthy Section which is probably to be regarded as the crown and coping-stone of his own comprehensive and diversified reflections on our condition in the future state.

But these suppositions are indeed no more than an extension of the rational and philosophical belief, which the greater part of the Christian Church has always held respecting the laws which govern the condition of the believing dead. The Church has walked in the path opened for it by St. Paul through his prayer on behalf of Onesiphorus [1]. It has condemned our accepting what is termed the sleep of the soul; a speculation amounting to a suspension of human existence, and alike at variance with Scripture, which describes active enjoyments and even sufferings of the dead, and with reason, which exhibits to us our nature as constituted with a view to discipline and advance through the prolongation of existence, and through the action it entails. The Christian dead, then, are in a progressive state; and the appointed office of the interval between death and resurrection is reasonably believed to be the corroboration of every good and holy habit, and the effacement of all remains of human infirmity and vice. The extension suggested by Butler amounts to this : that, while the view of the Church in general only extends to those who have before death given evidence of repentance and faith such as the human eye can reasonably appreciate; still, as he suggests, where this evidence falls short, the root of the matter may be there notwithstanding, and the Almighty may reserve to His own jurisdiction the development necessary to cover both the ground which a more palpable sanctification had in other cases visibly secured anterior to death, and that remainder of progress generally reserved for accomplishment hereafter, even by souls of a clearly manifested faithfulness to their Lord.

Under such a view as Butler's, then, of the teaching of our religion as to the dead, it would appear that there may be introduced, at the hour of final adjustment, to receive the Divine reward, a class whose position, relatively to that of the other believers, may in part be compared with that of

[1] 2 Tim. i. 16.

the labourers in the vineyard hired at the ninth and the eleventh hours. True indeed that, according to the parable, we are not entitled to say that these had known of, and had refused or neglected, any earlier offer. But then it may be also true of these, so to speak, belated spirits, that they, either as a class or in particular cases, owed their backward condition rather to the want of opportunity than to a greater perverseness of the will, or a more obstinate slackness to hear and to obey. Be this as it may, there are two things on which we may rest with considerable, if not indeed with undoubting, confidence. The first is, that there will be no murmuring against the Master's bounty, no grudge as towards those newly admitted to a share of the reward. The second, that, in all cases where the smaller degree of progress achieved has been due to the man, and not to the environment of the man, he will take no benefit by his delays. The aggregate of whatever enjoyments he may by them have unlawfully secured in this life will not in the least degree contribute to his final happiness or augment its sum total ; but, on the contrary, will have left behind tracks of the course that has been trodden, and will have impressed tendencies, or left stains upon the soul which have had to be reversed or effaced by a process of discipline, happy indeed in its result, but of which we have no right to assert, as indeed we have no such right in other cases of departed spirits, that the redeeming and consummating process will be accomplished without an admixture of salutary and accepted pain.

I have slightly sketched one class of cases, by way of illustrating Butler's supposition, where much good had been generated by the discipline of life, but where it had still remained defective in its relation to the central good, and may have sorely lost thereby. There are many other classes, to our eyes yet more dubious, on which there would be no advantage in descanting. The fundamental idea, lying at the root of his conception, is this : that the appreciation of character and of moral action is a high matter, in which our means of judgement are scanty and feeble ; that we are therefore not competent to pronounce, in the intermediate region between manifest excellence and glaring sin, upon the state of souls; that, as they may be worse, so they also may often be better, than the evidence available for our use would warrant our declaring or assuming; that, while the determining impulse may have been received during life, the direction of the resulting movement may not as yet have been exhibited in our sight; and that this awful reckoning, which will set the last first, and the first last, is not committed to us, but is reserved for eyes more penetrating as well as more just.

It may be thought, and perhaps justly thought, by persons of more experience and perspicacious reflection than myself, that, while professing to follow the footsteps of Butler into the Unseen, I have not succeeded in conforming to his Christian and philosophic circumspection. Should this be so, I can only regret my being unequal to discharging the duty of an intelligent disciple; and I cherish the hope that my errors are not either wanton or contumacious. The master himself, at least, is here open to no charge.

His speculations on behalf of departed spirits which have not while in the flesh given evidence cognizable by us of their reunion with God, are not loosely projected into space. They are for those only who are 'capable of amendment, and being recovered to a just sense of virtue.' If we have no adequate means of judging who these may be, our incapacity may suggest the further question: Why should we have such means? The premature possession of them might bring about a relaxation of the bonds of moral obligation. Such is the account I should presume to give of the pregnant thoughts expressed by Butler in the remarkable Section we have now had before us. He avoids, it will be seen, the dangerous figment of those who please their imaginations by gratuitously supposing, to the grave disparagement of the Scriptures and the great redemption, that a new state or states of probation for us lie beyond the dread barrier of the grave. The question he raises is not that of a new probation, but only whether the present probation may take more complete effect under circumstances more felicitous for virtue and goodness than those of the terrestrial life. He does not add anything to the Incarnation, but he asks a guarded question as to the manifestation of results, which in their essence have been already wrought though not developed; and he gives us hope of hereafter rescuing a wider domain from the sway of evil or of its consequences, without weakening in the present critical state the laws of righteous award.

As a general apology for the papers now about to be brought to a close, I advance a proposition which, at least in its general terms, will not be gravely contested. Those who are conscious of their inability to solve a problem or close a controversy, may, nevertheless, render a real, though limited, service if they can eject from it matter gratuitously imported; can draw jealous attention to conceptions by which it has been both widened and perplexed; can relieve it from the pressure of unwarranted assumptions; can secure upon a field of doubtful speculations a temper of sobriety and even reserve; and can make contributions at least towards narrowing the issues, upon which men have found or thought themselves to be divided.

In pursuit of this general aim, the following measures have here been adopted.

1. To call into question the title of what is termed natural immortality to the place which it now largely holds in the religious mind of our generation; to endeavour to strip it of its acquired character as a doctrine of religion, and to exhibit it as a contested and undecided matter of philosophical speculation, upon which we do not possess material sufficient to warrant the assertion of any religious duty either to affirm or to deny.

2. To point out that early Christianity was not saddled with the responsibilities attaching to this opinion, and therein possessed a freedom which has been impaired by its unauthorized encroachments, and by its tacit usurpation of the field as a tenet to be accepted on the authority of the Christian faith.

3. To show that the Christian religion, properly so called, the

> Bella immortal benefica
> Fede ai trionfi avoezza [1],

is less directly implicated in these contentions than has been

---

[1] Manzoni, *Cinque Maggio.*

commonly supposed; and thankfully to put under view the wisdom and moderation of the early Christian Church in the construction of its Creeds.

4. To describe the three formally developed modes now chiefly prevalent in the presentation of the subject, and leave it to be considered whether there is not good reason sometimes firmly to eschew and condemn, and sometimes at least to stop short of affirming, various propositions which one or other of them has advanced.

5. To point attention to the diversities of phrase and idea, with which the lot of those rejected in the world to come is set forth by our Lord. My mind is swayed towards the belief that the combined effect of the several declarations is to indicate a Divine purpose of reserve as to all which lies beyond the broad and solemn utterance hereinbefore cited from St. Paul; and that the firm assertion and enforcement of the truth conveyed in that utterance might possibly be found more effective for the practical repression of sin, than its development into more copious and detailed, but less certainly authorized, expositions.

6. To bring into view the guarded and circumspect enlargement of the common field of view, which Butler has conjecturally supplied, and in which he abates nothing from the efficacy of the Incarnation of the Saviour, but adds to the sum of its beneficent results.

All this the present writer has set out as subject to correction, worthy at most only of being deliberately pondered, in the hope that the wheat may be duly winnowed from the chaff. A similar sense of the evils and dangers of self-confidence governs him in the attempt to sketch the frame of mind into which, not as a teacher of religion, but as a private Christian, obliged like his brethren to serve the truth as best he can, he now seeks to cast his own contemplation of the subject.

The future life, says Butler[1], is the foundation of all our hopes and all our fears, such hopes and fears as are worthy of any consideration. We are invited to assume an immense inheritance, of which the portion withheld from present view is of such extended range, as to throw the present

[1] *Anology*, Introd. § 17.

bounded scene, not indeed into insignificance, but into comparative minuteness. In what St. Paul described as the fullness of time, a Gospel was proclaimed, tidings of joy and gladness, with a background, it is true, of penal retribution for the obstinately disobedient, but still with joy and gladness for their principle, their determining character; inasmuch as, had it been otherwise, the great gift, so long detained for the maturing process in the womb of time, would have not been an *evangelion*, but a *dusangelion* to man. The leading office of the Gospel, in its bearing on the world to come, was to make known, not misery, but salvation. Its direct concern was with the moral and spiritual part of man; the part in which he had received a deadly wound; the part which supplies the true enduring basis of what he *is*, the basis of his character. To heal that wound, to supply that character with a fund of enduring vitality, it did not furnish him with particular information as to the conditions of the life to come : but, leaving his ignorance to be dispelled at the proper season when it shall arrive, revealed the one great secret which comprised in itself every other that concerned him, the mode and means of his reunion with God.

But in the shadow of this glorious teaching lay another inevitable question : What shall be the lot of those who reject it ? This question was small and remote for the hundred and twenty elect souls [1] in the upper room, set upon pursuance of the truth and the right. But it gradually grew large and larger still for the Church, as it spread from land to land, and obtained the world's confessed, or professed, allegiance. The provision for meeting this question was ready to hand. It lay, in a certain sense, outside the Gospel ; and was anterior to it, like the other laws of our human nature, and of the government of the world by its Author. But this law, like all other antecedent and perpetual laws, was acknowledged by the Gospel; it was the law of ' indignation and wrath, tribulation and anguish, upon every soul of man that doeth evil [2].' But it was acknowledged with a sorrow which is shown by the comparatively fluctuating or shadowy manner in which this sad reverse of

[1] Acts i. 15.   [2] Rom. ii. 8, 9.

the picture is presented; the inseparable but obscure under-side, so to speak, of the great foundation-stone of our peace and happiness. How much do we know of the lot of the perversely wicked? They disappear into pain and sorrow; the veil drops upon them in that condition. Every indica-tion of a further change is withheld; so that, if it be de-signed, it has not been made known, and is nowhere incor-porated with the Divine teaching. Whatever else pertains to this sad subject is withheld from our too curious and unprofitable gaze. If men cannot restrain their thoughts, their affections, from further speculation, let them take good heed that, as it is necessarily weak and shadowy, so it be deeply tinged with modesty and awe. Let there not be the presumption of assimilating hope or surmise with the solid truth of the great revelation. The specific and limited statements supplied to us are, after all, only expressions in particular form of immovable and universal laws, on the one hand, of the irrevocable union between suffering and sin; on the other hand, of the perfection of the Most High; both of them believed in full, but only in part disclosed, and having elsewhere, it may be, their plenary manifesta-tion, in that day of the restitution of all things, for which a groaning and travailing creation yearns.

CHAPTER V

1. THAT the natural immortality of the soul is not taught in Holy Scripture.

2. Neither is it commended by the moral authority of the *quod semper, quod ubique, quod ab omnibus,* even after placing that comprehensive *dictum* under such limitations as it reasonably admits.

3. Neither is it affirmed or enjoined by any of the great assemblies of the undivided Church, or by any unanimity, actual or moral, of Decrees and Confessions posterior to the division of the Church into East and West.

4. The immortality of the soul is properly to be regarded as holding its place in religion from its being a gift or endowment due to the Incarnation of our Lord.

5. The survival of the soul after death is in itself distinct from the immortality of the soul, and is included in the doctrine of the Resurrection; and was so treated by the earlier Fathers of the Church.

6. Also, the existence of the soul after death, which was so largely believed in old religions outside the Hebrew revelation, was a belief in survival, and was not associated with any formal examination and adoption of an absolutely endless life.

7. The presumptions of the case, apart from the Gospel, are favourable to a belief in this survival; but they can hardly, as such, be said to amount to demonstration.

8. If we set out from the belief that Christ both reveals and gives immortality, which is exemption from death, and is life without an end, it is plain that the first application of this doctrine is to the righteous, because the assurances of their future condition do not seem to rest upon the expressions used in Scripture as to the duration of future

happiness, but rather upon the announcement that they are restored to the image of God, in which man was originally formed; according to the announcement of our Lord in a single passage, which may be taken as *instar omnium*: 'Thou in me, and I in thee, that they also may be one in us [1].'

9. So that the immortality of the righteous, habitually associated in Holy Scripture with bliss, rests on no matter of disputed construction, but upon the clearest, highest, and surest ground conceivable; and is by no means simply parallel or identical with the declarations of the eternal punishment of the wicked.

10. The declarations contained in the Scriptures of both Testaments respecting the duration of the future state, either generally or after the resurrection and the day of judgement, do not appear to go to the extreme limit of the powers of human language in describing it so as to correspond strictly with the idea of a duration, or of time, prolonged continually and without end.

11. In regard to future punishment, it is plain that great differences of opinion have prevailed at different periods of the history of the Church, the first centuries presenting a view of a different colour from that which may be said to have prevailed over others from about the time of St. Chrysostom and St. Augustine.

12. Apart from the question of the degrees of authority respectively due to the Scriptures, the Creeds, and the acknowledged tradition of the undivided Church, it does not appear safe to apply the term traditional theology to the largely developed opinions of later ages on future punishment, as compared with the more reserved conceptions of an earlier period.

13. In approaching the contemplation of future retribution, the *axioma summum*, the axiom of axioms, which we should not only carry with us, but keep ever ready and fresh in our minds, is the conviction that God is eternally, immovably, and universally just, and that every provision ordained by Him is subservient to, and every conclusive adjustment is to be in direct accordance with, the ὑψίποδες νόμοι, His own ethical laws.

[1] John xvii. 21.

14. Good and evil doing are not propounded to us for formal consideration unless within the limits of the Christian Revelation ; inasmuch as the great law that covers all beyond it, has been comprehensively and conclusively, but separately, laid down for us in the clearest (though in general) terms by St. Paul, in his Epistle to the Romans [1].

15. It is therefore an apparent mistake to speak of the disputed questions on Scripture texts concerning future retribution as involving the fate of the vast majority of mankind, it being plain that the large majority for any age, and the enormous majority when we take all ages together, are placed altogether beyond the scope of these disputes, and of the parable of the Last Judgement.

16. A collateral question of great interest arises upon the twofold declaration of St. Peter [2] that our Lord preached to certain disembodied spirits, and that these were the spirits of the men who had been disobedient in the days of Noah, and whose disobedience brought upon the earth the judgement of the Flood : for, since God is constant to Himself, the question arises whether He may not give equivalent opportunities to the dead at large who have not upon earth enjoyed the light of the Christian Revelation.

17. A further deduction from the scope of our controversies is to be made for those who, even within the Christian precinct, are placed by infancy, early childhood, or mental insufficiency, or hindrances not dependent upon themselves, beyond the limit of responsible action.

18. Wherever, within the bounds now established, the condition of the wicked after death is expressly touched upon in Scripture, it is described as (*a*), with respect to quality, a condition of greater or less, and mostly of great, suffering ; and as to duration (*b*), as a condition of death, or (*c*) by imagery that annexes to it no idea of a termination.

19. It is rash to declare as cognizable by us that, even if eternity be truly conceived in the popular idea, there can be no such thing as suffering, of whatever kind, through eternity except by God's departing from a principle of justice.

20. For, besides considering punishment as stripes inflicted from without, we have to consider the future state of the un-

---

[1] ii. 6–16. [2] 1 Pet. iii. 19, 20.

righteous as governable by causes operating from within, and therefore, possibly, self-determining by a fixed natural law.

21. And all modern thought and knowledge tend to attach greater weight to the regular and fixed operation of these self-determining causes.

22. In particular, we have before us the great doctrine of habits, under which, even by unconscious, and yet more by deliberate, use and wont, we continually approximate to a condition which, when the formation of it has been promoted or tolerated by the will up to a certain extreme point, becomes finally incapable of correction by the will, and therefore, as far as we know, unchangeable.

23. Nor can it be allowable in reason to plead that this condition may conceivably be terminated by some miraculous agency of the Almighty, as this would be simply to suppose the destruction of the freedom of the will when it had been most fully used, and would be contrary to all experience and to the whole analogy of nature, so far as it is placed before us by our experience. We are hardly fit judges beforehand when extraordinary agency, such as miracle, is proper to be employed; but we may sometimes see plainly that it is not.

24. Inasmuch as evil hath been allowed to enter the world we are bound to suppose that it has been for some exemplary or other sufficient purpose : but, if there may be a sufficient purpose for its being here now, our knowledge cannot suffice to warrant our determining that no conditions are in the nature of things possible, under which that purpose might involve its presence otherwise or always. We have not competency to lay it down, that evil in time limited, however long, is compatible with the Divine idea, but evil in time unlimited is not.

25. It must always be borne in mind, if we project some theory which purports to have for its aim an acquittal of the Almighty in respect of the presence of evil, and to turn upon its perpetual duration, that we do not escape from the question by means of any scheme for dealing with the future condition of unrighteous men ; for this as well as other reasons, that there is still before us the presence of perpetuated evil in the fallen angels, inhabitants of God's universe.

26. If it be true that in this, and in any other matters,

there may be secrets of the Divine counsel and resource possibly applicable to our future condition, they are secrets, inaccessible to us, which we must suppose to be advisedly withheld from us, and wherein we can neither speculate nor infer.

27. The case of the fallen angels appears to establish a fatal flaw in the theory commonly termed Restitutionism or Universalism : whether as founded on any declaration of Scripture, or as aiming at a vindication of the Divine character by the expulsion of evil from the universe ; unless, indeed, there be boldness enough to include all these unhappy beings together with unrighteous men in the catalogue of the blest.

28. This theory founds itself, so far as Scripture is concerned, on declarations such as that of St. Paul in 1 Cor. xv. 26–28, that there shall be a time when all things shall be subdued unto God, that He may be all in all. To which, perhaps, it may be replied, that the Apostle is speaking of putting an end (ver. 26) to death, and makes no reference to sin or its annihilation. And more at large these declarations of a happy state of things may very conceivably be understood of the state of things subsisting for the regenerated creation, out of whose condition and environment every jarring element will have been expelled.

29. On the other hand, and apart from any argument from the nature of death, which the unrighteous are to undergo, it seems impossible to fit this theory, which has never obtained any amount of steady or responsible countenance in the Christian Church, into any rational conception of religion. For, as it teaches, the unrighteous are subjected to an indefinite amount of terribly demoralizing experience in evil, and to a definite condemnation, as to which none can pretend that it makes them better than they would have been without it, and which, if so, seems to be in no way recommended by reason for assumed admission into a scheme devised by Divine wisdom.

30. But the fact which seems *in limine* to condemn Universalism is its flagrant contradiction to the declarations of our Lord : such as that there is a sin against the Holy Ghost which shall never be forgiven, either in this world or in the

world to come; and especially that there has been in the
world a soul for which it had been preferable never to have
been born. The first of these is categorical, and if it can be
circumvented these words are powerless for their proper
purpose: and, as to the second, existence is manifestly a
good to any one whose suffering has bounds, and whose
bliss has none.

31. The ordinary and principal description of the future
state of the unrighteous is that conveyed in the word death.
This word in its ordinary signification bears the sense of an
extinction or cessation of some kind. It might mean cessation for the wicked of life itself. During the largest portion of Christian history it has been expressly or tacitly
taken to mean not an extinction but a continuance for ever
of existence, with the element of suffering superadded.
These are contradictory conceptions: but either of them is
alike fatal to Restitutionism.

32. What Restitutionism requires is to read into each and
all of the multitude of passages denouncing death against
the wicked such words as these: [death] ' which is no death
but a suspension of life, and of a life which is thereafter to
be indissolubly joined with enjoyment.'

33. The Scriptures set forth a course of discipline and
education for the human soul. On the supposition of Restitution they become a riddle; and some other Bible surely
ought to be devised to set out what is another and totally
different course of training.

34. The popular definition of death, as applied to the
wicked in the future state, appears abstractedly liable to
these two objections: (1) It takes away from death that
idea of cessation and extinction, which its ordinary meaning always in some form includes: (2) It adds an idea of
suffering, amounting largely to misery and torment, which
the original sense of the word in no manner contains.

35. Restitutionism is to be considered with reference to
what is matter of observation as well as to revealed truth.
In this light, it strikes at what all believers in a future
state consider as the grand and central truth of the subject,
this, namely, that we are living in a state of probation.
Now probation signifies not only discipline, but such dis-

cipline as implies a decisive and conclusive test, analogous to those tests of inanimate substances, which are employed in order, once for all, to ascertain their essential quality. But under Restitutionism all idea of essential quality as a distinctive mark disappears, and therefore all idea of genuine probation.

36. The *dictum* of Paley that the worst condition in heaven may be faintly distinguishable from the best condition in hell, and that of Mr. Mivart who describes the state of ' Happiness in Hell,' do not harmonize with the religious sentiment, or with the language or spirit of Holy Scripture, and seem to recommend humble reliance on the Divine justice, in preference to pushing forward into the shadows of death for the production of no better results than these.

37. It is not wise or safe to pronounce, as within our own present knowledge, and faculty of judgement, that none but a temporary punishment, whether of infliction or privation, whether by decree or by natural sequel, can, without isolation of Divine justice, ever be inflicted on the creature in respect of acts done and responsibility incurred within the limits of time.

38. The notion of Universal Restitution is, then, not supported by Scripture, or by Christian tradition, or by any sound philosophy of human nature, which by its constitution tends to an ever-growing fixity of habits.

39. The nature and limits, if any, of time, and the signification of the word eternity, have not been opened to us so largely as is assumed in popular language and ideas.

40. The metaphysical doctrine of a natural indefeasible immortality of the soul, as an immaterial existence, has come, unawares and gradually, to reckon, or to be assumed, as a doctrine of Faith, and no longer as only a philosophical opinion.

41. The idea that existence may be worn out and finally fail through depravation of its central principle seems to have in it nothing at variance with the foundations of philosophy, but is not taught by the Christian religion.

42. The assumption that imputations on the Divine justice in connexion with future punishment are disposed of by simply introducing a limit of time is unwarranted.

43. This whole controversy wherein Divine justice is arraigned tends to run up into the general controversy on the origin of evil, which presents to the limited powers of the human mind insurmountable barriers in the way of effectual inquiry.

44. The central and final stronghold of believers is faith in the indefeasible and universal justice of the Divine Being, and to fall back upon this stronghold is more wise and safe than to present imperfect solutions in matters not entrusted to us to examine.

CHAPTER VI

NECESSITY OR DETERMINISM

THE scheme of Necessity or Fatalism, though largely dealt with by Butler from his own point of view, has also as a scheme of thought been dismissed by him with a disrespect amounting to contempt. The scheme itself, and the application of it, are both of them summarily treated as absurd [1]. It is very rarely that Butler allows himself to employ language with respect to the propositions he resists which can be taken to imply so severe a judgement. He does it however in the case now before us; and we may be sure that, when such a sentiment escapes from him, it is one which he has strongly and advisedly entertained. In this instance it is the more striking because of the respectable countenance which had already been given to the necessarian theory.

Not indeed by the ancients; who thought it enough to body forth an overhanging Fate, which might counterwork and defeat the designs of men, and indeed of Deity [2]. They had not a sufficient store of supererogatory wits to devise a system which, in nullifying the will and responsibility of man, should deprive his nature of its dignity, and his life of purpose. We can understand how such a system could commend itself to the mind of Holbach and thereby furnish a twin engine of destruction for all that is best in manhood. He had not written when Butler constructed the *Analogy*. But a very different person, and a fervent Christian, Jonathan Edwards, had from the barren heights of Calvinism planted a battery against the inward freedom of man, and had worked it with intensity of zeal and much wasted force of dialectic. It may perhaps be enough, in the way of reviewing past periods, if I pass by several names, famous in

[1] *Analogy*, I. vi. 1, 8. [2] Æsch. *Agam.* 996.

various degrees, (such as those of Luther, Hobbes, and Priest-
ley,) and associated with the championship of the 'slavery
of the will,' and touch only upon the two I have named,
after first referring to the most artful among the advocates
of the necessarian system.

Hume, at the outset of his Essay on Liberty and Necessity [1], begins by contending that the controversy upon them
is purely verbal, and that all men have always been agreed
in upholding both according to the only reasonable sense
which can be put upon the terms [2]. But, in this apparently
equitable adjustment as between the two, the share allotted
to liberty is a meagre one. It means the liberty 'which is
universally allowed to belong to every one who is not a
prisoner or in chains [3]'; that is to say, it is liberty from
external constraint. Could so acute a man, so fond of
arguing as a mole burrows, namely out of sight, have supposed that any single free-willer would accept for grain
chaff such as this?

His real argument is as follows. We know nothing
of causation, except by conjunction. This conjunction is
always found, when the whole of the case is taken into
account, to be uniform, so as to enable an inference to be
drawn: and these two, conjunction and inference, make up
one idea of causation; (for which it would appear that we
may safely substitute sequence). In physics, this is manifest to every observer. Mental operations are also seen to
exhibit an antecedent and a consequent. But here we have a
class of disputants who seek to insert between them a power
which they call will: whereas the antecedents of action,
'ambition, avarice, self-love, vanity, friendship, generosity,
public spirit [4],' have always been, and still are, the sources
of action among mankind. His language is not quite consistent: for presently he allows the word will, and in a note [5]
seems to carry over his necessity from agents to observers,
admits our seeming to feel 'that the will itself is subject to
nothing,' and seems perplexed with the image of *relleity*.
However, he returns to his point, and argues thus. We

---

[1] 'An Inquiry into the Human Understanding,' sect. viii : *Philosophical Works*, vol. iv. p. 48. Boston and Edinburgh, 1854.
[2] Page 93.   [3] Page 100.   [4] Page 94.   [5] Page 98.

admit necessity in physics, because we can discover nothing that intervenes between antecedent and consequent. The same incapacity attends our examination of mental operations [1]; so that we have in the two cases one and the same reason for admitting the existence of necessity, which, he boldly states, has been universal among philosophers [2]. The Essay ends with an apparent endeavour to refer the direct causation of evil to the Almighty Will, and with the usual artifice to avert reproach.

It is indeed self-evident, that between antecedent and consequent nothing can intervene ; for if there were any intervening power, they would no longer be consequent and antecedent. But what Hume does, as in my citation above, is to string together as motives a vitally defective list of the factors which determine human action. We have, it is true, convictions and emotions. But these do not of themselves govern conduct. They are liable to be summoned, and are summoned, before the tribunal of the higher faculties, especially of Conscience and Intellect, which are as it were the right and the left hands of Will. When these have acted, then the mental operation is complete ; and in every true definition of that mental operation its freedom is included. For of will, apart from several subsidiary questions, freedom in assent or refusal, together with propelling power, seem to constitute the essence.

I come now to Jonathan Edwards, who associated necessity with strictness and fervour in religion, and who has left upon record what may perhaps be considered the closest of all the schemes of argument ever framed in support of the idea. Its date is 1754 [3].

The will, according to Edwards, is that 'by which the mind chooses any thing [4]': and will can never be in disaccord with desire. In contemplating this identification of the will with choice, we are reminded of the Greek προαίρεσις, and of its entire distinctness from βουλή [5] and its deriva-

---

[1] Pages 96 *seqq.*, 105.
[2] Page 105.
[3] *A Careful and Strict Inquiry into the Modern Prevailing Notions of that Freedom of Will, which is supposed to be essential to Moral Agency,* Virtue and Vice, Reward and Punishment, Praise and Blame. 1754.
[4] *Works* (London, 1817), vol. i. p. 127.
[5] Hom. *Il.* i. 5.

tives. Its determining cause is 'that motive, which, as it
stands in the view of the mind, is the strongest[1].' 'The
will always is as the greatest apparent good.' And good,
as he here uses it, is what appears agreeable or pleasing[2].
The will always follows 'the last dictate of the . . . whole
faculty of perception or apprehension[3].' Necessity is that
which absolutely will be, which is certain[4]. Philosophical
necessity is 'the full and fixed connexion between the subject and predicate . . . of a proposition which affirms something to be true[5].' Liberty is 'the power that any one
has to do as he pleases[6].' This, he says, is true; but he
appears to speak only of external liberty. The false notion,
propagated by Arminians and others, is 'that it consists in
a self-determining power of the will,' 'a certain sovereignty
which the will has over itself and its own acts, whereby it
determines its own volitions[7].'

He has now come fairly into sight of the enemy; and
availing himself, with a skill only equalled by his perti-
nacity, of an open joint in the armour of definition, he propounds what may justly be called his main and central
argument; with a great redundance indeed of iteration, but
such a redundance as might appear more and more to shut
up the reader to his conclusion. In this account of will, he
discovers exactly what he wanted, a subject and a predicate,
indissolubly wedded by necessity. And so he goes to work.

It is plainly absurd, he contends, to suppose 'that the will
itself determines all the acts of the will.' 'If the will determines all its own free acts, then every free act of choice is
determined by a preceding act of choice, choosing that act.'
But that preceding act had, in its turn, a predecessor. So
every posterior act of choice, in series, is determined by a
prior act of choice. If not, we arrive at last at some act of
the will, determining all the consequent acts, but not in itself
self-determined, and therefore *ex hypothesi* not free. The
will, determining its own acts, determines them as it determines other things that are under its command. But
that first or original act, which we suppose, not being self-
determined, is not free. And if it be not free, then, as it

<hr />

[1] *Works*, i. 131.   [2] *Ibid.* p. 133.   [3] *Ibid.* p. 138.   [4] *Ibid.* p. 139.
[5] *Ibid.* p. 142.   [6] *Ibid.* p. 152.   [7] *Ibid.* p. 153.

governs all the rest, their freedom is tainted at its source, and so the Arminian notion crumbles into dust [1].

They speak, he says, of a sovereignty of the will. Be it so : this will is either active or inactive in determining volitions. If there be no action, there is no freedom ; but if the will be active, then there is one will-act determining another [2].

Throughout, the force of his argument depends upon the word ' self-determining,' and upon an illegitimate analysis of that word. He will have something that determines, and something that is determined, and he claims to separate the one from the other. He proceeds to make them subject and object, agent and patient. It amounts simply to this. He does not confute self-determination ; but he denies it. He declines to look at it as it is. There is no ground for this arbitrary denial, unless it be the *prima facie* likelihood, that where there is action, and a power set up by that action, there is a true plurality, and we may accordingly argue from the one to the other as separate entities. It is plausible to say that, wherever something double is to be noted, there is a double agent. But it is untrue. On the same ground all spontaneity should be denied ; for, wherever spontaneity exists, it is the self that sets the self in motion. The freedom of the will is essentially postulated, and whatever cancels that freedom destroys the idea, and establishes one of those contradictions, which Edwards is fond of charging upon his Arminians. But the most effective answer to his contention for a plurality inherent in the will itself is perhaps to be found in the phenomenon of consciousness. Here there is an act of perception, and there is a thing perceived ; but the one cannot be severed from the other either in idea or in action. The process of consciousness, as it exhibits itself in analysis, wherein the percipient perceives itself, thus far begins and ends within the same faculty, and raises metaphysically no presumption of an originating action from without. If in truth we substitute the word ' originating ' for the word 'self-determining,' we sweep away at once that structure of argument, which Edwards has reared upon the basis of a fallacy. That fallacy is due

---

[1] *Works*, i. 157–159.   [2] *Ibid*. p. 161.

to the particular form chosen for the construction of a phrase apparently on account of its easy significance, and it finds no *prise* if we employ another phrase, less popular but more exact.

Edwards contends that foreknowledge implies necessity. It would seem that here he is entangling himself in the consequences of the relation he has arbitrarily set up between necessity and certainty. It appears to me that in setting up this proposition he unwittingly forswears his own scheme. For foreknowledge no otherwise implies certainty than as it is implied by all knowledge; and Divine knowledge carries it no more than human. *A* knows that *B* is at dinner; but this knowledge is in no manner or degree the cause of his dining. Therefore we have here a necessity without causation. What title therefore have we, on the showing of the fatalists themselves, anywhere to draw in necessity in order to supply a cause? Why associate necessity with cause, when we find that through its relation to certainty it operates in full while standing in no connexion with causing? As we have seen that necessity does not imply causation, it follows that, where cause is lacking, necessity does not fill the gap.

In the whole of these remarks it must be steadily borne in mind that will, when we speak of freedom of the will, means that paramount agency which takes effect after deliberation, and has no connexion with that lax use of the term in which it is made to include a multitude of impelling forces such as bias, prejudice, inclination, impulse, sympathy, desire, not yet co-ordinated and placed in line by the action of the higher faculties.

D'Holbach, writing (1770) [1] after Hume (1751), reproduces many of his ideas, but with inferior skill and without his subterfuges. He pleads the equality at all points of physical and mental laws [2]. There is one idea of will, a *prétendu sens intime*; but it is totally delusive. If I have a burning thirst, I am compelled to drink [3]. Mucius Scaevola, in his strange action, could not help keeping his hand

---

[1] D'Holbach (pseudonym *Mirabaud*), *Système de la Nature*, Part I, chaps. xi, xii. Two vols.
[2] Vol. i. pp. 186, 211.   [3] Pages 190, 215.

in the fire, any more than if it had been held there by force [1]. Choice is a phantom. Deliberation is only suspension. All irregularities are explained by going up to the source, which is always necessary [2]. Our acts are very various, but the spring of them is uniform [3]. The source of error lies in regarding will as the *premier mobile* [4]. Once he thinks he has found a summary adjustment of the whole matter [5]. 'It is will that somehow (*telle quelle*) makes men deliberate : deliberation leads to choice, and choice to action.' But here he makes will play the part of *premier mobile* in the wrong place. It is affection, passion, knowledge, prejudice, and the like, which put the mind in motion. Will becomes the *premier mobile* immediately before action. He employs the term fatalism with freedom ; which Hume had prudently avoided.

He is most diffuse in the detailed application of his arguments, without adding in the least to their force. He praises, and indeed to cover the nakedness of his system he is compelled to praise, virtue, experience, education. But, as to everything that is to be done in this world, why does he not fold his arms, and spare himself the trouble of deliberation or speech or anything else ? For necessity will do his work on his behalf. When the issue has been fixed beforehand, why deliberate ? There is, as Butler observes, much waste in the universe : but, under the scheme of fatalism, is not all deliberation waste ? It produces no result ; but ought any philosophy to acknowledge or admit operations which have no result, means which exercise no influence over ends ? If I am told the means are pre-appointed as well as the ends, I reply that of that I am already aware ; that is not the point of the objection : the objection is, that the system of fatalism is loaded with a weight of what it reduces to merely cumbrous and useless paraphernalia : for no purpose is served by the immense *apparatus* which, under the established system of human life, is put into play before action. If I am told that deliberation trains character, I reply that all training power depends on the freedom

---

of choice, which is its basis and pre-condition at every step [1].

The opinions of Mr. Leslie Stephen on the question of Determinism are those of a very recent, as well as able expositor. As they have been declared in his recent article [2], they may be summed up as follows :

1. Acts, done under coercion from without, are neither moral nor immoral.

2. Free-will confounds causation with coercion, and breaks the chain of natural causation.

3. How can man, if constantly governed by an omnipotent Being, be other than a puppet ?

4. Action proceeds from character; and character is not made by us, but determined by the Creator.

The first of these propositions may be admitted as to all true coercion; such as the case cited by Mr. Stephen, where physical force guides the pen of an unwilling writer.

But the advocate of free-will, while admitting that it works at a presumptive disadvantage owing to the degeneracy of nature through sin, and to difficulties of environment, entirely denies that it is destroyed or vitally disabled; nay, under the Christian scheme, asserts that its infirmities are repaired, and the obstacles to its action neutralized, by a Divine aid, open without stint to those who ask it.

In man, character is a growth, the result of acts performed in series. For the choices of those acts, and the shaping of his character through them, he is provided with governing faculties : with conscience to sever right from wrong by internal action, and with the self-determining power of will to accept or repudiate the authority of conscience, and to place action in harmony or in conflict with it.

Mr. Stephen's argument assumes that a government by omnipotence must be an absolute government. Not only is this denied by the advocates of freedom in the will, but it

---

[1] It was the method of D'Holbach (see *Biogr. Universelle*) to publish his works, when he was apprehensive of consequences, under the names of dead men, and with supposititious names of place. The *Système de la Nature* is expressly ascribed to him by Grimm. It appeared in 1770 : but he had already set out, without publishing, its main principles in a *Catéchisme* dated 1765.

[2] *Nineteenth Century*, Jan. 1896, pp. 111-117.

involves a fallacy so hopeless as to amount to a palpable solecism. For it assumes that a Being, omnipotent *ex hypothesi*, has not power to bring into existence any agent who shall be an originating agent.

The necessarian argument belongs, in truth, to that method of abstract reasoning which is in all cases so unsafe a weapon in hands like ours: and uses it, too, for purposes which, as I have shown, stand self-condemned.

On the other hand, the advocate of free-will stands on the ground of the general experience of mankind, which attests its own existence by the only kind of knowledge that in general we possess; not a direct perception of essences, but an experience of conditions and effects [1].

The necessarian theory now most commonly passes under the name of Determinism. This appellation does not appear to have merits sufficient to render it preferable to the older titles which the system had borne, and may therefore seem as if it had been invented in order to give a certain freshness and respectability to what had been heavily battered and somewhat discredited. With this fact before me I offer a few remarks upon it.

For persistence and tenacity in pressing the necessarian argument, Jonathan Edwards may still be cited. If human action be immediately dependent upon the will, the will as he would urge is determined by a balance of reasons. That is to say reasons are placed, like weights, in scales, and the overweight invariably in the last result carries the will and determines action. In vain do we plead that there is in the mind something extraneous to and apart from the considerations which are compared and weighed one against another, namely, the power, resulting in the act, of decision. It is admitted that the mind has estimated the reasons, and ultimately behaves to each of them according to this estimate.

---

[1] The most forcible part of Mr. Stephen's argument appears to be that in which he deals with another subject, the narrative in Genesis, chapter iii, of the temptation and transgression of primitive man. The doctrine of Christian theology being that the fault impressed by sin upon human nature has been transmitted from Adam to his descendants, Mr. Stephen contends that such an ingrained fault could not be represented as the consequence of a single act, but only of continued and habitual transgression; and therefore that the narrative must be taken as parabolical.

But we are now dealing with the eventual act which takes place after they have all been brought into juxtaposition, and have had their several ranks and values assigned to them. And at this stage of the proceedings, as it is urged, the final act, decisive as to result, adds nothing to any of the reasons either way. They remain as they were; and as the decision follows upon them without having anything added, but in simple accordance with the overweight, whichever way it may incline, it must be due to that overweight; and is a mere expression of it, as the hands on the face of the clock exhibit the exact preponderance at the moment in the action of the works, and is not a cause, but only an effect.

It may perhaps even be conceded, in reply to the foregoing argument, that the action of the will is in accordance with the overweight or apparent overweight of reasons, and adds nothing of the like kind to the weight already lodged in either scale. It would be necessary, in order to its making such an addition, that the thing we call will should be homogeneous with the things we call reasons, so far at least that they should be commensurable; capable of being described, or measured, under common terms. But the reasons are the pleading power, and the will is the separate sovereign and deciding power; and they may be compared respectively to the advocates on one side and the judge on the other, the comparison only requiring that we regard the judge's decision *ab extra*. We do not, for the present purpose, enter into the interior action of the several minds.

It is admitted that, in general, the human being as an agent acts under the habitual and unquestioning impression that he is free; and so nearly does this belief approach to universality that, if it be untrue, the case is without example as an instance of profound and cruel fraud perpetrated by nature upon her children. But minds that are capable of resting in the necessarian opinion are not likely to be displaced from it by apprehension of such a consequence. Nor is there any necessity for resort to this particular topic. The advocate of free agency, who may be called in respect to subjective impressions the advocate of the human race, has only to face the facts as they stand. The will is a causal agent. I will not say it is incapable of being

subjected to pressure, nor deny that the pressure may be
long, severe, and trying in the extreme. Nay more, it may
be that, when a character of feeble tissue has been long
indulged in the habit of remissness, the will like other
disused and neglected organs may dwindle, and its faculty
may descend to a point indefinitely low. Or it may be that
the will requires for its normal action the support of the
moral faculties in whose interest it has been given, and that,
when these have sunk into impotence, or are perverted into
a wrong direction, they may become the means of paralyzing
or undermining its action, so that the forces of inducement,
deception, and intimidation may carry the man away as he
would be carried when not on his feet by a current which,
in the erect position that nature gave him, he might have
withstood. To admit this is to admit that through original
weakness, combined with evil environment, and still more
through the growth of depraved habit originally tolerated
and at length growing to be tyrannical, our humanity may
lapse into a condition so abnormal, as to require that even
the mapping out of our elementary faculties should be re-
adjusted. But the cases we are now considering are, from
the higher and more normal ranks down to those of average
action in average men, cases of things done not in passion
but with some moderate degree of reflection. This is the
way with ordinary human action ; we may deal separately
with extremes. And we may here fearlessly observe that the
will is the commander and the arbiter of all those cruder
forces by which it may be surrounded and solicited, but by
which, except when it has forgotten self-assertion and abdicated supremacy, it cannot be dethroned. And only then, if
at all, in consequence of defects which might have been
supplied, or of concessions which might have been withheld.

I need not undertake metaphysically to examine the
nature of that heterogeneity by which the deliberative will
of man is exempted from the danger of forcible supersession.
In few words, we may say, that it is a force not
homogeneous with the forces that can be brought against it.
Its primary and ordinary aspect is that of a difference
analogous to those differences of natural species which
disable them from intermingling. So that a will cannot

be coerced, as an idea cannot be burned, nor an inundation confuted. Whether this is or is not so in ultimate analysis, need not now be inquired. There might conceivably be other adjustments by which the same end might be secured. It is I suppose conceivable that, without an absolute incommensurability between will and motives such as have usually been placed in competition with it, there might be some limit upon the amount of force which these might attain, while the will might be so profoundly and inextricably rooted in the general structure of the living agent as to make it ineradicable without tearing away the life itself: so that it would be as secure against violence, as the rock upon the coast towering on high is secure against the puny efforts of those, be they few or many, who might struggle by thrusting to displace it. I do not rest upon any alternative hypothesis, but revert to what I have called difference of species. So the will stands as a primal cause, and its freedom as an ultimate fact, neither requiring nor admitting any outlying explanation except this, that thus it was launched into existence by the sovereign providence of God.

Romanes, in his *Thoughts on Religion* [1], presents, without adopting, the objection that if the will be causal, the multitude of first causes must produce 'a new and never-ending stream of causality' which sooner or later must throw the kosmos into a chaos, 'through the cumulative intersection of the streams.' The supposed danger seems to depend on the idea that the aggregate result of these limited individual causalities might be either infinite, or so great as to threaten the security of the natural order. But we see man possessed of a power, to which no limit can be assigned, of evolving independent forces which he marshals and organizes under his own direction with a command, or grip, such as he could never exercise over the consequences of his volitions generally. He does this by his knowledge of existing physical antecedents, or causal agencies. Yet the forces of nature remain undisturbed and supreme. Again, the effect of human volitions, as a general rule, is not, like the snowball, to gather as they roll, but rather,

[1] Page 130.

like the stone thrown into the water, to produce a series of concentric circles with lengthening radius but diminishing efficiency, and soon becoming imperceptible; or, like the same stone thrown upwards into the air, and gradually but soon losing its upward motive force by friction and the regular influence of gravitation, which brings its movement to an end. And, more generally, if there be a providential adjustment of the aggregate of all existing forces such as to produce an equilibrium of the mundane system, if the inner contents of the earth do not beyond narrow limits disturb its crust, why must we apprehend the insufficiency of the power which has hitherto proved sufficient, both in the material and in the moral sphere, to maintain the balance of forces needed for the natural order. Nay more. Whether these volitional forces be caused or uncaused, there is no difference in their amount, and the admission in philosophy of the freedom of the will makes no objective change whatever, either in that freedom or in its force. So there is nothing here to disturb the doctrine that the true idea of will is that of a faculty which, in its usual condition and operation, is not determined from without, and carries along with it in full the consequence of moral responsibility for its acts.

In the department of thought, nothing is of more vital consequence than truly to apprehend the nature of volition. For it is to this agency that believers in religion ascribe not only the movement of the universe but the fact of its existence. The will of God is the fountainhead, up to which we may, but beyond which we cannot, trace any question of agency or of act. The only question, which for us can lie beyond it, is that of the relation between the Divine will and the moral principle in accordance with which it works, it being, according to Butler,[1] 'determined' by the reason of the case. But when our author uses that expression I do not imagine that he intends to treat the morality of the Divine character as to assign to the will only a position of subordination, or to enter upon the ground of the arguments of Cudworth which may seem to have that tendency. We should, 1

[1] *Analogy*, I. vi. 16 *n.*

think, understand the Bishop to refer simply to the absolute certainty of the accordance of the two; if so, the
phrase 'determined by' means is in entire accordance or
harmony with, and there is no reference to any question
either of priority or of superiority as between these two
great factors : nor, I think, should either of them be regarded as extraneous to the other in any sense known
to us.

When we think or speak of will as it exists in the Deity,
we are in little danger of confusing its true nature, as being
in us the sovereign faculty which immediately determines
action, and takes cognizance of those inclinations, desires,
or propensions which predispose us to it. These, however
jejune our notions of a God may be, we exclude from all
interference *ab extra* with Divine action. But, when we
come to argue upon the constitution or acts of the human
species, we find ourselves in the midst of an almost hopeless confusion, not due to the nature of the case, but arising
from the habitual neglect to distinguish between these sub-
altern impulsions, and the power which is seated in a region
above them, which calls them to account, and rules or, if
need be, overrules them.

The proper office of the will, in its proper sense, is to
direct thought into action, or, in other words, to direct action, both mental and external, in accordance with the laws
of right in the spiritual and moral sphere, of truth in the
region of the intellect; and of beauty, as some would add,
in its own proper department ; but this last we need not
include in the present discussion. The will, therefore, is
something entirely distinct from the reason as understood
by Butler, which includes the whole investigating faculty,
in whatever province it may be employed. With investigation the will has nothing to do, save this, that it has
rightfully to accept, or wrongfully to refute and disallow its
proper results. As it is the action of the will, whether
positive by determination, or negative by the abdication of
its office, and handing over the reins to some other directing power, which entails responsibility, so the law of duty
is the principal object appointed for the standing cognizance
of the will. Not only does will in us lie next to action, but,

as external action may be intercepted by overruling power, to will is truly to act; and no other acts than those so done amount to action in its duly developed sense.

How then stands the will in relation to faith, belief, or opinion?

And I may be permitted also to disclaim at the outset even the remotest shade of concurrence with those who set up an opposition between faith and reason ; sometimes in a premature anxiety to prevent the intrusion of one faculty into the province of another, but sometimes also, under cover of an affected anxiety to save faith from invasion by the understanding, in such a manner as to undermine it altogether by leading us to understand that there is a radical antagonism between the two. It is indeed a remarkable circumstance that the same age and country should have produced on the one hand Bishop Butler, who perhaps of all Christian writers has most boldly declared the prerogatives of reason and the reasonableness of faith ; on the other hand the two men who have gone such daring lengths in setting up the false and mischievous idea, that faith works upon principles which will not bear rational investigation. It is sad to connect with such tendencies the two distinguished names of Hume and Gibbon.

It is sometimes held [1] that there cannot be faith without a strong concurrent action of the will. This proposition appears to me to miss its aim through failing to distinguish between the several stages or degrees, if not kinds, of faith. In advancing from one of these stages to another, the composition of faith comes to be enriched and enlarged by the attraction of new ingredients. Initial faith is one thing, and *fides formata*, faith full formed, is in this sense another, that it includes what infant faith did not include. A distinction of this kind is recognized in the remarkable definition furnished by the Epistle to the Hebrews [2]; 'Now faith is the substance of things hoped for, the evidence of things not seen.' By the word translated evidence appears to be intended mental sight. But this description of sight may surely accrue without a process strictly moral : whereas when we deal in the first part of the definition, which is

[1] *Thoughts on Religion*, p. 138.   [2] Heb. xi. 1.

indeed twofold, with the mention of things hoped for, we at once perceive that moral elements have been already introduced into the case. For hope implies inclination or desire. This, however, and not the sovereign action of will, the propension towards heavenly things, is the moral element supplied. These things hoped for, which are future and remote, faith brings into the present; this definition dealing with the matter of time, as the other does, so to speak, with space. We have here the affection which draws us towards certain things, and the understanding finds it reasonable that we should thus be drawn. Action is not involved, and the will as an active faculty has as yet no place, except it be in so far as it may give its sanction to the findings of the intellect.

But the graver branch of the question is whether there can be any act of faith without the concurrence of the acting and governing will. I submit that there may. I think that an apt illustration of the frame of mind now in my view is supplied by the remarkable words recorded of Napoleon the Great, who said : ' Je ne crois pas aux religions ; mais qui est ce qui a fait tout cela ? ' For here we have on the one hand a full satisfaction of the intellect upon the question whether there is a God ; on the other hand no recognition of any of His moral titles, of any obligation to regard His word or will. Thus far then we have an act of faith, but one not presenting to us as it stands any element properly moral. The force of the teleological argument, either from nature or at any rate from the providential dispositions, with which man is girt about in the ordinary government of the world, may perhaps without any movement specifically moral, and on grounds of pure reckoning only, lead a man, as a rational being, to the conclusion that, whether he will or not, he has to deal in the experience of life with a power able to control his destinies, and actually exercising an influence upon them, which seems likely to be constant throughout his present existence, and at the very least to suggest the prolongations of that life beyond the grave, with continued and possibly much nearer relations in the future state to that power.

There is nothing, as it appears to me, either impossible or strange in the supposition I am about to sketch in outline.

Let us suppose a person of good intelligence and education, whose mind, from circumstances, has never been turned at all to religion, and is a blank with regard to it. He reads that part of the *Analogy* which refers to the natural government of the world; and he is struck by the indications of system and the signs of direction to certain ends which it presents. This is a consideration limited in its nature by the subject of the powers it exhibits to us; and, anterior to any consideration of moral elements, he is struck by the question of calculation, by the *pros* and *contras*, as he might with real, but in no way moral, attention and concern examine the risks and likelihoods of a journey by a particular route. He comes, on a principle of common sense, a sense of his own interest, without any religious bias, to the conclusion that the matter is one which deserves further consideration. As that consideration is resumed and prolonged, and as it comes to include, together with the exterior facts, the balances of suffering or enjoyment, a pretty clear view is obtained of the moral elements of the case, and the general laws under which, not uniformly, but on the whole sensibly, good fortune, or at the least hope and solace, appear to accompany the path of virtue, and uneasiness, growing into misery, the path of sin. The door into his whole mind has now been opened, and the moral picture, by its affinities with the better parts of our nature, assumes an aspect of beauty and attraction in his eyes, so that he becomes a believer, and follows the subject onwards, even to the acceptance of the entire Christian Revelation. Thus we have before us one continuous growth, the character of which is largely modified as it advances. When it began, and in the first of its stages, there was either no moral element involved, or it was so slight as to be imperceptible; but it passed on from embryo to a kind of infant consciousness, and then, through many more stages, into a full-formed conviction, backed by all the energies of heart and mind. It is hard, or not even possible, to trace these stages. 'The wind bloweth where it listeth, and thou hearest the sound thereof, but canst not tell whence it cometh, and whither it goeth: so is every one that is born of the Spirit [1].' It may be difficult to pronounce whether, before emotion and desire came to be

[1] John iii. 8.

excited, faith had in such a case rudimentally begun; but it is surely plain that the basis of the operation in its inception was, at the very least, mainly intellectual; that conviction at least of a duty to persevere in the investigation may have preceded any longings for a particular conclusion, and that only in its riper state is faith saturated with morality. First it opens the door to Christ, then it falls down and worships Him, at last it forsakes every adverse attraction and desire to follow Him, with the full concurrence of the will properly so called, which stamps the covenant, and sets the man free for collected action.   So much for faith.

Belief, in its popular use, is understood to imply faith as a living knowledge, together with an harmonious will as to the matters believed; and unbelief is commonly named so as to imply, in the region of the will, a flavour of aversion. But if we take belief more strictly, it is defined by Bishop Pearson[1] to be assent to that which is credible, as being credible.   This seems to be a definition requiring no moral qualification, a vision without love, or even possibly with the reverse of love: 'the devils also believe, and tremble[2].'   Here it is evident that no moral element whatever is engaged. Belief seems to be doubly related to conviction; in that, firstly, it demands less absolutely the exclusion of doubt and the undisputed possession of the entire mental field: and secondly, agreeing with it in being capable in the last resort of complete severance from moral elements.

Opinion is a word of larger range and looser texture.   As belief falls, in the respect just indicated, before conviction, so opinion falls below belief, has a larger toleration of doubt, does not acknowledge in as stringent a form the obligation to consequent action, is scarcely applicable with any propriety to truth when at once obvious and necessary, belongs to the early stages of investigations as yet but partially developed, obtains no wide favour in the higher regions of philosophy, and, as to theology, remains wholly (so to speak) in the outer courts.

If it be said that this exposition on faith and its congeners is separate from the direct issue raised by determinism, I shall not contest the point; but only observe that an

---

[1] *On the Creed.*   [2] James ii. 19.

analysis of these mental operations, and an exhibition of the active relations they exhibit between the human soul and a personal Deity, place us in view of a state of things which if touched by the hard mechanical forces of necessity seems like a garden blasted into a desert by a whirlwind. If it be replied that this scheme was embraced by the piety of Calvinism, I answer in my turn that that acceptance cannot well be appraised, without an examination of the whole subsequent history of Calvinism.

The fundamental contention of this essay is, that the will is a faculty not homogeneous with intellect, passion, affection, or conscience; possessed of an originating power of self-action; entitled and enabled to carry with it the whole man; the immediate precursor of his action; and eventually incommensurable with what are commonly (for example, by Jonathan Edwards) called motives, and may also be called inducements.

If objection be taken to my claim of incommensurability between two descriptions of human faculty or energy admitted to have a power of interaction inherent in them, I reply by what seems to me an answer conclusive. If there be some other case where such interaction (or if not such interaction, yet a true action, commanding or influential) is undeniable, and while yet there is an incommensurability that cannot be denied, then all semblance of objection to my contention, drawn from this source, is done away. Now nothing can be more plainly, and nothing more absolutely, incommensurable than the will on one side, and the muscles of the body on the other. The exertion of the muscles is the immediate antecedent of our bodily actions. Behind them lie the nerves, which supply a channel or vehicle for the commands of the will, and transmit them to these unresisting instruments. Behind the nerves we have the brain. If there be in this case any other intermediary, it is one which has hitherto remained too subtle for detection. But the material point is not whether the links that form the chain are more or fewer: it is whether the connexion of the chain itself with that to which, through universal and familiar experience, we know it to be attached, is clear and indisputable. Of course I do not deny that there is also involuntary operation of the muscles also: partly normal, as, for example, in the action of the heart (which, however, may be suspended or even stopped by the will), and the circulation of the blood depending on it: partly abnormal, like walking in sleep. But there is also a large and habitual action of the muscles in obedience to the will, where the incommensurability is one of the very plainest facts of psychology, and where the power of command is paramount. A relation of incommensurability like this in essence, though not attended with· all the same conditions, is exactly what I assert to exist between ordinary motive or inducement, and the faculty of will sovereign in the active, as that of conscience is in the judicial sphere.

If I am asked for authorities on behalf of this contention, I may admit that among the ancients, as the freedom of the human will, within the circuit of the faculties of man, hardly ever was denied, so its attitude and office in relation to the rest of those faculties may never have been strictly formulated. At the same time, I am disposed to suggest that the προαίρεσις, or choice, of Aristotle, even if nowhere scientifically defined, seems to discharge not indeed the whole, but a part both vital and the first in order of the exact office which I have here treated as belonging to the will. And this προαίρεσις, or choice, is never subjected to coercion from within. Amongst the moderns it is obvious that necessarianism is the opinion of a sect at most, perhaps only of individuals sporadically distributed: and every one who upholds the freedom of the will, asserts in substance the contention now upheld, whether the assertion be formal or only implied. I suppose the truth to be that never, or perhaps never until quite lately, has necessarianism weighed so sensibly in the aggregate of human thought, as to require more to be done in reply than to furnish (as Butler for one has furnished) the practical confutation of the doctrine.

But objection may also be taken at a point nearer to the source, and we may justly be called upon to specify how far we demand for this incommensurable will a power of giving effect to its behests without limitation, failure, or control. For such is the nature of the command which the will exercises over the muscles of the body. Do we claim for its office, in regard to motives and inducements generally, such prerogatives at large ?

I answer by distinguishing. So far as the empire over motive and inducement are concerned, the will is absolute, as in some despotic countries, given their admitted traditional usages, there is absolutely no provision for resistance to the orders of the sovereign. But in the sovereign himself there may be something, or there may be the lack of something, which defeats the sovereignty and makes it ineffective. Only, the something, which disables, does not lie in any intrinsic force lying outside the will in the motives and inducements.

Were the will so conditioned as in every case, or possibly as in any case, to exclude the action of all disabling causes, it would be out of analogy with all other human faculties of the present dispensation, inasmuch as it would be perfect. These disabling causes may be numerous. They are certainly grave ; as will appear sufficiently from the cases of disability, or reduced ability, that I shall quote. The will may be subject to surprises ; subject to inertness ; subject to decay ; without being subject to coercion. And so it may be that, from the want of timely and sufficient action of the will, it may fail to take its legitimate place between motive or inducement on one side, and conduct on the other ; and conduct may be moved, or may be guided, by the forces inherent in, or allowed to belong to, motive or inducement. These impulsions upon conduct may bear a certain analogy to the action of will upon muscle, as for example in this that, in the absence or dormancy of the legitimate sovereign, they may exercise over conduct an absolute command, limited only by the amount of the forces they possess, as, in the case of the muscles, the action of the will is limited by their physical capacity.

Take the first of the disabling causes I have mentioned. The will may be subject to surprises. It is but imperfectly and partially that we discharge the office of rational and deliberative beings. The will may be asleep, like a sentry on his post, though it ought always to be awake ; even as Zeus, the Olympian sovereign who, agreeably to his office, is awake amid the slumbering gods in the Second Iliad, but is inveigled into sleep in the Fourteenth, and befooled accordingly. During this dormancy of the will, passion, affection, interest, misconception, may carry the man into action without the proper warrant.

I also submit for consideration whether the will may in certain cases be defeated, be in fact outrun, by mere rapidity of action on the part of an inferior faculty. The most ready illustration is perhaps to be found in the case of hot and hasty temper, especially when it is only a question of words, for words are winged in a sense, or to an effect, that blows can rarely be. It is usually the function of the judgement to be the immediate arbiter of temper by repressing its undue action : but the suppression of judgement by temper appears very commonly to be absolute, and this not upon a struggle, but by anticipation and rapidity. If the same thing may in fact apply to the will, we must be conscious that there is here no relief from responsibility, since a standing discipline of temper is among the most obvious of human duties.

Again, why may we not suppose that the will is subject to something in the nature of exhaustion and fatigue ? As we find a stalwart reasoner like Butler occasionally adopting a bad reason, though it be with him as a black swan (for example, that of the probabilities against the life of Caesar as it actually was), it is conceivable that lapses of this kind may be due to a fatigue of will, which has been brought about by severe and long-continued coercion of choice in abstruse or nicely balanced subject-matter; or, and perhaps more commonly, amidst great difficulties of environment. It is true that in such a case the faculty or power is not withdrawn. If it is subjected to a momentary abdication, that abdication is not involuntary. It might have been avoided, for instance, by a summons at the moment for more strength, which is among the satellites of the will, or by a better adjustment beforehand between time and labour. A faculty going astray is not on that account to be treated as a cancelled faculty : even a careful calculator will sometimes fall into an error in a sum.

But further, and in a more general way, I suppose we may maintain that the will is, like every other portion of the human constitution, capable of being modified in con-

U

nexion with habit; is capable of, and liable to, education. It may become more or less prompt, more or less vigilant, more or less vigorous, more or less persistent, more or less comprehensive in survey before action, more or less accurate in its apprehension of the rights and wrongs presented to it with authority by the conscience, though not forced upon it; of the true or false, the beautiful or deformed, the isolated or the sympathetic, the pleasurable or the painful, submitted to it for acceptance or rejection in all cases where they are associated with conduct, or where they demand a recognition other than that of simple apprehension. In a word there is a discipline and probation of the will as of the other faculties; but with a case which, though it may be regarded as a counterpart or reflection of theirs, also differs from theirs in this that, while it presides over the whole of their training, its own is self-administered.

Brief notice may be taken of another question, lying between the will and all the other faculties which bring as it were to the tribunal of choice all matters of motive or inducement. It has been part of the hypothesis above explained that there exists in the human being a separate will-force which, as a superior in kind, overrules and overrides all the forces belonging to motives and inducements, considered in themselves. It seems also conceivable that the will is concerned in the award of those forces themselves to the separate faculties, and thus in the exercise of a preventive, as well as an ultimate and overruling power. But if there be any truth in this alternative view, I do not regard it as disposing of the whole case; for it seems an established fact of experience that the will may be *de facto* in abeyance, and that conduct is, or may be, prompted in part by passion without will. It therefore follows that, when we speak of the freedom of the will, we deal with that which in the abstract is true universally, but which in particular and exceptional cases may fail to be operative.

And, after all, we may be pressed with the extreme nature of the difficulties against which will has to contend. sometimes under the most adverse circumstances. It is constantly compelled to acknowledge that the conclusion which it rejects is sustained by considerations, which are at once legitimate and forcible in themselves, though they are certainly or probably outweighed, in either or both respects, by the reasons on the other side. Here there is a doubt in fact, but none in principle. Doubts in principle arise, when the reason cannot formulate a firm, even if obscure, moral judgement upon particulars. These become more frequent as we ascend into the higher circles of life. It is perhaps difficult to name a case more palpable than that supplied by the case of Charles the First in assenting to the Act for the attainder of Strafford. Yet even such a case does not perhaps exhibit at its maximum the amount of pressure which may solicit the will, and may even seem in some minds to apply a *force majeure* to its action, and wring from it a consent it declines to give. Such cases may occur in the form of extreme physical torture, or of the lapse of women into sensual vice as an alternative to starvation. Surrender under such circumstances ought often to disarm absolutely the judgement of man. They recur at their extreme point, by disabling the conscience which is the informant of the will, and thus by effacing for the moment the distinction of right and wrong on the particular point, rather than by any invasion of the general truth of the freedom of the will, which under such circumstances is widowed of the material whereupon to act. If there be a general collapse of the moral agent, the question as to freedom of the will is hardly brought into view. In many even of such cases, where repentance follows, there comes with it a frank admission that, while there might be plea for excuse and sense of pressure, there is no absolute justification, for there was not in strictness an abolition of freedom. It might perhaps be added that, if there have been or might be instances in which fear or weakness mounted up to a true necessity, such instances would no more affect the general doctrine of free volition than eclipses of the sun are taken into account in making estimates of its general operation.

Of course this particular aspect of the subject, which treats of the self-action as against the bondage of the will in the extremities of trial, must be held carefully apart from the cognate but wholly different question which arises as to the relation between the application of such trial to our frail humanity, and the doctrine of a paternal Providence, governing the world.

So much for those extreme cases, which at the outset I separated from the average or ordinary function presented to the will in the common course of life.

CHAPTER VII

BUTLER supplies the teleologist with his text, in a manner resembling that, in which he himself had been supplied by Origen. ' All observations of final causes, drawn from the principles of action in the heart of man, compared with the condition he is placed in, serve all the good uses which instances of final causes in the material world about us do [1].'

There is a notion, highly popular with the champions of negation, that the argument from final causes, which formerly held its head so high, has been effectually maimed by the establishment of the doctrine of physical sequence. This objection was urged by Mr. Romanes, only however in the earlier period of his life ; but it may be found to admit of a conclusive answer, and this singularly able champion saw reason, before his much lamented death, to abandon it.

But negation, usually vigilant enough, appears to have overlooked the fact that, although the argument of design took its rise within the precincts of the physical order, it did not end there. And Butler has here laid down for us the cardinal principle on which is founded its extension to the moral universe, so far as that moral universe lies within our cognizance. It remains, however, to point out (1) that here we at once escape from the apparent difficulty which for a time was used to baffle the argument, inasmuch as there is not in the moral order anything which essentially corresponds with physical sequence ; (2) that this extension has itself two departments : one which deals with the human species as individuals; the second which regards them as gathered into societies, and which is itself susceptible of a subdivision between single societies, which constitute the individuals of this compartment of the subject, and the grand

[1] *Sermon*, vi. 1 ; also *Analogy*, I. iii. 1.

combination at large of the societies known to history and forming the 'Parliament of man,' the great evolution of the world.

With these prefatory observations, I pass to the question of the argument of teleology as it has been commonly handled, in conjunction with the dispositions of external nature: that is to say, to physical antecedents known by experience to be capable in each case of producing the effects alleged in argument. And, accordingly, it is contended that, wherever there is such an assemblage of physical antecedents, we lose sight of the argument of design; for while their adequacy, taken individually, is indisputable, the question remains whether their juxtaposition may be due only to chance.

But it must be observed, before we proceed farther, that we are here touching only a very small portion of the field which is covered by the argument of teleology. For we are dealing with inorganic nature only. But from inorganic nature we ascend to organisms; from organisms to intelligence; from intelligence to morality; and, with or beyond this, to the comprehensive idea of the spiritual life, or the image of God. It is plain that the argument against design in the realm of inorganic nature ceases to have any corresponding force as we rise into the higher divisions of created things, unless and until it be shown that in those higher divisions the phenomena, which appear in combination, and which accomplish a purpose, are themselves immediately due to a concurrence of antecedents as necessarily connected with the several constituent items, as those which the natural inorganic world supplies for the uses of the argument against design. So that, if the argument of design be applicable to the inorganic world, it may be applicable *a fortiori* to those worlds which are above it.

Having this caution solidly laid down in the first instance, let us proceed to examine how far design in the natural world is really touched by the hostile reasoning.

The objector succeeds in referring the combination to a set of antecedents, which are adequate, when taken together, to produce the result, but which are severally such as cannot be referred to any special purpose; and whose action, if taken separately, conveys not so much as an inkling of a moral aim. Yes : but how did the antecedents themselves come to be combined ? Does not the juxtaposition of such antecedents, as are combinedly capable of producing consequents that accomplish a purpose, as effectually, though more remotely, suggest the argument of design ? For we ask how was it that the antecedents came into their admitted collocation ? A man is the child of his grandfather as truly as of his father. It is admitted that the antecedents have a power and a special fitness to produce the combination. That fitness growing out of the relation among the antecedents, regarded as a whole, in its turn implies purpose ; and purpose implies a moral agent.

The set of antecedents, which thus require us to shift the standing-ground backwards by a stage, has, for each of its items, other sets of physical antecedents, and the great argument of design, which is now most commonly described by the phrase I have already employed, may be simply and concisely represented by these words ; adaptation, which is essentially comprehensive, implies purpose ; and purpose, in its turn, implies an agent. Adaptation carries the idea of something distinct from mere power or capacity. For these latter may be predicated of a single and uncompounded energy, whereas adaptation, in which energy may or may not be included, requires that a number of parts be placed in connexion with one another, and that the aggregate be endowed with a fitness, not included in the parts if taken singly, to perform a function, or produce an entity, beyond itself. So the argument holds good that adaptation, thus understood, implies purpose ; and purpose is the intention of a moral agent to accomplish an end by the use of the appropriate system of means.

We must not allow ourselves to become the sport of words. Chance has no real objective existence. It simply signifies events of which we cannot trace the sequence. For us, the sparrow falls to the ground by chance, for we can observe no purpose in connexion with the event. And so it may be with cards or dice. It is conceivable that in the aggregate a series of these indications may have a very serious purpose ; and who shall say that any fraction of a serious purpose is not serious? But in an inquiry of this kind, we may justly say, *de minimis non curat lex*: a certain magnitude is requisite to bring the argument of design within our mental range, as a physical magnitude, which the microscope might catch, may be too small for the eye.

Chance, therefore, cannot be a competitor with purpose, in regard to teleology or the argument from design.

But now it is contended by some, that the investigations of science, or of natural science (and it is most important to bear in mind that wherever the substantive is used alone, it is used in regard to natural science exclusively [1]), have laid open the facts of physical causation; that they have demonstrated to us that there are a multitude of adaptations in nature which are immediately due to what religion would call the operation of second causes; and that the same will hold as we move onwards and upwards in an ascending scale. Let the first set of antecedents be a, the next will be a^1, the next behind this a^2, and so on to a^n. Thus we should have before us so many sets of combinations of antecedents, multiplying themselves as we ascend in geometrical progressions. This being so, it follows that, if our query as to the first combination or juxtaposition of antecedents have a solid foundation, then, the farther we carry the pursuit of these combinations, the more is that foundation deepened and strengthened.

Before proceeding to another stage, let me say I do not proscribe the idea that even to the original and crude material forces before their differentiation, on account of the capacities for combination and result which, when differentiated, their constituent parts will exhibit, the argument of design might in a measure be applicable.

It is fundamental with Mr. Romanes, in the anti-teleological argument which he maintained at an early period of his distinguished career, rigidly to exclude the admission of design when only a single combination is concerned: be it that of the sea-bay. or that of the eye, the illustrations with which he deals [2]. But he makes a considerable admission for

---

[1] In obedience to an established though (as I think) faulty usage; which has left us, I believe, without a term to describe knowledge in its strictest sense.

[2] *Thoughts on Religion*, pp. 45, 56 seq. I will here cite the interesting passage which serves as a basis for the argument of the early essay of Mr. Romanes (p. 56). He introduces

the adverse case when the floor is widened, and a combination of combinations, or a multitude of combinations, is contemplated. The bringing together of all the combinations so arranged as to exhibit adaptation to an end, is with him conclusive, at least *prima facie*, in favour of the inference of agency; that is to say, of an agent.

Thus far Mr. Romanes is led by the distinction which he draws between general and special design; between special adjustments, and the general laws of nature[1]. It appears plain, however, to me that his concession ought in consistency to have been carried farther. Let us take his case of

an observer, who walks down to the sea-shore : —

'First, he observes that there is a beautiful basin hollowed out in the land for the reception of a bay ; that the sides of this basin which, from being near its opening, are most exposed to the action of large rolling billows, are composed of rocky cliffs, evidently in order to prevent the further encroachment of the sea, and the consequent destruction of the entire bay : that the sides of the basin, which from being successively situated more inland are successively less and less exposed to the action of large waves, are constituted successively of smaller rocks, passing into shingle, and eventually into the finest sand : that, as the tides rise and fall with as great a regularity as was exhibited by the movements of the watch, the stones are carefully separated out from the sand to be arranged in sloping layers by themselves, and this always with a most beautiful reference to the places round the margin of the basin which are most in danger of being damaged by the action of the waves. He would further observe, upon closer inspection, that this process of selective arrangement goes into matters of the most minute detail. Here, for instance, he would observe a mile or two of a particular kind of seaweed artistically arranged in one long sinuous line upon the beach ; there he would see a wonderful de-posit of shells ; in another place a lovely little purple heap of garnet sand, the minute particles of which have all been carefully picked out from the surrounding acres of yellow sand. Again, he would notice that the streams which come down to the bay are all flowing in channels admirably dug out for the purpose ; and, being led by curiosity to investigate the teleology of these various streams, he would find that they serve to supply the water which the sea loses by evaporation, and also, by a wonderful piece of adjustment, to furnish fresh water to those animals and plants which thrive best in fresh water, and yet by their combined action to carry down sufficient mineral constituents to give that precise degree of saltness to the sea as a whole which is required for the maintenance of pelagic life. Lastly, continuing his investigations along this line of inquiry, he would find that a thousand different habitats were all thoughtfully adapted to the needs of a hundred thousand different forms of life, none of which could survive if these habitats were reversed. Now, I think that our imaginary inquirer would be a dull man if, as the result of all this study, he failed to conclude that the evidence of design furnished by the marine bay was at least as cogent as that which he had previously found in his study of the watch.'

[1] *Thoughts on Religion*, p. 60.

the sea-bay, produced, as he has shown, by the action of a number of immediate physical causes, independent one of another. Now he would admit that each of these antecedents has its own antecedent; let us call it a pre-antecedent. There was then a collection of these pre-antecedents, which stood in the same relation to the later, and immediate or proximate antecedents, as these later or more immediate antecedents held to the sea-bay. And they hold, as we have seen, to that sea-bay a relationship 'once removed' but not the less real because it becomes operative through one medium or through more than one. For they in their turn had been due to a prior set of antecedents, antecedents of a third order; and so forth until, in the upward movement, we arrive at the original ὕλη, or matter in its primal condition. So that here we have the very thing postulated for the admission, namely, a combination of combinations, although they all eventuate in one result; and as the combination of combinations is admitted to raise a presumption of design, it is evident that the sea-bay, if not by virtue of its immediate parentage, yet by virtue of its long line of ancestors, or its atavism, effectually raises that presumption; every one of the antecedents in the successive stages having been in itself independent of every other, by which, and by the progenitors (so to call them) of which, it was accompanied, and this independence is just as complete as the independence of the physical causation in one department of nature can be of the physical causation in another, for it is absolute and entire [1]; and we are entitled to press the physicist with his own interrogatory, 'How is it that all [these] physical causes conspire, by their united action, to the production of a general order of nature?' And take again the suggestion conveyed in the following words: 'The resultant is determined as to magnitude and direction by the components. Yes: but what about the magnitude and direction of these components [2]?'

So the supreme directing cause is intelligence. In fact, the introduction of antecedents, intended to overset the argument of design, ends by imparting to it a large accession of strength. As it originally was urged, it rested on

---

[1] *Thoughts on Religion*, p. 67.   [2] *Ibid.* p. 70.

the final combination only. But we now find that there is a long or indefinite series of combinations: and a series of combinations is in itself a new combination; apart from the force which attaches to each of them when viewed separately, and only in relation to its immediate consequent. A like argument applies to the final union of all the separate combinations, that make up the general order of nature.

But this conclusion is followed by observations, which deprive it of practical value. This intelligence, we are told, is different from anything that we know of mind in ourselves. Different, not in degree only, but in kind. Finding its onward way with the aid of Mr. Herbert Spencer, the argument holds that, for the purpose in view, 'Mind must be divested of all attributes by which it is distinguished,' in other words, 'mind is a blank [1].' Surely one of the most unfortunate of arguments. We have arrived in our inquiries at a combination which requires nothing less than what we call and know by experience as mind. But, to meet the case before us, we are required to postulate something still greater, and much greater than our mind can be pretended to be. We cannot grasp the dimensions, nor follow the operation, of this great creative mind. Therefore, though we see its results, in us and before us, for us it is no mind at all. A bewildering, nay, a befooling conclusion.

Let us proceed to test it. Strange as it may seem, the argument appears to be no other than this. Were the object before us one produced by the thought and hand of man, we should, it seems, be entitled, at the stage we have previously reached in the argument, to say that this must be recognized as proving design: design limited in its character as proceeding from a limited agent, yet still true design. In dealing, however, with the order of nature, we become acquainted with products which, taken in severalty and in simple forms, lead to a like conclusion; but which taken as a whole are not only more large, subtle, complex, and diversified, but are all these in a way transcending all measure, and are the products of a power which passes beyond comprehension. Let us view this power, by way

[1] *Thoughts on Religion*, p. 74.

of illustration, as if it were a line projected into space.
Let us cut off from it some limited and moderate space.
Such is the productive force of the human intellect, compared with that of the Unseen. What are we to conclude?
One should say we may reasonably cherish a devout amaze-
ment at the infinite excess of the Divine over the human.
But no, says the adversary. The limited line is all very
well and is a true line, and he that drew it was capable of
designing: but the endless one, even though it produce
what (taken singly) is analogous to the products of the
limited, cannot be recognized as proceeding from a Power
capable of purpose, as acting upon design, and is, in the
view of the present discussion, no mind at all. If this be
the *cul de sac* of our inquiries, surely reason has abdicated
her throne.

Let us next proceed to that intermediate region of nature
which may be termed the animal, and which lies between
the human and the inorganic. It appears to be admitted
that, within the bounds of this region, the adjustments of
means to ends are more numerous, nicer, and more elaborate,
than in the realm of inanimate nature. But it is contended
that the argument in favour of design is no stronger on that
account. Here, again, the phenomena presented to us are
said to be accounted for by their antecedents; and, whether
this can be demonstrated or not, it probably cannot be denied with demonstration. On the other hand, another class
of arguments indicating purpose can be more effectively
developed at the next stage of our inquiries, and is accordingly reserved.

Passing onwards, then, we come to the case of man, the
lord of the visible creation. And here, as it seems to me,
the argument of the teleologist rides triumphant, I may
almost say unassailed, from the very first. Not as regards
the adaptations of his bodily constitution; for here, I suppose, no more can be said than that, as the animal adaptations surpass the inorganic, so the human corporal adaptations (take the wonderful case of the hand for example)
transcend those of the animal world at large. But whereas,
for animals, we were not enabled to draw our arguments from
any higher region, the position is now altered in its very

foundation. We rise from the animated to the intellectual and the spiritual part of man, and from his material composition to his environment, and to his condition as a whole.

And now the argument of design appears before us in a shape altogether new. Man finds himself placed not in a chaos of accidents, but in what he finds to be on the whole, though only in partial and imperfect development, a *kosmos* of experiences and events so ordered as to present a certain character and to produce certain results. Before examining the argument of design as it arises out of the relation between man and his environment, or experience, let us for a few moments consider it in connexion with his composition or constitution. The proposition that reference of facts to antecedents is, as a rule, one thing in the inorganic world and another in the higher orders of being, cannot perhaps be better illustrated than by observing the conditions of our human lineage. I see no reason to doubt that heredity is here largely traceable. But more largely in physical than in mental peculiarities, and sometimes under the most singular forms [1]. It is more easy to find the tradition of physical beauty in particular families than continuity of mind. Some are fond of referring the characters of great men to their parents; but such references commonly cover no more than a very small part of the ground. Little is known of the parents of Shakespeare; but it seems plain that the space by which his genius went in advance of ordinary mental endowments was in no degree bridged over by them, and was indeed nothing less than immeasurable. Napoleon had a beautiful and energetic mother, and a notary of some ability for his father. The former is a clear case of heredity as to physical beauty : but as to mental characteristics no common measure can be found between the Corsican parents and this colossal man. Political ability affords, in the mental

---

[1] A gentleman, rather well known in the (still) present century, had the peculiarity, when asleep, of emitting breath in short and light puffs, which raised part of the upper lip. No one in his sphere was known to do the same, or even to have heard of any one who did. But one of his sons reproduced this non-voluntary habit, and was equally solitary in it. So the reproduction of a single white lock amidst a mass of dark hair is alleged at this time to characterize a Roman family of high rank and historic name.

order, the most marked and frequent instances of evident
transmission. But, as a rule, antecedence here entirely fails
us as an instrument for rendering account in the greater
cases ; and the floor is left clear and unincumbered for creative power and the manifestation of design. That vacant
floor is at once filled by the great world-historic fact of the
singular and palpable adaptation between the apparition of
men having the highest greatness, and the demands made
by the order of circumstances into which they were born.
Indeed, I have read, in a negative treatise of great ability,
the remark that, were it not for our living in a time when
all Divine interference with the order of nature has been
disproved, it might almost be supposed to be established by
this particular class of phenomena.

Let us now turn to the other portion of the field of argument. Speaking generally, the position in which man finds
himself placed seems to be adapted to his instruction and his
improvement. Like the sea-bay, it presents a combination
of parts accommodated to particular purposes ; and, like the
structure of the sea-bay, so the combination of these parts
can be submitted to an analysis. We find from experience
that the human character is tested, exercised, and matured by
some, perhaps by all, of the combinations it presents ; for its
elevation and its felicity, if they are turned to account in one
way, for its degradation and destruction, if they are handled
in another. External fortunes likewise arrive not by chance,
but, for the most part, under the operation of certain laws
of sequence. Prudence and forethought issue in success,
extravagance and neglect in ruin or in failure. The observance of justice and truth brings about good repute and
general respect, often gratitude and the return of benefits ;
while the opposite qualities are regarded with disfavour,
and create indifference or dislike, or rouse opposition.
All these rules, it is true, seem to fail, and even to be
reversed, in particular cases. But Wesley predicted with
justice that the effect of reclaiming large bodies of men
from ignorance, idleness, debauchery, and irreligion to
habits of sobriety and diligence, and to a sense of piety,
would be so fundamentally to alter and improve their
condition on the whole, as to bring in a new set of dan-

gers and temptations, which lurk in the train of prosperity. Even amidst the dark fortunes of the early Church, the Apostle gave the assurance [1] that godliness had the promise of the life that now is. Through all the following centuries this declaration has been echoed back by the prevailing tenor of the facts of life. Christianity, born in a manger, has attracted to itself, in overwhelming proportion, the power, the wealth, and the commanding influences of the world. In the battle of good and evil, Providence, though it may seem to be fighting in disguise, chooses its side and makes known its choice.

Here, then, is a scheme of moral adaptation, which though imperfect is universal and perpetual. And here there is not, as in the case of the sea-bay, any such collection of physical antecedents, as can be set up by way of competitors with the action of the Almighty, or can furnish some sort of substitute for design. And there is no aggregate of moral antecedents capable of being picked out from among the threads of the tangled web of life with any approach to the uniformity and clearness necessary to demonstrate the relation between moral causes and their effects. In regard to the most important of all the benefits to be gained, the very highest are those exhibited by the formation of character. But these are often indiscernible until they have reached a considerable degree of ripeness, and it would be impossible to establish such an analysis of them, or of the experiences amidst which they were evolved, as in any tolerable degree to affiliate particular effects to their particular causes. The evidence is, as a rule, essentially general, but the educative process is broad and undeniable. The fortress of design is so planted in the wide expanse of human life, as to be alike unassailable by its enemies and conspicuous in the eyes of every rational and impartial observer. Besides the fatally enhanced difficulty, which philosophy finds in assigning consequents to moral antecedents from general defect of exactitude in the evidence of connexion, another power intervenes to defeat the process of calculation. That is the power of will. For it is often found to happen that two men will, in circumstances which appear to

[1] 1 Tim. iv. 8.

the observer identical, arrive at decisions, and follow lines of conduct, absolutely contradictory. It is true that the opposition in the modes of action may have regard, and may even in a certain sense be due, to inward springs of character and impulse. But these influences, besides being infinitely diverse, manifold, and also complex, are effectually hidden, sometimes wholly, sometimes in a large degree, from the eye of human observation, and cannot therefore be made evidence in the case. Whereas, on the other side, it is ingeniously urged that in every physical adaptation, the union of conditions presented to us can be finally, and unequivocally, traced up to the action of the two great postulates, matter and force [1].

The argument of design in the intelligent order may be said to begin not with man, but in the sphere of the lower animals, and in connexion with their instincts. It has a larger and clearer application to the case of men taken individually. But the chain of extension does not end here. We pass from man individually into a new sphere of argument, when we consider man introduced to the adaptations of union in the social body, and to the purposes, ever multiplying among progressive races, of advanced political development.

Besides the difference already pointed out on behalf of intelligent and moral, as compared with physical, teleology, we should, I conceive, reckon this capacity of development in its combinations. The adaptations in the inanimate, inorganic world are, for the purposes of common observation, stationary. Even in the organic departments inferior to man, the range assigned to progress is very limited. It may indeed be disclosed to us hereafter that physical combination may, as in the case of the earth we inhabit, or of other heavenly bodies, form portions of larger and more complex developments. In the case of the human being, we have them already placed before us. What a marvellous thing in itself, and apart from any conclusion as to the manner of its use, is the development or education of a genius, like that of Goethe, in his long

---

[1] The argument from physical adaptation is comprehensively stated in some of the Bridgwater Treatises, e. g. those of Whewell and Bell.

life of fourscore years, with the marked changes it included, and notwithstanding its great and important deficiencies. When we contemplate many of the political societies, such as the Roman, the British, the American, their movement through successive stages is astonishing. But each of these stages is a new presentation of the argument of design; and the combination of the stages among themselves is a new presentation of it in a new form. So that besides the inference deducible from each combination by itself, the combinations ascend with the force of multiplication. We have a hierarchy of combinations.

Greatest and last of all, within the range of the intelligent and moral order, is the great drama of world-history. It is, indeed, not as yet placed fully within our view. But Christendom perceives that it has a centre in the Incarnation and the Advent; and the adaptations offered us by history, in preparation for these events, are so salient and palpable, that it may be supposed difficult, even for non-Christians, altogether to deny them. The most palpable of the auxiliary arrangements which ' prepared the way of the Lord, and made straight in the desert a highway for our God [1],' were the general dominance of the Greek language, consequent mainly, but by no means wholly, on the conquests of Alexander the Great, the introduction of the literary and thinking world to the Old Testament through the Septuagint, and the network of facile communication with all the apparatus of a dominant intelligence, which was supplied by the grand itinerary of the Roman Empire. More important still, if less obvious and salient than these, were the intellectual contributions ready to hand for the formation of Christian thought and action through the Greek and Roman mind respectively. A concurrence after the fact, greatly subserving the purposes of revealed religion, is, as I should plead, to be found in the remarkable assemblage of the ancient Sacred Books, belonging to religions outside the pale of the Bible, and materially sustained, as I should further plead, by other manifestations of primitive religion, also foreign to the geographical precinct embraced by the Scriptural record. All this is of

[1] Is. xl. 3.

course to amass particulars, not in rivalry with but in subordination to, the mighty and long-lived evangelical preparation presented to us by the Hebrew history. What may
yet further have to be made known in the complement of the
great time-cycle not yet filled up, it is impossible to say,
and would be hazardous even to conjecture. But as the
plays or tales of poets and romancers may indicate the
essence of their plot long before they have been fully exhibited or perused, so we have had already submitted to our
view the historic drama of the human race in what are to
all appearance its highest and its governing sections, in a
degree and on a scale of vast dimension and immeasurable
complication of parts, such as offers to us the facts of combination, and the argument of design, with an extension
almost mocking the human faculty, but yet with a clearness
such that he who runs may read.

It is this fortress of design, as exhibited in the natural,
the moral, and the spiritual government of the man as such,
that Butler, without having it for his professed and principal aim, and indeed without detailed exposition, has exhibited to us more forcibly, in point of essential principle, than
any other writer: so that it is no exaggeration to decorate
him with the chieftainship of Christian Teleology. Paley,
as I conceive, as a sturdy wrestler, overthrows his antagonists within the compass of his arm, while Butler soars
high into the heaven above them as an eagle on the wing.

Two other matters call for observation before bringing
these remarks to a close.

First, a favourite subject of discussion in the philosophical world is that which passes by the name of evolution.
It is not a very convenient name, for it does not in itself
indicate the idea of which it is meant to be the vehicle. In
itself it may be said to mean the sequence of events, but it
really has reference to the order of causation. It might be
said, as it is now used, to mean the sequence of events
through the operation of second causes ; but this language
may not be agreeable to those who do not accept the suggestion it seems to make of a first cause lying behind them.
The evolution we have now before us would perhaps in
Christian terminology be called devolution, for it would

mean that the Almighty has entrusted to that system of nature, which He has designed and put into action, the production and government of effects at large : as the watchmaker has entrusted to the mainspring and machinery of a watch the discharge of its essential function, namely, the indication of time.

In many quarters it appears to be either asserted or taken for granted that this method of action, this production of natural effects from natural causes, is a heavy if not a deadly blow to religion, and in particular to the argument of design. We are told that the theory which evolution displaces was a theory of sudden or special creation : phraseology which has been devised by negationists, and of which those arguing from an opposite point may perhaps be allowed to say that it seems unphilosophical, if not indeed almost nonsensical. For an effect produced in the course of nature is no more sudden and no more special if produced by the action of a force flowing direct from Deity, than if it result from the action of (as it were) a store of force lodged in some intermediate agency. It is only the wildest spirit of assumption which can suppose that government by forces coming straight from the fountain-head must needs be government by fits and starts, and that order and method cannot be had except by the action of what are known as instrumental causes.

But such action of second causes is not a thing which believers in religion ought to be inclined to view with jealousy. In the history of thought, it is pre-eminently they who have taught the existence and power of the will in created agents, of a separate originating source of action, and of many and grave effects ; of an order, in short, of second causes which is of the greatest force and dignity among them all. Take, for example, the will of Alexander the Great in the invasion and conquest of Asia. In itself a first cause, it was, notwithstanding, relatively to the counsels of God, a second cause : for it was through this second cause, that is, through its foreseen results, that the Almighty brought about some events, which were most powerful factors in the accomplishment of His counsels for the redemption of the world. If, then, we see that Almighty wisdom can thus make the force and independent action of man effectuate the purposes of His government, why should it be imagined, by either friends or foes, that devolutions of power to other created agencies, not spontaneous, but working only upon the lines of an order which He himself has predetermined, can involve the smallest derogation from His supremacy ?

Let us take, for example, the whole upward movement of organic life, from its lowest forms of mollusc or zoophyte, or be they what they may, to the highest of those orders which were included in the preparation of the earth for the residence of man. On the one supposition, the Almighty was alike and equally concerned in every one of the infinitesimal exercises of force by which the ascent was gradually achieved. On the other supposition, portions of that force were delegated to initial forms of natural agency, with all the conditions of their advancement fore-ordained, including its interruptions and its failures, and that the results were achieved by a heaven-born necessity, precisely as they would have been under the method first proposed. The difference thus set up by us has, as it regards the Divine omnipotence, not an atom of result. If the modes of operation differ, the method and effect are the same. It may, however, perhaps be said that in relation to us they seriously differ : that, in its manifestation to us, the former method represented government by occasion ; the latter method, government by scheme or system. The one did not preclude the idea of change, the other betokened fixity, and encouraged anticipation and prediction. Be it so : the fixity being, however, one liable at any moment to displacement, like that order of climatic or terrestrial phenomena which, amidst marrying and giving in marriage, was rudely interrupted by the deluge ; or like that regulated existence of heavenly bodies which, at the proper time, find its consummation in the discharge of their shattered fragments through unmeasured space. But let us regard the scheme or system apart from these contingent changes. Ought our tracing of the widespread operation of second causes to darken our conception of Deity ? As it seems to me, it should do exactly the reverse. The more we have of system and fixity in nature, the better. For, in the method of natural second causes,

God as it were takes the map of His own counsels out of the recesses of His own idea, and graciously lays it near our view ; condescending, as it were, to make us partakers of His thought, so that, seeing more and more His qualities in His acts, we may, from knowing their large collocation, be more and more stirred to admiration, to thankfulness, and to love.

And although the overthrow of religion by evolution has been loudly proclaimed in the name of science, it would be injustice no less than folly to charge this shallow conception on men of science taken at large, or as represented by their most distinguished authorities [1].

Next and lastly, in connexion with the great argument of design, the illustration from the instance of a watch found on a heath has become famous, and has also come to be closely, perhaps for this country inseparably, associated with the name of Paley, a writer so well known, among other qualities, for the felicity of his illustrations.

In the year 1873, however, Lord Neaves, a well-known Scottish judge, delivered to an association at Carlisle a lecture on Paley, in which he showed that the illustration was not original, but borrowed. In announcing the circumstances, Lord Neaves is careful to state that his discovery in like manner is borrowed from one or more preceding inquirers.

Bernard Nieuwentyt, a Dutch philosopher, published simultaneously in Dutch and English, in the year 1715, an able and learned work, *The Existence of God demonstrated by the wonders of Nature*, which book, a few years afterwards, was translated into English by John Chamberlayne, and published under the title of *The Religious Philosopher*.

When the respective passages in the two works are compared, they show a relationship in detail, besides the identity of the general idea. Paley's apology is this ; that it was his general practice, after having made his own notes on a subject, to consult the works of others, and to publish what he had extracted, 'commonly without the name of the author [2].' The application of his rule was in this instance

---

[1] See Dr. Zahm's *Evolution and Dogma*, Part II. chaps. vii, viii.

[2] Lord Neaves, *Lecture on Paley*, pp. 25-27. Blackwood, 1873.

most unfortunate, for he seems to have been forcibly struck with the force and beauty of the illustration, or he would hardly have selected it, as he has done, to take its place in the opening paragraph of his work.

But although the proprietary title of Nieuwentyt to the illustration, as against Paley, is thus firmly established, this argument itself is far older, and has been admirably set forth by Cicero in the following passage [1]. 'Quis enim hunc hominem dixerit, qui, cum tam certos caeli motus, tam ratos astrorum ordines, tamque inter se omnia connexa et apta viderit, neget in his ullam esse rationem, eaque casu fieri dicat; quae quanto consilio gerantur, nullo consilio assequi possumus? an, cum machinatione quadam moveri aliquid videmus, ut sphaeram, ut horas, ut alia permulta, non dubitamus quin illa opera sint rationis? cum autem impetum caeli cum admirabili celeritate moveri vertique videmus, constantissime conficientem anniversarias vicissitudines cum summa salute et conservatione rerum omnium; dubitamus quin ea non solum ratione fiant, sed etiam excellenti divinaque ratione? licet enim iam, remota subtilitate disputandi, oculis quodammodo contemplari pulchritudinem rerum earum, quas divina providentia dicimus constitutas.'

[1] Cicero, *de Natura Deorum*, II. 38.

CHAPTER VIII

MIRACLE

HUME has stated his argument against miracles in a variety of successive paragraphs, as if he were afraid to startle and repel his reader, unless he adopted the method of disguised approaches. No one, however, can complain that he is not outspoken as he approaches his conclusion. Evidently bearing in his mind the alliance so firmly compacted by Butler between faith and reason, he begins his final assault by placing the two in violent opposition; and leaving faith aside in a νεφελοκοκκυγία of its own, he pronounces the verdict of 'reason,' by way of example, on the miracles of the Pentateuch, which he describes as follows :

'A book, presented to us by a barbarous and ignorant people, written in an age when they were still more barbarous, and, in all probability, long after the facts which it relates, corroborated by no concurring testimony, and resembling those fabulous accounts which every nation gives of its origin [1].'

Every particular of this tirade may be at this date successfully contested, and some of them were even at Hume's date marked by gross incaution. He has not, however, provided us with a full synopsis of his own argument, and I cannot do better, as I conceive, than present to the reader that which has been framed by Cardinal Newman, in his *Grammar of Assent* [2].

'It is experience only which gives authority to human testimony, and it is the same experience which assures us of the laws of nature. When these two kinds of experience are contrary the one to the other, we are bound to subtract

---

[1] Hume on Miracles : *Philosophical Works* (Boston and Edinburgh, 1854), vol. iv. p. 149.

[2] Pages 298 *seqq.*

the one from the other. We have no experience of the violation of natural laws, and much experience of the violation of truths. So we may establish it as a maxim that no human testimony can have such force as to prove a miracle, and make it the foundation of a system of religion.'

I will not refer to the succinct but striking argument offered by Newman in reply. But turning to the position which he controverts, I find Hume's first proposition to be that experience, which gives authority to human testimony, also assures us of the laws of nature. If we grant for a moment that Hume's contention is unassailable from this point forwards, it still appears to me that the proposition I have cited is infected with a fatal flaw. Experience, it appears, assures us of 'the laws of nature.' Does it assure us of all the laws of nature? At what date did it begin to supply us with this comprehensive knowledge? Clearly not, for example, before the Copernican system, which, with its consequents, has brought up new laws of nature and has reversed the old, which we had previously thought ourselves assured of. Now, unless we know all the laws of nature, Hume's contention is of no avail; for the alleged miracle may come under some law not yet known to us. One law of nature traverses and controls or reverses another. The law of capillary attraction contradicts, wherever it operates in certain directions, the law of gravitation; for it draws matter upwards which, under the force of gravitation, would pass downwards. Suppose, for argument's sake, a state of things in which the law of gravity was known, but capillary attraction unknown. And suppose a narrative were told, which was based upon capillary attraction. On the principle advanced by Hume, that narrative would be condemned *in limine* as false. And so it is that miracle is condemned. Particular laws of nature we may know, but we do not always know the limits of those laws; and future experience may reveal to us other laws now unknown, but (at least) bounding and curtailing, nay perhaps traversing, those which we think we know, so as to leave spaces open for miracle without contravention of law, which at present appear to be closed.

The fact seems to be that, creeping on from step to step, we learn a little, and again a little, of natural laws; and we

build them into a system of knowledge, to which great value
may belong without its having reached the stage of perfection or of infallibility. We hear much of the uniformity of
nature. But does this phrase mean more than that wide
regions are made known to us, within which her action is
uniform; and that her extremest variations may at some
time be reducible to some high and comprehensive rule, at
present hidden from our eyes? Under what law of nature,
now known to us, is it that parthenogenesis has been allowed to occupy a portion of the field, which was supposed to
be wholly given up to the ordinary law of sexual generation
from a pair? Does there not here accrue to us a lesson,
which seems to teach that there may be generalizations
bringing into methodical relations with one another all the
phenomena of nature: but that, for us of the present day
and the present conditions, what we are conversant with is
not uniformity of nature, but certain uniformities of nature,
which, as revealed to us, vary from one another? And
vary, not under plainly known rules like the domesticated
pigeons, but under rules wholly unknown; so that the uniformities we know are, as related one to another, truly
varieties; and the rules, so far as we know them at present,
are rules subject to exception.

This is in truth no more than a partial unfolding, perhaps
an expansion, of what Butler has suggested as a possibility
of the future state; when he observes to us that what is
here and now reckoned supernatural may hereafter be found
to fall into a natural order[1]. So, under our present life-
dispensation, things that warrant or require the introduction of the supernatural in order to present them even as
conceivable, in one given state of our knowledge, may in
another state of our knowledge be found to fall within the
range of ordinary human resources. Ariosto, in the sixteenth century, invokes preterhuman aid to transport a
British army in one day from Picardy to Paris[2]: but it is
now a journey of a few hours. A French engineer assured
me, at the last Paris Exhibition in 1891, that if the *chemin
de fer glissant*, of which he was in charge, and which was
there put in action, could be perfected it might (with all

[1] *Analogy*, I. i. 31.   [2] *Orl. Fur.* xiv. 96.

proper subsidiary arrangements) conceivably reduce the
time required for a journey to London down to the limit of
two hours.

In the proposition associated with the name of Hume,
there is a clear *petitio principii*, which entirely cancels its
force. 'Miracles cannot be true, because they are contrary
to experience.' To whose, and to what, experience? On
Hume's own ground we are entitled to say that, until the
powers and bounds of natural law are exhaustively known,
we never can be certain that it is at any point or in any
sense contravened by this or that alleged miracle. Even
this consideration does not reach the full scope of the
offence against logic, with which the argument is chargeable. This experience, which we are said to possess, and
which shuts out miracle, is not only not such an experience
as draws the line with accuracy between what the laws of
nature in their totality allow and what they prohibit, but
it does not even include the whole of such experience as has
in the aggregate of times and places fallen to the lot of man.
Let *A* come and allege his miracle. *B* denounces it as false,
because it is contrary to experience; that is, to *B*'s experience. But how does *B* know that it is contrary to *A*'s
experience? As in the famous illustration of ice asserted
in the tropical plains to exist elsewhere, what is impossible
for the one may be familiar to the other.

There is undoubtedly much plausibility, and even a good
share of force, in the contrast drawn between the carelessness, folly, and mendacity, which so often vitiate human
testimony, and the honesty and frankness with which nature reveals her treasures. But even here we must be on
our guard against precipitate concessions to the astuteness
of an adversary. Human testimony, liable as it is to failure
in so many forms, is the main instrument by means of which
human affairs are carried on. True, it is frequently subject
in many cases to the check of verification; but in many
cases it is not so checked; and yet, with such precautions
as the circumstances may admit, it is here also received and
believed, and shown by experience to be rightly so received
and believed. The *crux* in Hume's case is this. He has to
prove that miracle as such — that is to say, an event not to

be accounted for by the known laws of nature — is impossible; for in all things, except the impossible, human testimony is received. Doubtless, when improbability exists,
then it is only received with an amount of care and jealousy
in proportion to that improbability; yet the door is ever
open to acceptance after the demands of such care and jealousy have been met. But the impossibility, which shuts
out the testimony altogether, never can be shown except by
proof that every avenue is blocked by which the miracle
might come in. Any law of nature, or created things, might
open such an avenue: and Hume's argument is of no avail
until we have shown that we know every such avenue that
is now in existence, and know that all of them are blocked.

Now if it be true that these miracles are anomalies in
nature, it may be that there exist, although at present hidden
from us, good reasons for such anomalies in the importance
of the purposes which may be served by them. I have often
observed in woodcutting that when a tree threw out near
the ground beginnings of roots unusually large, this was
a cautionary provision made by nature to compensate, by an
outward projection of unusual strength, for the weakness
produced by some rot latent in the interior trunk. So it is,
I believe, that in the case of a broken arm nature commonly
aims at making up, by an extension given to the ordinary
mass of bone, for a loss of tenacity resulting from some want
of the compactness originally belonging to the composition of
the limb. In the first of these cases, the enlargement is liable to be more or less in the nature of a deformity. In the
second, I presume it to be always a mild example of mal-
formation. We shall have to ask whether compensation may
not atone for such deformity. It may be that for all natural
anomalies whatsoever there are good reasons in reserve. Let
us also suppose it possible that there are no such reasons,
when we know at least that none are within our view. But
this at least seems obvious, that anomalies such as those last
noticed, which serve purposes of marked utility, can plead
a justification for their admission to a place in nature, as
compared with any anomalies (and there are many such)
which can render no justifying account of themselves.

Now let it be admitted that miracles, as at present known

to us, are an anomaly in nature. But have they no justifying
pleas, which they can exhibit on their own behalf? Surely
there is such a plea, and one of overwhelming importance.
For sin is in the world. And its ejection from the world
would at once cover nine-tenths of the way towards the
solution of the problems which most perplex and afflict
humanity. And the Christian, in concert with the Jewish,
religion urges that the miracles, which it alleges to have
been performed, were performed, and have operated with
great and probably indispensable power, towards the attainment of that very end. This subject is so weighty that it
may be proper to adopt a fresh point of departure, and to
open it more at large.

I have spoken of the laws of uniformity within the narrow
limits known to us. Under what law of uniformity were
the Siamese twins organically united so as to be inseparable,
and so that they were incapable of being separated by a
surgical operation without the gravest danger to life? Now
here was a variation from natural order, which utterly contravened utility. Think of what the world would be if it
were, in whole or in part, inhabited by assemblages of such
twins. It was a variety which might, at any rate on the
surface, be called freak, or absurdity; and we know not what
there was or could be below the surface to make the desig-
nation improper. What, again, is the law of uniformity in
nature which permits two trees to run organically into one
another, most commonly at the stages nearest the roots and
next above the ground, but occasionally, though very rarely [1],
at a higher elevation? What crook or cranny in this alleged uniformity permits an infant occasionally to be born
with six fingers instead of five; nay, even to be formed in
embryo with two heads instead of one? Farther still: we
are informed this very year of the birth in France of a living
child with two heads, which has been treated, in Holy Baptism, as involving a duality of persons [2]. Or, again, while
the pen of Molière was able to exhibit as the *ne plus ultra*
of absurdity the idea that the heart was by medical ordinance

---

[1] I happen to know of only two
cases, one of them at the place where
I myself reside.

[2] See the public journals of Paris
at the corresponding date, January,
1896.

to be placed on the right side instead of the left, how comes it that a case has been known, in which an adult now alive has actually had the heart so placed? and in whom, to crown the anomaly, it has shifted from the one side to the other [1]. But I recur to those cases which I have named first in the preceding enumeration. They are in sharp contradiction to natural laws. They are disbelieved by none, though they have only been verified, even in the case of the Siamese twins, by a small portion of mankind; and they have now become incapable of verification in any shape, now that death has put in his sickle. But they bring into view an argument not hitherto touched, which appears to me to be of great force against Hume's negation.

The miracles of the Christian religion, not to say of the Scriptures generally, are admitted to have had commonly in their direct aim purposes of great utility as works of corporal mercy; apart from one or two which may be regarded as having been, in the main, simple indications of power in their first aspect, but with a great ulterior design. If we look onward to their common indirect purpose, in supplying mankind, and especially the current generation, with evidence of the truth of the Gospel, we give additional breadth to the reasonable allegation that these miracles were miracles of purpose. On the other side we have to admit that they lay outside the known laws of nature, nor are we justified, under this head, in saying more than that they may have lain within the scope of other laws which were, or still are, unknown. That they should be unusual, and therefore startling, was, we may own, even of their essence.

This foreignness to natural law is the point of objection confidently urged against the Christian miracles. Now I venture to urge these three propositions with reference to some of the exceptional phenomena I have cited. First, that these phenomena are in no less sharp conflict with the established laws of nature, than the miracles of the Gospel generally. Even apart from the subject of purpose, what an uproar would they not have made, could we have met them on the pages of the Evangelists. But secondly, while

---

[1] My authority for this statement is an able and esteemed physician now practising in London.

the Gospel miracles were full of purpose readily appreciable by us, we labour in vain to suggest any purpose whatever in the case of the departures from the natural sequence now before us; and we feel that, if such purpose exist, it is at any rate entirely withholden from our view. And thirdly, it seems absolutely plain that the multiplication of such cases as two-headed children and pairs of Siamese twins would not only be productive of inconvenience, but would, within their spheres, derange or destroy the necessary conditions of practical life. But a multiplication, even a considerable multiplication, of the Gospel miracles might conceivably have occurred, with only benefit, or let us say with a large balance of benefit, to such portions of men as might be within their range, while the general laws of personal and social life would in no way have been disturbed.

Can it for a moment be denied, if we admit the two sets of phenomena (a large admission from my point of view) to be fundamentally in the same relation to the known laws of nature, that the Gospel miracles are clogged with a smaller amount of antecedent improbability to weigh down the testimony in their favour, than these recent and recurring portents? And yet the recent portents are believed wholesale by the very persons, who exhort us to disbelieve the Christian miracles, or cast floods of ridicule upon those who believe them!

It is common, among the opponents of miracle, to take very high ground; sometimes even to consign all who admit their possibility to the class of intellectual impotents and imbeciles. There undoubtedly have been times, when treatment equally rough would have been awarded to the followers of Hume. But it is unnecessary to pursue this line of thought. Have these champions, bold and loud as Rodomonte, duly measured the efficacy of mental force in directing, developing, and releasing for action, physical force through the energy of the will? Nay, have they taken into due account the office and effects of will upon and amidst physical laws, or asked themselves with a sufficient persistency how and when any absolute limit can be assigned to the effects which that energy of will may conceivably produce?

Let us recommence; and present the matter in another form.

A book is resting on a table by my side. It is kept in its position by the unfailing action of the law of gravity. But I desire at some given moment to consult it; and my will issues an order to the muscular power of my arm accordingly. This command is conveyed through the brain to the muscle, which in the normal condition of the body unfailingly obeys, and the book is accordingly lifted off the table by a force which counteracts and overpowers the law of gravity. The intermediate motor, by which gravitation is thus overcome, is a force proceeding from the muscular adjustment of my arm ; but the true and original motor is an invisible force, wholly incommensurable with it, but acting conclusively upon it.

It is recorded in the Gospel of St. Mark, that there arose upon the Sea of Tiberias a violent storm when our Saviour had embarked upon it in a small vessel, and had fallen asleep[1]. Being aroused, 'He rebuked the wind, and said unto the sea, Peace, be still.' And the storm abated thereupon. Is this really more difficult to believe than a familiar occurrence such as my lifting the book ? The main difference is that there is one factor only, the personal will of our Saviour which acts upon the passive sea without any intermediate instrument, such as the muscles by which the book is raised. But is not the substance of the matter one and the same ; the same in essence, if not in degree ? In both the cases an unseen mental force produces a visible physical result so as to alter for the time being an ordinary natural law. With the one form of incident we are familiar daily, and, while it is brought about for some small or trivial purpose, it excites no surprise. But the other is rare ; and, being rare, it provokes our incredulity. It is a great exercise of power instead of a small one, and the natural forces, represented as passive and obedient, are of a form not subject to our control. Is there, however, any real disproportion between them ? That can only be answered by our comparing the agent in each case with the action, and the means employed with the end in view. In the one case a limited agent proceeds with a limited aim to an exercise of force suited to the nature of that aim. In the other

[1] Mark iv. 37–39.

case the agent is by the supposition omnipotent instead of
limited, and the act (we may say) gigantic instead of small.
But it forms a portion of a process which is far more gigantic, for it has in view the regeneration of the world. Is it
not in at least as just a proportion to that purpose, as the
movement of the arm is to the raising of the book ? The
proceeding is rare, and no wonder : for it is an ingredient
in a vast and comprehensive plan, which is the crown of
the world's history, and to which all the most striking parts
of that history stand visibly and harmoniously related.

Let us take another very simple case. Moved by a decision of the will, we mount a ladder twenty feet high, or
lift a weight of a hundred pounds from the ground. Here,
to use Hume's happy expression, we must subtract the
effects of one law from those of another. The energy, which
antecedently to the action of will had slept, is stirred into
life under the command of that sovereign faculty, and lifts
the whole weight of the body, or the hundred pounds mentioned in the question, in direct defiance (so far as it goes)
and active contradiction of the law of gravity. Deduct the
force of gravity, and a true and sufficient force remains.
The weight I carry, combined with the distance through
which it is carried, forms an effective subtraction from the
law of gravity. True, such subtraction is often brought
about under the action of ordinary natural laws, as when
a wind is raised through some change in the atmospheric
temperature, and this wind raises leaves from the ground,
and tosses them in the air. But the essential point in the
reasoning now before us is that conflicts between natural
laws, deductions by one of them from the ordinary operation of another, can be and incessantly are brought about in
the sphere of our common experience by the action of the
human will. These conflicts are prosecuted to a very wide
extent. For example, every building (not to say every
bird's nest) on the face of the earth, together with the
immense preliminary operations, is due to them. The entire mass of that command over external nature, in which
we so much boast of our progress, results from the power
of the human will thus exercised and applied. But this
power, so great in its aggregate effect, is, when brought into

comparison with the power of the Divine will, exhibited in creation, and in the laws which govern creation, but infinitesimally small. Does it not then, at the very first blush, appear to be an act of questionable rationality for the insect-like human being to pronounce with respect to the Divine will, 'Thus far it can go, and no farther'?

It will be alleged, and with apparent justice, that Hume's reasoning does not postulate a denial of the Divine omnipotence. But why is the pretentious argument from the fallibility of human testimony employed for this particular purpose, if not because miracle is alleged to impose a special strain upon belief? And what is the nature of that imagined strain? Is it because miracle is alleged in order to accredit an evil purpose? Or because it is a waste of power for no purpose at all? Or is it because it places in the hands of Deity a power which we do not know that God possesses, and which we cannot safely assume Him to possess, inasmuch as there has never been any proof of its exercise? True, these propositions are outside the argument of Hume. The first may be dismissed at the present stage, since the purposes of the Christian miracles claim to be beneficent. And the second, since, aiming at the introduction of a regenerative system, the aim they have in view is manifestly one of great elevation. But the third? Now this, though outside the argument of Hume, is by no means outside the habit of mind which the acceptance of that argument has powerfully tended to engender. The true upshot of that argument is that there exist no means by which miracle can be made known to man at large. For, all that we know, in the world of fact, we know either by experience or by testimony. Man at large, that is to say each and every man, cannot know miracle by experience; for, if the experience of them were universal they would cease to be miracles, and would scarcely possess that evidential value which is the paramount reason of their existence. So again, men in general cannot know them by testimony, for testimony, which is good for all ordinary purpose, is declared to be of insufficient force for establishing the existence of miracle.

It is futile, then, to show that Hume's argument does not in itself deny God's omnipotence. For it does all, which could be done by the denial. It proves, if valid, that the Divine power is a rusted weapon no longer available for use, which has no practical existence for us : inasmuch as it does not provide Him with any means of making Himself known to us afresh, and thus of nearly operating upon us as reasonable beings ; He can only act on man through the existing laws of nature. For anything outside of them is a miracle, and subject to all the disabilities by which miracle as such is affected.

The argument still gives us leave, or does not take away our leave, to see God in the laws of nature themselves. But this part of the work of negation has been done by coadjutors whom Hume himself has done much to invite into the field. His argument shut off one of the manifestations of God, that which may be called extraordinary or occasional. For the other, or ordinary, exhibition of God in His works, the first step is to cover regularity and sequence with the name of law, as a name savouring of compulsion, and excluding choice. The next is to point to the origin of these laws as co-ordinate with the beginning of the universe, and to remit the entire action of the Creator to that date. From that time, He is a neutral power. He has acted (it seems) like an incompetent Ruler, who has handed over all His powers to a regency, and has from that date no farther concern in affairs. By a process moderately graduated, but effectual, the Almighty is placed in the condition of the sinecure gods, whom Epicurus could afford to leave in heaven. Only one farther step remains to land us in absolute and blank negation ; and it is plain that this step is unimportant in comparison with those which we have already left in our rear : for what is the difference, relevant to the present subject, between deities whom the law of nature binds in perpetual abeyance, and no deities at all ?

It is, therefore, material to bear proximately in mind the omnipotence of God who supplies, in whatever form, the forces necessary to sustain, as well as those necessary to establish, in the world, the sequence and order that we term natural law. And next we should recollect that miracle is not disbelieved because the miraculous thing requires some greater exercise of Divine power than this or that natural object or process, but solely because we have not, as is alleged, the same power of verifying the thing asserted, and we ought not to believe where we cannot verify.

Let us test this proposition by comparing with miracle all the facts scientifically ascertained in connexion with what we may call the two infinities, that of greatness upwards, and of smallness downwards. Take the heavenly bodies and their distances, with their laws of motion in the region upwards; and the particles on which the scent of dogs appears to operate upon the scale running downwards. In what sense is the first-named congeries of facts verified by us? The disciple of Hume says, 'Miracle I disbelieve, for it is admitted that at once, or in a limited time, it passes away, and leaves us no means of verification. Astronomical marvels of distance I believe, for they can be and have been verified.' Let us suppose the disciple to be one of the common mass of men. With his case in view, I ask, By whom have they been verified? The answer is, by highly educated men, who have mastered the secrets of the calculus. For each of that handful of men, the verification avails in the particular case. But how as to all the other wonders of nature? Each class has been verified by its own specialists for their own behoof, but no man, unless such a prodigy as would be somewhat like a miracle, can be a specialist with regard to them all, or can acquire in each and every branch enough of specialism to allow of a real verification. Why then does the specialist in A accept all the secrets of nature in B, C, D, E, and so forth? He receives them on the faith of human testimony: and if he did not so receive them he would justly be regarded as a fool. Therefore he does, in the wide range of natural knowledge, the very thing which, in all the majestic pride of this new philosophy, he is forbidden to do with regard to miracle.

The reply may be made that here the acceptance upon testimony is warranted, on the ground that there is no antecedent improbability, for the propositions accepted are within the laws of nature; or that they are experimentally attested. But the reply is utterly futile. For how does the *idiotes* know these laws of nature? It is not a knowledge born with him, or with any one, but only acquired by a large expenditure of time, which, under the necessities of life, he cannot bestow, and by the devoted application of faculties, which, in the overwhelming majority of cases, he does not possess.

This vaunted resource, then, of verification comes to be eventually convicted of being a mere pretext, for the purposes of the argument before us. What, on Hume's principle, is absolutely necessary in order to warrant the belief in all the great facts of nature, hidden from mankind in general, but said to be established through the possession of special knowledge, is that each and every man should, for himself, possess the faculties and devote the time necessary to give him an original, and not merely a derived, knowledge of the particular law or laws of nature by which the alleged fact is redeemed from the disqualification of improbability. This being impossible, reason, within the walls of the Humian school, forbids him to believe the movements of the heavenly bodies throughout the universe. But the reason of mankind at large, based upon the necessities of life, requires him to believe, where the Humian school forbids; and this upon pain of being set down by his fellow-creatures at large as *non compos*. Therefore the argument of Hume, being totally unsusceptible of impartial application, is in direct conflict with the reason of mankind at large upon the matter of verification.

As I have shown, the specialist himself, if a votary of Hume, is in this lamentable condition with regard to all specialisms, except those which he has made his own. And the whole mass of men, if and so far as they have strayed into the same error, are involved in the same unhappy consequence.

And let it be observed what the nature of our reasoning process has been. I have provisionally admitted Hume's principle. He allows that human testimony has value. But then its strength does not suffice to float us, when we swim beyond the range of the known laws of nature. From that point onwards we are encountered by an antecedent improbability which alters to the negative side the scale of just judgement formerly verging to the affirmative. Now it has been shown that the results of these propositions are absurd. Therefore the propositions themselves are untenable.

On the assumed conflict with the laws of nature, and on the fallibility of human testimony, it is only necessary to observe that until Hume has met our demand upon the first of these points, he is not entitled to open his case upon the other. But the demand is one which cannot be met.

There are some of his subsidiary points, on which his pleas are not unreasonable. For example, when he props himself by the authority of Bacon in maintaining that accounts of signs and miracles are especially to be suspected, when they have been got up in the interest of religion. This is true : and it is also true that religion has a force in generating not only fanatical partisanship, but also fanatical antagonism, of which the pages of Hume himself supply some striking examples, notwithstanding his general calm and self-possession.

I have admitted all along in these remarks that miracles are abnormal. It is no wonder that they should lie outside the methods of teaching, which an all-wise Governor might be expected to use in the education of innocent and docile pupils. But in this case the pupils are neither innocent nor docile, as we know too well from their offences, not only against God, but against one another, and (without meaning it) against themselves. But a miracle, if a thing foreign to our ordinary experience, and so far out of the range of comparison with phenomena that fall within it, is a specialty on account of this strangeness, rather than on account of its appearing to require an exercise of Divine power unusually great. For it may seem on inquiry that there are other phenomena in the world which, but for their commonness, we might deem to be, so to speak, in themselves more arduous performances. If, for example, we take the case of men lost in trespasses and sins, and consider what a marvellous thing it is to reverse the moral drift of a character, with its courses of desire and the force of its habits, and apply this to men wedded to the world, does it not seem probably or possibly more difficult to furnish and apply the spiritual powers necessary for the true effectuation of such a change than to bid the waves of Gennesareth rise and swell, or relapse into stillness ? A character misset, a will misdirected, is perhaps the most formidable antagonist that the Almighty, in the field of providential government, ever, in ordinary and familiar action, betakes Himself to overcome.

In the closing paragraph of this Essay, Hume deals with prophecy; to which he probably remembered that Butler assigned, along with miracle, the highest rank among the evidences of religion [1]. He begins with the daring assertions that every prophecy is a miracle, and that all he has said against miracle may be said against prophecy, 'without any variation.' Now the term miracle is used in more senses than one. It has been said by Butler that the Incarnation is a miracle, but a miracle that proves nothing, and that requires to be proved itself. This is not the stamp of miracle with which Hume's Essay deals. For him, and he follows the ordinary use of the term, a miracle is an exercise of Divine power not only outside of ordinary law, but also made visible to the eyes or ears of men, and thereby capable of being largely and generally reported by human testimony. Before the miracle, I observe a man blind; after it I find that he sees, and I report accordingly. Only in this form can Hume bring his artillery to bear upon it. What are we then to say when we find that in order to include prophecy in his damnatory argument, he shifts his definition of a miracle without a word of notice, and declares prophecy to be miracle while knowing quite well that prophecy, as a rule and on the larger scale, is entirely without that kind of appeal to the individual mind, made through or with the sense, which alone is obnoxious to the assault of Hume? When our Lord told the disciples He would rise from the dead, this prediction was no miracle for them, until its fulfilment. But in the great bulk of cases the prophecy is delivered to one generation, and its accomplishment takes place in another. It is in both cases a question of fact: and neither of the alleged facts is under any semblance of conflict with the laws of nature, so that while human testimony operates in full force when prophecy has been fulfilled, there is on the other side no improbability to be set against it.

When we consider that Hume has included all prophecy in his description, it might, perhaps, be difficult to find in the whole compass of polemical argument a grosser case, in a famous writer, of an abuse of logic and of language, than is supplied by his paragraph on prophecy.

[1] On Miracles : *Philosophical Works*, vol. iv. p. 150.

CHAPTER IX

ON THE MEDIATION OF CHRIST: AN ADDENDUM

[This short chapter may be reckoned as an Addendum to the arguments of Butler on Mediation, which it is in no respect intended to qualify. It bears upon a point which had not been widely raised at the date of the *Analogy*.

Under the head marked I, the argument is like a flight in an ether too thin to sustain us. The word 'Person' is quite inappropriately used. It is in truth *ultra vires*, or beyond our office and competency, to treat of inter-personal relations in the Deity, though Milton has done it: and this whether the language used may tend either towards identification, or towards severance.

The same phrase may be applicable to the word 'passions' used further on, for which 'affections' ought to be substituted.

The general argument was suggested by Butler's Chapter, and I think will hold, though the language used may require some correction. The paper was written in an interleaved copy of the *Analogy* about July, 1830, and is now printed with a very few purely verbal amendments.]

I. Much of the objection to the doctrine of redemption is founded upon the assumption that the Redeemer, as being an innocent yet the suffering party, is treated unjustly by God.

If we consider the oneness of the Father and the Son, this difficulty may perhaps be obviated.

For, if *A* inflicts punishment upon himself to serve *B*, can he be said to suffer injustice? Surely not.

And, in Christianity, the same party suffered punishment as the Victim, and inflicted it as the Judge; His prayer in the Garden being the result of superinduced feelings and propensities constituting His human nature.

Therefore the case is at least equally strong with that in the instance quoted. Perhaps it may appear even stronger, if we consider that, in this individual instance, and this alone, not only the executors of the law, and the sacrifice it demanded, were the same person, but also that person was the very source, and sanction, and strength of the law itself.

II. Even without this, however, the objection might be thought to vanish from the following considerations.

1. The offering up of the Victim was in accordance with His own free will.

2. If it be answered : 'Yes, but men often hurt themselves willingly, and it ought to be the business of the Supreme Arbiter to prevent an innocent Being's so hurting Himself : ' it is to be remembered, that the whole force of this argument rests on the consideration that man, as an imperfect being, may err in judgement, and through error, do himself a mischief. If a man wishes to do himself injury αὐτοῦ ἕνεκα, we call him mad, that is to say, one who has lost his understanding.

Apply the argument. therefore, to the case of a being of perfect judgement, which is the nature of the case under consideration, and from the want of this essential feature of imperfect judgement, the argument falls to the ground at once.

III. But it does not appear to me that even this is required in order to meet the objection. For it seems to presuppose and assume, as the primary principle on which it is to be built, the proposition that *pain is essentially or at least universally an evil* (for pain is what our Blessed Lord brought upon Himself). But this, it seems to me, ought to be denied. Pain is not in its nature an evil in the proper sense, nor is it universally attended with evil as a consequence, any more than pleasure is universally a good, or attended with it.

Pleasure and pain have not in themselves the nature of good and evil. Properly indeed, and in perfect states of being, pleasure is attached to good, and pain to evil, both of them invariably : but, in this perturbed and unnatural state of things, the alliances are broken respectively ; and we are rather to consider pleasure and pain, in relation to ourselves, as δυνάμεις, that is to say, as being contingent in reference to the ends for which they will be employed, and each capable of multiplying either to us.

Now, to a good being, pleasure is not an evil, for it augments his gratitude to the Giver of pleasure, and thereby it causes him to energize in his best and holiest feelings, and by that energizing strengthens, extends, and increases them.

To a being partially good, but under the dominion of a good principle, which is gradually assimilating his nature to its own, upon the whole, rather than a bad one, the same effects will accrue, but in an inferior degree.

To a being perfectly evil, pleasure will be a δυνάμεις productive of evil, inasmuch as it calls forth his feelings of self-love and desire of self-gratification, and will increase his evil by causing him to energize these. (I say increase his evil, though above he is called perfectly evil, because, though the essence is perfect, or is entirely ποίη τις, of a certain character, yet its quality and intensity may admit of variation.)

To a being partially evil, and on the whole under the ascendency of a bad principle rather than a good one, the like effects will accrue, in proportionable measure.

Pain, on the other hand, will be a δύναμις αὐξητική of evil to a being perfectly evil, and in the main under an evil principle, because it will cause him to energize in vindictive feelings towards the inflictor of the pain, and thereby augment the evil; that is to say, make him more evil than he was before.

(Thus do we assimilate the objects, with which we come in contact, to our own nature, or rather operate upon our own nature by them.)

Lastly, and to come to the point which concerns the present question; to a being, in the main under the direction of a good principle in some degree, and to a perfectly, or entirely, good being in a degree proportionably higher, pain will be a δύναμις αὐξητική of good, because it will cause him to energize in those feelings of self-mortification and self-sacrifice, which are his best, and will thus again, by the process heretofore referred to, increase his goodness.

Such a being, it is needless to say, was our Saviour in His human nature. To Him, therefore (if we reject the as it seems to me false, fearfully prevalent, and most dangerous doctrine, that pain is in itself an evil), in that human nature the bitterness of His cross, the physical and the mental torture, and the buffets, and the taunts, and the scorn, were no evil, if we look closely at the right meaning of the term, but a good; not indeed essentially, but consequentially, as good; so that, we may well suppose, it was in reference to this that our Saviour exclaimed, ' For their sakes I sanctify myself [1]; ' and that thus the Apostle has told us that ' the Captain of our salvation was made perfect through sufferings [2].' For it is obvious, from many passages of Scripture, that our Saviour's state, in His human nature, was (1) probationary, and (2) progressive. So entirely was the human nature, with its conditions except sin, attached to the Divine Being. We are told —

in Luke ii. 52, that He grew in wisdom . . . and in favour with God. . . .

in Heb. v. 8, 9, ' *Though* he were a Son, yet learned he obedience by the things which he suffered; and being made perfect, he became the Author of eternal salvation unto all them that obey him.'

in Luke xiii. 32, ' I do cures to-day and to-morrow, and the third day I shall be perfected.'

in Phil. ii. 8, 9, ' And being found in fashion as a man, he humbled himself, and became obedient unto death, even the death of the cross : wherefore God also hath highly exalted him, and hath given him a name which is above every name.'

In His human character, then, His kingdom is the reward of His obedience. All this must fall, if the proposition that pain is not essentially an evil, falls; and I think it will stand, if that stand.

It seems to me that most of our difficulties arise from the laxity of the ordinary sense, in which the term evil is used ; for it is now more commonly applied to pain than to sin; and good, on the other hand, to advantage more than to godliness. No doubt we may trace through this very

<hr />

[1] John xvii. 19.   [2] Heb. ii. 10.

remarkable transfer of significations, that deeply rooted and audacious tendency of the human heart, the desire to put a veil over our eyes, to disguise the truth as we cannot destroy it, to create darkness where we hate light, ignorance where we cannot endure reflection. The appropriation of these terms to what we like or dislike respectively, is at the same time a tacit homage to the great God of good and of truth, exacted by the remains of that sense of right and wrong, which still bears unavailing testimony to the fact that man was made in the image of God, but compromised and rendered nugatory by that prevailing depravity, which does indeed, while it seeks pleasure, submit to calling it by the name of good, and is perhaps startled at the notion of seeking nothing but its own pleasure, when this is put in plain terms : but which, to make amends for its nominal condescension, exercises all the realities of an iron despotism over the soul.

It would appear then, if what has been urged is true, that in the scheme of redemption there was, on the part of God, mercy indeed and love abundant and unspeakable ; incomprehensible in that Christ descended from the right hand of His Father's glory, and the bosom of His love, and took upon Him the passions [1] of humanity, lived a life of sorrow, and died an ignominious and a painful death, attended with mental agony far more terrible than the ignominy, or the pangs of His lingering tortures or of His closing struggle ; so that He atoned for our sins by His death, He gave a pattern for our characters by His life, He instructed us to copy it by His teaching, and He exemplified, though at a height which we can only gaze upon from afar, in His own person, by the attaching of a human nature to a Divine Essence, the possibility, *a fortiori*, of engrafting a Divine principle upon a human soul. All this it is wonderful indeed that He did and suffered, for though He need not have felt or cared for the pain, yet for our sakes He put Himself in a situation to feel and care for, as well as basely suffer it. But, in all this, there was no evil done Him. We cannot say there was, any more than we could say evil was done to a person, to whom God should send His merciful chastisements to awaken him

[1] See Prefatory Note.

to a sense of spiritual things. Therefore, though the mercy was indeed mysterious, and incomprehensible from its vastness, there is no injustice, nor the semblance of it.

(Pascal says, 'Let us term nothing evil, but what turns the sacrifice of God into the sacrifice of Satan [1].')

So that I trust we may glory in the cross of Christ, unmolested by any notion that there is the smallest presumption or symptom of injustice connected with that wondrous sacrifice. In this case there is nothing to contradict our notions of justice, however much there may be to transcend them. There is a mystery, deep hid in the bosom of God, but it is a mystery of love, of love eternal, love unbounded, and love alone.

IV. All mental pain seems to be to the mind what medicine is to the body; at least, all mental pain in this probationary state. Pain and evil seem to me to be so clearly distinguishable, that I should not call the bad taste of medicine, *abstractedly* considered, in any degree an evil. But, waiving this question, surely few would hesitate to admit that the *complex* idea of medicine, as an instrument working beneficial ends by painful means, is that of a good. And, on the same principle, surely men in general ought to admit that the complex idea of pain, in a probationary state, as a similar instrument applied to the mind, displays the same character.

V. There is one objection, however, which seems likely to be raised against a theory of this kind, and which, if it be possible, it is also highly desirable to answer.

It is this: 'If this pain was a good to our Saviour, in any sense of the term, what sacrifice did He make in coming upon earth?' Consequently our views of the greatness of the sacrifice will be weakened; and also our views of the occasion for it, and thus of our own sinfulness.

Though we are treading upon dangerous ground in endeavouring to treat of matter which depends upon the distinctions of our Saviour's two natures, thus much, I think, may be said. The sacrifice our Saviour made was primarily His taking upon Him the human nature, and all its sympathies and sensibilities to pain; and when we consider Him

[1] *Thoughts on Death.*

as really and truly a Man, endued with these sensibilities, and think how deep and bitter was the cup of His affliction, we shall not, I think, see any reason to lower our views of the greatness of His love.   For we are to remember —

1. That man's chief revulsion is from pain ; and

2. Very little, comparatively, from evil considered independently of pain.

And though our Saviour did not take on Him this indifference to sin, yet He did take on Him in full the revulsion from pain ; and here His struggle lay.

So that the question which has been touched, whether pain be essentially an evil or not, has no effect either in diminishing or enhancing our views of the greatness of the sacrifice, which are left precisely as they may have been. The point affected by the decision of this question is the notion of supposed injustice done to Christ by the scheme of redemption, and that alone.

Juvenal perceived, and has recorded in the most unequivocal terms, the difference between pain and evil, considered simply :

> Nec poenam sceleri invenies, nec digna parabis
> Supplicia his populis in quorum mente pares sunt,
> Et similes, *ira* atque *fames* [1].

[1] Juv. *Sat.* xv. 129–131.

CHAPTER X

PROBABILITY AS THE GUIDE OF LIFE[1]

1. THE doctrine of Bishop Butler, in the Introduction to his *Analogy*, with regard to probable evidence, lies at the root of his entire argument; for, by the analogy which he seeks to establish between natural religion and that which is revealed, he does not pretend to supply a demonstrative proof of Christianity, but only such a kind, and such an amount, of presumptions in its favour as to bind human beings at the least to take its claims into their serious consideration[2]. This, he urges, they must do, provided only they mean to act with regard to it upon those principles, which, in all other matters, are regarded as the principles of common sense. It is therefore essential to his purpose to show what are the obligations which, as inferred from the universal practice of men, probable or presumptive evidence may entail.

2. But indeed the subject-matter of this Introduction has yet a far wider scope. It embraces the rule of just proceeding, not only in regard to the examination of the pretensions of Christianity, but also in regard to the whole conduct of life. The former question, great as it is, has no practical existence for the vast majority, whether of the Christian world, or of the world beyond the precinct of the Christian profession. It is only relevant and material (except as an exercise of sound philosophy) to three descriptions of persons; those whom the Gospel for the first time solicits; those who have fallen away from it; and those who are in doubt concerning its foundation. Again,

[1] First published in, and reprinted from, the *Nineteenth Century*, for March, 1879.

[2] The title of Bishop Butler's book is *The Analogy of Religion to the Constitution and Course of Nature*. But, in the Introduction, § 3, the Bishop describes his postulate in close correspondence with the phrase I have used in the text.

there are portions of these classes, to whose states of mind other modes of address may be more suitable. But every Christian, and indeed every man owning any kind of moral obligation, who may once enter upon any speculation concerning the grounds which dispose him to act, or to refrain from acting, is concerned in the highest degree with the subject that Bishop Butler has opened incidentally for the sake of its relation to his own immediate purpose.

3. The proposition of Bishop Butler, that probability is the guide of life, is not one invented for the purposes of his argument, nor held by believers alone. Voltaire has used nearly the same words : —

Presque toute la vie humaine roule sur des probabilités. Tout ce qui n'est pas démontré aux yeux, ou reconnu pour vrai par les parties évidemment intéressées à le nier, n'est tout au plus que probable. . . . L'incertitude étant presque toujours le partage de l'homme, vous vous détermineriez très-rarement, si vous attendiez une démonstration. Cependant il faut prendre un parti : et il ne faut pas le prendre au hasard. Il est donc nécessaire à notre nature faible, aveugle, toujours sujette à l'erreur, d'étudier les probabilités avec autant de soin, que nous apprenons l'arithmétique et la géométrie.

Voltaire wrote this passage in an Essay, not on religion, but on judicial inquiries [1]: and the statement of principle which it propounds is perhaps on that account even more valuable.

4. If we consider subjectively the reasons, upon which our judgements rest, and the motives of our practical intentions, it may in strictness be said that absolutely in no case have we more than probable evidence to proceed upon; since there is always room for the entrance of error in that last operation of the percipient faculties of men, by which the objective becomes subjective; an operation antecedent, of necessity, not only to action, or decision upon acting, but to the stage at which the perception becomes what is sometimes called a 'state of consciousness [2].'

5. But, setting aside this consideration, and speaking only

---

[1] 'Essai sur les probabilités en fait de Justice.' *Works* (4to, Geneva, 1777), vol. xxvi. p. 457.

[2] *Nineteenth Century*, for April, 1879, pp. 606, 607.

of what is objectively presented as it is in itself, a very
small portion indeed of the subject-matter of practice is or
can be of a demonstrative, or necessary, character. Moral
action is conversant almost wholly with evidence, which in
itself is only probable. So that a right understanding of the
proper modes of dealing with it is the foundation of all
ethical studies. Without this, it must either be dry and
barren dogmatism, or else a mass of floating quicksands.
Duty may indeed be done, without having been studied in
the abstract; but if it is to be studied, it must be studied
under its true laws and conditions as a science. Now, probability is the nearly universal form or condition, under
which these laws are applied: and therefore a sound view
of it is not indeed ethical knowledge itself, but is the *organon*, by means of which that knowledge is to be rightly
handled. He who, by his reasonings, at once teaches and
inures men to the methods of handling probable or imperfect evidence, gives them exercise, and by exercise strength,
in the most important of all those rules of daily life, which
are connected with the intellectual habits.

6. Different forms of error concerning probable evidence
have produced in some cases moral laxity, in others scrupulosity, in others unbelief.

To begin with the last named of these. It is a common
form of fallacy to suppose that imperfect evidence cannot
be the foundation of an obligation to religious belief, inasmuch as belief, although in its infancy it may fall short of
intellectual conviction, tends towards that character in its
growth and attains it when mature. Sometimes, indeed, it
is assumed by the controversialist, that belief, if genuine, is
essentially absolute. And it is taken to be a violation of
the laws of the human mind that proofs which do not exclude doubt should be held to warrant a persuasion which
does or may exclude it. Indeed, the celebrated argument of
Hume, against the credibility of the miracles, involved the
latent assumption that we have a right to claim demonstrative evidence for every proposition which demands our
assent. From this assumption it proceeds to deny a demonstrative character to any proofs, except those supplied
by our own experience. And the answer, which Paley has

made to it, rests upon the proposition that the testimony adduced is such as, according to the common judgement and practice of men, it is rational to believe; but he passes by without notice the question of its title to the rank of speculative certainty.

7. Next, with regard to the danger of scrupulosity. This has perhaps been less conspicuous in philosophical systems, than in its effect on the practical conduct of life by individuals. There are persons, certainly not among the well-trained and well-informed, who would attach a suspicion of dishonesty to any doctrine, which should give a warrant to acts of moral choice upon evidence admitted to be less than certain. Their disposition is deserving of respect, when it takes its rise from that simple, unsuspecting confidence in the strength and clearness of truth, which habitual obedience engenders. It is less so when we see in it a timidity of mind, which shrinks from measuring the whole extent of the charge that it has pleased God to lay upon us as moral agents, and will not tread, even in the path of duty, upon any ground that yields beneath the pressure of the foot. The desire for certainty, in this form, enervates and unmans the character. Persons so affected can scarcely either search with effect for duties to be done, or accept them when offered, and almost forced upon their notice. As a speculative system, this tendency has appeared among some casuists of the Church of Rome, and has been condemned by Pope Innocent XI.

8. The position of many among her divines with reference to the danger of moral laxity opens much graver questions. The *Provincial Letters* of Pascal gave a universal notoriety to the doctrine of Probabilism. Setting apart the extremes to which it has been carried by individuals, we may safely take the representation of it, as it is supplied in a Manual [1] published for the use of the French clergy of the present day. According to this work, it is allowable, in matters of moral conduct, that if of two opposite opinions, each one be sustained not by a slight but a solid probability, and if the probability of the one be admittedly more solid than that of the other, we may follow our natural lib-

---

[1] *Manuel des Confesseurs.*

erty of choice by acting upon the less probable. This doctrine, we are informed, had been taught, before 1667, by 159 authors of the Roman Church, and by multitudes since that date. It appears to stand in the most formal contradiction to the sentiments of Bishop Butler; who lays it down without hesitation that the lowest presumption, if not neutralized by a similar presumption on the opposite side, and the smallest real and clear excess of presumption on the one side over the presumptions on the other side, determines the reason in matters of speculation, and absolutely binds conduct in matter of practice. Such being the scope of the subject, and such the dangers to which it stands related, let us now proceed to its examination.

9. First we have to inquire, what is probability? Probability may be predicated whenever, in answer to the question whether a particular proposition be true, the affirmative chances predominate over the negative, yet not so as (virtually) to exclude doubt. And, on the other hand, improbability may be predicated, whenever the negative chances predominate over the affirmative, but subject to the same reservation that doubt be not precluded. For, if doubt be precluded, then certainty, affirmatively or negatively, as the case may be, must be predicated. In mathematical language, certainty, affirmative or negative, is the limit of probability on the one side, and of improbability on the other, as the circle is of the ellipse.

10. The relations of probabilities among themselves may be most clearly expressed by mathematical symbols. Let a represent the affirmative side of the proposition to be tried, b the negative, and let the evidence be exactly balanced between them. Then

$$a : b : : 1 : 1, \therefore \frac{a}{b} = 1.$$

Let the evidence so preponderate on the affirmative side that out of one hundred and one cases presenting the same phenomena, in one hundred it would be true. Thus the expression is

$$a : b : : 100 : 1, \therefore \frac{a}{b} = \frac{100}{1} = 100.$$

Again, let the evidence be such that, out of one hundred and one cases presenting the same phenomena, in one hundred the proposition would turn out to be false : then the expression becomes

$$a : b : : 1 : 100, \therefore \frac{a}{b} = \frac{1}{100}.$$

And it is clear that —

(1) When the second side of this equation consists of an integer or an improper fraction, the proposition is probable.

(2) As the numerator becomes indefinitely great it represents probability approaching towards certainty. This it can never adequately express : but no fixed limit can be placed upon the advances which may be made towards it.

(3) When the second side of this equation consists of a proper fraction, the proposition is improbable.

(4) As the denominator becomes indefinitely great, it represents improbability approaching towards negative certainty, or, as it is sometimes, perhaps improperly, called, impossibility.

11. But the sphere of probability, according to Bishop Butler, includes not only truths but events, past and future : and it likewise comprehends questions of conduct, or precepts, which may be said to form a class apart, both from truths and from events : whereas the definition here given turns simply upon the preponderance of chances for the truth or falsehood of a proposition. How shall we broaden that definition ?

The answer is that truths, events past and future, and questions of conduct, may all be accurately reduced into the form of propositions true or false, by the use of their respective symbols : for the first, the symbol *is* ; for the second, *has been* or *will be* ; and for the third, *ought to be.* In one or other of these forms, every conceivable proposition can be tried in respect to its probability.

12. It is necessary also to observe upon an ambiguity in the use of the term probable. It has been defined in the sense in which it is opposed to the term improbable ; but, in a discussion on the character of probable evidence, probable and improbable propositions are alike included. When, for this purpose, we are asked what does probability designate ?

the answer is, that which may or may not be. We have no word exclusively appropriated to this use. In the Greek, Aristotle conveniently designates it τὸ ἐνδεχόμενον ἄλλως ἔχειν, as opposed to τὸ ἀδύνατον ἄλλως ἔχειν. Sometimes this is called contingent, as distinguished from necessary, matter; and safely so called, if it be always borne in mind that we are dealing with propositions, with certain instruments supplied by human language, and adapted to our thoughts, but not with things as they are in themselves; that the same thing may be subjectively contingent and objectively certain, as, for example, the question whether such a person as Homer has existed: which to us is a subject of probable inquiry, but in itself is manifestly of necessary matter, whether the proposition be true or false. So, again, in speaking of future events, to call them contingent in any sense except with regard to the propositions in which we discuss them, is no less an error; because, whether upon the necessitarian or the ordinary Christian hypothesis, future events are manifestly certain and not contingent; it remaining as a separate question whether they are so fixed by necessity, or as the offspring of free volition. It may be enough, then, for the present to observe that the ' probable evidence' of Bishop Butler reaches over the whole sphere, of which it is common to speak as that of contingent matter; and that the element of uncertainty involved in the phrase concerns not the things themselves that are in question, but only the imperfection of the present means of conveying them to our minds. To the view of the Most High God, who knows all things, there is no probability and no contingency, but 'all things are naked and open unto the eyes of Him, with whom we have to do.'

13. In His case, and in every case of knowledge properly and strictly so called, the existence of the thing known is perceived without the intervention of any medium of proof. But evidence is, according to our use of the term, essentially intermediate; something apart both from the percipient and the thing perceived, and serving to substantiate to the former, in one degree or another, the existence of the latter. Thus we speak of the evidence of the senses, meaning those impressions upon our bodily organs which are made by objects visible, audible, and the like. These respectively make,

as it were, their assertions to us; which we cross-examine by reflection, and by comparison of the several testimonies affecting the same object. And, with regard to things incorporeal, in the sphere of the probable, it seems that, in like manner, the impressions they produce upon our mental faculties, acting without the agency of sense, are also strictly in the nature of evidence, of presumption more or less near to demonstration, concerning the reality of what they represent; but subject always to a similar process of verification and correction.

14. The whole notion, therefore, of evidence seems to belong essentially to a being of limited powers. For no evidence can prove anything except what exists, and all that exists may be the object of direct perception. The necessity of reaching our end through the circuitous process implies our want of power to go straight to the mark.

15. And it further appears that the same idea implies not only the limitation of range in the powers of the being who makes use of evidence, but likewise their imperfection even in the processes which they are competent to perform. The assurance possessed by such a being cannot be of the highest order, which the laws of the spiritual creation, so far as they are known to us, would admit. However truly it may be adequate, and even abundant, to sustain his mind in any particular conviction, it must be inferior to science in its proper signification, that of simple or absolute knowledge, which is the certain and exact, and also conscious, coincidence of the intuitive faculty with its proper object. For it is scarcely conceivable that any accumulation of proofs, each in itself short of demonstration, and therefore including materials of unequal degrees of solidity, should, when put together, form a whole absolutely and entirely equivalent to the single homogeneous act of pure knowledge.

16. The same conclusion, that imperfection pervades all our mental processes, at which we have arrived by a consideration of their nature, we may also draw from the nature of the faculties by which they are conducted. For there is no one faculty of any living man of which, speaking in the sense of pure and rigid abstraction, we are entitled to say that it is infallible in any one of its acts. And no combina-

tion of fallibles can, speaking always in the same strictness, make up an infallible; however, by their independent coincidence, they may approximate towards it, and may produce a result which is for us indistinguishable from, and practically, therefore, equivalent to, it.

17. Certainly that which is fallible does not therefore always err. It may, in any given case, perform its duty without fault, and as though it were infallible; just as a sum in arithmetic, that is rightly worked by one of us, could not be more right if it were worked by an infallible intelligence. The fallibility of our faculties therefore may not prevent our having knowledge that in itself is absolute. But at the least it prevents our separating what may be had with such knowledge from what we grasp with a hold less firm. In any survey, or classification, of what we have perceived or concluded, since the faculty which discriminates is fallible, the reservations, which its imperfection requires, must attach to the results we attain by it. So that, although we might have this knowledge, if we consider knowledge simply as the exact correspondence of the percipient faculty with its proper object, we could not make ourselves conscious of the real rank of that knowledge in a given case; we could not know what things they are that we thus know, nor consequently could we argue from them as known.

18. Since, then, nothing can be known except what exists, nor *known* otherwise than in the exact manner in which it exists, knowledge, in its scientific sense, can only be predicated — first, *of* perceptions which are absolutely and exactly true, and secondly, *by* a mind which in the same sense knows them to be absolutely and exactly true. It seems to follow, that it is only by a licence of speech that the term knowledge can be predicated by us as to any of our perceptions. Assuming that our faculties, acting faithfully, are capable in certain cases of conveying to us scientific knowledge, still no part of what is so conveyed can, when it stands in review before our consciousness, carry the certain indefectible marks of what it is. And since there is no one of them, with regard to which it is abstractedly impossible that the thing it represents should be otherwise than as it is represented, we cannot, except by such licence of speech as afore-

said, categorically predicate of any one of them that precise correspondence of the percipient faculty, with the thing perceived, which constitutes knowledge pure and simple.

19. It is desirable that we should fully realize this truth, in order that we may appreciate the breadth and solidity of the ground on which Bishop Butler has founded his doctrine of probable evidence. We ought to perceive that, observing his characteristic caution, he has kept within limits narrower than the basis, which the laws of the human mind, viewed through a medium purely abstract, would have allowed him to occupy. His habit was to encamp near to the region of practice in all his philosophical inquiries; that he might appease, and thus gently reclaim, the contemptuous infidelity of his age. A rigid statement of the whole case concerning our knowledge would probably have startled those whom he sought to attract, and have given them a pretext for retreating, at the very threshold, from the inquiry to which he invited them. Considerations of this kind are, indeed, applicable very generally to the form in which Bishop Butler has propounded his profound truths for popular acceptation. But it is manifest that, if he even understated the case with regard to probable evidence, his argument is simply corroborated by taking into view all that residue, which he did not directly put into requisition.

20. He was engaged in an endeavour to show to those, who demanded an absolute certainty in the proofs of religion, that this demand was unreasonable; and the method he pursued in this demonstration was, to point out to them how much of their own daily conduct was palpably and rightly founded upon evidence less than certain. The unreasonableness of such a demand becomes still more glaring in the eyes of persons not under adverse prepossession, when we find by reflection that no one of our convictions, or perceptions, can in strictness be declared to possess the character of scientific knowledge. Because, if such be the case, we cannot rebut this consequence: that, even if a demonstration intrinsically perfect were presented to us, the possibility of error would still exist in the one link remaining; namely, that subjective process of our faculties by which it has to be appropriated. This (so to speak) primordial element of

uncertainty never could be eliminated, except by the gift of inerrability to the individual mind. But such a gift would amount to a fundamental change in the laws of our nature. Again, in the particular case of belief, such a change would obviously dislocate the entire conditions of the inquiry, which appears to turn upon the credibility of revealed religion as it is illustrated by its suitableness to — what? not to an imaginable and unrealized, but to the actual, experienced condition of things.

21. To the conclusion that scientific knowledge can never be consciously entertained by the individual mind, it is no answer, nor any valid objection, to urge that such a doctrine unsettles the only secure foundation on which we can build, destroys mental repose, and threatens confusion. For, even if a great and grievous fault in the condition of the world were thus to be exposed, we are not concerned here with the question whether our state is one of abstract excellence, but simply with the facts of it, such as they are. We cannot enter into the question, whether it is abstractedly best that our faculties should be liable to error. That is one of the original conditions under which we live. No objection can be drawn from it to an argument in favour of revelation, unless it can be shown either, first, that, on account of liability to error, they become practically useless for the business of acting or of inquiring; or else, secondly, that the materials to be examined in the case of Revelation are not so fairly cognizable by them, as the materials of other examinations which, by the common judgement and practice of mankind, they are found to be competent to conduct and determine.

22. But the state of things around us amply shows that this want of scientific certainty is, in point of fact, no reproach to our condition, no practical defect in it. Rather it is a law, which associates harmoniously with the remainder of its laws. The nature of our intelligence makes no demand for such assurance; this is evident, because we are not capable of receiving it. Nay, we cannot so much as arrive at the notion of it without an effort of abstraction. Our moral condition appears still less to crave anything of the kind. If we allow that sin is in the world (no matter, for

the purpose of this argument, how it came there), and that we are placed under the dominion of a moral Governor who seeks by discipline to improve His creatures, it is not difficult to give reasons in support of the proposition that intellectual inerrability is not suited to such a state. One such reason we may find in the recollection, that the moral training of an inferior by a superior either essentially involves, or at the least suitably admits of, the element of trust. Now the region of probable evidence is that which gives to such an element the freest scope; because trust in another serves to supply, within due limits, the shortcomings of direct argumentative proof; and when such proof is ample, but at the same time deals with materials which we are not morally advanced enough to appreciate, trust (as in the case of a child before its parents) fulfils for us a function, which could not otherwise be discharged at all. I must not, however, attempt to discuss, at any rate on the present occasion, the subject, a wide and deep subject, of the shares, and mutual relations, of intellectual and moral forces in the work of attaining truth.

23. Passing on, then, from the subject of scientific certainty, let us observe that the region next below this, to which all the propositions entertained in the human mind belong, is divided principally into two parts. The higher of these is that of what is commonly called *necessary* matter: and certainty would, in its ordinary sense, be predicated of all that lies within its range. That is to say, certainty with a relation to our nature: a certainty subjectively not defective: a certainty which fixes our perceptions, conclusions, or convictions, in such a frame as to render them immovable: a certainty not merely which is unattended with doubt, but which excludes doubt, which leaves no available room for its being speculatively entertained, which makes it on the whole irrational. With this certainty we hold that bodies fall by the force of gravity; that air is rarefied at great altitudes; that the limit of human age established by all modern experience is not very greatly beyond a century; that the filial relation entails a duty of obedience. The certainty repudiated in the antecedent argument is only that of the Stoical 'perception.' In the words of the Academical

philosophy, 'Nihil est enim aliud, quamobrem nihil *percipi* mihi posse videatur, nisi quod percipiendi vis ita definitur a Stoicis, ut negent quidquam posse percipi, nisi tale verum, quale falsum esse non possit[1].' But certainty of an order so high, as to make doubt plainly irrational, applies to various classes of our ideas.

24. This is the region of the ἐπιστητόν of Aristotle[2], and the faculties employed in it are chiefly, according to him, νοῦς[3] for principles, ἐπιστήμη for inferences from them. It has been defined as the region of the *Vernunft* in the modern German philosophy, of the Reason by Coleridge. It seems to be largely recognized by the most famous schools of the ancients. It contains both simple ideas, and demonstrations from them. It embraces moral, as well as other metaphysical, entities. It had no place in the philosophy of Locke. As regards the distinction of faculty between Reason and Understanding, *Vernunft* and *Verstand*, I am not inculcating an opinion of my own, but simply stating one which is widely current.

25. The lower department is that in which doubt has its proper place, and in which the work of the understanding is to compare and to distinguish; to elicit approximations to unity from a multitude of particulars, and to certainty from a combination and equipoise of presumptions. It is taken to be the province of all those faculties, or habits, of which Aristotle treats under the several designations of φρόνησις, τέχνη, εὐβουλία, σύνεσις, γνώμη, and others[4]; of the *Verstand* of the Germans, of the Understanding according to Coleridge. It embraces multitudes of questions of speculation, and almost all questions of practice. Of speculation: as, for example, what are the due definitions of cases in which verbal untruth may be a duty, or in which it is right to appropriate a neighbour's goods. Of practice, because every question of practice is embedded in details: if, for example, we admit that it is right to give alms, we have to decide whether the object is good, and whether we can afford the sum. Because, even where the principles are ever so absolute, simple, and unconditioned, they can rarely be followed

1 Cic. De Fin. v. 26.
2 Eth. Nicom. vi. 3, 2.
3 Ibid. vi. 6, 2.
4 Ibid. vi. 4, 5, 9, 10, 11.

to conclusions, either in theory or practice, without taking into view many particulars, with various natures, and various degrees, of evidence. This is the region of probable evidence.

26. The highest works achieved in it are those in which the combinations it requires are so rapid and so perfect, that they are seen, like a wheel in very rapid revolution, as undivided wholes, not as assemblages of parts; in a word, that they resemble the objects of intuition. Towards this, at the one end of the scale, there may be indefinite approximation: and below these, there are innumerable descending degrees of evidence, down to that in which the presumption of truth in any given proposition is so faint as to be scarcely perceptible.

27. From what has now been said, it is manifest that the province of probable evidence, thus marked off, is a very wide one. But, in fact, it is still wider than it appears to be. For many truths, which are the objects of intuition to a well-cultivated mind of extended scope, are by no means such to one of an inferior order, or of a less advanced discipline. By such, they can only be reached through circuitous processes of a discursive nature, if at all. In point of fact, there appear to be many who have scarcely any clear intuitions, any perceptions of truths as absolute, self-dependent, and unchanging. If so, then not only all the detailed or concrete questions of life and practice, to which the idea of duty is immediately applicable, for all minds, but likewise the entire operations of some minds, are situated in the region of probable evidence.

28. The mode in which the understanding performs its work, within this region, is by bringing together things that are like, and by separating things that are unlike. To this belong its various processes of induction and discourse, of abstraction and generalization, and the rest. Therefore Bishop Butler teaches that the chief element of probability is that which is expressed 'in the word likely, i. e. like some truth or true event.'

29. The form of assent, which belongs to the result of these processes, may properly be termed belief. It is

bounded, so to speak, by knowledge on the one hand, where it becomes not only plenary, so as to exclude doubt, but absolute and self-dependent, so as not to rest upon any support extrinsic to the object. It is similarly bounded on the other side by mere opinion; where the matter is very disputable, the presumptions faint and few, or the impression received by a slight process and (as it were) at haphazard, without an examination proportioned to the nature of the object and of the faculties concerned. Of course no reference is here made to the case in which, by a modest or lax form of common speech, opinion is used as synonymous with judgement. Opinion, as it has now been introduced, corresponds with the δόξα of the Greeks: and approaches to the signification in which it is used by St. Augustine, who, after commending those who know, and those who rightly inquire, proceeds to say, 'tria sunt alia hominum genera, profecto improbanda ac detestanda. Unum est opinantium ; id est eorum, qui se arbitrantur scire quod nesciunt[1].'

30. It may indeed, or may not, be convenient to attach [2] the name of belief to such judgements as are formed where some living or moral agent, and his qualities, enter into the medium of proof; inasmuch as in such cases there is a power to assume false appearances, which complicates the case : and inasmuch as the process must be double, first to establish the general credibility of the person, then to receive his particular testimony. This seems, however, more properly to bear the name of faith, with which belief is indeed identical in the science of theology, but not in common speech. For faith involves the element of trust, which essentially requires a moral agent for its object. Apart from any technical sense which the word may have acquired in theology, and more at large, human language warrants and requires our applying the name of belief to all assent which is given to propositions founded upon probable evidence.

31. The tastes of many, and the understandings of some, will suggest that this qualified mode of statement is dis-

---

[1] *De Utilitate Credendi*, c. xi.
[2] With Bishop Pearson. *On the Creed*, Art. I. § 1.

paraging to the dignity of conclusions belonging to religion and to duty. But let not the suggestion be hastily entertained. It is in this field that moral elements most largely enter into the reasonings of men, and the discussion of their legitimate place in such reasonings has already been waived. For the present let it suffice to bear in mind that there is no limit to the strength of working, as distinguished from abstract, certainty, to which probable evidence may not lead us along its gently ascending paths.

32. There is, therefore, a kind of knowledge of which we are incapable: namely, that which necessarily implies the existence of an exactly corresponding object.

There is a kind of knowledge, less properly so called, which makes doubt wholly irrational; and which may often be predicated in a particular case, whether it be by an act of intuition, or by a process of demonstration.

There is, thirdly, a kind of mental perception or impression, to which also in common speech, but yet less properly, the name of knowledge is frequently applied. It is generically inferior to knowledge, but approaches and even touches it at points where the evidence on which it rests is in its highest degrees of force: descending below this to that point of the scale, at which positive and negative presumptions are of equal weight and the mind is neutral. There is a possibility that the very same subject-matter which at one time lies, for a particular person, in the lower of these regions, may at another time reside in the higher.

33. If, then, it be allowable, and it is not only allowable but inevitable, to collect the laws of the human intelligence by the observation of its processes, which in fact grows to be an induction from universal practice, it is manifest that we are so constituted as to yield assent to propositions having various kinds and degrees of evidence. We agree to some as immediate, and (to our apprehensions) necessary: to some as necessary but not immediate: to some as originally neither necessary nor immediate, but as presenting subsequently a certainty and solidity not distinguishable from that which appertains to the former classes. Again, we yield our assent to others of a different class, which falls into sub-classes. These have various degrees of likelihood

in subject-matter infinitely diversified; some of them so high as to exclude doubt, some admitting yet greatly outweighing it by positive evidence, some nearly balanced between the affirmative and the negative : but in all cases with a preponderance on the former side. All these are formed to attract legitimate assent, according to the laws of our intellectual constitution; which has universal truth for its object, and affirmation and rejection for its office. With other processes, such as assent given under blind prejudice against probability, or purely arbitrary conjecture, or the *quasi*-truths of the imagination, we have in this place nothing to do.

34. The doctrine that we are bound by the laws of our nature to follow probable truth, rests upon the most secure of all grounds for practical purposes, if indeed the consent which accepts it is in fact so widely spread in the usual doings of mankind, that it may well be termed universal. The very circumstance that there are exceptions confirms the rule, provided it may be maintained that the exceptions are of a certain kind. For conversely, if there be a practice invariably followed by those who are known to be wise in kindred subject-matter, it is often doubtful whether this can be said to derive any positive confirmation from the concurrent course of persons who are known to be of an opposite character. Again, if there be an universal agreement concerning any proposition among those who have no sinister bias, the fact that others who are known to have such a bias differ from them does not impair their authority, but may even appear rather to constitute an additional evidence of their being in the right. Now this is exactly the kind of consent which may justly be said to obtain among men with regard to the following of probable truth. For every one acts upon affirmative evidence, however inferior to certainty, unless he be either extremely deficient in common understanding, or so biassed the other way by his desires as to be incapable of an upright view of the case before him. Even the last-named class of excepted instances would generally take the form rather of an inability, under the circumstances, to perceive the evidence, than of a denial of its authority.

35. But the doctrine itself appears to be as irrefragably established in theoretic reasoning, as it is in the practice of mankind. We may, however, distinguish those propositions which are abstract, from such as entail any direct consequences in our conduct. With regard to the former, suspension of judgement is allowable in all cases where serious doubt appears before examination, or remains after it. Whether Rome was built 753 years before our Lord, whether King Charles the First wrote the *Eikon Basilike*, whether Caligula made his horse a Consul, whether St. Paul visited Britain, — these are questions which present no such evidence as to bind our judgement either way, and any decision we may form about them has no bearing on our conduct. But to doubt whether the empire of the Caesars existed, or whether King Charles was beheaded, or perhaps whether he said ‘remember’ to Bishop Juxon on the scaffold, or whether Michael Angelo painted the ‘Last Judgement’ in the Sistine Chapel, — this, after the question had once been presented fairly to our minds, would be a violation of the laws of our intellectual nature. It would be in any case a folly, and it would even be a sin if moral elements were involved in the judgement, for instance if the disbelief arose from a spirit of opposition, and self-assertion, predisposing us unfavourably to conclusions that others have established, and that have obtained general acceptance.

36. At the least, I say, it would be a violation of the law of our intellectual nature; if indeed the one obligation of that nature is to recognize truth wheresoever it is fallen in with, and to assent to it. The effect of the obligation cannot be confined to cases of immediate or intuitive knowledge. For, in the first place, this would be to cast off the chief subject-matter of our understanding, or discursive faculty. If we admit the current definition of the term, it would even be to leave all that organ, in which the mind chiefly energizes, without an office, and therefore without a lawful place in our nature. But, in the second place, let us observe how the denial of all assent to probable conclusions will comport with our general obligations. A great mass of facts from some history are before us. There may be error here and there in particulars, but their general

truth is unquestioned; and upon a given point, taken at random, the chances are probably a hundred to one or more that it is true. Of two persons, each having a hundred such facts, independent of one another, before him, one, acting upon the ordinary rule, receives them; and he has the truth in ninety-nine cases conjoined with error in one: the other, rejecting them, has neither the one error, nor the ninety-nine truths; his understanding has refused its work, and lost its reward in the ninety-nine cases, for fear of the failure in the one. And further we are to remember that the error in the one is material only, not formal. It has not of necessity any poisonous quality. It is more like a small portion of simply innutritious food received along with the mass of what is wholesome.

37. The case has indeed here been put upon the hypothesis of very high probability. What shall we say to propositions, of which the evidence is less certain? The answer is, that no line can be drawn in abstract argument between them: that the obligation which attaches to the former attaches to the latter: that it must subsist, so long as there remains any preponderance of affirmative evidence, which is real, and of such a magnitude as to be appreciable by our faculties. But at the same time, although this be true in the cases where it is necessary for us to conclude one way or the other, it is not applicable to the multitude of cases where no such necessity exists. Sometimes a total suspension of judgement, sometimes a provisional assent, consciously subject to future correction upon enlarged experience, are the remedies offered to our need, and very extended indeed is their scope and use for prudent minds. Of course it remains true that the understanding, when it has to choose the objects of its own activity, may justly select those on which a competent certainty is attainable, instead of stimulating a frivolous and barren curiosity, by employing itself on matters incapable of satisfactory determination by such means as are ordinarily at our command.

38. Whether, then, we look to the constitution of our nature, and the ὕλη or matter provided for it to work upon, together with the inference arising from the combined view of the two; or whether we regard the actual results as

realized in the possession of truth ; we find it to be a maxim
sustained by theory, as well as by the general consent and
practice of men, that the mind is not to be debarred from
assent to a proposition with which it may have cause to
deal, on account of the circumstance that the evidence for
it is short of that which is commonly called certain ; and
that to act upon an opposite principle would be to contra-
vene the law of our intellectual nature.

39. But now let us deal, so far as justly belongs to the
purpose of this paper, with that part of the subject-matter
of human inquiry where moral ingredients are essentially
involved.   For hitherto we have spoken mainly of such
kind of obligation as may attach to geometrical investigations, in which usually the will has no concern either one
way or the other.

With regard to moral science properly so styled, whether
it be conversant with principles, when it is called ethical,
or whether it be concerned with their application to particulars, when it becomes casuistry, although the whole of
it is practical, as it aims to fix the practical judgements and
the conduct of all men, yet obviously the whole cannot be
said to be practical in regard to each individual.   For the
experience of one person will only raise a part, perhaps a
very small part, of the questions which it involves.   So far,
then, as moral inquiries properly belong to science and not
to life, they are pursued in the abstract, and they are subject to the general laws of intellectual inquiry which have
already been considered ; only with this difference, that our
judgements in them are much more likely to be influenced
by the state of our affections and the tenor of our lives, by
our conformity to, or alienation from, the will of God, than
where the matter of the propositions themselves had no
relation to human conduct.

40. But, for the government of life, all men, though in
various degrees, require to be supplied with certain practical judgements.   For there is no breathing man, to whom
the alternatives of right and wrong are not continually present.   To one they are less, perhaps infinitely less, complicated than to another ; but they pervade the whole tissue
of every human life.   In order to meet these, we must be

supplied with certain practical judgements. It matters not
that there may have existed particular persons, as children,
for instance, who have never entertained these judgements
in the abstract at all; nor that many act blindly, and at
haphazard, which is simply a contempt of duty; nor that
there may be another class, into whose compositions by
long use some of them are so ingrained, that they operate
with the rapidity and certainty of instinct. Setting these
aside, it remains true of all persons of developed understanding that there are many questions bearing on practice,
with regard to which, in order to discharge their duty
rightly, they must have conclusions, and these not necessarily numerous in every case, but in every case of essential
importance, so that they may be termed 'a savour of life
unto life, or a savour of death unto death.'

41. Now it is in this department that the argument for
the obligation to follow probable evidence is of the greatest
force and moment. It has been seen, how that obligation
may be qualified or suspended in the pursuit of abstract
truth ; so much so, that even the contravention of it need
not involve a breach of moral duty. But the case is very
different when we deal with those portions of truth that
supply the conditions of conduct. To avoid all detail, such
as may dissipate the force of the main considerations, is
material. Let it therefore be observed that there is one
proposition in which the whole matter, as it is relevant to
human duty, may be summed up : that all our works alike,
inward and outward, great and small, ought to be done in
obedience to God. Now this is a proposition manifestly
tendered to us by that system of religion which is called
Christianity, and which purports to be a revelation of the
Divine will. It is the first and great commandment of the
Gospel, that we shall love God with the whole heart, and
mind, and soul, and strength [1]; and whatsoever we do, we
are to do all to the glory of God [2]. And as every act is, *ceteris
paribus*, determined, and is at the very least in all cases
qualified, by its motive, this proposition concerning an
universal obedience as the ground and rule of conduct, is
of all propositions the one most practical, the one most

---

[1] Mark xii. 30 ; Luke x. 27.   [2] 1 Cor. x. 31.

urgently requiring affirmation or denial according as the evidence may be in favour of or against its truth.

42. We seem, then, to have arrived at this point: the evidences of religion relate to a matter not speculative, not in abstract matter, which we may examine or pass by according to our leisure. It is either true or false: this on all hands will be admitted. If it be false, we are justified in repudiating it, so soon as we have obtained proofs of its falsity, such as the constitution of our minds entitles us to admit in that behalf. But we are bound by the laws of our intellectual nature not to treat it as false before examination. In like manner, by the laws of our moral nature, which oblige us to adjust all our acts according to our sense of some standard of right and wrong, we are not less stringently bound to use every effort in coming to a conclusion one way or the other respecting it: inasmuch as it purports to supply us with the very and original standard to which that sense is to be referred, through a sufficient revelation of the will of God, both in its detail, and especially in that with which we are now concerned, the fundamental principle of a claim to unlimited obedience, admitting no exception and no qualification.

43. The maxim that Christianity is a matter not abstract, but referable throughout to human action, is not an important only, but a vital part of the demonstration, that we are bound by the laws of our nature to give a hearing to its claims. We shall therefore do well to substantiate it to our consciousness by some further mention of its particulars. Let us then recollect that we have not merely the general principle of doing all to the glory of God, declared by the Bible in general terms: but this is illustrated by reference to the common actions of eating and drinking[1]. 'Whether ye eat or drink, or whatsoever ye do,' thus the passage runs, ' do all to the glory of God.' Now surely, one should have said, if any acts whatever could have been exempt from the demands of this comprehensive law, they should have been those functions of animal life, respecting which, as to their substance, we have no free choice, since they are among the absolute conditions of our physical existence. And by the

[1] 1 Cor. x. 31.

unbeliever it might consistently be argued that, inasmuch
as food and drink are thus necessary, it is impossible to
conceive that any question relating to the different kinds
of them (unless connected with their several aptitudes for
maintaining life and health, which is not at all in the
Apostle's view) can be of any moral moment. But the
allegation of Scripture is directly to a contrary effect: and
apprises us that even such a matter as eating or refrain-
ing from meat, has a spiritual character. 'He that eateth,
eateth to the Lord, for he giveth God thanks; and he that
eateth not, to the Lord he eateth not, and giveth God
thanks. For none of us liveth to himself, and no man
dieth to himself[1].' Not only (as the entire passage seems
to mean) where a special scruple may be raised by the facts
of idol worship; not only in the avoidance of pampered
tastes and gross excesses; but in the simple act of taking
food, the religious sense has a place. The maintenance of
life, though it is a necessity, is also a duty and a blessing.

44. And to the same effect is the declaration of our
Lord: 'But I say unto you, That every idle word that men
shall speak, they shall give account thereof in the day of
judgement[2].' The 'idle word' is perhaps the very slightest
and earliest form of voluntary action. Consider the fertility
of the mind, and the rapidity of its movements: how many
thoughts pass over it without or against the will; how
easily they find their way into the idle, that is, not the
mischievous or ill-intended, but merely the unconsidered
word. So lightly and easily is it born, that the very forms
of ancient speech seem to designate it as if it were self-
created, and not the offspring of a mental act[3],

'Ατρείδη, ποῖόν σε ἔπος φύγεν ἔρκος ὀδόντων;

and as we say, such and such an expression 'escaped him.'
Thus then it appears that, at the very first and lowest stage
of scarcely voluntary action, the Almighty God puts in His
claim. In this way He acquaints us that everything, in
which our faculties can consciously be made ministers of
good or evil, shall become a subject of reckoning, doubtless
of just and fatherly reckoning, in the great account of the
day of judgement.

[1] Rom. xiv. 6, 7.　　　[2] Matt. xii. 36.　　　[3] *Iliad*, iv. 350.

45. Further, it appears that there are many acts, of which the external form must be the same, whether they are done by Christians, or by others; as for instance those very acts of satisfying hunger and thirst, of which we have spoken. If these, then, are capable, as has been shown, of being brought under the law of duty, a different character must attach to them in consequence; they must be influenced, if not intrinsically, yet at least in their relation to something else, by their being referred to that standard. The form of the deed, the thing done, the πρᾶγμα, is perhaps, as we have seen, the same; but the action, the exercise of the mind in ordering or doing it, the πρᾶξις, is different. It differs, for example, in the motive of obedience; in the end, which is the glory of God; in the temper, which is that of trust, humility, and thankfulness. Accordingly, it appears that Christianity aims not only at adjusting our acts, but also our way of acting, to a certain standard; that it reduces the whole to a certain mental habit, and imbues and pervades the whole with a certain temper.

46. Not therefore at a venture, but with strict reason, the assertion has been made, that the question, whether Christianity be true or false, is the most practical of all questions: because it is that question of practice which incloses in itself, and implicitly determines, every other: it supplies the fundamental rule or principle (*Grundsatz*) of every decision in detail. And, consequently, it is of all other questions the one upon which those, who have not already a conclusion available for use, are most inexorably bound to seek for one. And, by further consequence, it is also the question to which the duty of following affirmative evidence, even although it should present to the mind no more than a probable character, and should not, *ab initio*, or even thereafter, extinguish doubt, has the closest and most stringent application.

47. Now the foregoing argument, it must be observed, includes and decides the question for what is commonly called the doctrinal part of the Christian religion; for those objective facts, which it lays as the foundation of its system, and which are set forth in the historical Creeds of the Catholic Church. It is not necessary here to enter upon the

inquiry how far the internal evidence about suitableness to our state, which the nature of those facts offers to us, may constitute a part or a proof of, or an objection to, the truth of the Christian Revelation. I have not in any manner prejudged that question by the foregoing observations ; I have shown its claims to nothing (where there is no conviction already formed) beyond a hearing and an adjudication. But in those claims the doctrinal part of the revelation, that which is distinct from the law of duty, has a full and coequal share with the moral part. The Christian system neither enjoins nor permits any severance between the two. Being inseparably associated, and resting upon the testimony of precisely the same witnesses, they on that account stand in precisely the same authoritative relation to our practice. Accordingly, when we accept or reject the Christian law of duty as such, we accept or reject also the system in which, and as a part of which, it is revealed. Whether we refer to the Scriptures, or to the collateral evidence of history and of the Church, we find it to be undeniable as a fact that Christianity purports to be not a system of moral teaching only, but, in vital union therewith, a system of revealed facts concerning the nature of God, and His dispensations towards mankind. Upon these facts, which centre in our Lord and Saviour, moral teaching is to rest, and to these it is to be indissolubly attached. Thus the part of Christianity, called doctrinal, has that claim to enter into our affirmative or negative decision, which belongs to a question strictly practical. It is, therefore, one, to which we inevitably must daily and hourly say Aye or No by our actions, even if we have given no speculative reply upon it.

48. To point out more clearly this connexion of the Christian dogma with practice, I may remark that the principal part of the matter of the Christian Creeds is a declaration of the nature of God, who is the object of our Faith : along with the main facts of that Incarnation of our Lord, which is the appointed medium of our reunion with Deity. Subjoined hereto is simply a declaration of belief in the Church, as the society in which we claim membership with Christ, and with one another ; in the Baptism, whereby we find

entrance into that society; and in the Resurrection, which connects the present with the eternal Kingdom of our Lord. It is no paradox to suggest that a religion, which purports to open the means of reunion with God, and to restore the eternal life which we have lost, by means of a spiritual process wrought upon us, should propound, as essential constituents of that process, a faith to be held concerning the nature and attributes of Him whose image we are to bear; concerning the assumption of our nature by the Redeemer, which makes the image approachable and attainable; concerning the dispensation of time for forming our union with Him; and the dispensation of eternity, in which the union with Him becomes consummate and imperishable. Christianity is the religion of the Person of Christ; and the Creeds only tell us from whom He came, and how He came and went, by what Agent we are to be incorporated into Him, and what is the manner of His appointed agency, and the seal of its accomplishment.

49. But there is a latent notion in the minds of some men, that a matter so important as Christianity ought to be presented with the fullest evidence: that it would be unworthy of it, and of its Author, to suppose any revelation from Him imperfectly attested. But, in the first place, such an objection is of no value whatever, unless it will carry us so far as to warrant our holding such language as the following: 'Although there be, apart from this notion, a balance of evidence in favour of Christianity over anything urged against it, yet I will reject it, upon the ground that I consider it unworthy of the Almighty to propound anything for acceptance without demonstrative proofs of it made immediately accessible to us.' Now who, that admits the general recognition of probable evidence as a guide to human practice, will think that the particular subject of the evidence of religion can be exempted from a law so comprehensive, on account of an assumption formed in an individual mind, and by no means having, or even pretending to have, anything like that general sanction from mankind, which belongs to the law that it proposes to supersede? We need not inquire into the piety, or even the decency, of setting up, under any circumstances, an opinion of our own upon the

question what the Creator ought to have done, against a communication of what He has done; because such considerations scarcely belong to the present stage of this inquiry. The case now before us is that of setting up such an opinion, founded upon a measurement which has been made, by one or more individual minds, of the universal nature of things, without any support from the general sense of mankind; nay, against what that general sense, and what even the objectors themselves, in other subject-matter, usually accept as a valid law for the discovery of truth; namely, the law of probable evidence. Such a proceeding is plainly irrational. It offends against the laws of the general reason of our race.

50. But unless the objection can be carried to that point, it is worthless for the question at issue. For the matter to be examined is not whether the revelation is in all its accompaniments, or in all its particulars, such as is thoroughly agreeable to us, exactly such as we approve, or such as we should have anticipated; but, whether or not it be a revelation from God. According to the decision of this last-named question, it must be accepted or rejected; and there can be no reference to the prior topic, otherwise than as it may enter into the decision in what spirit we are to receive such a revelation when its proof has been supplied. Such considerations might conceivably diminish the satisfaction with which the Gospel is acknowledged to be Divine, and the cheerfulness with which it is accepted. This is plainly their legitimate scope when they shall have been proved, and nothing beyond this.

51. The case would indeed be different if the nature of the difficulty were such that the Gospel was found to present contradictions to the moral law graven on the heart of man. There are undoubtedly principles so universally accepted, and of such authority, that a demonstration of anything, be it what it may, which should overthrow them, would leave no firm resting-place in the human mind even for its own reception. It would break down the stays and pillars of all truth within us. But such is not the character of the objection we are now considering. It has not an universal acceptance. It does not relate to moral subject-matter. It is a condition laid down by some few persons as

being in their view necessary to preserve a due dignity in that intellectual process, which is to be the avenue of the truth of God to the soul.

52. It is, however, perhaps not difficult to show that the objection is in itself ill-founded. It assumes that the force of the proofs ought to increase with the importance of the subject. But this is an assumption, which is wholly foreign to the law of probable evidence. That law takes no cognizance of the absolute magnitude of the propositions in question, but only of the relative likelihood of an affirmative or a negative concerning them. This proportion is equally applicable to all subject-matter, however great, or however small. The law, therefore, of credibility has no more dependence upon the magnitude of the questions tried than have the numbers on the arithmetical scale, which calculate for motes and for mountains with exactly the same propriety. At either extremity, indeed, the nature of our faculties imposes a limit. Practically numbers are bounded for us. We cannot employ them to count the sands of the sea-shore; nor again by any fraction can we express the infinitesimal segments, into which space is capable of being divided. And just so in the case before us. If the objection be that the proportion of affirmative and negative evidence upon any given question approaches so nearly to equality as to be indistinguishable from it, and if, when the whole elements of the case are taken into view, this can be made good as their general result, then in truth, but only then, the obligation of credibility may cease and determine.

53. But indeed the objection may even be inverted. When, as here, the matter in question is very great, the evil consequences of a contravention of the law of probability are enhanced. It is not necessary to maintain that any essential difference in the obligation to follow the apparent truth is thus produced : but it is manifest that, the larger and more serious the anticipated results, the more natural and becoming, to say the least, is it for us to realize beforehand our position and duties with regard to the question, and by a more vivid consciousness to create an enhanced and more sharply defined sense of our responsibility. So that both the danger and the guilt of refusing to apply to the evidences

of religion the same laws of investigation, which we obey
in all other departments of inquiry and of action, are not
mitigated, but aggravated, in the degree in which it may be
shown that the matter at issue transcends in its importance
all those which are ordinarily presented to us.

54. Further. The most reasonable presumptions are positively adverse. If we admit that man by free will and a
depraved affection fell away from God, which is the representation addressed to us by the Gospel, nothing can be more
consistent with it, than that he should be brought back
to God by ways which give scope for the exercise of will
and affection, and for their restoration, through exercise, to
health. But surely it is plain that this scope is far more
largely given, where the proof of revelation involves moral
elements, and grows in force along with spiritual discernment,
than if it had the rigour of a demonstration in geometry, of
which the issue is accepted without any appeal, either to
affection or volition, in the appreciation and acceptance of
the steps of the process. And yet more specifically. If it
be true that we are to be brought back, as the Gospel says,
by a Divine training to the image of God, if that which is
crooked is to be made straight, and that which is feeble
strong, by the agency of a Perfect on a fallen being, nothing
can be more agreeable to our knowledge of our own state
than the belief that such a process would be best conducted
in the genial climate and atmosphere of a trustful mind;
that reliance or faith (always being reasonable reliance or
faith) in another would greatly aid our weakness; that we
should thus realize in the concrete Divine qualities before
we can comprehend them in the abstract. But this faith
essentially involves the idea of what we have called probable
evidence : for it is 'the substance of things hoped for, the
evidence of things not seen;' and 'what a man seeth, why
doth he yet hope for [1]?'

55. It may be that, despite of all reasoning, there will be
pain to many a pious mind in following, even under the
guidance of Bishop Butler, the course of an argument which
seems all along to grant it as possible, that the argument in
favour of the truth of Divine Revelation may amount to no

1 Heb. xi. 1 ; Rom. viii. 24.

more than a qualified and dubious likelihood. But as, when the net of the fisherman is cast wide, its extremity must lie far from the hand that threw it, so this argument of probability aims at including within the allegiance of religion those who are remote from anything like a *normal* faith. It is no mere feat of logical arms; it is not done in vainglory, nor is it an arbitrary and gratuitous experiment, nor one disparaging to the majesty and strength of the Gospel. The Apostle, full of the manifold gifts of the Spirit, and admitted already to the third heaven, condescended before the Athenians to the elementary process of arguing from natural evidences for the Providence of God [1]. The Gospel itself alone can fit us to appreciate its own proofs in all their force. It is addressed to beings of darkened mind and alienated heart. The light of truth indeed is abundant; but the clouded and almost blinded eye can admit no more than a faint glimmering. But if even that faint glimmering be suffered to enter, it will progressively train and fit the organ, that it has entered, to receive more and more; and although at first the glory of the Lord could scarcely be discerned in a twilight little short of night itself, yet by such degrees as the growth of the capacity allows, it 'shineth more and more unto the perfect day [2].'

56. Moreover, it is necessary to comment upon the declaration of Bishop Butler, that in numberless instances a man is called upon to act against probability, and would be thought mad if he declined it. The meaning is, that we may be bound by duty, or led by prudence, in obedience to a more comprehensive computation of good and evil, of benefit and loss, to act in opposition to that particular likelihood which lies nearest at hand. To take an example in moral subject-matter. We are bound to avoid occasions of anger; and yet, for the vindication of truth, it may be a duty to enter into debates, which we know from experience will stir our passions more or less. If we look merely at the likelihood of that excitement, we ought to refrain: but if we look onwards to the purpose in view, it makes the other scale descend.

57. Again, in a matter of worldly prudence. The mer-

---

[1] Acts xvii. 24-31.   [2] Prov. iv. 18.

chant hears of a valuable natural product on the coast of Africa. The chances are estimated by him to be two to one against his finding it on the first attempt; but when he finds it, the gain will repay tenfold the expense of the voyage. It may be prudent in such a man to equip and send his vessel, though the likelihood of its failure be two-fold greater than the chance of its success. So that cases, which apparently depart from the law of probability, do in fact only, when we include a greater range of calculation, illustrate its comprehensiveness and universality.

58. It is a deeply important question whether, and how far, the law of probable evidence governs the means by which provision has been made for the determination of questions touching Christian doctrine as they may arise from time to time. This is a great controverted question of Theology, which it could not but be advantageous to discuss in the light, tranquil as it is, supplied by the philosophy of Butler. It cannot now be attempted, however well it may deserve a separate effort. For the present; it only remains to deal with a question belonging to the region of Ethics. For the doctrine of the authority of probable evidence in practical subject-matter is impugned not only by those who require absolute certainty in lieu of it, but likewise by those who, not as just now stated, but in the wider sense of the word, permit and warrant moral action against probability. These are the teachers of what is called Probabilism.

59. Probabilism is by no means the universal or compulsory doctrine of the Roman theologians. It has been combated even by Gonzales, a Jesuit, and a General of the Order [1]. It is confronted by a system called Probabiliorism : which teaches that, when in doubt among several alternatives of conduct, we are bound to choose that which has the greatest likelihood of being right. And there is also in the Latin Church a rigid school of those who pass by the name of Tutiorists. These hold that even such likelihood is insufficient, and that certainty is required as a warrant for our acts. But the popular doctrine seems to be that of Probabilism. It would be wrong to assert that it is a doctrine consciously held and taught for purposes adverse to

---

[1] Ravignan, *De l'Existence et de l'Institut des Jésuites*, p 84.

morality or honour. Without venting any such calumny, let us regard it purely in the abstract, and not as having become parasitical to a particular Church. For my own part I know not how, when it is so contemplated, to escape from the impression that, when closely scrutinized, it will be found to threaten the very first principles of duty ; or to deny that, if universally received and applied, it would go far to destroy whatever there is of substance in moral obligation.

60. The essence of the doctrine is, the licence to choose the less probable. Is it not, then, obvious in the first place that it overthrows the whole *authority* of probable evidence ? No probabilist, it must be supposed, could adopt and urge the argument of Bishop Butler's *Analogy* for the truth of revelation. For his opponent would at once reply by the plea that there are certain real and unsolved difficulties about the theory of religion ; that these constituted a solid, even if an inferior, probability ; and that he could not, on the principles of Probabilism, be blamed for vindicating the right of his natural freedom in following the negative. If the view here taken of the range and title of probable evidence be correct, it is fearful to think what must be the ultimate effects upon human knowledge, belief, and action, of any doctrine which either overthrows or saps its title to our obedience. I say the ultimate effects : for, when thought moves only within prescribed limits, a long time may elapse before the detail of a process is evolved, and it is the ultimate effect, in moral questions, which is the true effect. It would even seem as if any, who are, consciously or unconsciously, impairing the authority of probable evidence, must also, however unconsciously, be clearing the ground for the fell swoop of unbelief in its descent upon the earth.

61. Next, we are surely justified in being to the last degree suspicious of a doctrine which sets up the liberty of man as being not only a condition of all right moral judgement, but a positive ingredient in the claim of one alternative to be preferred over another ; an element of such consideration, as to give the preponderance to what would otherwise be the lighter scale. Duty, or the δέον, is that which *binds*. Surely, if there is one idea more pointedly expressive than another of

the character of the ethical teaching of Christianity, if there is one lesson more pointedly derivable than another from the contemplation of its model in our Blessed Lord, it is the idea and the lesson that we are to deny the claim of mere human will to be a serious ground of moral action, and to reduce it to its proper function, that of freely uniting itself with the will of God. This function is one of subordination : one which manifestly it never can perform, so long as it is to be recognized as something entitled to operate in determining moral choice, and yet extrinsic and additional to, and therefore separate from, His commands.

62. Again, what can be more unnatural, not to say more revolting, than to set up any system of rights or privileges in moral action, apart from duties ? How can we, without departing from our integrity before God, allege the right of our natural freedom as sufficing to counterbalance any, even the smallest, likelihood that His will for us lies in a particular direction ? Scripture, surely, gives no warrant for such a theory; nor the sense of Christian tradition ; nor the worthier schools of heathen philosophy. Is it not hard to reconcile the bare statement of it with the common sense of duty and of honesty, as it belongs to our race at large ?

63. And more. Is it possible to go thus far, without going much further ? It is granted and taught, not indeed that where there is an overwhelming, yet where there is a sensible and appreciable superiority of likelihood in favour of one alternative against another, there, on account and in virtue of our inclination for that which has the weaker evidence, we may choose the latter with a safe conscience. That is to say, eliminating, or excluding from the case, that portion of likelihood which is common to both alternatives, there remains behind on the one side not a great but an appreciable probability ; on the other a simple predilection ; and shall the latter be declared by a system of Christian ethics to outweigh the former ? How is it possible, either, firstly, to establish the right of mere *will* to be set against presumptions of duty ; or, secondly, when once that right has been arrogated, to limit, by any other than an arbitrary rule, the quantity of such presumptions of duty, which may be thus outweighed ?

If an ordinary inclination may outweigh so much of adverse presumption of duty, may not a bias tenfold and twentyfold stronger outweigh a little, or a good deal, more ? And then, where is this slippery process to terminate ? Where is the clue to this labyrinth ? What will be the rights, and what the assumptions, of inclination in this matter, when it has been stimulated by the countenance of authority, and when through indulgence it has become ungovernable ?

64. But, as our sense of the obligations of human relationship, though lower, is also less impaired than that of our duty towards God, let us illustrate the case by reference to this region. Will a licence to follow the less probable alternative bear examination, when it is applied to the relative obligations which unite man with man ? An enemy brings me tidings that an aged parent is in prison and at the point of death, without solace or support. The same person has before deceived and injured me. It is probable that he may be doing so again : so probable that if he had communicated any piece of mere intelligence, not involving a question of conduct, it would, upon the whole, have appeared most safe not to believe the statement. Let it then even be more likely that he now speaks falsehood than truth. Will that warrant me in remaining where I am, or is it possible to treat with neglect a call which *may* reveal the want and extremity of a parent, without an evident, gross, and most culpable breach of filial obligation ? The answer would be No ; and it would be immediate and universal. And yet the case here put has been one not of greater but of inferior likelihood. How then, we may ask, by the argument *a fortiori*, is it possible to apply to the regulation of our relations towards God a theory which explodes at the first instant when it is tested by a case of lower yet of just obligation, namely, by perhaps the deepest among all the original instincts of our nature ?

65. It is indeed true that the doctrine of Probabilism is guarded by two conditions. The first is, that it is to apply only to questions of right, not to those, as I find it expressed, where both fact and right are involved. The question of the validity of a sacrament is not to be tried by it ; and ' de même, un médecin est tenu de donner les remèdes les plus

éprouvés, et un juge les décisions les plus sûres [1].' But this reservation appears rather to weaken, than to strengthen, the foundations of the doctrine itself. Is it not sometimes difficult to decide on the validity of a sacred rite? Do the judge and the physician never doubt? Why are the rules for the investigation of truth which bind them, otherwise than obligatory on other personal conduct? Is not the foundation of duty to others strictly and immutably one with the foundation of duty to our own selves? Again, obligation to a fellow-creature cannot be stronger than obligation to our Father in heaven; therefore, if the liberty of a man is a good plea against a doubtful command of God, why may it not equally warrant a doubtful wrong to a patient or a suitor? if it be good in that part of our relations to God, which embraces the immediate communion of the soul with Him, why not also in that other part, when the intercourse is through the medium of holy rites? It is not difficult to see that neither the Church, nor civil society, could bear without derangement the application of Probabilism to the relations between them and the individual. But then it is more than ever difficult to conceive how such a relaxation of the moral law is to be justified; and justified, moreover, in the department of conduct which is inward, in which we are our own judges, and in which therefore we may even have need to be aided against temptation by a peculiar strictness of rule.

66. The other limitation of the doctrine is, that the probability we are to follow, though inferior to that of the competing alternative, must be intrinsically a solid one: and must not be glaringly, though it may be sensibly, inferior to the opposing argument. 'Quoique, comparativement à la probabilité contraire, la vôtre soit inférieure, il faut qu'elle soit, absolument parlant, grave, et solide, et digne d'un homme prudent; comme une montagne relativement à une autre peut être plus petite, mais néanmoins être en soi, et absolument, une assez grande masse pour mériter le nom de montagne [2].' And this doctrine is supported by the very strange reason [3], that it is more easy to determine whether the probability in favour of a given alternative belongs to

---

[1] *Manuel des Confesseurs*, p. 74.   [2] *Ibid.* p. 75.   [3] *Ibid.* p. 86.

the class of solid or of faint and inadmissible probabilities, than whether it be superior or inferior to the probability in favour of some other alternative. This proposition is one which requires to borrow support, rather than one which can afford to lend it. To me it has the sound of egregious paradox. However difficult it may sometimes be to compare the reasons adducible in support of opposite alternatives, the line between them, it is evident, can rarely be finer and more hair-drawn than that which is to distinguish, in the technical and abstract order, the general traits of a faint from those of a solid probability.

67. But upon the doctrine itself let me record, in concluding, these three remarks. In the first place, the cases are innumerable in which there is evidence in favour of a given alternative, which would amount to a solid, aye a very solid probability, if it stood alone : if it were not overthrown by evidence on the opposite side. But if we are to regard it absolutely, and not relatively, we must on this account fall into constant error. Secondly : to know that our duty is to follow the safest and best alternative, is at least to possess a determinate rule, and one eminently acceptable to a sound conscience ; one which gives us a single and intelligible end for our efforts, though the path of duty is not always, even for the single eye, easy to discern. It becomes a tangled path indeed, if we invoke the aid of Probabilism. For this requires the decision of at least two questions : first, whether the alternative which it is meant to follow has a solid, not a feeble, probability in its favour ; secondly, whether the alternative to be discarded has a notable and conspicuous, or only a limited and moderate, superiority over it. For the step cannot, by hypothesis, be taken, until both these questions have been determined. In the third place, it is painful to recollect that when we are dealing with the most difficult parts of duty, namely those which we transact wholly within ourselves, the appetite for self-indulgence should be pampered by encouragement from without. We are already apt enough to conjure into solid probabilities the veriest phantasms of the mind, provided only they present an agreeable appearance. Here is a new premium set upon this process, alike dangerous

and alluring. The known subtlety of such mental intro-
spections excuses many failures in those who do not create
their own embarrassments; but, for those who do, such a
system appears capable of colouring error, which might
have been blameless, with the darker hues of wilfulness
and guilt.

[In an early part of this volume[1], reference has been
made to a supposed remark by Mr. Pitt, that the *Analogy*
suggested to him more doubts than it solved. I have not
there touched on the merits of the remark in itself. It
is not to be treated as frivolous or captious. No other
work written to promote belief, had then, or within my
knowledge has now, been written, which before answering
objections brings them so fully and clearly into view. We
were then still at the commencement of the critical or questioning period; and to many minds (probably, for example,
to the mind of Mr. Wilberforce) these objections may have
been new. The man who first propounded and brought
home the idea that the system under which the world is
governed is not ideally perfect, spoke, without doubt, a
formidable word. So the man who first propounded and
brought home the idea that the text of the Holy Scriptures
is not absolutely exempt from error, he, too, spoke a formidable word. A third case may be noted; the first promulgation of the heliocentric system, and the revelation of a
number of sister worlds, may have disturbed the faith of
many minds, though hardly of any strong minds. Such
disclosures can hardly fail to impart a shock at the outset,
unless where minds are clothed in the compound panoply
of faith and reason. But the terror of Copernicus, we may
hope, has entirely passed away, and the kindred and more
recent alarms should now, so far as believers are concerned,
be on their road to extinction — 1896.]

1 Page 30.

OXFORD: HORACE HART
PRINTER TO THE UNIVERSITY